BUSINESS ENGLISH

WRITING FOR THE GLOBAL WORKPLACE

DONA J. YOUNG

Boston Burr Ridge, IL Dubuque, IA New York San Francisco St. Louis
Bangkok Bogotá Caracas Kuala Lumpur Lisbon London Madrid Mexico City
Milan Montreal New Delhi Santiago Seoul Singapore Sydney Taipei Toronto

BUSINESS ENGLISH: WRITING FOR THE GLOBAL WORKPLACE
Published by McGraw-Hill, a business unit of The McGraw-Hill Companies, Inc., 1221 Avenue of the Americas, New York, NY, 10020.
Some ancillaries, including electronic and print components, may not be available to customers outside the United States.
This book is printed on acid-free paper.
Printed in China
2 3 4 5 6 7 8 9 0 CTP/CTP 11 10
ISBN 978-0-07-354542-4 (student edition)
MHID 0-07-354542-2 (student edition)
ISBN 978-0-07-329194-9 (annotated instructor's edition)
MHID 0-07-329194-3 (annotated instructor's edition)
Vice President/Editor in Chief: *Elizabeth Haefele*
Vice President/Director of Marketing: *John E. Biernat*
Associate sponsoring editor: *Natalie J. Ruffatto*
Developmental editor: *Kristin Bradley*
Marketing manager: *Keari Bedford*
Lead media producer: *Damian Moshak*
Media producer: *Marc Mattson*
Director, Editing/Design/Production: *Jess Ann Kosic*
Project manager: *Rick Hecker*
Production supervisor: *Jason L. Huls*
Designer: *Srdjan Savanovic*
Photo research coordinator: *Jeremy Cheshareck*
Media project manager: *Mark A.S. Dierker*
Interior and Cover design: *George Kokkonas*
Typeface: *10/12 Times Roman*
Compositor: *Precision Graphics*
Printer: *CTPS*
Cover credit: *Corbis*
Photo Credits: Part 1 Jim Frazier/Images.com; Chs.1, 7 Lisa Zador/Getty Images;
Chs. 2, 3, 9 Royalty-Free/Corbis; Parts 2, 3, Ch. 5 Digital Vision/Getty Images;
Ch. 4 Images.com; Ch. 6 Eric Peterson/Images.com; Chs. 8, 10 Photodisc/Getty Images

Library of Congress Cataloging-in-Publication Data

Young, Dona J.
Business English : writing for the global workplace / Dona J. Young
p. cm.
Includes bibliographical references and index.
ISBN-13: 978-0-07-354542-4 (student edition : alk. paper)
ISBN-10: 0-07-354542-2 (student edition : alk. paper)
ISBN-13: 978-0-07-329194-9 (annotated instructor's edition : alk. paper)
ISBN-10: 0-07-329194-3 (annotated instructor's edition : alk. paper)
1.English language--Business English. 2. Business writing. I. Title.

PE1115.Y68 2008
808'.06665--dc22

2007007210

The Internet addresses listed in the text were accurate at the time of publication. The inclusion of a Web site does not indicate an endorsement by the authors or McGraw-Hill, and McGraw-Hill does not guarantee the accuracy of the information presented at these sites.

www.mhhe.com

DEDICATION

To Jack and Margie McCartan
who gave me the freedom and resources to begin my journey of inquiry

ABOUT THE AUTHOR

DONA J. YOUNG

As a teacher and facilitator, Dona has a passion for making learning exciting and relevant. In addition to teaching college classes, she also facilitates writing programs at major corporations. Previously, Dona was the director of general education at Robert Morris College, Chicago and Springfield, Illinois. She was responsible for curriculum development, faculty training, and program management of general education studies.

Dona has been a speaker at conferences and conducted numerous training programs throughout the country. She holds a B.A. in Sociology (with minors in secondary education and business education) from Northern Illinois University, a Teacher Education Program certificate from the Chicago Institute for Psychoanalysis, and an M.A. in Curriculum and Instruction from The University of Chicago. Dona considers herself a lifelong learner, believing that who we become is a result of what we learn. Beyond that, her dog Reggie keeps her from taking work, or life, too seriously.

BRIEF CONTENTS

CONTENTS

PREFACE

What kind of job do you want to get when you graduate? If you were going on a job interview tomorrow, would you feel confident about your speaking and writing skills? One thing is certain, regardless of where you live, you will need to speak and write Business English with proficiency if you want to have a *successful* career.

People from around the world—from India to Japan to Germany—use English to communicate with other people from diverse cultures. Now think of your immediate surroundings. How many people do you know from countries other than your own? What language do you speak in a formal environment? Your answer is likely to be English, but it's not just any brand of English—it is formal English, which is also known as Business English.

For a moment, reflect on the language variety you encounter on a daily basis. If you live on the East Coast, you can hear several different varieties of English within a 100-mile radius. If you live in the Midwest, you use language slightly differently than people who live in the South, East, or West. If you "hop the pond" and compare one of the many varieties of British English with American English, the differences are more dramatic.

Every one of us speaks a local language to some degree or another, especially when we are with friends and family in informal environments. In fact, the language used in text messaging can even be considered a local language: it certainly isn't a form of Standard or Business English.

Even though local language is more accepted today than at any other time in our cultural history, the person who can shift from informal to formal language patterns at will has the advantage. And that's what these materials are designed to help you do. By refining your use of language, you are improving your career opportunities for the rest of your life.

With this text, you will use your local language (or dialect) to become more proficient with Business English. You can achieve this by comparing and contrasting the two language systems, "building a wall" between Business English and your local language and attaining the best of two worlds. The key is to match the language you use with the environment you are in.

This book provides you with the tools you need for the global workplace. When you have mastered the principles presented here, you will have a solid foundation in speaking and writing Business English to people from around the world.

Dona Young

ACKNOWLEDGMENTS

CONTRIBUTIONS

Linda Schreiber, whose vision and leadership inspire everyone to give their best; Natalie Ruffatto, whose vibrant energy drives our process; Peter Vanaria, whose enthusiasm and professionalism help us exceed our goals; Elizabeth Anderson, whose creative talent adds a fresh dimension; and James Riley, whose keen insight and expertise enhance the product as well as the process.

ACKNOWLEDGMENTS

Elaine C. Weytkow, a cousin, friend, mentor, and devil's advocate who offers good advice; Trisha Svehla, an excellent consultant but a better friend; Kathleen Sutterlin, whose passion provided the vital link; Tom DiPietropolo and Michelle Lopane, sales reps with enthusiasm and finesse; Denny Spisak and Dave Fosnaugh, colleagues from long ago who support the best in education; Ben Johnston, who shares my love for FEW; Tom Nimtz, a man who honors integrity; Charles Yanulevich, whose strength and integrity were surpassed only by his love; Rose and Robert Lindsey, who always pushed me to my best; Charles C. Young, my hero; a few good friends who assisted along the way: Janet Skoda, Carol Glasco, Jean Gibb-Smith, Gerry Nangle-Reece, Jane Curry, and Dave Wondra. And finally, my colleagues at LaSalle Bank ABN AMRO and Blue Cross and Blue Shield who support writing instruction at the corporate level; my colleagues at the former Bank One, American Dental Association, and Chicago Title and Trust, where much of the original research was done.

SPECIAL PEOPLE WITH SPECIAL TALENT

Many extraordinary people worked behind the scenes to make this book the best it can be. Molto grazie to Kristin Bradley, developmental editor, Keari Bedford, marketing manager; Rick Hecker, senior project manager; Jason Huls, production supervisor; Sidj Savanovic, designer; Megan Gates, marketing specialist; and Jeremy Cheshareck, photo research coordinator, along with others who have done excellent work throughout this process.

TEACHERS WHO MADE A DIFFERENCE

Fred E. Winger, whose passion for teaching and love for students remains unequaled; John Ginther and Ralph W. Tyler, great teachers whose wisdom is timeless; Doris and Floyd Crank, who made every student feel important; and finally the "old team" who placed students at the top of the organization chart, giving their best always: Janet Day, Carolyn Webb, Gladys Jossell, Feranda Williamson, Beverly Carter, Angelia Millender, Marsha Swalek, Rutha Gibson, Adeline Sangineto, Kathy Viollt, Deb Brody, Deb Dahlen, Lynn Schumacher, Cynthia Reynolds, Vern Sims, Janice Caudy, and all the wonderful teachers who make a difference in their students' lives every day.

The following teachers deserve a special thank you for adding quality to the text through their thoughtful and insightful reviews:

Edwin F. Cummings, Jr., *Bryant & Stratton College*
Diana K. Gunderson, *Institute of Business & Medical Careers, Inc.*
Nancy A. Johnson, *Clark College*
Jackie Marshall, *Tri-State Educational Systems, Inc.*
Karen Ann Myers, *Fisher College*
Loreen Ritter, *The Salter School*
Judith Rozarie, *Gibbs College*
Kate Sawyer, *Lincoln Educational Services*
Judy Scire, *Stone Academy*
Minna Seligson, *Briarcliffe College*
Donna Slaughter, *Bryant & Stratton College*
Bonnie J. Tuggle-Ziglar, *Brookstone College of Business*
Melanie Whiton, *Long Island Business Institute*
Paul E. Winters, *DeVry University*
Karen Zempel, *Bryant & Stratton College*

GUIDED TOUR

Business English: Writing for the Global Workplace uses local language as a springboard for learning Business English, connecting with students personally as it leads them to use language more professionally. The text ties grammar to writing style by focusing on the sentence core, offering a real method to achieve writing success for students of all levels. Using this technique, the text creates the context and thus the urgency for language proficiency, providing a built-in rationale for student motivation.

PRACTICAL APPLICATIONS

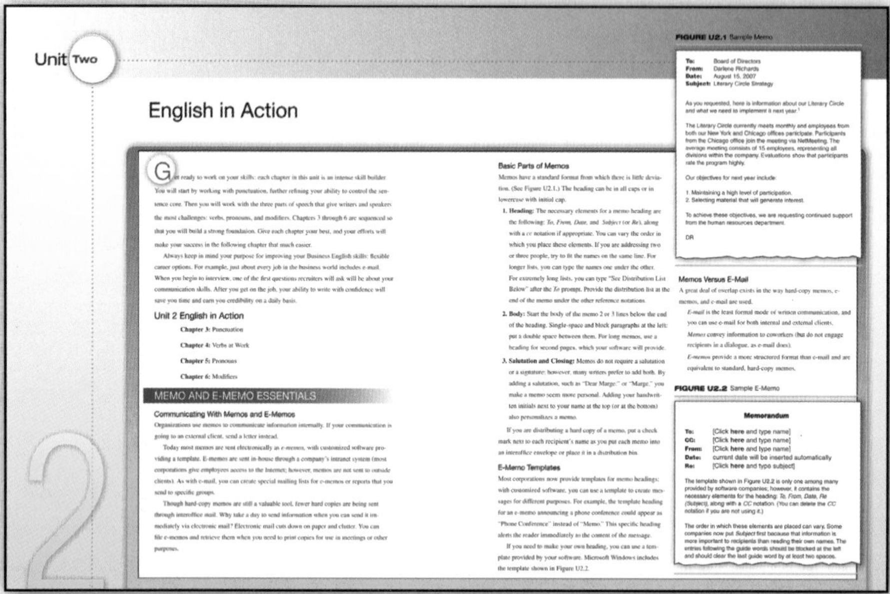

Unit Two

English in Action

Get ready to work on your skills: each chapter in this unit is an intense skill builder. You will start by working with punctuation, further refining your ability to control the sentence core. Then you will work with the three parts of speech that give writers and speakers the most challenges: verbs, pronouns, and modifiers. Chapters 3 through 6 are sequenced so that you will build a strong foundation. Give each chapter your best, and your efforts will make your success in the following chapter that much easier.

Always keep in mind your purpose for improving your Business English skills: flexible career options. For example, just about every job in the business world includes e-mail. When you begin to interview, one of the first questions recruiters will ask will be about your communication skills. After you get on the job, your ability to write with confidence will save you time and earn you credibility on a daily basis.

Unit 2 English in Action

Chapter 3: Punctuation

Chapter 4: Verbs at Work

Chapter 5: Pronouns

Chapter 6: Modifiers

MEMO AND E-MEMO ESSENTIALS

Communicating With Memos and E-Memos

Organizations use memos to communicate information internally. If your communication is going to an external client, send a letter instead.

Today most memos are sent electronically as *e-memos*, with customized software providing a template. E-memos are sent in-house through a company's intranet system (most corporations give employees access to the Internet; however, memos are not sent to outside clients). As with e-mail, you can create special mailing lists for e-memos or reports that you send to specific groups.

Though hard-copy memos are still a valuable tool, fewer hard copies are being sent through interoffice mail. Why take a day to send information when you can send it immediately via electronic mail? Electronic mail cuts down on paper and clutter. You can file e-memos and retrieve them when you need to print copies for use in meetings or other purposes.

Basic Parts of Memos

Memos have a standard format from which there is little deviation. (See Figure U2.1.) The heading can be in all caps or in lowercase with initial cap.

1. **Heading:** The necessary elements for a memo heading are the following: *To*, *From*, *Date*, and *Subject* (or *Re*), along with a *cc* notation if appropriate. You can vary the order in which you place these elements. If you are addressing two or three people, try to fit the names on the same line. For longer lists, you can type the names one under the other. For extremely long lists, you can type "See Distribution List Below" after the *To* prompt. Provide the distribution list at the end of the memo under the other reference notations.
2. **Body:** Start the body of the memo 2 or 3 lines below the end of the heading. Single-space and block paragraphs at the left; put a double space between them. For long memos, use a heading for second pages, which your software will provide.
3. **Salutation and Closing:** Memos do not require a salutation or a signature; however, many writers prefer to add both. By adding a salutation, such as "Dear Marge:" or "Marge," you make a memo seem more personal. Adding your handwritten initials next to your name at the top (or at the bottom) also personalizes a memo.

If you are distributing a hard copy of a memo, put a check mark next to each recipient's name as you put each memo into an interoffice envelope or place it in a distribution bin.

E-Memo Templates

Most corporations now provide templates for memo headings; with customized software, you can use a template to create messages for different purposes. For example, the template heading for an e-memo announcing a phone conference could appear as "Phone Conference" instead of "Memo." This specific heading alerts the reader immediately to the content of the message.

If you need to make your own heading, you can use a template provided by your software. Microsoft Windows includes the template shown in Figure U2.2.

FIGURE U2.1 Sample Memo

To: Board of Directors
From: Darlene Richards
Date: August 15, 2007
Subject: Literary Circle Strategy

As you requested, here is information about our Literary Circle and what we need to implement it next year.[1]

The Literary Circle currently meets monthly and employees from both our New York and Chicago offices particpate. Participants from the Chicago office join the meeting via NetMeeting. The average meeting consists of 15 employees, representing all divisions within the company. Evaluations show that participants rate the program highly.

Our objectives for next year include:

1. Maintaining a high level of participation.
2. Selecting material that will generate interest.

To achieve these objectives, we are requesting continued support from the human resources department.

DR

Memos Versus E-Mail

A great deal of overlap exists in the way hard-copy memos, e-memos, and e-mail are used.

E-mail is the least formal mode of written communication, and you can use e-mail for both internal and external clients.

Memos convey information to coworkers (but do not engage recipients in a dialogue, as e-mail does).

E-memos provide a more structured format than e-mail and are equivalent to standard, hard-copy memos.

FIGURE U2.2 Sample E-Memo

Memorandum

To: [Click **here** and type name]
CC: [Click **here** and type name]
From: [Click **here** and type name]
Date: current date will be inserted automatically
Re: [Click **here** and type subject]

The template shown in Figure U2.2 is only one among many provided by software companies; however, it contains the necessary elements for the heading: *To, From, Date, Re (Subject)*, along with a *CC* notation. (You can delete the *CC* notation if you are not using it.)

The order in which these elements are placed can vary. Some companies now put *Subject* first because that information is more important to recipients than reading their own names. The entries following the guide words should be blocked at the left and should clear the last guide word by at least two spaces.

UNIT OPENERS

Each unit opener stresses a different type of business document: E-mail, memos, and business letters.

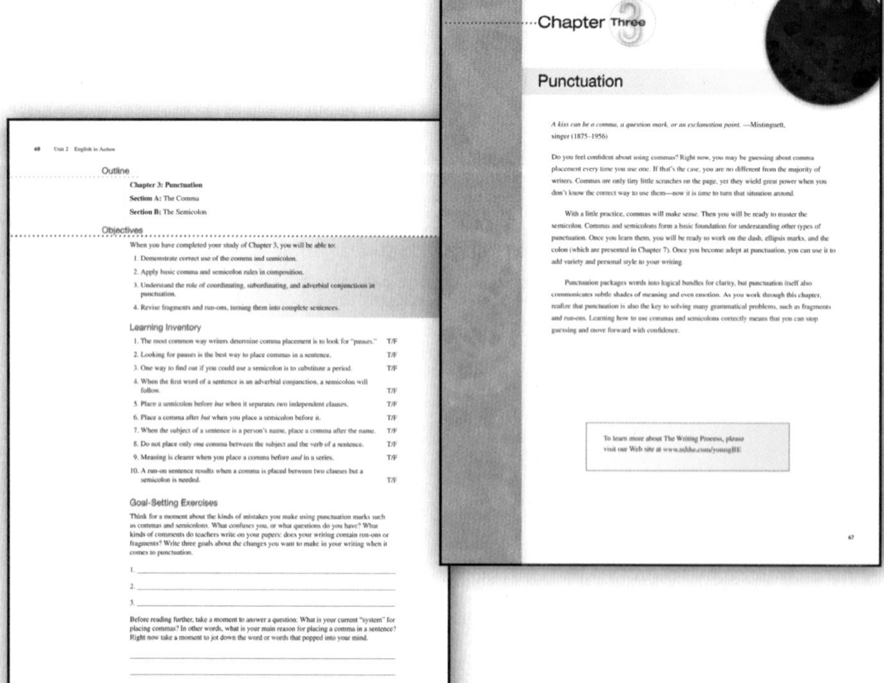

Outline

Chapter 3: Punctuation

Section A: The Comma

Section B: The Semicolon

Objectives

When you have completed your study of Chapter 3, you will be able to:

1. Demonstrate correct use of the comma and semicolon.
2. Apply basic comma and semicolon rules in composition.
3. Understand the role of coordinating, subordinating, and adverbial conjunctions in punctuation.
4. Revise fragments and run-ons, turning them into complete sentences.

Learning Inventory

1. The most common way writers determine comma placement is to look for "pauses." T/F
2. Looking for pauses is the best way to place commas in a sentence. T/F
3. One way to find out if you could use a semicolon is to substitute a period. T/F
4. When the first word of a sentence is an adverbial conjunction, a semicolon will follow. T/F
5. Place a semicolon before *but* when it separates two independent clauses. T/F
6. Place a comma after *but* when you place a semicolon before it. T/F
7. When the subject of a sentence is a person's name, place a comma after the name. T/F
8. Do not place only one comma between the subject and the verb of a sentence. T/F
9. Meaning is clearer when you place a comma before *and* in a series. T/F
10. A run-on sentence results when a comma is placed between two clauses but a semicolon is needed. T/F

Goal-Setting Exercises

Think for a moment about the kinds of mistakes you make using punctuation marks such as commas and semicolons. What confuses you, or what questions do you have? What kinds of comments do teachers write on your papers: does your writing contain run-ons or fragments? Write three goals about the changes you want to make in your writing when it comes to punctuation.

1. ____________________
2. ____________________
3. ____________________

Before reading further, take a moment to answer a question: What is your current "system" for placing commas? In other words, what is your main reason for placing a comma in a sentence? Right now take a moment to jot down the word or words that popped into your mind.

Chapter Three

Punctuation

A kiss can be a comma, a question mark, or an exclamation point. —Mistinguett, singer (1875–1956)

Do you feel confident about using commas? Right now, you may be guessing about comma placement every time you use one. If that's the case, you are no different from the majority of writers. Commas are only tiny little scratches on the page, yet they wield great power when you don't know the correct way to use them—now it is time to turn that situation around.

With a little practice, commas will make sense. Then you will be ready to master the semicolon. Commas and semicolons form a basic foundation for understanding other types of punctuation. Once you learn them, you will be ready to work on the dash, ellipsis marks, and the colon (which are presented in Chapter 7). Once you become adept at punctuation, you can use it to add variety and personal style to your writing.

Punctuation packages words into logical bundles for clarity, but punctuation itself also communicates subtle shades of meaning and even emotion. As you work through this chapter, realize that punctuation is also the key to solving many grammatical problems, such as fragments and run-ons. Learning how to use commas and semicolons correctly means that you can stop guessing and move forward with confidence.

To learn more about The Writing Process, please visit our Web site at www.mhhe.com/youngBE

CHAPTER-OPENING MATERIAL

Each chapter begins with an opening quote, a chapter outline, and chapter objectives. In order to prepare the students for the lessons, the chapter also opens with a learning inventory and goal setting exercises.

PRACTICAL APPLICATIONS

MARGIN FEATURES

Various margin boxes appear in each chapter to further explain the topics presented and reinforce skills that are vital to understanding Business English and its role in the workplace.

The Writer's Toolkit offers concrete tips and advice on improving one's writing for the workplace.

Internet Exercises give students extra chapter-specific practice by leading them to the book's Web site.

Language Diversity provides a glimpse into the broad range of language use—from Boston English to Spanglish to Black Vernacular English—and how these diverse local languages differ from Business English.

Vocabulary boxes stress building and refining a student's vocabulary with **Key Terms, Soundalikes, Word Usage,** and **New Words.**

Speaking Business provides pronunciation help with difficult words or phrases that are used in the everyday business world.

Communication Challenges offer additional information on practical uses of communication.

WRITER'S TOOLKIT

Conjunction Functions
The three types of conjunctions function as comma signals, indicating where to put a comma or semicolon.

A. *Subordinating conjunctions* are words and phrases that introduce dependent clauses and phrases. (Subordinating conjunctions show relationships.)

Examples: *as, after, since, unless, because, although, until, whereas, if, even though, while, as soon as, when, though, so that, before.*

B. *Adverbial conjunctions* introduce or interrupt independent clauses. (Adverbial conjunctions build bridges, helping the reader infer the writer's intent.)

Examples: *however, in addition, furthermore, consequently, therefore, accordingly, in conclusion, as usual, in general, usually, for example, unfortunately, of course.*

C. *Coordinating conjunctions* connect independent clauses or items in a series. *When needed*, put a comma *before* a coordinating conjunction, not after.

The Seven CCs: *and, but, or, for, nor, so, yet.*

Internet Exercise 3.1

Punctuation References: For information on punctuation resources—both online and on the bookshelf—go to the Web site at www.mhhe.com/youngBE. Select "Student Activities," and then click on the "Chapter 3" link to get started.

Language Diversity

Boston English: Best known for its habit of dropping the *r* and using a broad *A*, Boston English is the dialect not only of Boston but also of much of eastern Massachusetts. Boston English has much in common with the accents of Rhode Island, New Hampshire, and southern Maine, and it is frequently grouped with New York–New Jersey English, though there are subtle differences between the accents of Boston and New York.

Below is a list of words written as they are pronounced in the Boston English dialect. How many can you identify?

1. pahk	park
2. bah	bar
3. wiid	weird
4. lahge	large
5. wicked	very as in "wicked good"
6. sqwea	square
7. byd	bird
8. da tuneriz	the tuner (radio) is; the tuna (fish) is
9. stahtid	started
10. gidadaheah	get out of here (expression of disbelief)

Boston English: Wudja pahk da cah and gimmeah hand with dis hammah?

Standard: Would you park the car and give me a hand with this hammer?

SPEAKING BUSINESS

Vowel Sounds: Did you realize that whenever you pronounce a vowel sound your tongue is down and flat? Vowel sounds vary according to how much the lips and teeth are parted.

If you want to work on a particular vowel sound, first make a list of words that have similar and contrasting sounds.

For example, if you want to work on the way you pronounce the word *been*, make a list of words that rhyme with the traditional pronunciation of *been*, such as *then, ten, men,* and *hen*. Next, make a list of words that sound similar to your current pronunciation, which may sound like "bin"; for example, *spin, chin, Quinn,* and *pin*.

As you say each word out loud, notice how your tongue flattens and also notice how far you open your mouth and lips. For more practice, see EOC Activity 4 on page 92.

Ask Yourself: *Which vowel sounds do I want to work on?*

VOCABULARY: KEY TERMS

Antonyms, Synonyms, and Homonyms: Words that end with the suffix *nym* (from the Greek word *onoma*, for "name") often describe classes of words and the relationships between words. For example, the word *pseudonym* refers to an assumed, or false, name. The following are among the most commonly used *nym* words.

Antonyms are pairs of words that have opposite meanings, such as *early* and *late*, *accidental* and *intentional*, and *attack* and *defend*. Words can have more than one antonym; for example, *wise* and *clever* are antonyms of *foolish*. Can you identify antonyms of the following words?

absent	present
forget	remember
question	answer
abundant	scarce
quick	slow
exit	entrance

Synonyms are two or more words that have the same, or similar, meanings, such as *occupation, vocation,* an[d] ... Business writers use synon[yms] ... interest to their writing an[d] ... repetitive phrasing. Can yo[u] ... synonyms of the following ...

qualified	competent
hinder	delay
question	query
lost	missing
commence	begin
hearty	earnest

Homonyms are two or mo[re] ... sound the same but are (us[ually]) ... differently and mean differ[ent] ... as *bases, basis,* and *basses* ... *sites,* and *cites*. Here are a ... examples of homonyms:

flew	flue
peak	peek
rain	reign
weather	wether

VOCABULARY: WORD USAGE

Loan/Lend: Can you figure out what is wrong with the following?

I can loan you lunch money.

Alberto loaned me his notebook.

If you said using the word *loan* as a verb, you are correct. The word *loan* is a noun, and nouns cannot be used as verbs. Thus, you cannot "loan" anything to anyone. The correct word to use is *lend*. The past tense form of *lend* is *lent*, and so is the past participle.

I can lend you lunch money.

Communication Challenges

Pronoun Mistakes or Hypercorrections: Pronouns may create more problems for speakers and writers than verbs create. Most people who make mistakes with pronouns are not even aware of their mistakes.

There is widespread confusion between the use of *I* and *me*. As children, many people were corrected when they used *me* as a subject: "*Me and John* are going to the store." A correction might have followed immediately, "No, that should be '*John and I* are going to the store.'"

As a result, many people default to the more professional-sounding subjective case pronoun *I* at times when *me* is the only correct choice. This kind of response is called *hypercorrecting*. To a trained ear, using *I* in place of *me* can sound like nails scratching a blackboard. Using *myself* in place of *me* sounds even worse.

The improper use of *I* and *myself* in the object position may have reached epidemic proportions, and this erroneous construction is contagious.

Challenge: With a partner, develop several examples using *I, me,* and *myself* incorrectly, and then revise your ... so that they are correct. Answers will vary.

VOCABULARY: SOUNDALIKES

To/Too/Two: These words are frequently used incorrectly.

To is a preposition and part of an infinitive.

Mark went *to* the store.

To whom it may concern . . .

Tell them *to go* to the meeting.

Too is an adverb relating to quantity.

We have *too much* work.

This has happened *too many* times.

They have given us the wrong order *too often*.

Two is a number.

Please provide *two* packets of materials.

I would like *two* cheeseburgers.

It is *too late* for the *two* of us *to* argue.

To avoid confusion:

Follow *to* with a noun or a verb

Follow *too* with an adverb

Two is a number; can you substitute the number *2*?

VOCABULARY: NEW WORDS

Added to the *Oxford Dictionary of English* in 2005:

wiki, noun: A Web site or database developed collaboratively by a community of users, allowing any user to add and edit content.

podcast, noun: A digital recording, of a radio broadcast or similar program, that is made available on the Internet for downloading to a personal audio player.

Added to the *American Heritage Dictionary* in 2005:

yoctosecond, noun: One septillionth (10^{-24}) of a second.

BOX 8.1 The Editing Process

BEFORE

From: SystaProducts Customer Service
To: Della Reese
Cc:
Subject: Re: Your Order - Invoice # M778

Thank you for your recent inquiry.

Our return process is very simple. Please write the following code on the top of the box M778 this code is used to identify the package when it gets back to our warehouse, and please send it to the address below. We recommend shipping via UPS, FedEx or DHL because they supply tracking information automatically with their ground service (If you use USPS please request Delivery Confirmation and Tracking Service). Also please keep all shipping records and paperwork until your credit is fully processed. Please include a copy of your original packing slip with the M778 number as well as your full name and address on top. You will receive an e-mail notification once the package has been received by our warehouse system. Once the package has been received it takes approximately 14 business days for the credit to be fully processed but may still take 1 to 2 billing cycles to show on your card statement. We do not cover the cost of return shipping. Thank you for allowing us the opportunity to assist you.

SystaProducts
Attn: Returns A1835
4505 Wessley Pkwy
Boston, MA 2720

If you need further assistance, you may contact our Client Support Center by email at orders@systaproducts.net, by phone at 1-555-555-5353 or by visiting our web site at www.SystaProducts.net.
Thank you,

D.W.

AFTER

From: SystaProducts Customer Service
To: Della Reese
Cc:
Subject: Your Order In voice M778

Dear Della:

Our return process is very simple.

1. Send your package to the following address:

   SystaProducts
   Attn: Returns A1835
   4505 Wessley Parkway
   Boston, MA 27200

2. Send your package via UPS, FedEx, or DHL so that it will be tracked automatically if you use the USPS, request delivery confirmation so that you can track your package.
3. Enclose a copy of your original packing slip in the box.
4. Write your full name and address as well as the return code, M778, on top of the box.
5. eep all shipping records and paperwork until your credit is fully processed.

When we receive your package, we will send you an e-mail. Once we receive the package, it takes approximately 14 business days for the credit to be fully processed (but it may still take 1 to 2 billing cycles to show on your credit card statement). We do not cover the cost of return shipping.

If you need further assistance, you may contact our Client Support Center by e-mail at orders@systaproducts.net, by phone at 1-555-555-5343, or by visiting our Web site at www.SystaProducts.net.

Thank you for giving us the opportunity to assist you.

Dennis

Dennis Wilson
Customer Service Representative
SystaProducts
4505 Wessley Parkway
Boston, MA 27200
Phone: 555-555-5353

Here are examples of highly formal and professional writing:

THE EDITING PROCESS

shows a side-by-side comparisons of the same document both before and after proper edits were completed.

SECTION C CONCEPT CHECK

1. What does voice (active or passive) tell you about the subject of a sentence?

Voice tells whether the subject performs or receives action. In the active voice, the subject performs action; in the passive voice, the subject receives action.

2. When might it be more effective to use passive voice?

Passive voice might be more effective when you do not know who performed an action or do not want to call attention to that person.

3. Describe steps you can take to keep your subjects real and verbs strong.

Avoid expletive forms (*it is* and *there are*); use action verbs rather than state-of-being verbs; turn nominals (such as words ending in *tion* or *ment*) back into action verbs.

SECTION D: PARALLEL STRUCTURE

Using **parallel structure** means putting similar sentence elements in the same form. Parallel structure creates flow and consistency as it makes your ideas stand out. Writing that lacks parallel structure sounds choppy and disjointed and is difficult to understand.

In this section, you start with verbs as they appear in small units: words and phrases. Then you will work with sentences that shift from active to passive. Parallel structure is an important topic, and you will do more work with it in Chapter 8. For now, let's begin with a review of how to put similar elements in the same form by using gerunds and infinitives.

PARALLEL STRUCTURE WITH INFINITIVES AND GERUNDS

In Chapter 2, you learned that verbs could become nouns by changing form. Here's a brief review of two common ways that verbs become nouns:

- An **infinitive** is formed by adding the word *to* to the base form of a verb, as in *to go, to see, to be, to follow*.
- A **gerund** is formed by adding *ing* to the base form of a verb, as in *going, seeing, being,* and *following*.

One way writing can lack parallel structure is by presenting a list of items as a mixture of gerunds and infinitives. Here's an example:

Incorrect: Charley's favorite activities are *golfing, to fish,* and *swimming.*

Correct: Charley's favorite activities are *golfing, fishing,* and *swimming.*

VOCABULARY: NEW WORDS

Added to the *Oxford Dictionary of English* in 2005:

wiki, noun: A Web site or database developed collaboratively by a community of users, allowing any user to add and edit content.

podcast, noun: A digital recording, of a radio broadcast or similar program, that is made available on the Internet for downloading to a personal audio player.

Added to the *American Heritage Dictionary* in 2005:

yoctosecond, noun: One septillionth (10^{-24}) of a second.

Internet Exercise 4.2

Verb Worksheets: For more practice with the topics reviewed in this chapter, visit the Web site at www.mhhe.com/youngBE and select the "Chapter 4" link to get started.

CONCEPT CHECKS

The Concept Checks at the end of each section provide an opportunity for the students to immediately apply the material presented in the chapter.

PRACTICAL APPLICATIONS

PRACTICAL APPLICATIONS

EXPLORE, PRACTICE, APPLY

The Explore, Practice, Apply features are integrated into the text so that students apply what they are learning while the concepts are still fresh.

108 Unit 2 English in Action

Communication Challenges

Business English vs. Local Language: When you use a verb differently from its prescribed usage in Business English, you are using your local language.

Identify where your local-language verb patterns differ from those in Business English, and then practice the Business English pattern until you feel comfortable.

To some degree or another, everyone speaks a local language. Grammar is only one aspect of how languages differ; another aspect is pronunciation. For example, do you say things such as "Wa jeet for lunch?" "Howja do on the test?" "Whoja go to the meeting with?"

Ask Yourself: *What local-language patterns have I noticed in my speech or writing?*

APPLY

Instructions: Select five verbs that you use differently in your local language than you do in Business English. For each verb, compose three sentences in local language and then translate your sentences into Business English. Try to use both the past tense and the past participle forms.

Verbs in Present Tense: The *S* Form

Verb Principle 3: *In simple present tense, apply the s form correctly to third-person singular verbs.*

Third-person singular verbs are also known as the ***s* form** because they *all* end in *s*. Many people consistently make errors with the *s* form. For example:

Incorrect: The service department *have* the right attitude about business.

Correct: The service department *has* the right attitude about business.

Incorrect: Wilson *don't have* the information we need.

Correct: Wilson *does not (doesn't) have* the information we need.

VOCABULARY: KEY TERMS

Transitive and Intransitive Verbs: Have you ever wondered about the difference between the verbs *lay* and *lie?* These verbs are confusing and rarely used correctly.

The verb *lay,* which means "to place," is transitive and needs an object. The verb *lie,* which means "to recline," is intransitive and cannot be followed by an object.

- Transitive verbs need a direct object.
- Intransitive verbs cannot have a direct object.

Most verbs can be used with or without a direct object, but a few verbs are *only* transitive or *only* intransitive. The verbs that are especially tricky are the ones that seem to come in pairs, such as *lay* and *lie* or *sit* and *set*. Here are some examples of transitive and intransitive verbs.

	Base	Past Tense	Past Participle
Intransitive	lie	lay	lain
Marcus felt ill so he had lain *down.*			
Transitive	lay	laid	laid
Sue laid the *book* on the table.			
Intransitive	sit	sat	sat
Izzy sat *down.*			
Transitive	set	set	set
Fred set the *book* on the table.			

In these examples, the adverb *(down)* modifies the intransitive verbs, but the direct object *(book)* follows the transitive verbs.

PRACTICE

A. Instructions: Correct the simple present tense sentences below. **For example:**

Incorrect: Their accountant have all of the information.

Corrected: Their accountant *has* all of the information.

1. Our sales representative don't always complete the reports on time.

   Our sales representative *does not (doesn't)* always complete the reports on time.

2. While Jolie work on a solution, Peter wait for an answer.

   While Jolie *works* on a solution, Peter *waits* for an answer.

3. The training director always follow the guidelines for the course.

   The training director always *follows* the guidelines for the course.

4. The director haven't analyzed the data from their department.

   The director has not (hasn't) analyzed the data from their department.

5. Meredith say that my expense account have not been turned in yet.

   Meredith says that my expense account has not been turned in yet.

Verbs in Past Time: Helper Verbs

Verb Principle 2: *When using verbs in past time, do not use a helper verb with th[e] tense form; however, you must use a helper verb with the past participle.*

With *regular verbs,* the past tense and past participle are the same; they both end [...] result, with regular verbs in past time you cannot make an error based on using o[r] a helper verb. However, with irregular verbs, this kind of error is common.

- When using the past participle form of an irregular verb, you *must* use a helper.
- When using the past tense form of an irregular verb, you *cannot* use a helper.

Listed below are a few irregular verbs that are used in the examples that follow. [...] helper verbs were randomly chosen.) For a more complete list of irregular verbs, se[e ...]

Base	Past Tense	Past Participle
choose	chose	(has) chosen
do	did	(have) done
freeze	froze	(had) frozen
go	went	(is) gone
see	saw	(are) seen
speak	spoke	(was) spoken
write	wrote	(were) written

For *irregular verbs,* here are the two most common errors:

1. *Type 1 error:* Using an irregular past tense form with a helper.

   Incorrect: Your budget *is froze* until next year. *(is frozen)*

   Incorrect: The director *has spoke* about that problem. *(spoke or has [...])*

   Incorrect: Marty *has* finally *did* the paperwork for the proposal. *(did o[r ...])*

   Incorrect: The report *had went* out yesterday. *(went or had gone)*

2. *Type 2 error:* Using an irregular past participle without a helper.

   Incorrect: Margaret *seen* Bob at the conference. *(saw or had seen)*

   Incorrect: They *done* the work last week. *(did or had done)*

   Incorrect: Barbra *chosen* the décor for the new office. *(chose or has [...])*

   Incorrect: Alice *been* the director for a year now. *(has been)*

Here is how to stop making errors with irregular verbs:

1. Know the correct past tense and past participle form of each irregular verb.
2. When using the past tense form, *do not use* a helper or auxiliary verb.
3. When using the past participle, *use* a helper.

If you do not have a problem with the verbs presented here, diagnose your ow[n] language pattern to know which verbs give you problems.

EXPLORE

Instructions: Observe speech patterns in a public place (in a restaurant or an elevator, on a bus or train, on the street). Listen until you hear five local-language statements involving verbs. Make a list of the verbs or of the statements and bring them to class for discussion.

END-OF-CHAPTER ACTIVITIES

At the end of each chapter, after a chapter summary and checklist, students will find several activities to reinforce the lesson, including review questions, speaking exercises, and a vocabulary list. The activities also contain a Process Memo, serving as an important communication tool, and team exercises and a key to the Learning Inventory from the beginning of each chapter.

CHAPTER 5 SUMMARY

Pronouns are challenging—maybe more challenging than you first realized when you began this chapter. However, through diligent practice, you have now made another major stride in your skill growth.

By continuing to observe how you use pronouns in your local language, you can build a wall between the way you use pronouns in Business English and the way you use them in your local language. Table 5.2 summarizes the critical aspects of pronoun use. Review it now, and use it in the future as a quick reference about pronouns.

CHAPTER 5 CHECKLIST

__ Subjective pronouns are functioning as subjects
__ Objective pronouns are functioning as objects
__ Reflexive pronouns refer to subject pronouns
__ Point of view (I, you, we, they) is consistent
__ Pronouns agree with their antecedents
__ Collective nouns have correct agreement with their verbs
__ Indefinite pronouns have correct agreement with their verbs
__ Writing is gender neutral

CHAPTER 5 END-OF-CHAPTER ACTIVITIES

ACTIVITY 1: PROCESS MEMO

INSTRUCTIONS: Write your instructor a short message indicating the kinds of changes you are now making with pronouns in your speaking and writing. Are you more confident using pronouns? What questions or problems do you still have?

If you have Internet access, you can complete this exercise online at www.mhhe.com/youngBE and then send an e-mail to your instructor.

ACTIVITY 2: PRONOUN WORKSHEETS

WORKSHEET A: USING CASE CORRECTLY

INSTRUCTIONS: In the following sentences, correct any errors in pronoun case. For example:

Incorrect: Allison gave the report to Lou and I this morning.

Corrected: Allison gave the report to Lou and *me* this morning.

1. Yesenia and me met with two prospective clients yesterday.

   Yesenia and *I* met with two prospective clients yesterday.

2. Both prospective clients decided that they would like to work with Yesenia and I.

   Both prospective clients decided that they would like to work with Yesenia and *me*.

154

PRACTICAL APPLICATIONS

THE INBOX

COMPOSING

In a magazine or newspaper, find a photograph that has people in it. Write a paragraph describing the activity taking place in the photo. Try to write the paragraph without using *any* pronouns.

REFLECTING

Consider the paragraph you wrote about the photo. How difficult was it to avoid using pronouns? What is the effect of writing without pronouns?

Rewrite the paragraph using pronouns where you feel they would be appropriate. How has your paragraph changed? Do you like one paragraph better than the other? Why or why not?

DISCUSSING

1. Some writing experts think that the overuse of pronouns weakens writing. The theory is that writers should insert noun phrases in place of some pronouns to break up the monotony of repetitious and vague pronouns. Here's an example:

   The writer spent several years on *her* first novel. *She* was finally happy with *it* after endless hours of revising.

   The writer spent several years on *her* first novel. *She* was finally happy with *the final edition* after endless hours of revising.

   Do you think inserting a noun phrase in place of a pronoun makes a difference? Have your group discuss this question, and then present three examples supporting your view.

2. The Preamble to the United States Constitution states:

   > We the People of the United States, in Order to form a more perfect Union, establish Justice, insure domestic Tranquility, provide for the common defence, promote the general Welfare, and secure the Blessings of Liberty to ourselves and our Posterity, do ordain and establish this Constitution for the United States of America.

   As you read through this famous proclamation, notice the use of pronouns. Think about the historical setting against which the Preamble was written. Think about the Preamble as it applies to citizens today. Who are the "we" in "We the people"? For whom are the "Blessings of Liberty" being secured ("us")? Discuss how the use of pronouns can hinder or aid legal documents by the nature of their vagueness. Would the United States be a different country today if the Preamble had actually avoided the use of pronouns and stated the antecedents to which *we* and *our* refer?

165

THE INBOX

Located at the end of the activities is The Inbox, where students can continue to practice and hone their skills in both writing and editing. Each Inbox has sections on composing a document, reflecting and discussing what was written, and finally editing other passages. For Chapters 7-10, The Inbox also includes a section on creating documents for a career building portfolio.

Writer's Reference Manual

For further detail on any topic reviewed in this reference manual, please refer to *The Gregg Reference Manual*.

CONTENTS

ABBREVIATIONS

Abbreviations are shortened forms of words or phrases, such as *Mr.* (for the word *Mister*) or *R.S.V.P.* (for *Repondez s'il vous plait*). Writers use conventionally accepted abbreviations to shorten repeated references to the lengthy names or terms the abbreviations represent. For example, in a newspaper article about the North American Free Trade Agreement, using the abbreviation *NAFTA* after the first reference saves time for both the reader and the writer.

344

WRITER'S REFERENCE MANUAL

At the end of the text is an easy to use reference manual for writing. The manual is organized alphabetically to quickly find guidance on important topics. Each chapter also contains an activity that refers to the manual so that students can become familiar with using reference manuals.

PRACTICAL APPLICATIONS

ONLINE LEARNING CENTER

The Online Learning Center (OLC) is a Web site that follows the text chapter-by-chapter. OLC content is ancillary, supplementary, and relevant to the textbook.

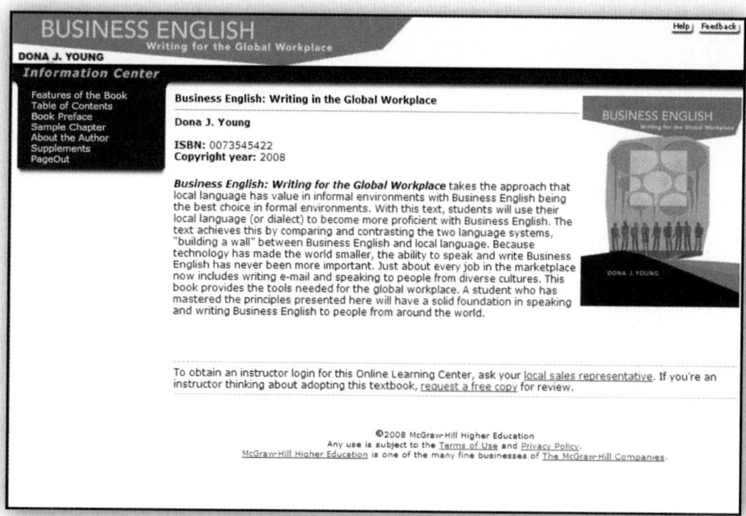

BUSINESS ENGLISH
Writing for the Global Workplace
DONA J. YOUNG
Help | Feedback

Information Center

- Features of the Book
- Table of Contents
- Book Preface
- Sample Chapter
- About the Author
- Supplements
- PageOut

Business English: Writing in the Global Workplace

Dona J. Young

ISBN: 0073545422
Copyright year: 2008

Business English: Writing for the Global Workplace takes the approach that local language has value in informal environments with Business English being the best choice in formal environments. With this text, students will use their local language (or dialect) to become more proficient with Business English. The text achieves this by comparing and contrasting the two language systems, "building a wall" between Business English and local language. Because technology has made the world smaller, the ability to speak and write Business English has never been more important. Just about every job in the marketplace now includes writing e-mail and speaking to people from diverse cultures. This book provides the tools needed for the global workplace. A student who has mastered the principles presented here will have a solid foundation in speaking and writing Business English to people from around the world.

To obtain an instructor login for this Online Learning Center, ask your local sales representative. If you're an instructor thinking about adopting this textbook, request a free copy for review.

©2008 McGraw-Hill Higher Education
Any use is subject to the Terms of Use and Privacy Policy.
McGraw-Hill Higher Education is one of the many fine businesses of The McGraw-Hill Companies.

ANNOTATED INSTRUCTOR EDITION

The Annotated Instructor Edition (AIE) offers instructional strategies that reinforce and enhance the core concepts presented in the student text. These include an introduction to each chapter, called "The Teaching Workshop," answers to the Practice and Concept Check sections, and an answer key to some of the activities at the end of the chapter.

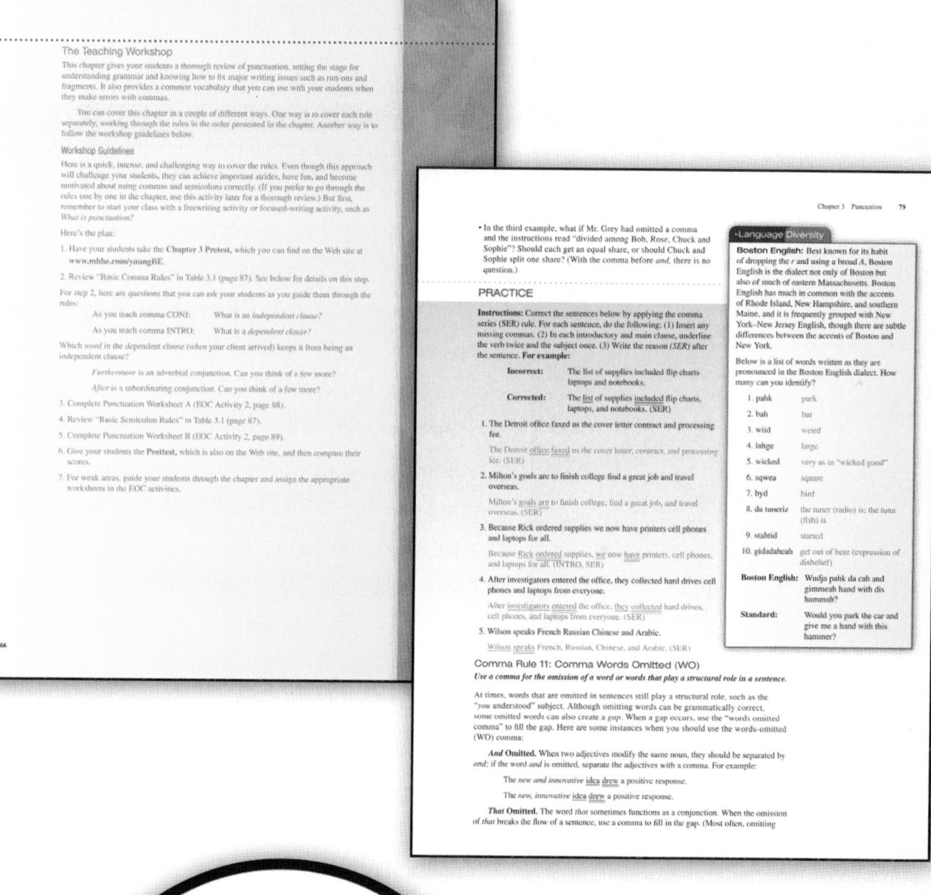

The Teaching Workshop

This chapter gives your students a thorough review of punctuation, setting the stage for understanding grammar and knowing how to fix major writing issues such as run-ons and fragments. It also provides a common vocabulary that you can use with your students when they make errors with commas.

You can cover this chapter in a couple of different ways. One way is to cover each rule separately, working through the rules in the order presented in the chapter. Another way is to follow the workshop guidelines below.

Workshop Guidelines

Here is a quick, intense, and challenging way to cover the rules. Even though this approach will challenge your students, they can achieve important strides, have fun, and become motivated about using commas and semicolons correctly. (If you prefer to go through the rules one by one in the chapter, use this activity later for a thorough review.) But first, remember to start your class with a freewriting activity or focused-writing activity, such as *What is punctuation?*

Here's the plan:

1. Have your students take the **Chapter 3 Pretest,** which you can find on the Web site at **www.mhhe.com/youngBE.**
2. Review "Basic Comma Rules" in Table 3.1 (page 87). See below for details on this step.

For step 2, here are questions that you can ask your students as you guide them through the rules:

As you teach comma CONJ: What is an *independent clause?*

As you teach comma INTRO: What is a *dependent clause?*

Which *word* in the dependent clause (*when* your client arrived) keeps it from being an independent clause?

Furthermore is an adverbial conjunction. Can you think of a few more?

After is a subordinating conjunction. Can you think of a few more?

3. Complete Punctuation Worksheet A (EOC Activity 2, page 88).
4. Review "Basic Semicolon Rules" in Table 3.1 (page 87).
5. Complete Punctuation Worksheet B (EOC Activity 2, page 89).
6. Give your students the **Posttest,** which is also on the Web site, and then compare their scores.
7. For weak areas, guide your students through the chapter and assign the appropriate worksheets in the EOC activities.

66

Chapter 3 Punctuation 79

- In the third example, what if Mr. Grey had omitted a comma and the instructions read "divided among Bob, Rose, Chuck and Sophie"? Should each get an equal share, or should Chuck and Sophie split one share? (With the comma before *and,* there is no question.)

PRACTICE

Instructions: Correct the sentences below by applying the comma series (SER) rule. For each sentence, do the following: (1) Insert any missing commas. (2) In each introductory and main clause, underline the verb twice and the subject once. (3) Write the reason *(SER)* after the sentence. **For example:**

Incorrect: The list of supplies included flip charts laptops and notebooks.

Corrected: The list of supplies included flip charts, laptops, and notebooks. (SER)

1. The Detroit office faxed us the cover letter contract and processing fee.
   The Detroit office faxed us the cover letter, contract, and processing fee. (SER)
2. Milton's goals are to finish college find a great job and travel overseas.
   Milton's goals are to finish college, find a great job, and travel overseas. (SER)
3. Because Rick ordered supplies we now have printers cell phones and laptops for all.
   Because Rick ordered supplies, we now have printers, cell phones, and laptops for all. (INTRO, SER)
4. After investigators entered the office, they collected hard drives cell phones and laptops from everyone.
   After investigators entered the office, they collected hard drives, cell phones, and laptops from everyone. (SER)
5. Wilson speaks French Russian Chinese and Arabic.
   Wilson speaks French, Russian, Chinese, and Arabic. (SER)

Language Diversity

Boston English: Best known for its habit of dropping the *r* and using a broad *A,* Boston English is the dialect not only of Boston but also of much of eastern Massachusetts. Boston English has much in common with the accents of Rhode Island, New Hampshire, and southern Maine, and it is frequently grouped with New York–New Jersey English, though there are subtle differences between the accents of Boston and New York.

Below is a list of words written as they are pronounced in the Boston English dialect. How many can you identify?

1. pahk	park
2. bah	bar
3. wiid	weird
4. lahge	large
5. wicked	very as in "wicked good"
6. sqwea	square
7. byd	bird
8. da tuneriz	the tuner (radio) is; the tuna (fish) is
9. stahtid	started
10. gidadaheah	get out of here (expression of disbelief)

Boston English: Wudja pahk da cah and gimmeah hand with dis hammah?

Standard: Would you park the car and give me a hand with this hammer?

Comma Rule 11: Comma Words Omitted (WO)

Use a comma for the omission of a word or words that play a structural role in a sentence.

At times, words that are omitted in sentences still play a structural role, such as the "*you* understood" subject. Although omitting words can be grammatically correct, some omitted words can also create a *gap.* When a gap occurs, use the "words omitted comma" to fill the gap. Here are some instances when you should use the words-omitted (WO) comma:

***And* Omitted.** When two adjectives modify the same noun, they should be separated by *and;* if the word *and* is omitted, separate the adjectives with a comma. For example:

The *new and innovative* idea drew a positive response.

The *new, innovative* idea drew a positive response.

***That* Omitted.** The word *that* sometimes functions as a conjunction. When the omission of *that* breaks the flow of a sentence, use a comma to fill in the gap. (Most often, omitting

INSTRUCTOR'S RESOURCE CD-ROM

The Instructor's Resource CD-ROM (IRCD) is an electronic version of all the instructional material from the AIE. It will include materials such as PowerPoint presentations, Lecture Notes, and additional instructor materials.

Unit One

Language in Context

In today's global business culture, English is the "unofficial official" language. People all over the world are speaking and writing English to each other for international commerce. For example, when businesspeople from India speak to their counterparts in Japan, they might use English as a common ground. Your ability to speak and write English has never been more important in determining your success in business.

English comes in many different forms: American English, British English, and numerous other varieties. This text gives you grounding in *Business English,* which is the language of the boardroom. Business English is rooted in *Standard English,* which is "standardized": everyone who studies it learns the same rules of grammar and word usage. Though pronunciation varies on the basis of geographic location, even some aspects of pronunciation are standardized.

The term *Business English* lets you know immediately that it is the language of the workplace, not necessarily the home. At home or with friends, most people speak a different variety of English, which can be tagged as a *dialect* or *local language.* Local languages follow their own rules of grammar, word usage, and pronunciation. Local languages express their own style and identity. In the process of improving your Business English, you will also get in touch with your local language, identifying how it is similar to and different from Business English.

If you apply yourself in this course, you will learn to use Business English proficiently; at the same time, you will be encouraged to continue speaking your local language when you are at home or with friends. Your goal is to learn to apply language the way you now select your wardrobe, using the language system—formal *or* informal—that works best for the situation.

To become proficient in Business English *and* retain your local language, you need to practice what you are learning in real-world environments. That's partly what this unit's title, "Language in Context," means. *Book learnin' ain't enough:* adapting lifelong language patterns requires practice, practice, and more practice. So when you think about learning language in context, focus on applying your new skills through speaking *and* writing, shifting your language style according to the environment you are in.

Learning—or changing one's skills, behaviors, and ways of thinking—can be difficult, at times bringing out fears and self-doubts. To make changes in the way you use language, you will need to tap into your greatest strengths and your highest qualities. The more flexible, patient, committed, and optimistic you are, the greater strides you will make in achieving your goals.

Unit 1 Language in Context

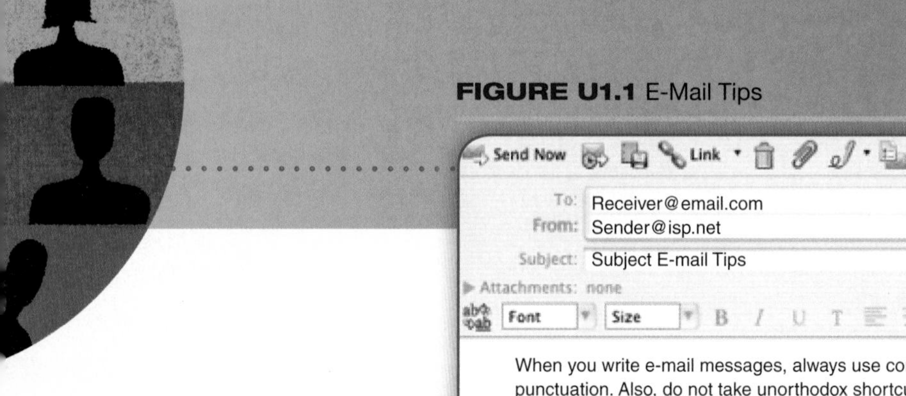

Send Now
Link
Insert
To: Receiver@email.com
From: Sender@isp.net
Subject: Subject E-mail Tips
Attachments: none
Font
Size
When you write e-mail messages, always use correct grammar and punctuation. Also, do not take unorthodox shortcuts: follow standard rules for capitalization, and do not abbreviate unnecessarily. Keep information short and to the point. Also, don't press the Send button if you have any doubts about your message. If you feel unsure, either save your message as a draft or make a phone call.
Resist the urge to add "personality" to your business communications through the use of *emoticons* such as smileys or sad faces [:) or :( ], and do not use slang. Since your message can be forwarded up the chain of command without your knowing it, always keep your messages professional in tone and appearance.

FIGURE U1.1 E-Mail Tips

E-MAIL ESSENTIALS

Basic Parts of E-Mail

With e-mail, software templates provide the heading; writers need only fill in the necessary information. However, there is still room for misuse. Here are some tips to keep in mind:

- Use an accurate **subject line,** and update it as your conversation evolves.
- Use a **greeting,** even if it is as simple as the person's name.
- Keep the **body** (or message) short.
- Use a simple **closing.**
- Include a **"sign-off,"** or **signature,** that lists your company name, address, and phone number.

See Figure U1.1 for additional e-mail tips.

E-Mail Format

Although e-mail standards are still evolving, all business writing must follow standard rules for grammar, punctuation, and abbreviation. Though more casual than a business letter, e-mail is a business document that portrays an image of you and your company. Thus, do not be too casual with e-mail. (In other words, do not use abbreviations or other shortcuts to save time.)

Salutation

The purpose of the first part of any business document is to connect with the reader. To connect with your reader, start an e-mail with a salutation or greeting. Since e-mail is less formal than a business letter, you have many choices. Any of the following would be appropriate, depending on what you want to achieve.

Dear Michael: *or* Michael:

Dear Michael, *or* Michael,

Many professionals even use a salutation such as "Hi Michael," when they communicate with people on a regular basis.

If you do not know the recipient and your e-mail is your first communication, follow the most formal guideline: Use the recipient's last name preceded by *dear*. (For example, *Dear Mr. Stevens:*)

Message

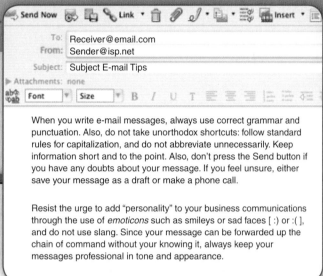

When you follow basic guidelines with e-mail messages, your communication will be more successful. Consider these points:

- Keep your message short, about one screen in length.
- Limit each message to one main issue.
- Start with the most important information and get right to the point.
- If you need the reader to take action, identify the needed action at the beginning of the message.

Closing

E-mail does not have rigid rules and protocols as business letters do. Standard closings such as *Sincerely* or *Sincerely yours,* while appropriate in letters, are too formal for most e-mail messages.

When you are writing to someone for the first time, be conservative and use a closing such as *Regards* or *Best regards,* followed by a comma. When writing in less formal situations, you can be a bit expressive by using a short statement such as the following: *Take care. Let's talk soon. Hope your day goes well. Thanks for your help.*

Ask Yourself: *What are some interesting closings I have used or seen? What closing do I typically use?*

Note: See the Web site for more detailed e-mail guidelines.

Chapter One

English for Business Today

The limits of my language mean the limits of my world. —Ludwig Wittgenstein, philosopher (1889–1951)

To succeed in most parts of the world today, regardless of your career choice, you will need to speak and write formal English. "English dominates international business, politics, and culture more than any other language in human history."[1]

For the sake of their future international business careers, millions of young students around the world are learning English as their second language; in fact, the number of people who speak English as a second language may already exceed the number of native speakers.[2] Those students are learning **Standard English**—considered the "universal" way of speaking English because it is "standardized" and studied formally; it is also the root language of other varieties of English used around the globe. **Business English** is a form of Standard English and is the language used in formal situations in the workplace; more specifically, Business English is the language of the boardroom.

Most English-speaking people are fluent in varieties other than formal English, even when they are not aware of it. In fact, most are **bidialectal**, speaking two or more varieties of English.[3] Think about the way you speak when you are with family and friends. Now think about the way you speak when you are in a classroom. Here are a few questions to consider:

- Are you more aware of your speech when you are in a formal situation?
- Are you sometimes unsure if the grammar of your speech or writing is correct?
- Do you speak differently in informal situations than you do in formal ones?

Most people around the world speak more than one variety, or **dialect,** of their native language, regardless of whether their home tongue is English or Spanish or Russian or Chinese or any other language. The use of **local language** (another term for *variety* or *dialect*) is prevalent throughout the world, regardless of the language being discussed.

This book will help you build language awareness and skills. You will learn to speak and write formal English confidently *without* giving up your local language. In professional, academic, and international environments, you will be prepared to speak "the queen's English." And when you are with your friends or family, you will be comfortable speaking any way you want; in fact, the best language to use with friends and family is your local language. However, when you improve your Business English, your career opportunities will soar.

To learn more about The Writing Process, please visit our Web site at **www.mhhe.com/youngBE**

Outline

Chapter 1: English for Business Today

Section A: What Is English?

Section B: What Role Does Local Language Play?

Section C: Learning Language in Context

Objectives

When you have completed your study of Chapter 1, you will be able to:

1. Understand the difference between Business English and local language.
2. Recognize and identify formal and informal language patterns.
3. Develop an understanding of what it means to be bidialectal.
4. Understand that Business English is the international language of commerce.
5. Recognize which language pattern to use in formal and informal environments.
6. Begin to acquire the ability to shift language patterns at will.

Learning Inventory

1. Most people speak differently with friends or family than they do at school or work. T/F
2. Repeating the same writing mistakes over and over again relates to local-language use. T/F
3. When you write e-mail for business, using shortcuts such as "lol" is acceptable. T/F
4. Most people speak a local language when they are with family and friends. T/F
5. British English differs from American English in grammar. T/F
6. Formal, written English is consistent in grammar usage everywhere in the world. T/F
7. As your formal English improves, you should continue to use informal language with friends. T/F
8. When you write, you should edit your work as you compose. T/F
9. Mistakes come in patterns because writers use local language. T/F
10. *Variety* is another term for *dialect,* which is another term for *local language.* T/F

Goal-Setting Exercises

For a few minutes, think about the kind of job you want to get when you finish school. Now give serious thought to the kind of speaking and writing skills you will need to enter your new career and progress up the corporate ladder. What kinds of changes would you like to make in your writing and speaking? Would you like to feel more confident? How would you like your first employer to describe your spoken and written language skills? Write three goals that will bring you closer to achieving your career objectives.

1. ______________________________

2. ______________________________

3. ______________________________

SECTION A: WHAT IS ENGLISH?

In this section, you will first examine characteristics of language in general terms. Then you will work toward defining specific qualities of your own unique language system and how your language system fits into the broader scheme of language usage.

LANGUAGE IS A SYSTEM

Have you ever wondered why people from different parts of the same country speak differently? Have you ever thought that there was a "right way" to speak, and has that thought made you feel uncomfortable about the way you speak? Language is a complicated issue. As you work through this chapter, you will see language in a broader context; and you are encouraged to enjoy the language voyage you are now beginning.

Language is defined as "an *arbitrary system* of vocal symbols by which members of a speech community communicate and cooperate."[4] Language is **arbitrary** because words take on meaning based on "the agreement of the speakers of a given language," and thus words for the same things can vary greatly among languages. Language is **systematic** because words follow a structure; they are not used randomly. This is true of modern languages as well as ancient ones.

Thus, a language is arbitrary and systematic in the way in which words string together to create meaning.[5] Once again, *arbitrary* means that words are based on mutual agreement. So when you use a word such as *bad* with friends, as in "That's a *bad* shirt," the word *bad* means something different than it does when you say to a teacher, "That's a *bad* question." Another example is *cool.* Speakers use the word *cool* to refer to the temperature in a room or to describe how they feel about a person or event. In each case, both the speaker and the listener understand the meaning based on their unspoken agreement of what the word means at that moment.

The *systematic* aspect of language refers to the grammar, with speakers stringing words together in the same format. For example, in English, sentences follow the systematic pattern of "subject-verb-object" (SVO). For Romance languages such as French, Spanish, and Italian, the systematic structure is "subject-object-verb" (SOV). In Chinese, verbs do not have tenses; another word in the sentence indicates the time frame. Every language has its own systematic ordering of words, or **grammar,** and that includes the various local languages that spring from it.

Because it depends on the mutual agreement of its speakers, language is a "living organism." Because they are *alive,* all spoken languages throughout the world change over time, with some languages changing more than others. This organic quality of language allows some words to be added while others fall out of use; even geographic pronunciation, or accents, changes over time. For example, the way people spoke English 100 years ago in your part of the world sounded very different from the way you and your friends speak English today. (See Figure 1.1.)

FIGURE 1.1 English Language Timeline

There are many varieties of English spoken in the world; this timeline shows the evolution of English over the last 1,500 years.

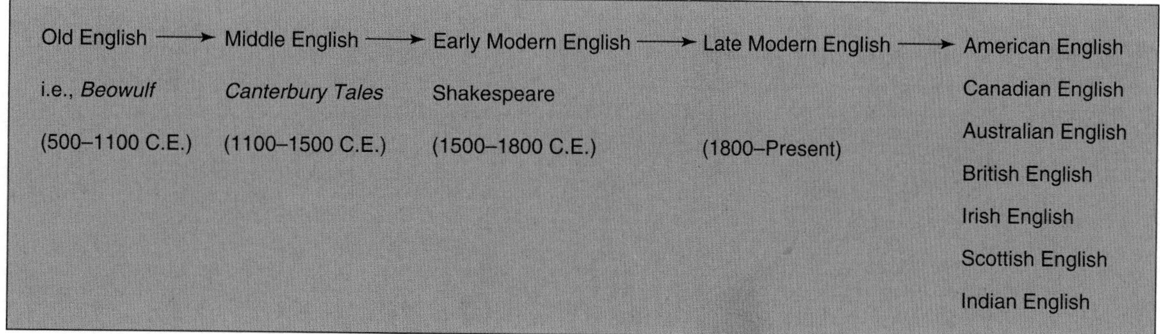

VARIETIES OF STANDARD ENGLISH

"Whereas the English-speaking world was formerly perceived as a hierarchy of parent (Britain) and children ('the colonies'), it is now seen rather as a family of varieties."[6] Even British English, the original source of the numerous varieties of English spoken around the world, is now considered only one of the family of English varieties.

This perception of language differences dates back to the early 1800s. In 1808, John Jamieson published the *Etymological Dictionary of the Scottish Language* in which he recognized that there was a difference between the Scottish variety of English and the English of England.[7] The 1848 publication of *Bartlett's Dictionary of Americanisms* was further documentation that a distinct variety of English was spoken in America.

Varieties Among Countries

How does American English differ from British English and all the other varieties, such as its Canadian, Irish, Scottish, Australian, and New Zealand cousins? There are three components to compare:

1. Grammar
2. Pronunciation
3. Word usage

Let's examine each one of these components in terms of the use of Standard English around the globe.

Grammar Written English does not vary from country to country on the basis of its structure; all formal varieties of English follow the same grammar. Regardless of what country you are in, you could use the same handbooks, reference books, and textbooks. In fact, *the least likely component of any language to change over time is its grammar.*

For the past couple of hundred years, the grammar of English has not changed significantly. However, certain aspects of English grammar are not applied as rigidly as they once were. For example, distinguishing between *who/whom* is now not done often in informal contexts, and ending sentences with prepositions is now acceptable in most circumstances.

Pronunciation In every country, English words take on different pronunciation; in fact, pronunciation even varies within each English-speaking country. British and American English differ primarily in the way vowels are pronounced. The difference is referred to as "the great vowel shift," which is thought to have occurred some time around 1400 C.E. For example, Americans pronounce the word *dog* as "dawg"; whereas the British pronounce it as "dohg," with a long *o* sound. This example is just one among many of how American and British vowel sounds differ. Some words are pronounced differently for no logical explanation, such as the word *schedule;* the British say "shejule" and the Americans, "skejewel."

> **• Internet Exercise 1.1**
>
> **The Great Vowel Shift:** To find out more about the "great vowel shift," go to the Web site at **www.mhhe.com/youngBE** and select the "Chapter 1" link to get started.

Canadian and American pronunciations are similar to each other but also differ in some vowel sounds, specifically the *ou* sound as in *house.* In the States, the *ou* is pronounced as "ow," so *out* is pronounced "owt"; in Canada, *ou* is pronounced "oo," so *out* is pronounced "oot."

In some areas of England and the eastern United States, speakers systematically leave off the *r* sound after vowels within words; *mark* would be pronounced "mahk." They add the *r* sound after a vowel that ends a word; *idea* would be pronounced "idear."

People who seek careers in broadcasting or acting often go to voice coaches to lose their accents. In reality, accentless speech is nonexistent; in other words, every geographic region has its own accent. Like it or not, we all have an accent unless we've gone to a voice coach to eliminate it—and then there's no locale in the world where people actually speak that way.[8]

Word Usage Every English-speaking country has its own unique words that people from other countries may not understand. For example, in Great Britain, a car has a "boot," whereas in America, a car has a "trunk." Here are a few more examples:

British	American
barrister	attorney
bank holiday	legal holiday
lift	elevator
single ticket	one-way ticket
account card	charge card
post code	zip code

Some words are also spelled differently, as in the following:

British	American
centre	center
theatre	theater
organise	organize
colour	color
practise	practice

The examples in this section are just a small sampling. Many more words and phrases differ in pronunciation and spelling, and it would take a linguistic study to cover all the differences. However, the important point to remember is this: For the most part, *varieties of Standard English around the world are more similar than they are different.*

Varieties within the United States

Variety can be used for the word *dialect* or for the term *local language*. In their book *Do You Speak American?* Robert MacNeil and William Cran examine the broad range of language variety spoken in the United States and how the dialects are constantly changing.[9] They examine the use of the **vernacular** (another word for *dialect*) around the country, giving a realistic picture of language usage today. Some of the varieties of English found in America today include the following:

Appalachian

Boston English

Black Vernacular English

Cajun

Chicano English

Gullah

Hawaiian pidgin

Southern dialect

Spanglish

But this partial list of dialects does not tell the whole story. Many local languages in the United States are dying out, and new ones are being added faster than linguists can officially record them. Local languages change much more rapidly than does standard language partly because standard language is established through formal study. "The dialects of New York, Philadelphia, Detroit, Chicago, Saint Louis, Dallas and Los Angeles are now more different from each other than they were 50 or 100 years ago."[10]

TABLE 1.1 | Indo-European Language Tree

The language-tree model begins with a theorized original tongue from which all the world's languages evolved. In this language tree, "Proto-Indo-European" refers to a descendant of that original tongue. This table shows the branches that include Latin and the modern Romance languages as well as the Germanic languages and their descendants (many people think that the roots of English come from Latin, but in fact English is a Germanic language). Other descendants of the Proto-Indo-European language (not listed) are the Indo-Iranian languages, including Hindi and Sanskrit; the Slavic languages; the Baltic languages; the Celtic languages; and Greek.

PROTO-INDO-EUROPEAN				
Latin	**West Germanic**		**East Germanic**	**North Germanic**
Catalan	Low German	High German	Gothic	Gothic Old Norse
French	Modern Low German	Modern High German		Danish
Italian	Frisian	Yiddish		Swedish
Portuguese	**English**			Farnese
Provencal	Dutch			Norwegian
Romanche	Flemish			Icelandic
Romanian	Afrikaans			
Spanish				
Galician				

Communication Challenges

What Is Communication? When you communicate, you are sending a message; but that's only one part of the communication process. When you communicate, you are using your words and your listening skills to build relationships. Here are some key points about communication:

- Communication is about building relationships.
- Communication builds relationships through establishing trust, which develops over a period of time.
- Communication relates to the environment in which it occurs. The environment constantly changes; as a result, communication changes or evolves over time.

Building relationships through communication also relates to developing understanding. As you discuss an issue with one other person or an entire group, you may be doing more than just expressing your view: you may also be constructing (or reconstructing) your perceptions as well as the perceptions of those with whom you are communicating. By affecting perceptions, communication helps people form their view of the reality of a situation.

The process of communication is complex and involves more than words alone. Communication is an art, not a science; so you can learn guidelines about communication, but you cannot use guidelines as recipes. Communication is a live process that changes on the basis of the people and circumstances involved. Outcomes cannot always be planned or predicted, and it can take a lifetime to master the *art* of communication.

This book focuses primarily on the difference between Business English grammar and the grammar of local languages, which do differ significantly. In future chapters, you will become more aware of the specifics of how they differ. To understand the ancient roots of modern-day English, see Table 1.1. This language-tree model shows how various languages, including English, evolved from one language.

EXPLORE

Instructions: Take a moment to consider the following questions: What happens when you do not understand what someone is saying? How do you feel when you do not understand the words or the meaning? Recall a situation in which you were among people who spoke differently from one another. What were the challenges? What were the benefits?

ENGLISH READILY ADAPTS TO CHANGE

One of the reasons English has turned into *the* global language is that it is so adaptable to change. English is unique among languages in terms of its adaptability, with the English vocabulary containing words derived from just about every language on earth. Once a foreign word enters the English vocabulary, speakers incorporate the new word as if it were their own. The foreign word can usually be pronounced with the same sort of **intonation, inflection,** and **rhythm** as the rest of the English vocabulary.

Most other languages are not as adaptable: when a new word is added, it usually sounds awkward, standing out like a "sore thumb." For example, the word *pizza* entered the American vocabulary after World War II when soldiers returned home from Italy. Today the word *pizza* fits into the vocabulary of English speakers as well as any of the other 200,000-plus words that are in common use.[11] (The *Oxford English Dictionary* contains 615,000 words.)

Probably around the time that Americans started using the word *pizza,* Italians started using the word *weekend.* Words originating in Italian are pronounced with a rhythm and intonation different from those of English. No matter how long the word *weekend* is spoken as part of an Italian sentence, it will not sound like an authentic Italian word. The same is true with other languages; for example, a word such as *weekend* would stand out in Japanese, French, Russian, Chinese, Swahili, and so on.

Though the irregularity of English is a characteristic that makes it adaptable to change, its irregularity also creates serious drawbacks. For example, everyone has difficulty learning how to read and write English because of its irregularity, which results from the multitude of exceptions to its rules. As a result, many words and phrases that seem to violate all basic grammar and spelling rules are considered correct—and for no logical reason.

Consider the extraordinary number of irregular verbs that follow no consistent pattern of conjugation. Also consider the huge number of English words with silent letters. Only a fraction of English words follow the language's spelling rules; in fact, only about 40 percent of English words are pronounced on the basis of phonetics. Is it any wonder that reading and spelling are difficult challenges, even for kids who grow up in English-speaking countries?

So the key point is this: English takes in words from other languages and makes them its own. Other languages do not have that versatility, partly because of political reasons but mostly because of the regularity and consistency in their grammar and spelling: a more consistent and less irregular language cannot incorporate new words without having those words sound distinctively different from the rest.

▸Language Diversity

Melting-Pot Language: The ability of English to adapt may stem from a philosophy that remains receptive to words and concepts from other languages. In the United States, for example, French terms such as *menu, soup de jour, science, dance, hotel, bandages, diplomat, beef,* and *bulletin* (among many others) have become part of standard American English usage.

In contrast, some countries work hard to keep foreign terms from having too great an influence on the character of their language. In France, the French Academy is frequently coining new terms for public officials to use in place of foreign phrases that have crept into their language. Terms such as *le Big Mac, le compact disc, le aftershave, le cash flow, le hot-dog, le cowboy, le weekend,* and *le bluejeans* are banned from official governmental use.

Ask Yourself: *What new words have I heard recently that came from another language?*

FORMAL ENGLISH IS THE GLOBAL STANDARD

People who study English as a second language (ESL) learn formal English. ESL speakers do not become proficient with slang and clichés used around the world, which vary significantly from city to city. People from diverse cultures, even if they are fluent in English, have difficulty understanding local-language varieties of English. If a person is not fluent in English, even slight variations in pronunciation can cause confusion and misunderstanding. When the differences are more pronounced and seem intentional, people can feel excluded and hurt.

Business English gives communication a common ground so that meaning is clearer and speakers can identify with each other. Imagine you are in a business meeting with people from countries such as Great Britain, South Africa, and New Zealand. Using Business English is the only way to ensure that these participants from diverse cultures—even if they are all English-speaking—understand the message. Even when people understand the words, every communication is open to interpretation. Of course, interpreters and translators employ formal, standardized English.

In addition, formal English is the "unofficial official language" of the Internet. See Figure 1.2, which shows the percentage of Web content for the various languages used throughout the world.

As a business professional, you are likely to encounter many different varieties of English as you communicate globally. When people speak differently from each other, one result can be a lack of understanding or identity. In the business world, misconstrued meaning and feelings cost money. One solution to this communication dilemma is to focus on using Business English—a variety of Standard English—but also to keep an open mind about language usage in general.

FIGURE 1.2 Web Content, by Language

Because the Internet was first established in the United States, much of its content is in English. As more countries increase their presence online, the percentages are expected to change in the next decade.

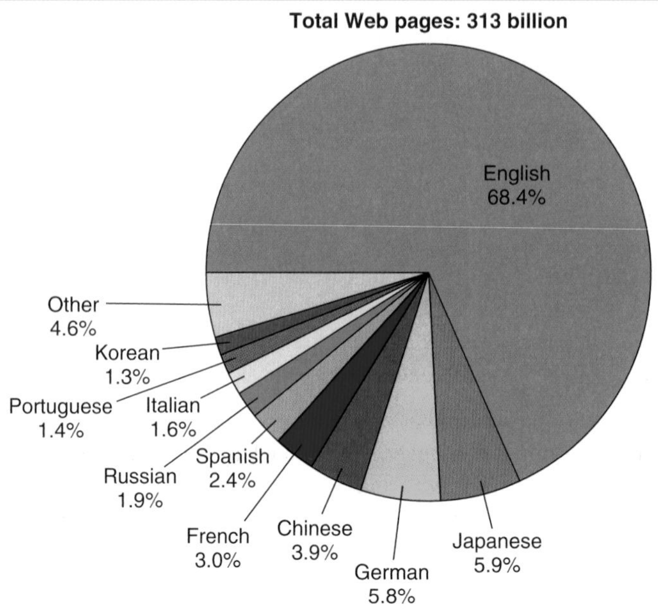

Source: Global Internet Statistics, http://www.global-reach.biz/globstats/index.php3, accessed January 1, 2006; http://www.Vilaweb.com, as quoted by eMarketer.

EXPLORE

Internet Exercise 1.2

History of English: Log on to the Web site at www.mhhe.com/youngBE to find out more about the evolution of English, including links and activities.

Instructions: Do some research about English to answer the following questions:

1. Find a text written in Old English, such as *Beowulf,* and read parts of it aloud. What are some of the differences between old English and modern English?
2. Find a text written in Middle English, such as *The Canterbury Tales*. Is Middle English easier to read than Old English? What are some of the differences between Middle English and modern English?
3. In which countries is English the primary language?
4. What are some major countries in which English is the second language?

SECTION A CONCEPT CHECK

1. What are some examples of how American English differs from British English?

2. Name some dialects that are spoken in the United States today.

3. *Language* is defined as being *arbitrary* and *systematic*. Explain what these two words mean.

SECTION B: WHAT ROLE DOES LOCAL LANGUAGE PLAY?

Often when people make "mistakes," more is going on than what first appears obvious. Mistakes in the formal voice are often "correct" patterns of speech from one's home language. Let's take a moment to understand the difference between the *formal voice* of a language and an *informal voice*.

FORMAL AND INFORMAL LANGUAGE

The standard voice, or **formal voice,** is the language used in international business transactions. An **informal voice** of a language is a local language that a person uses in relaxed, informal situations with friends and family.

In most countries *other than* the United States, people are consciously aware of whether they are speaking their own informal local language or the standard, formal language. This includes other English-speaking countries such as England. Have you ever heard of the play *Pygmalion,* written by George Bernard Shaw in 1916? If not, maybe you have heard of its musical version, *My Fair Lady*. The setting is turn-of-the-century England. Eliza Doolittle, a common flower girl, speaks a dialect that varies significantly from "the queen's English." When Professor Henry Higgins encounters her, he makes it his goal to teach her to speak English "properly." His mission is considered next to impossible to achieve because of the mistaken belief that language patterns cannot be changed. The play and movie elevated language awareness to new levels.

To summarize the qualities of each language system, here are formal definitions of Business English and local language:

- *Business English* is Standard English (which is also known as Edited American English), the formal language pattern that is used in textbooks, professional journals, local and national news, nonfiction books, and professional journals. Business English consists of the grammar rules presented in handbooks and reference books. Less formal terms for Business English are "school talk" or "work talk." Word usage is loosely restricted to words found in abridged dictionaries, and pronunciation reflects phonetic guidelines that appear in dictionaries.
- *Local language* is a term that can be used for any language pattern that differs from its standard version. Some common terms for local language are "community dialect," "home talk," or "talkin' country." Local languages take many different forms, varying dramatically from one community or geographic region to another. Novels and short stories often incorporate dialect or slang into dialogue and, at times, even the narrative. Several local languages have been labeled and formally documented as to their grammar, pronunciation, and word usage; for example, Black Vernacular English, Appalachian and Ozark dialects, Creole, and Spanglish, to name a few.

The term *local language* artificially bundles various informal varieties of English together, without distinguishing one variety from another. The United States is not unique in the scope and variety of its local-language patterns. Canada, Great Britain, Australia, and New Zealand, as well as all global communities that study English as a second language, have their own forms of local language. As you work through this book, you will identify how and when your language patterns vary from standardized English. Your goal is to "build a wall" between your informal speech patterns and your formal speech patterns so that you can shift from one language pattern to another at will.

EXPLORE

1. Choosing the language you speak is like choosing your wardrobe. With a partner, discuss how you would dress for a formal occasion such as going on a job interview. Now compare that outfit with what you would wear to a sports event or an evening out with friends.

VOCABULARY: KEY TERMS

Idioms: An *idiom* is a word or phrase that has a different meaning from its literal meaning. For example, *put up with* translates to "tolerate or endure."

Examine the following and identify the sports idioms that are part of the message:

Pat, your team will need to come up with a strategy to ensure that we don't lose the game before we get to first base. You may have to pass the ball or at least touch base with me if it looks as if the lights are going out. Then again, we may hit a home run before we even get to the 7th inning stretch.

If Pat has never played or watched sports, she could be at a total loss as to what is expected of her. What is "first base" or a "home run"? Think of the numerous idioms that are part of everyday conversations, such as:

- turn over a new leaf
- fit as a fiddle
- right as rain
- hit the road
- slept like a log

The list is practically endless. Idioms contribute to miscommunication, particularly when English is not the primary language of the person hearing them.

Communication Challenges

Communication Exchange: One way to explain communication is through the **telegraph model.** The telegraph model explains communication as consisting of a "sender" and a "receiver"; in other words, a **speaker** (sender) and a **listener** (receiver). When two people are communicating, they are both speakers *and* listeners. To communicate, they must hear and understand each other's point of view.

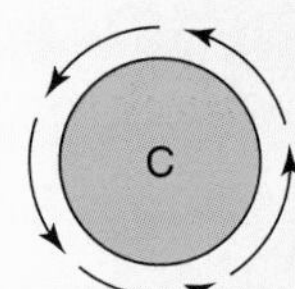

To understand another's point of view, you do not need to agree with it. When one person tries to change another person's point of view, issues can occur. Instead, think of communication as a process to clarify meaning. When people work toward understanding each other, communication flows more effectively.

Communication occurs in **cycles** until those involved reach an understanding and are ready to move on. If you speak to someone and that person does not connect to your message through an appropriate response, you cannot assume that communication occurred. If you reflect on the role communication plays in your life, you may find that communication has the potential to bring incredible joy as well as immense frustration.

2. Develop a list of informal words or phrases that you would use with your friends but that you would not use in a formal situation.
3. Use the list from Exercise 2 to develop a formal equivalent for each informal term.

THE BIDIALECTAL APPROACH: BEING VERSATILE WITH LANGUAGE

By applying the material in this book, you will enhance your proficiency with Business English and at the same time retain your local language. To achieve this, you will need to identify the differences between your informal home talk and Business English. Here's the reasoning: As a learner, you do not need to improve your use of informal language patterns, but you don't want to lose them either—more of your life is spent in informal situations than formal ones. However, because success in the global business world depends on it, using Business English confidently will enhance your potential for success.

It is important for you to apply this concept: As you make changes in the way you speak formal English, do not correct family or friends in their language use or encourage them to change the way they speak. In fact, make a special effort *not* to change the way you speak with family and friends. Reserve formal language for formal, business environments and informal language for informal, casual environments.

Language Choice: A Matter of Degree

At times, everyone speaks informally, using slang and clichés and dropping endings. If most people stopped to think about it, they would have to admit that whether they speak a local language is not a matter of yes or no but, rather, is a matter of "to what degree."

Most people become bidialectal without even realizing it. They unconsciously make language decisions, primarily speaking one way at work and another way with friends and family. In other words, people automatically choose their language on the basis of the environment they are in.

• Internet Exercise 1.3

Language Patterns: Log on to the Web site at www.mhhe.com/youngBE to find more information about dialect, including links and activities.

By becoming more in tune with language use, you are developing a higher level of awareness that will result in a higher level of choice. Your goal is to become as confident with Business English as you currently are with informal speech.

Language Flexibility: Enhancing Opportunity

The more flexibility a person has with language, the more business opportunities he or she will have. Let's consider someone we all know—Oprah. Oprah Winfrey's success is global. When Oprah is doing a formal interview, most of the time she speaks formally. However, when she intends to be particularly expressive, she uses informal language to convey meaning as well as emotion. Oprah loves speaking local language, as anyone can see by observing her when she expresses herself informally—she emotes deep feelings, with her body language changing along with her words.

The way Oprah uses language is the goal for all of us: use Business English for formal situations and local language for other situations, especially when friends and family are involved.

Oprah's love of language variety can also be seen through her ties to *The Color Purple*. Oprah played the role Harpo in the 1985 movie produced by Steven Spielberg; then in 2006, Oprah produced the Broadway production of the play. *The Color Purple* by Alice Walker is a piece of literature that uses language variety, creating an amazing experience for readers who feel culture and emotion beyond the literal meaning of the words on the page.

But Oprah's use of language and her success are not unique. Turn on the daily morning shows or the evening news. Regardless of their home talk, all hosts and most guests speak Business English. What is not so obvious are the numbers of business professionals who speak Business English at work while speaking another variety of language at home. Being bidialectal is an asset—use it to your advantage.

EXPLORE

Instructions: Get a copy of *The Color Purple* and translate a paragraph or two into Business English. How does the tone change? Could the book have been written effectively in Business English?

LANGUAGE VARIETY IN YOUR LIFE

Understanding Language Variety

The difference between formal and informal language is common knowledge among Europeans; however, that understanding of language is not a common part of American thought. In Europe, when a person speaks informally, it is understood that the person is not making mistakes with the standard language, or "mother tongue," but, rather, is speaking a variety of the standard language.

Anyone of Spanish heritage understands that there is a difference between the language spoken at home and the formal Spanish that is spoken in the courts and classrooms. The Spanish dialects spoken in Mexico differ from those spoken in Spain or in Spanish-speaking countries in South America. The same kinds of differences between the formal and informal exist in all other languages around the world.

So, to make progress, embrace your local language and realize that "fixin'" your speech or writing is more complicated than "correcting your errors." As mentioned earlier, focus on building a wall between your home talk and your school talk—your formal and informal language—so that you become as proficient with formal language as you are with informal language. That is what you'll be working on in several chapters of this book.

Communication Challenges

Communication and Relationships: A primary purpose of communication is to build relationships. In your personal life, you may take relationships with family and friends for granted; that is, you have established patterns of relating. Some of those patterns are effective; others are not. You may not be aware of the extent to which your communication patterns affect your relationships; some relationships may even feel out of your control.

To be successful in the business world, you must remain aware of how your communication affects others and work toward constructing good, consistent relationships. You can make progress toward this end by:

1. Recognizing what another is trying to communicate to you and acknowledging the communication.
2. Responding to another's communication through words or actions.
3. Respecting another's point of view by keeping an open mind, even when you don't agree.
4. Taking responsibility for your words and behavior; if you make a mistake, correct the situation by saying you are sorry.

Communication is a *live* process that is *ever changing*. Short of telepathy, there is no way to ensure with 100 percent success that your message will be received as you intended.* Communication intertwines feelings, expectations, and behaviors of people with diverse interests. Expect challenges in an ever-changing world that gives you many opportunities to show your best.

* V. A. Howard and J. H. Barton, *Thinking on Paper,* Quill/William Morrow, New York, 1986, p. 21.

Dropping the Criticism

Many people criticize language that is different from their own. If you pass judgment on language on the basis of style, you probably criticize yourself as much as you criticize others. In fact, you probably feel embarrassed when you make mistakes in public. The way you pronounce a word or conjugate a verb is not a moral issue: don't turn it into one by feeling bad about yourself.

Instead of being critical of local languages, examine some of the benefits of speaking one. People express certain feelings and emotions far better in a local language than they do in formal English; for example, extreme sadness, joy, or anger. Family and friends identify with one another through language patterns. You can even find affinity among strangers who speak the same language patterns you speak. And remember, to a greater or lesser degree, *everyone* speaks a local language. No one speaks formal English perfectly all the time—doing so isn't even possible.

Always keep in mind that your goal is to become bidialectal, appreciating the beauty and contributions cultural differences bring to every situation.

SPEAKING BUSINESS

Reading Between the Lines: Micromessages are the silent "subtle, semiconscious, universally understood behaviors that communicate to everyone what the speaker really thinks."*

Micromessages can lead to either positive results or negative results. For example, imagine you are with a group of people who start speaking a foreign language that you cannot understand. No one stops to explain the conversation to you, and the conversation goes on for a long time. What is the micromessage? Was being left out of the conversation a positive experience or a negative experience?

Keep in mind that the person sending a micromessage is not necessarily aware of it. Regardless, when you feel as if you are being treated unfairly, this can have a negative impact on personal relationships.

Ask Yourself: *What micromessages have I received lately? Were they positive or negative; in other words, how did they make me feel? How did I respond?*

*Barbara Davis and Bobbie Krapels, Association for Business Communications conference, Greensboro, North Carolina, Spring 2005.

EXPLORE

1. With a partner, share some of your language experiences. Focus on the times when you felt unsure of your speech patterns and how you would be judged.
2. Think of a time when you were feeling intense emotion. What kinds of words did you use to express yourself—did you speak in a formal or an informal voice?

SECTION B CONCEPT CHECK

1. Does everyone speak a local language or only a select few?

2. What are some benefits of speaking a local language?

SECTION C: LEARNING LANGUAGE IN CONTEXT

Learning about the history of English and how it varies around the world is interesting and helps you put your own language use in context. However, your purposes for studying English are personal. If you improve your use of English—both speaking and writing skills—your opportunities at home and abroad improve significantly.

Language is at the core of every subject you will study and every job you will have. Improve your language use and you improve your future. This section helps you understand the rationale for the work you will do using this textbook.

HOW TO USE THIS BOOK

In this chapter, your goal is to explore how you feel about language study on the basis of your experiences. In the end-of-chapter exercises, Activity 2, in which you write your "history as a writer and speaker," is critical. In Chapter 2, you will begin to review the structure and usage of Business English. Unit 2 reviews principles for using verbs, pronouns, and other troublesome parts of speech, comparing their informal and formal language uses. In Unit 3, you will apply what you are learning in real-life exercises.

By the time you finish this textbook, you will be ready to write professional e-mail messages and speak with confidence on any job interview. However—and this is an important point—you will have retained your informal speech patterns so that you can express yourself with pride in any situation.

Communication Challenges

Speaking in Gestures: Do you use your hands when you communicate? Human resource managers have their own codes for interpreting behaviors such as tapping your fingers or fiddling with a piece of string during an interview.

Likewise, people from other cultures may have different interpretations of your gestures than you may intend. In England, for example, flashing the *V*-for-victory symbol with the palm facing inward is considered an insult; in Japan, giving someone the "thumbs up" might bring you an order of five of something; in Brazil, the "OK" sign is considered obscene.

Ask Yourself: *Am I conscious of how I use my hands in face-to-face conversation? Do I use my hands differently when I am speaking to a group? What do I think I am communicating with these gestures?*

A PROBLEM-SOLVING PROCESS: EXPLORE, PRACTICE, APPLY

This textbook breaks most activities into one of the following three categories: *explore, practice,* or *apply*. These concepts are an extension of the learning theory developed by Alfred North Whitehead, a British mathematician and philosopher. Here is how to apply these concepts to a problem-solving strategy:

- **Explore** relates to considering ideas without evaluating them. Drop expectations and notions about what you should achieve. Let innovative, creative ideas enter the mix of topics that relate to solving the problem.

Exploration involves becoming familiar with a problem *before* you consider how to solve it. Exploration bypasses the serious aspect of problem solving and allows a bit of fun to enter the process. When you explore a topic in a group or team, do not feel pressured to produce an immediate answer: you and your teammates are acquainting yourselves with one another and the topic; each member of the group is developing interest and motivation, connecting to the project's mission in a personal way. Exploration leads to *thinking outside the box*.

- **Practice** relates to precision: getting the precise details down correctly—the cold, hard facts, so to speak. Practice takes focus and determination. Practice involves developing specific skills by repeating a concept until you thoroughly learn it and can use it confidently in new situations.

Practice also entails research: developing details about the difficult concepts you discovered through exploration and building the body of knowledge you need to solve the problem. Practice is the tedious, mechanical part of any project; but once you and your team explore a topic and connect with its mission, the practice phase flows naturally. In addition, the practice phase provides the *foundation* for developing a solution.

- **Apply** relates to creating an innovative, unique solution drawn from the research and skill you acquired in the practice phase. Neither you nor your group should consider solutions final until you have *explored* and *practiced* sufficiently.

Are all three of these phases necessary in solving a problem? Alfred North Whitehead thought so. In fact, Whitehead believed the most critical phase was *exploring*. Unless you and your team members buy into the mission

WRITER'S TOOLKIT

The Dictionary

Every business writer needs to have a comprehensive dictionary that will provide answers to questions related to word usage. Most authorities prefer an **unabridged** dictionary, which is considered the most comprehensive and complete of dictionary sources. An **abridged** dictionary is one that has been condensed or shortened for space considerations. Merriam-Webster, for example, publishes an unabridged dictionary featuring 470,000 words as well as abridged dictionaries—such as dictionaries of synonyms, English usage, and slang—that contain only some of the definitions found in the unabridged edition.

In general, dictionaries provide the following information:

- *Spelling:* Dictionary entries show how words are spelled.
- *Definition:* A good dictionary lists all of a word's definitions, usually in the order in which they developed historically. Often, the dictionary provides examples of the word's use in different senses.
- *Capitalization:* The dictionary shows whether a word is to be capitalized when it is not the first word of a sentence.
- *Hyphenation:* Dictionary entries usually indicate the correct places for breaking or dividing words.
- *Pronunciation and division into syllables:* Immediately after the regular spelling of a word, the dictionary shows the word's *phonetic spelling*. This feature indicates how the word should be broken into syllables, how each syllable should be pronounced, and which syllable or syllables should be accented.
- *Inflectional forms and derivatives:* **Inflectional forms** are forms of a word that show tense, number, and other meanings. For example, *flies* is an inflectional form of *fly*. A **derivative** is a word formed from another word. For example, *confirmation* is a derivative of *confirm*. The dictionary shows the irregular plurals of nouns, the past tense and participial forms of irregular verbs, and the comparative and superlative forms of irregular adjectives and adverbs. The entry for the irregular verb *speak,* for example, gives its past tense, *spoke;* its past participle, *spoken;* and its present participle, *speaking*.
- *Synonyms:* Some dictionaries list **synonyms**—words that have almost the same meaning as the entry.
- *Signs and symbols:* This section, found in most dictionaries, consists of signs and symbols frequently used in such fields as astronomy, biology, business, chemistry, data processing, mathematics, medicine, physics, and weather.
- *Biographical names:* Some dictionaries include the names of famous people, each with the proper spelling and pronunciation. Biographical data such as dates of birth and death, nationality, and occupation are also provided.
- *Geographical names:* This section provides information about places—name, pronunciation, location, population, and so on.
- *Grammar rules:* Included in this section are basic rules on punctuation, italicization, capitalization, and plurals; citation of sources; and forms of address.

Although numerous online dictionaries are available and useful, a comprehensive, bound dictionary is an indispensable tool for writers who know how to use it.

• WRITER'S TOOLKIT

The Thesaurus

A **thesaurus** can be a tremendous aid for business writers who want to expand their vocabulary. Thesauri provide lists of specific words and expressions you can use to convey a general idea; some writers use a thesaurus to avoid repeating a word or phrase too often.

As with dictionaries, you can access online versions of thesauri on the Internet; however, you may also want to keep a bound copy of a thesaurus on hand for quick reference. *Roget's International Thesaurus* and *Merriam-Webster's Collegiate Thesaurus* are two popular thesauri.

For information on online thesauri, see Internet Exercise 1.4 on page 20)

or importance of a project, you may not commit to the intense work in the practice phase that leads to creating an innovative, quality product. *Explore* opens the door to creativity (and possibly passion); *practice* provides the details; and *apply* assembles the pieces in a novel way to generate a truly effective response.

These phases are cyclical, not linear. As you work through your project, at various points take note of which phase describes where you are. For example, you may find yourself exploring ideas in the application phase of the cycle. At the end of the chapter, you will find activities relating to each of these concepts. By using these concepts in a creative way rather than a linear 1-2-3 approach, you will achieve good results.

THE CHALLENGE OF CHANGING LANGUAGE PATTERNS

Though you may have spoken English all your life, you probably have not studied English in the way you will study it in this book. In each chapter, you will be asked to identify the kinds of mistakes that you commonly make in your speech and writing in an academic environment. These "mistakes" may systematically recur in your speech and writing because they are patterns of your local language, the informal variety of English that you speak regularly with your friends and family.

Remember that the term *informal* refers to local language whereas the term *formal* refers to Business English. You are encouraged not to think of the differences between your informal language and Business English as mistakes. Instead, you will learn to "translate" your informal speech patterns into Business English so that you develop more confidence for speaking in formal workplace environments. You will be asked to create sentences and messages using informal language and then to write the parallel structure in Business English. You should have fun with these drills, but always remember that career success is serious business.

Modifying lifelong language patterns is difficult, to say the least. If you want to make progress with your speaking and writing skills, you will need to apply yourself 100 percent. Change can also be emotional, so be aware of your feelings and honor them.

Give your best efforts: the more motivated you are, the more your skills will grow. No one can *teach* you to change your language—such change is for you to *learn* through study and application. The more you practice the principles in real-life situations, the stronger your skills will become.

SOME TECHNIQUES TO GET YOU STARTED

Applying new principles in your writing and speaking is the most powerful way to achieve your goals. In fact, the principles that you don't apply will be lost—you might as well spend your time on something else if you don't use what you are learning.

Writing is challenging, and you may or may not be familiar with writing techniques to help you push through writer's block. One tool that you will use is mind mapping. Unlike writing a formal outline, creating a mind map helps you capture your ideas in a free-flow manner.

- *Mind mapping:* Originally known as clustering, **mind mapping** is a free-form way to get your ideas on the page (see Figure 1.3). First, write your topic in the middle of a page and draw a circle around it. Next, cluster related ideas around the topic circle, branching off into any direction your ideas take you. Stay focused on your mind map for about 3 minutes.

  Exploring ideas through a mind map provides freedom and creative energy. Mind mapping feels exciting because it takes on a creative energy of its own. A mind map shows relationships to help you organize and prioritize your information; you get a bigger picture much faster. (You can also do a mind map before you make an important phone call; or you can start your day by doing one to plan your time, mapping the various activities you need to accomplish.) The mind map in Figure 1.3 explores the relationships among the concepts in this chapter.

FIGURE 1.3 Mind Mapping

Map It Out: *Mind mapping is an organizational technique that offers freedom and creativity in exploring ideas.* Take 3 minutes to create a mind map about a topic that interests you.

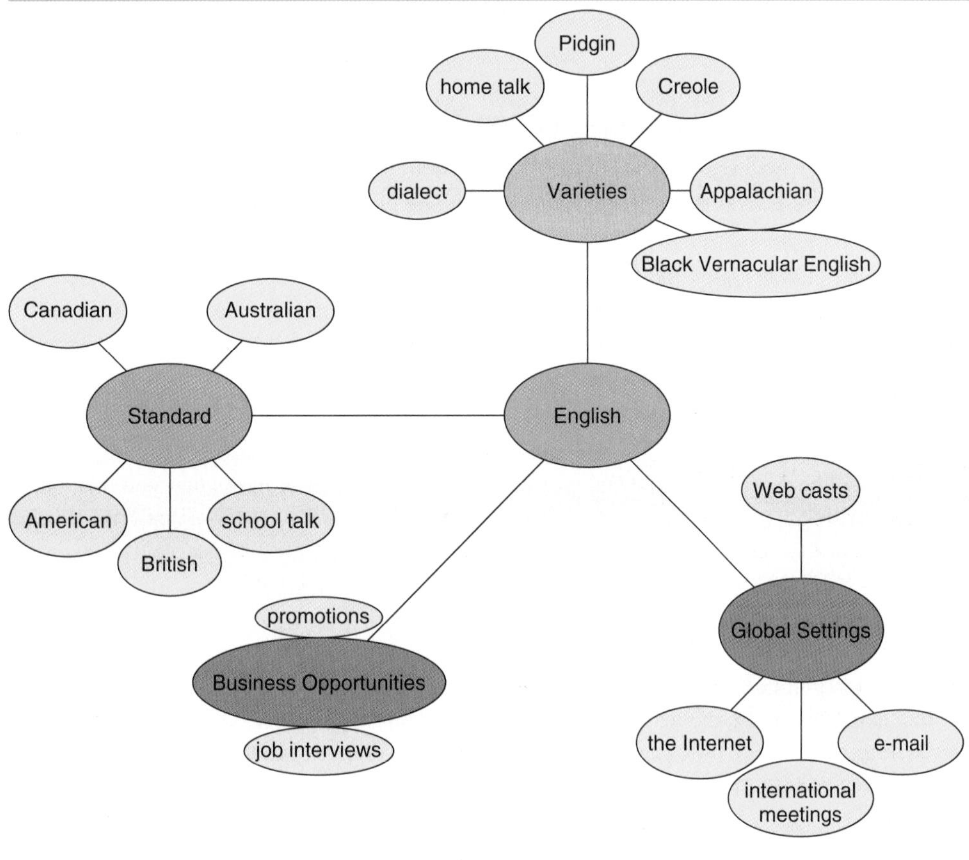

Next, you will learn some techniques to help you develop your ideas in complete, but not necessarily correct, sentences.

- *Freewriting:* **Freewriting** involves putting whatever is on your mind on paper in a free form. You are free-associating, not screening your thoughts. Bounce around from one idea to another if that is what is going on in your head. If you do not know what to write about, write, "*I don't know what I'm writing about . . .*" When you let go of your anxiety, ideas will start to jump onto the page.

  Freewriting is similar to some types of journal writing. Write to release your feelings, thoughts, and stress and to gain insight into unresolved issues. You do not need to go back and make sense of what you wrote; put your finished product through a paper shredder if you wish. There is an ancient saying, "If you hold it in, it will destroy you; if you let it out, it will free you." The value of freewriting comes from doing it; you need achieve no other goal.

- *Focused writing:* **Focused writing** is more structured than freewriting: it involves only one topic. Choose your topic *before* you begin writing and focus only on that topic. Set a limit for yourself—for example, two to three pages or 10 to 20 minutes—and let the ideas flow. If you work much longer than 20 minutes or three pages, you may begin to avoid this activity. Keep it short and simple; do not set expectations. You are not trying to produce something you will use; you are simply getting your ideas on the page without losing your train of thought.

  This activity helps you start a writing assignment sooner so that you do not wait until the last minute. The sooner you start to work, the farther away the deadline will seem.

You may find that after you have gotten some ideas on the page, the assignment does not seem so intimidating. Your creative thinking skills will take over, and you will begin to solve the problems the assignment presents. Get into action, and you may be surprised how much progress you make.

EXPLORE

1. Spend 8 to 10 minutes freewriting. Allow your mind to jump from topic to topic, and do not worry about grammar, punctuation, or the "right word." Write whatever comes to mind, and keep your pen moving the entire time. Did you enjoy freewriting, or did it feel frustrating?
2. Select a familiar topic (one you would enjoy writing about). Spend 8 to 10 minutes doing a focused writing. Stay on the topic and keep your pen moving; do not worry about grammar, punctuation, or the "right word." Did you enjoy focused writing? How did it differ from freewriting?
3. Consider purchasing a notebook that you can use as a journal for the various freewriting and journaling activities that you will do as part of the End-of-Chapter Activities. Your work will be more organized and you will see the consistent progress that you make in your writing.

• Internet Exercise 1.4

Electronic Editing Tools: Log on to the Web site at **www.mhhe.com/youngBE** to learn about the promises and pitfalls of spell checkers, grammar checkers, online thesauri, and other editing tools accessible by computer.

PRACTICE IN WRITING SKILLS: COMPOSING VERSUS EDITING

Writers often find themselves stuck because they multitask: they work on different types of writing activities simultaneously. To make progress, consciously focus on only one phase of the writing process at a time: *composing* or *editing*. You do not need to complete an entire paper before editing, but try to complete one or two pages first.

Do you stop to edit as you compose? When you stop to correct grammar, punctuation, or spelling as you compose, your ideas may evaporate. If you start to revise before your ideas are mapped out, you may be wasting time and energy. After you learn specific editing skills, editing will become easier than composing. Allow yourself to make mistakes when you compose; force yourself to correct mechanics and reshape your ideas when you edit and revise.

This point cannot be stressed enough: When you compose, just keep writing. Force yourself to ignore finding the right word or words to express an idea. If you stop editing as you compose, you will feel less stress and your results will improve immediately and dramatically.

You will spend time learning how to proofread and edit in each chapter of the rest of this book. When an exercise asks you to compose, stay focused and let go of your critic. Don't try to write your words perfectly as you compose: the purpose of editing is to reshape and correct your writing.

Communication Tool: Process Memo

A *process memo* is a tool you can use to communicate with your instructor. In a process memo, you relate information about your learning process. For example, you could discuss the concepts and principles that are helping you make progress with your writing and the areas of writing that still cause you problems.

For your instructor, the process memo is a diagnostic as well as a communication tool. By knowing more about what gives you difficulty with writing, your instructor can assist you more effectively with your learning process. Periodically, your instructor may ask you to compose a memo about the concepts and principles you are learning or the areas that you find difficult. Your instructor may also ask you to attach a process memo to a paper you are resubmitting so that you can describe changes and corrections you made.

Here is an example of a process memo:

To: Ms. Young

From: Reggie Glasco

Date: November 5, 2007

Subject: Learning Update

So far, I have learned about the difference between Business English and local language. I have been noticing how I speak differently when I am with my friends than when I am in class. I like the idea of becoming bidialectal because speaking a local language is fun when I am with my friends but I also want to speak formally when I go on job interviews.

Writing doesn't seem as difficult as it did before because now I start with a mind map. Thank you for asking about my progress in this class.

In the End-of-Chapter Activities, the process memo assignment is the first assignment listed.

PRONUNCIATION LESSONS

In every chapter, you will find a *Speaking Business* sidebar and an end-of-chapter exercise that you can use to refine your pronunciation. These lessons will highlight words and sounds that are often pronounced differently in business than they are in local languages.

Some lessons will take you step-by-step through a specific sound as it is formed in your mouth. You will pay attention to the movements of your tongue, teeth, lips, and throat so that you can become aware of what it takes to pronounce every part of the sound. Make sure when you practice the new speech patterns that you are in an environment where you feel comfortable and relaxed.

Repetition is one of the best ways to learn a new skill: repeat a word pattern or sound over and over again until you learn it thoroughly. New sounds and ways of speaking will sound strange to you at first. You must get accustomed to hearing your own voice speak the sounds and word patterns until you feel comfortable. Working on speech patterns is only partly an intellectual exercise and mostly an experiential one: you need to apply what you are learning in the context in which you will use the new skill.

SECTION C CONCEPT CHECK

1. What are some ways to get your ideas on paper before you start writing?

2. Why is it important not to edit as you compose?

3. What is the method to use when you are practicing difficult word sounds?

CHAPTER 1 SUMMARY

Language is a complicated topic because of the language diversity that exists throughout the world and even among close friends and relatives. The English language is organic, changing all the time. However, the grammar of formal English remains consistent. Though words may be added and dropped, English grammar not only remains consistent over time but also remains consistent from country to country.

You have focused on the difference between formal and informal language patterns, learning that Business English is formal and local language is informal. To retain your informal language as you build skills with formal language, you will need to build a wall distinguishing differences between the two language systems. As you improve your proficiency in Business English, you will also improve your career opportunities. Though "speaking business" enhances your career opportunities, retaining your local language keeps you in tune with your culture, family, and friends.

CHAPTER 1 CHECKLIST

___ Are you conscious of the language patterns you speak?

___ Do you spend time translating your informal speech into formal English?

___ Have you considered the importance of speaking formally in global situations?

___ Do you feel more confident about what you need to do to speak confidently in formal business settings?

___ Have you taken the time to consider the benefits of formal language as well as informal language?

___ Are you willing to communicate with others without correcting their speech?

CHAPTER 1 END-OF-CHAPTER ACTIVITIES

ACTIVITY 1: PROCESS MEMO

INSTRUCTIONS: Following the steps described below, write a process memo to your instructor identifying what you want to achieve in this class. What are your goals as they relate to speaking and writing? How do these goals relate to your future career goals?

1. First take 3 minutes to do a mind map, and then take 8 to 10 minutes to do a focused writing.
2. Before giving the memo to your instructor, follow the model on page 21 to format it correctly.

If you have Internet access, you can complete this exercise online at **www.mhhe.com/youngBE** and then send an e-mail to your instructor.

ACTIVITY 2: MAKING THE CONNECTION: MY HISTORY AS A SPEAKER AND WRITER

INSTRUCTIONS: Now that you have considered the broader qualities of language as a system, it is time for you to examine the role of language in your own life. Write a short paper describing the kinds of mistakes you make when you write and speak in formal academic situations. Break the topic into two parts so that you can focus on each area more thoroughly. You may find that you have some similar challenges in speaking and in writing.

A: WHAT'S DIFFICULT ABOUT SPEAKING?

Think about how you feel when you are speaking in formal situations such as in class or at work. What makes you feel uncomfortable: Are you afraid of losing your train of thought? Are you afraid of making a mistake with your grammar or pronunciation? What kinds of corrections have you been told to make in your speaking?

B: WHAT'S DIFFICULT ABOUT WRITING?

Think about the challenges you have when you write. Even if you don't write very much, that in itself says something. Why don't you write? What do you struggle with when you write? Do you prefer to write an outline first, or do you have problems writing an outline? Do you jump right into a task, or do you put it off until the last minute? Do you write a "first and final draft," or do you allow time to edit? Describe the process you go through to get a paper written. What kinds of errors do you make?

The more details you provide, the better. You may use this information in a classroom exercise in which you share your experience with a classmate or two.

ACTIVITY 3: SPEAKING/LISTENING DRILL

A

INSTRUCTIONS: Go to a public place and listen for words and phrases that are part of a local language. Write down as many as you hear in a period of about 5 minutes. Bring your list to class so that you can share it with a partner or the entire class.

B

INSTRUCTIONS: Use a digital or cassette recorder to record 5 to 10 minutes of a conversation between two or more people. When you are finished, play back the dialogue and make a transcript of a part of the conversation, enough to fill a page. Then do the following:

1. Underline words and phrases that are part of a local language.
2. Circle instances of slang, clichés, and idiomatic expressions.
3. Be prepared to discuss any observations you've made about the way people use English in conversation.

ACTIVITY 4: SPEAKING BUSINESS

Here is your first lesson on sounds that are often pronounced differently in formal English than they are in local language. The first sound is the *sk* sound that is part of words such as *ask, task, bask,* and *flask.*

Focus on pronouncing the word sounds step-by-step, noticing how each sound is formed in your mouth. Pay attention to the movements of your tongue, teeth, lips, and throat so that you become aware of each part of the sound. Practice the new patterns in a place where you feel comfortable and relaxed. Now let's start with *ask* and then work on the other words.

Ask is a challenging word; if you want to say "a-s-k" in professional environments, practice each sound individually, noticing all the movements that are going on in your mouth and throat.

1. For *ask,* notice how the *s* sound is formed in your mouth by blowing air through your front teeth.
2. Next notice how the *k* sound is made at the back of your throat.

3. Repeat "s-k" several times, feeling the *s* followed by the *k* located at the back of your throat.
4. Finally, stretch out the *a* sound at the beginning of the word, and then follow it with the *s* and *k*.

Repeat the sounds over and over again until you feel comfortable, realizing that it will sound strange to you at first. Practice until you get accustomed to hearing your own voice speak the sounds and word patterns. Now repeat the procedure for other words ending in *sk,* such as *task, bask,* and *flask.*

1. Focus on extending the vowel sound in the middle of the word by stretching it out; for example, "t a . . ."
2. Follow it with the *s* and *k* sounds.

Working on speech patterns is mostly experiential, which means that you need to apply the new pronunciation in the real world. Now give yourself a pat on the back for accomplishing something challenging.

ACTIVITY 5: E-WRITING

INSTRUCTIONS: Translate the following text messages into readable messages:

1. Hey, J. ru going to the mtg this am to rap about nw plcs? i cnt be there so fl me in whn you gt bk in the early pm. lol with your proposal. thx. BJ

___

___

2. Gar-

Thx for tdy.. Everything esp. The good words in front of The Prez. C you nxt Fri. E me a time to mt. Audi

___

___

3. Alisa—Cn u e the Swalzes' docs by 5 pm est?

___

4. D.P: Plz snd copies new doc rtntn plcy to all brnch mngrs ASAP.

___

___

5. All:

Note the nu mtg hr and suite # on 2nd day at Obsrvtry. Drs to opn at snset Sat Jan 9.

___

___

ACTIVITY 6: THESAURUS DRILL

INSTRUCTIONS: Writers keep the reader's interest by using a variety of words. To achieve variety, writers use *synonyms:* words that have similar meaning. For example, the word *difficult* could also be represented by words such as *hard, challenging, complicated,* or *complex.*

In some chapters, you will find a short exercise to help you develop skill with synonyms. For each word listed, write two or three similar words or phrases that come to mind.

1. good
2. expensive
3. grammar
4. describe
5. listen

ACTIVITY 7: THE "WRITER'S REFERENCE MANUAL" DRILL

BACKGROUND: The last part of this book consists of a short "Writer's Reference Manual." At the end of each chapter, you will use that reference manual to learn about a topic and then complete an exercise.

INSTRUCTIONS: Find the topic "articles" in the "Writer's Reference Manual," review the material, and complete the exercise below by putting in the correct article, *a* or *an,* to modify the word that follows.

_____ apple	_____ hope	_____ appetite	_____ natural
_____ unique	_____ idea	_____ NBC	_____ enemy
_____ hindrance	_____ list	_____ acorn	_____ elegant
_____ unusual	_____ honor	_____ understated	_____ uniform
_____ nuisance	_____ native	_____ unanimous	_____ elephant

ACTIVITY 8: VOCABULARY LIST

A. COMMONLY MISSPELLED WORDS

INSTRUCTIONS: The list below contains words taken from a compilation of the 500 most commonly misspelled words and from the chapter. Practice them until you can spell them automatically and use them correctly.

1. absence — (n) the state of being away; nonattendance; lack
2. accommodate — (v) to provide for; get used to; adapt; adjust; contain; assist
3. analysis — (n) a statement or report; breaking a whole into its parts to examine each part
4. arbitrary — (adj) subjective meaning through mutual agreement
5. believe — (v) to accept as true or real; to have confidence in or trust
6. connotation — (n) an implied or inferred meaning based on an emotional response

7. conscious	(n) aware
8. conscientious	(adj) thorough and painstaking; careful; meticulous
9. context	(n) environment; circumstances; history or background
10. denotation	(n) a word's literal, dictionary meaning
11. grammar	(n) syntax; structure; language rules
12. interrupt	(v) to break the continuity; to stop the action
13. language	(n) an arbitrary and systematic way to string words together to create meaning
14. possession	(n) control; the act or fact of possessing; wealth or property
15. systematic	(adj) orderly, organized

B. SIMILAR WORDS

INSTRUCTIONS: The list below contains similar words, some of which are profiled in the Vocabulary Builders in each chapter. Use these words in sentences until their meaning becomes clear.

affect/effect: *Affect* is a verb meaning "to influence"; however, *affect* is used as a noun in the field of psychology to mean "emotion." *Effect* is most commonly used as a noun meaning "result"; *effect* is also a formal but rarely used verb meaning "to cause to happen" or "to bring about."

The manager's mood *affected* our attitudes. (influenced)

The *effect* of the storm was devastating. (result)

That policy will *effect* important change. (bring about)

The doctor diagnosed her as having an *affective* disorder. (emotional)

accept/except: *Accept* is a verb meaning "to believe, receive, or approve of"; *except* can be a preposition, a conjunction, or even a verb. *Except* means "otherwise," "other than," "only," or "to exclude."

Everyone has *accepted* the invitation *except* Sam.

advice/advise: *Advice* is a noun meaning "counsel" or "recommendation"; *advise* is a verb meaning "give advice" or "make a recommendation."

The counselor *advised* you to follow your instructor's *advice.*

eminent/imminent: *Eminent* is an adjective meaning "noteworthy" or "famous"; *imminent* is an adjective meaning "about to happen."

Jordan is an *eminent* scholar in the field of immunology.

The meteorologist predicted an *imminent* disaster due to the hurricane's force.

could of/should of: Use ***could have*** and ***should have*** in written and formal communications.

THE INBOX

COMPOSING

Fold a piece of notebook paper in half vertically. Pretend that you have just now decided which college to attend. On the left side of the paper, write a brief note to a close friend telling why you chose that particular college (approximately one paragraph).

Here are some details you might want to include:

- You can mention the program of study you are interested in.
- You can discuss where you'll stay while attending the college.
- You can ask questions of your friend.

On the right side of the paper, address a letter to your former high school (or college) English teacher. Ask your former teacher to write a letter of recommendation for you to the college's admissions director (approximately one to two paragraphs—don't worry about the format).

Here are some details you might want to include:

- You are enclosing the information needed to write the letter.
- You should mention that you enjoyed the class or note what you learned in the class.
- You can mention that you scored quite well on your English entrance exams.

Sample:

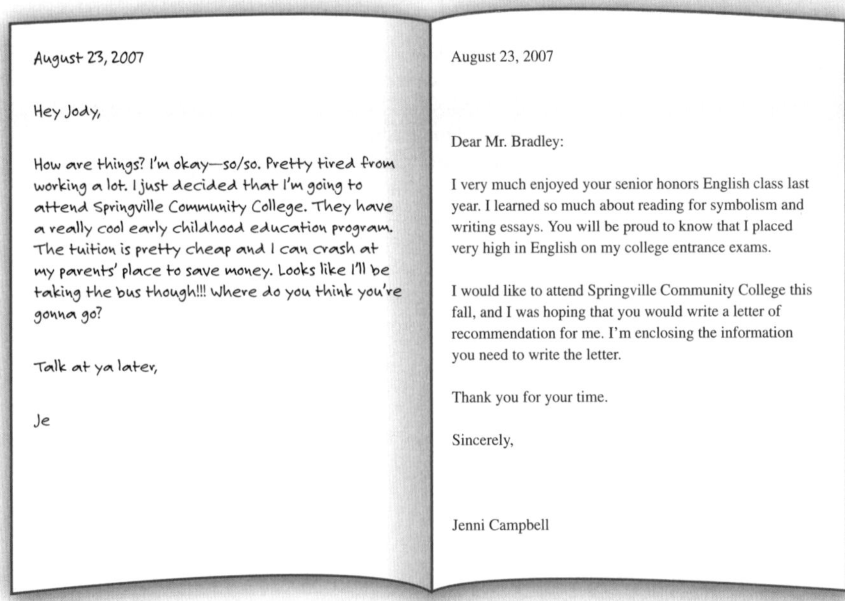

August 23, 2007

Hey Jody,

How are things? I'm okay—so/so. Pretty tired from working a lot. I just decided that I'm going to attend Springville Community College. They have a really cool early childhood education program. The tuition is pretty cheap and I can crash at my parents' place to save money. Looks like I'll be taking the bus though!!! Where do you think you're gonna go?

Talk at ya later,

Je

August 23, 2007

Dear Mr. Bradley:

I very much enjoyed your senior honors English class last year. I learned so much about reading for symbolism and writing essays. You will be proud to know that I placed very high in English on my college entrance exams.

I would like to attend Springville Community College this fall, and I was hoping that you would write a letter of recommendation for me. I'm enclosing the information you need to write the letter.

Thank you for your time.

Sincerely,

Jenni Campbell

REFLECTING

Now look at the two pieces of writing side by side. Underline the casual or local language phrases in your note to your friend. How are the two pieces different? How are they the same? To what extent does your audience influence your word choices? Write a brief journal entry reflecting on these two communications.

DISCUSSING

1. Exchange papers with another student. Discuss your and your classmate's approaches to both letters. Were the results similar? What is different about your classmate's writing? What is the same?
2. What factors determine the appropriate degree of formality? Together, brainstorm a list of writing situations in which informal language is appropriate. Next, brainstorm a list of writing situations in which formal language is appropriate.
3. What would be the result if Jenni Campbell (see the sample) had switched dialects in her letters? Do you think Mr. Bradley would have felt comfortable writing a letter of recommendation? How do you think Jenni's friend would have reacted to a more formal piece of writing from Jenni?

EDITING

Celina Huber needs a letter of recommendation from her former employer at Taco Heaven Restaurant in order to apply for a culinary scholarship. Ms. Claudia Menke owns Taco Heaven and has known Celina for three years. Celina was always punctual for work and was an exemplary employee. Now Celina asks you for help editing her letter to Ms. Menke. What suggestions do you have for Celina? Look for word choice as well as spelling.

July 12, 200-

Ms. Claudia Menke
Owner
Taco Heaven Restrant
4251East Drier Street
Springville, Ohio 45349

Hi Ms. Menke! How are you? I'm doing okay. I got into Taylor Culinary College and wow was I happy about it!!! But ya know what? The tuition is really really way out there and I gotta get a shcolarship. I really think I can get this culinary scholarship if you write me a good letter to recomend me for the scholarship. They wanna know if I got experience in the kitchen which I do from Taco Heven. You know I always worked my butt off for you and never ever complained. Please write me this letter and send it to Terri Radcliffe Director of Financal Aid at Taylor's. Would you let me know when you send it? You can text me or get my cell—555-0909.

Thanks Ms. Menke—you're the bomb!
Talk to ya later,
Celina

END CHAPTER 1 EOC ACTIVITIES

KEY TO LEARNING INVENTORY

1. T
2. T
3. F
4. T
5. F
6. T
7. T
8. F
9. T
10. T

CHAPTER 1 ENDNOTES

1. **http://www.PBS.org/speak/ahead/globalamerican/global**, accessed on December 7, 2005.
2. **http://www.askoxford.com/globalenglish/?view=uk**, accessed on December 7, 2005.
3. *American Heritage Dictionary of the English Language,* 4th ed., Houghton-Mifflin, 2000, updated 2003.
4. John P. Hughes, *Linguistics and Language Teaching,* Random House, New York, 1968, pp. 4 and 131.
5. Ibid.
6. **www.askoxford.com/globalenglish/worldenglish/?view=uk**.
7. Ibid.
8. **www.pbs.org/speak/seatosea/standardamerican**, accessed on February 15, 2006.
9. Robert MacNeil and William Cran, *Do You Speak American?* Doubleday, New York, 2005.
10. **http://www.ling.upenn.edu/phono_atlas/ICSLP4.html**.
11. **http://www.wordorigins.org/number.htm**, accessed on December 15, 2005. About 200,000 words are in common use today. An educated person has a vocabulary of about 20,000 words and uses about 2,000 in a week's conversation. (These estimates are not absolutes but vary widely depending on who is doing the counting.)

Chapter Two

Writing Effective Sentences

Write with nouns and verbs, not with adjectives and adverbs. The adjective hasn't been built that can pull a weak or inaccurate noun out of a tight place. —William Strunk and E. B. White, *The Elements of Style*

Are you able to write clear and correct sentences that speak to your reader? That is, are you able to write sentences that readers easily understand and that bring you good results?

In this chapter, you will begin your work with sentence structure, paying special attention to the sentence core. As you work through the exercises, notice how your local language or informal language patterns may vary from the structure of Business English.

When you can consistently write correct and clear sentences, you will have achieved one of the most difficult challenges of writing. On the surface, this statement sounds too simple to believe. Right now you may think that getting your ideas down is the biggest challenge because it feels so excruciatingly painful at times. But think about it—getting your ideas on the page is difficult partly because you are confused about writing decisions at the sentence level, such as using grammar and punctuation correctly or finding the right word.

Work hard to master the important principles in this chapter relating to the sentence core and conjunctions. These principles provide a foundation for your work in Chapter 3, "Punctuation," and they also provide a foundation to developing power in all your writing.

To learn more about The Writing Process, please visit our Web site at **www.mhhe.com/youngBE**

Outline

Chapter 2: Writing Effective Sentences

Section A: What Is the Sentence Core?

Section B: How Do Parts of Speech Work?

Section C: What Is a Sentence?

Objectives

When you have completed your study of Chapter 2, you will be able to:

1. Identify the sentence core: the subject and verb.
2. Recognize the various parts of speech.
3. Know the difference between action verbs and state-of-being verbs.
4. Recognize the main pronoun cases: subjective, objective, possessive, and reflexive.
5. Identify coordinating, subordinating, and adverbial conjunctions.
6. Know the difference between a sentence, a fragment, and a run-on.
7. Turn fragments and run-ons into correctly written sentences.

Learning Inventory

1. What are the two basic parts of the sentence core? _____________ _____________
2. Linking verbs are not followed by an object; they are followed by a _________ _________.
3. The three types of conjunctions are *coordinating, subordinating,* and *adverbial.* T/F
4. In statements, the subject generally precedes the verb. T/F
5. A dependent clause has a subject and a verb. T/F
6. An independent clause is an incomplete sentence. T/F
7. Pronouns are categorized by cases, such as subjective and objective. T/F
8. A dependent clause is a fragment. T/F
9. *Simple predicate* refers to the verb of a sentence. T/F
10. When identifying the sentence core, you should find the noun and then the verb. T/F

Goal-Setting Exercises

What kinds of problems do you have with writing sentences? On your papers, do teachers ever write comments that you have fragments or run-ons in your writing? What questions do you have about sentences? Review the chapter objectives, and then write three goals stating what you would like to achieve as you work through this chapter.

1. ____
2. ____
3. ____

SECTION A: WHAT IS THE SENTENCE CORE?

Did you know that every sentence has a *core?* The core of a sentence consists of its **subject** and **verb.** The **sentence core** is the powerhouse of the sentence. In this section, you will learn how to identify the sentence core so that you can gain control of your writing. To identify the core, you must first be able to identify verbs.

Verbs are complicated, and you will start by examining the verb in its role as **predicate,** the part of a sentence that expresses something about the subject. In Section B, you will learn more about the verb as a part of speech. Later, you will spend an entire chapter working with verbs (Chapter 4, "Verbs at Work"). Right now, let's examine the basics about verbs, covering enough information for you to become proficient at recognizing them. And don't let the word *predicate* scare you—*simple predicate* is just a bigger term for *verb.*

THE VERB AS PREDICATE

The predicate of a sentence expresses something about its subject. The **complete predicate** consists of a verb and other elements of the sentence such as objects or modifiers or complements of the verb.[1] The verb of a sentence is officially known as the **simple predicate.** From this point on, you can use the word *verb* rather than the word *predicate,* which can make grammar sound more complicated than it is.

Verbs provoke action and provide the motivating force behind a message. Verbs also create energy and direction. In fact, the verb determines the other core parts of the sentence: the subject and, when applicable, the object.

When asked what a verb is, most people will respond that a verb is an *action word.* Action verbs are *dynamic:* they transfer action from the subject to the object by introducing events and referring to something that happens.[2] In the following sentences (and in examples throughout this book), verbs are underlined twice:

Mel chaired the meeting.

Feranda managed the program.

Action verbs do not always need to be followed by an object; they can sometimes be followed by an adverb that modifies the verb. In the following sentences, adverbs are in italics:

The system ran *well.*

Melissa speaks *quietly.*

In addition, a sentence can be complete even when the verb does not have an object or a modifier. For example:

Bob arrived.

Rose left.

However, not all verbs transfer action. About 11 verbs in the English language are known as **state-of-being** verbs or **linking** verbs. Common linking verbs are forms of *to be (am, is, are, was, were), appear, become, seem,* and at times *smell, taste, feel, sound, look, act,* and *grow.* A linking verb is followed by an adjective, or a **subject complement.** In the following sentences, the adjectives, or subject complements, are in italics:

The report is *ready.*

I feel *good.*

• WRITER'S TOOLKIT

Phases (Not Stages) of Writing

Writers often find themselves stuck because they *multitask:* they work on different types of writing activities simultaneously. To make progress, consciously focus on only one phase of the writing process at a time: *composing* or *editing* or *revising.* Here's how the various phases differ:

A. **Composing:** creating, inventing, discovering, and molding your topic.

   1. **Prewriting:** researching, reading, and discussing a topic to gain insight; taking notes and mapping; thinking reflectively.
   2. **Planning:** organizing and prioritizing key ideas; clarifying purpose and audience.
   3. **Drafting:** getting your ideas on the page in narrative form.

B. **Editing:** making stylistic changes so that writing is clear, concise, and reader-friendly; proofreading for correct grammar, punctuation, or word usage.

C. **Revising:** restructuring, rethinking, or reorganizing content so that your message is effective.

Keep in mind that these are not distinct *stages* that you need to do in a specific order. You may find yourself going back and forth from *composing* to *editing* or *revising* throughout the entire production of a document. The *key* is doing only one activity at a time.

Unlike other words in English, verbs tell time by changing form, with the various verb tenses expressing differences in time. Verbs can include helpers to indicate whether an event *happened in the past, is happening in the present,* or *will happen in the future.*[3] You'll learn more about tenses and other qualities of verbs in Chapter 4. Your main goal now is to learn how to identify verbs within a sentence, so let's start the process.

Below is a list of 20 words. Pick out the words that are verbs by asking if the word involves an action. (Hint: One way to check whether a word is a verb is to put a subject in front of it, such as *you* or *I.* If it sounds as if you have the core of a sentence, then the word is probably a verb.)

speak	send	borrow	street	plant
drive	type	tree	write	watch
fun	walnut	manage	distribute	close
classify	throw	finish	lotion	manipulate

Now go through the list again, and identify which of the words above could also be nouns. You can determine whether a word is a noun by putting the word *the* in front of it, such as *the table.* You can see that some words, such as *plant* and *watch,* can be verbs as well as nouns. (Later in this chapter, you will learn that a word can play more than one role: how a word functions in a sentence determines its part of speech.)

In the spaces below, develop a list of ten action verbs.

________ ________ ________ ________ ________

________ ________ ________ ________ ________

The verb of a sentence determines the subject and also the object, if there is one. Focus on writing sentences so that the verb plays its role in a vital way. When you can, choose strong action verbs instead of linking verbs (such as *am, is, are, was, were, seem*) and weak verbs (such as *make, give,* and *take*).

PRACTICE

Instructions: Write a short, simple sentence for each of the verbs in your list above. Then do the following:

1. With a partner, read each of your sentences out loud.
2. After you read a sentence, pause to see if your partner can pick out the verb(s) in the sentence.
3. Work back and forth until each of you completes your list of sentences.

▸Language Diversity

Verb Patterns: Business English and most local languages differ in the way they employ some verbs. One pattern in local language is to leave off the *s* in third-person singular verbs; for example, "He speaks the truth" could be spoken in local language as "He speak the truth."

Many other differences occur in past and present tense forms of verbs between formal and informal language use.

Ask Yourself: *What are other examples of how I use verbs differently when speaking in informal situations as compared to formal situations?*

Compound Verbs

Some sentences have compound verbs. A **compound verb** consists of two or more verbs all relating to the same subject. In other words, one subject is followed by two or more verbs that create separate lines of thought about the subject. In the following examples, the subject is underlined once and the verb twice:

Rita arrived at the meeting by 9 a.m. and began speaking to the director.

Your invoice has been updated by our accountant and is enclosed.

To check whether you really have a compound verb, see if you can break the one sentence into two sentences, each with the same subject. Using the first sentence above as an example, you can create these two sentences:

Rita arrived at the meeting by 9 a.m.

Rita began speaking to the director.

Tips for Identifying Verbs

Even after reviewing verbs, you may still feel rusty about which words are verbs. Here are a few tips:

1. Some common verbs, such as **helping verbs** (also called *auxiliary verbs*), always function as verbs. When you see these words in a sentence, underline them twice so you immediately identify them as verbs.

   Be: am, is, are, was, were

   Have: has, have, had

   Do: do, did, done

2. The word *will* almost always functions as a verb (unless you are referring to someone named *Will* or you are using *will* as a noun as in "Last *Will* and Testament"). When used as a verb, *will* is usually followed by another verb, even though the two verbs can be interrupted by an adverb. The adverbs in the following examples are in italics:

   I will *definitely* negotiate the terms of the lease.

   Mary will contact them tomorrow.

   Our client will *happily* comply with the regulations.

3. The word *not* is an adverb that negates verbs; in effect, the word *not* modifies verbs. In a sentence containing the word *not,* you will find a verb on one or both sides of *not.* (Note: The verb *cannot* is usually spelled as one word and thus *not* is part of the verb.)

   George does *not* remember the correct terms of the contract.

   The carrier has *not* embarked on his journey yet today.

   The manager is *not* available until 3 p.m.

   Our insurance cannot increase for another year.

PRACTICE

Instructions: In the following sentences, underline each verb twice.

1. The administrator will not help us with our complaint.
2. Jane arrived an hour late and announced her resignation.
3. The plane departed on time.
4. My supervisor insists on proper etiquette at work.
5. Charles will advise us of the changes but will not assist us with them.

THE SUBJECT

You may have learned that to find the subject of a sentence, you should "look for the noun." But the object of a sentence can also be a noun. How do you know whether the noun you choose is the subject or object of the sentence?

"Looking for the noun" also limits you in other ways, because the subject of a sentence is not necessarily a noun: the subject can also be a pronoun or a phrase (which we'll discuss in Section C).

Here's information about subjects that will keep you on the right track. In well-written sentences, the subject expresses the topic of the sentence. The subject is a point of reference that the rest of the sentence gives information about. According to Karen Elizabeth Gordon, author of *The Deluxe Transitive Vampire,* "The subject is that part of the sentence about which something is divulged; it is what the sentence's other words are gossiping about."[4]

• Internet Exercise 2.1

Grammar References: In addition to a dictionary and a thesaurus, there is one more tool every business writer should have in his or her library: a grammar reference source. No one remembers all the rules all the time.

This book refers to the *The Gregg Reference Manual,* tenth edition, by William A. Sabin, but other comprehensive reference sources are available, both on the bookshelf and online. For more information, visit the Web site at **www.mhhe.com/youngBE**.

At the home page, select "Student Activities," and then click on the "Chapter 2" link to find instructions for getting started.

In the following sentences (and in examples throughout this book), simple subjects are underlined once:

The machine met all of our expectations.

A good proposal will bring us business.

Our building needs a new roof.

In some sentences, the subject is the "agent" of the verb. In other words, the subject is the "doer" of the action of a verb. As you read the following examples, see how the subject performs the action.[5]

Martha sings beautifully.

The dog barks loudly.

Our team welcomed the new manager.

Linking verbs, however, are not dynamic: they do not transfer action. The subject of a linking verb is the "identified" role.[6] As you read the following examples, notice how the word or words at the end of the sentence identify or describe the subject. With linking verbs, a **subject complement** (a word or several words that describe the subject), rather than an object, follows the verb. In the examples below, the subject complements are italicized:

William is my *supervisor.*

The cafeteria food is *good.*

Today feels *warmer than usual.*

At other times, a sentence does not begin with an "actor," "agent," or "participant" driving the verb; it begins with an **anticipating subject** such as *it* or *there.* In sentences that have *it* or *there* as the grammatical subject, the **real subject** often comes after the verb. To find the real subject, ask yourself what *it* or *there* stands for. In the sentences below, the italicized words are the real subjects:

It is a beautiful *day.* The day is beautiful.

There are five *cars* in the driveway. Five cars are in the driveway.

To sum things up, the **grammatical subject** precedes the verb. In some sentences, the grammatical subject is not the same as the real subject. The easiest way to identify the grammatical subject is to identify the verb first and then look for a word (or group of words) that precedes the verb. You will do more work with real subjects later; for now, just realize that there can be a difference between the grammatical subject and the real subject.[7]

Complete Subjects

A **complete subject** includes the simple subject as well as other words that modify it. In the examples below, the complete subject is in italics; the simple subject is underlined.

The young man at the end of the line requested the information.

An approach to consider when making decisions was suggested.

For all the exercises in this book, you will identify only the simple subject of a sentence.

Compound Subjects

Sentences come in many varieties, and so do subjects. A simple subject can also be a **compound subject** when two or more agents make up the subject. The words modifying the subject are part of the complete subject but not part of the simple subject. For example:

Tom and Jane arrived at the meeting together.

The director of marketing and his assistant will conduct the survey.

The new information and the old report are now contained in the packet.

PRACTICE

Instructions: Underline the compound subjects in the sentences below.

1. The director of finance and his new assistant arrived early.
2. My new supervisor and I will go to the meeting together.
3. Alfred from accounting and Martin from finance will have the information for you.
4. The handouts for the workshop and the books will arrive with Keari.
5. The summary of services and the invoice are both enclosed.

Understood or Implied Subjects

In some sentences, the actual subject does not appear in the sentence but instead is "understood." This type of structure can occur only when the subject is *you* or *I*. Think about it: when you directly address a person, you don't always include the pronoun *you* in a statement. In fact, at times including *you* or *I* sounds awkward. Here are some examples:

(You) Take the first seat available.

(You) Please inform the guests that the meeting is running late.

(You) Send your check in the enclosed envelope.

(I) Thank you for your assistance.

When you are identifying the subject of a sentence and cannot locate it, ask yourself if it might be an "understood" or "implied" subject. Understood subjects are common.

PRACTICE

Instructions: Write five sentences that have "*you* understood" as the subject. Assume that you are giving someone instructions to do something, such as "take out a pen," "start writing," "share your information." Then, with a partner, read each of your sentences out loud, and identify the verb in each sentence.

1.

2.

3.

4.

5.

THE SENTENCE CORE

As you now know, a sentence core consists of the verb and its subject. In the past, you may have learned to identify the subject first and then the verb. Now you are going to apply a new approach, one that will be easier and bring you better results. To identify the sentence core, *identify the verb first and then work backward to identify the subject.*

Here's the rationale: The verb determines the subject, and in statements the grammatical subject *almost* always precedes the verb. Here is the most efficient way to identify the sentence core:

1. *Identify the simple verb.* Look for a word or words that express action *(determine, identify, analyze)* or state of being *(is, are, was, were, seem, feel).* Underline the verb twice so that it stands out.
2. *Identify the simple subject.* After you have underlined the verb twice, work backward to identify the subject. Underline the subject once.

WRITER'S TOOLKIT

Implied Verbs

Just as sentences can have implied subjects, they can sometimes also have implied verbs. In other words, even if the verb is not spoken or written, structurally it is still part of the sentence.

The word *than* is a conjunction, and a subject and verb should follow it. Often, people leave out the verb in their speech and writing.

Bill is taller than Susan *(is tall).*

Michu speaks more highly of you than *(he does)* of me.

Another word that is used informally as a conjunction is the word *like.* (Use *as* or *as if* in formal writing.)

I wish I could work efficiently like you *(do).*

Everyone at work dresses like you *(dress).*

3. If you read the *subject* and *verb* out loud, they will give you a sense of what the sentence is about (you identify, you read, they should make).
4. To identify the subject and verb in a question, invert the order to statement form so that the subject comes before the verb, as in the following:

Will you go to the meeting with me? ⟶ You will go to the meeting with me.

Notice how much easier it is to identify the complete verb and its subject once the sentence is in statement form.

PRACTICE

Instructions: In the sentences below, identify the sentence core (simple subject and verb) of each main clause. First identify the verb, and underline it twice; then work backward in the sentence to identify the subject, and underline it once. If you have difficulty finding the subject, ask yourself if it is "*you* understood" (You) or "*I* understood" (I). For example:

Each sentence needs a subject and verb to be complete.

(You) Underline the verb two times and then the subject one time.

(You) Identify only the main subject and verb.

1. The members of the committee will determine the outcome.
2. Do not disperse information until after the merger.
3. Louise expected the appointment before the end of this year.
4. The CIO sent letters to employees about the job cuts.
5. After the discussion, the librarian changed the hours and posted them on the door.

▸Language Diversity

Cajun: Cajun is a mixture of the French, American Indian, African, Spanish, and English languages. Cajun finds its origins with the descendants of French and Acadian people who settled in Louisiana from the seventeenth to the nineteenth centuries; in fact, the word *Cajun* is derived from a regional pronunciation of the word *Acadian.*

Below is a list of words written as they are pronounced in the Cajun language. How many can you identify?

1. beb
2. dat
3. bag daer
4. hose pipe
5. shah
6. tink
7. udder
8. tee
9. tree
10. dis

Cajun: Da udder boat bag daer is bigga den da res.

Standard: The other boat back there is bigger than the rest.

It is not uncommon for Cajun speakers to invert word order when asking questions:

Cajun	**Standard**
Where you at?	Where are you?
What time it is?	What time is it?

SECTION A CONCEPT CHECK

1. What are some ways to recognize verbs?
2. What is the easiest way to identify the simple subject of a sentence?
3. Not all verbs are action words; what is the other category of verbs?

SECTION B: HOW DO PARTS OF SPEECH WORK?

Now that you understand the sentence core, you can focus on reviewing parts of speech and the role each plays in a sentence. Though you have already learned how verbs function as predicates, you will now learn more basics about verbs and the different forms they take. In the previous section, you also learned about subjects, but you haven't yet covered information about nouns as a part of speech, so they are included in this section also.

In the past, when you learned about the various parts of speech, you may have memorized lists of words. Or you may have learned that some words can be more than one part of speech, depending on their role in the sentence.

In reality, the way a word *functions* in a sentence determines its part of speech. Here is a list of the parts of speech covered in this section:

- Nouns
- Verbs
- Pronouns
- Adjectives
- Adverbs
- Prepositions
- Conjunctions
- Articles

Let's briefly look at how the various parts of speech function and how some words shift roles. This section is only an introduction: an entire chapter is dedicated to each of the more complicated parts of speech, such as verbs, pronouns, and modifiers (adjectives and adverbs). Use the information here as a refresher or an introduction to later chapters: you are not expected to learn this information in depth.

NOUNS

A **noun** is a person, place, or thing, but it is also an idea or a thought or some other intangible "item" that can't be seen or felt, such as *wind* or *love* or *compassion.* Be flexible in the way you think of nouns.

One way to tell whether a word is a noun is to put the word *the* in front of it. If this combination makes sense and feels complete, then the word is likely to be a noun; for example, *the plant, the car, the book, the friend,* and *the economy.* Test this out for yourself. Write a list of words that you think are nouns and then put *the* in front of each word. Does the word combination make sense?

Nouns generally do not change into other parts of speech, but some words that are nouns can be verbs or adjectives, as you will see below.

In the following examples, specific words are highlighted: when they are nouns, they are in italics; when they are adjectives, boldface type. In addition, verbs are underscored twice and subjects are underscored once.

plant: The *plant* is green.

Marcia planted the vegetables next to the herbs.

My gift was the **plant** stand.

walnut: *Walnuts* are a healthful food.

The **walnut** chest is in the den.

light: The *light* is on.

Alex lights the candles for dinner.

The **light** jacket looks best.

figure: The *figure* seems too high.

He figured the expenses would be within his budget.

judge: The *judge* will decide the case.

Martha judged the situation incorrectly.

The **judged** event occurs at noon.

VOCABULARY: NEW WORDS

New to *Merriam-Webster's Collegiate Dictionary:*

McJob, noun: A low-paying, nonchallenging job with few benefits or opportunities, typically in the service sector.*

avatar, noun: An electronic image that represents and is manipulated by a computer user (as in a computer game or an online shopping site).

* Coined by Douglas Coupland, in his novel *Generation X,* after McDonald's fast-food chain.

Qualities of Nouns

Nouns can be categorized in various ways, and their category determines how they will be used. Here are the categories and a few details about some of them:

- **Proper nouns:** the official names of people, places, or things; for example, the days of the week, the months of the year, and the Declaration of Independence.

Proper nouns should be capitalized. Besides those mentioned above, can you think of other examples of proper nouns?

- **Common nouns:** general classes of places, objects, ideas, and qualities; for example, *town, car,* and *enthusiasm.*
- **Collective nouns:** groups such as *family, committee, team, company, firm, group, corporation, management, jury,* and *staff.*

In general, a collective noun can be singular or plural depending on the way the word is used. If the members of the group are acting as a unit, use the singular form of the verb; if they are acting separately, use the plural form of the verb. For example:

The committee meets later today.

The committee are not in agreement.

Notice that in the first sentence above, *committee* is singular because all the committee members are acting together, meeting as a unit. In the second sentence, the individual members are acting separately, disagreeing with one another. Here are a few more categories of nouns:

- **Concrete nouns:** things that can be experienced through the senses, such as *flower, dog,* or *rain.*
- **Abstract nouns:** things that are not knowable through the senses, such as *honor, integrity,* or *pride.*
- **Count nouns:** countable items, such as *cookies, friends,* and *tulips.*
- **Noncount nouns:** items that cannot be counted, such as *sand, water,* and *paint.*

This information on the types of nouns shows you that nouns fall into various categories. The most important distinction you will make is between common nouns and proper nouns. If you have the time, do the Explore exercise below.

EXPLORE

With a partner, think of a few more words to fit each of the categories listed below; then compare your list with others.

Common nouns: ________ ________ ________

Proper nouns: ________ ________ ________

Concrete nouns: ________ ________ ________

Abstract nouns: ________ ________ ________

Count nouns: ________ ________ ________

Noncount nouns: ________ ________ ________

Collective nouns: ________ ________ ________

VERBS

You have already learned that verbs express action and state of being. The base form of a verb is called an **infinitive;** for example, *to be, to see,* and *to enlighten.* Verbs are then conjugated into their first-, second-, and third-person singular and plural forms.

Infinitive: ***to walk***

	Singular	Plural
First person	I *walk*	we *walk*
Second person	You *walk*	you *walk*
Third person	He, she, it *walks*	they *walk*

Take special note of the following important points about verbs:

- All third-person singular verbs in Business English end in an *s;* third-person singular verbs are also known as the ***s*-form**.
- Verbs also have a **past tense form** and a **past participle form.** For regular verbs, both parts are formed by adding *ed* to the base of the verb. For *walk,* the past tense and past participle are *walked.* Notice that a helper is used with the past participle.

Base	Past Tense	Past Participle	
walk	walked	*has* walked	(regular)
prefer	preferred	*had* preferred	(regular)

However, many verbs are irregular, and their past tense and past participle are formed in various ways. For example, the verb *speak* is irregular, having a past form of *spoke* and a past participle form of *spoken.* In Chapter 4, you will do extensive work with irregular verbs.

Base	Past Tense	Past Participle	
speak	spoke	*have* spoken	(irregular)
throw	threw	*was* thrown	(irregular)

For the most part, verbs in the English language remain verbs; that is, they don't change to other parts of speech readily. However, some verbs transition into nouns by changing form. Two verb forms function as nouns:

- *The* ing *form:* The *ing* form is created by adding *ing* to the base form of the verb. This *ing* form of a verb functions as a noun and is called a **gerund.** For example, the gerund form of *walk* is *walking;* the gerund form of *speak* is *speaking.*
- *The nominal form:* Verbs also become nouns through their **nominal form,** which is created in different ways for different verbs. Sometimes the nominal form is created by adding *tion* or *ment* to the base of the verb.

Verb	Nominal	Verb	Nominal
act	action	distribute	distribution
argue	argument	entitle	entitlement
instruct	instruction	encourage	encouragement
treat	treatment	pay	payment

TABLE 2.1 | Verb Tenses

Verb tenses create a special problem for many. This chart indicates the various verb tenses. You may be surprised to learn that you don't have as much of a problem with verb tenses as you do with verb parts, especially the past tense and past participle forms of irregular verbs.

	Present	Past	Future
Simple	walk	walked	will walk
Perfect	have walked	had walked	will have walked
Progressive	is walking	has been walking	had been walking
Perfect progressive	have been walking	had been walking	will have been walking

Source: Lunsford and Connors, *The New St. Martin's Handbook,* Bedford / St. Martin's, Boston, pp. 180–185.

Nominals can be formed in various other ways; for example:

Verb	Nominal
serve	service
analyze	analysis
discover	discovery
resist	resistance
fail	failure

For the following verbs, first show the gerund form and then the nominal form:

	Gerund	Nominal
develop	developing	development
assist	________	________
facilitate	________	________
adapt	________	________
confuse	________	________
advise	________	________

Here are some nouns that are used as verbs in informal situations but not in formal ones:

	Informal	Formal
lunch	Let's lunch together this week.	Let's have *lunch* together this week.
lotto	Will you *lotto* this week?	Will you play the *lotto* this week?

▸Language Diversity

Pronouns: Some pronouns are used differently in local language than in Business English. One pattern in local language is to use *me* instead of *myself.* For example, "I'll leave *myself* a message so I don't forget" could be spoken in local language as "I'll leave *me* a message so I don't forget."

Other differences also occur with pronouns. In Chapter 5, "Pronouns," you will work on pronouns in depth, comparing and contrasting Business English with your local language.

Ask Yourself: *What are other examples of how I use pronouns differently when speaking in informal situations as compared to formal situations?*

PRONOUNS

A **pronoun** takes the place of a noun or another pronoun. Unlike some other parts of speech, pronouns remain pronouns; in other words, pronouns do not become verbs, adjectives, and so on. Pronouns are categorized by *case,* and the **pronoun case** determines how the pronoun, such as *I* or *me,* will be used in a sentence.

The main cases, or categories, of pronouns are *subjective* (sometimes called *nominative*), *objective, possessive,* and *reflexive.* With each pronoun case, speakers and writers make specific kinds of errors (which you will study in more depth in Chapter 5). There are also more categories of pronouns, such as demonstrative and relative (which you will also review in Chapter 5).

For now, here's the most important information you need to know about pronouns:

Subjective case pronouns function as subjects of verbs:

I, you, he, she, it, we, they, who

Objective case pronouns function as objects, primarily of verbs and prepositions:

me, you, him, her, it, us, them, whom

Possessive case pronouns show possession, and a noun usually follows them:

my, mine, your, yours, his, hers, its, ours, theirs

Reflexive case pronouns refer back to a subjective pronoun:

myself, yourself, himself, herself, itself, ourselves, yourselves, themselves

Here are some examples:

Subjective case: *They* arranged the meeting. *I* decided to attend.

Objective case: Bob handed *me* the agenda. Bob asked *her* and *me* to attend the meeting.

Possessive case: *My* brochure explains how they can solve *their* problems.

Reflexive case: **I** will do the proposal *myself;* **you** can do the other project *yourself.*

PRACTICE

Instructions: In the following sentences, identify each pronoun and also identify its case.

1. My manager asked me to arrive at work on time.

2. Sharon said that she was unable to attend her weekly meetings.

3. Blake gave his report to Marty, his manager.

4. Ms. Anderson and her assistant will complete their report on time.

5. They gave us an incomplete report about our transaction.

PREPOSITIONS

Prepositions show the relationship of a noun or pronoun to some other word in the sentence; prepositions are "go betweens" and result in **prepositional phrases,** having a noun or pronoun as their object.

Here are some common prepositions and phrases:

Preposition	Prepositional Phrase
about	about an hour
above	above the door
for	for an excuse
among	among the answers
at	at the meeting
before	before the game
behind	behind the car
between	between the two events
with	with the check

Create a prepositional phrase for each word in the list below:

after ________________________

from ________________________

in ________________________

into ________________________

of ________________________

on ________________________

SPEAKING BUSINESS

Greetings and Salutations: You can sometimes tell where people are from based on the way they express common greetings. In the South, "y'all" is used to address one or more people. In some areas, such as parts of Texas, that expression becomes "all y'all" when speaking to a group of people; for example, "How are all y'all doin'?"

In the East, you would more likely say, "you guys"; in parts of the Midwest, specifically Chicago, the greeting becomes "yous guys." That's right, in Chicago, people have been known to use the informal pronoun *yous* when talking to a group of people (which understandably drives some English teachers crazy). In other parts of the East and Midwest, the term becomes "you'ins."

In formal situations, you can simply use *you,* as in "How are you doing?"

Ask Yourself: *What do I say in my part of the country?*

over ______________________________

through ______________________________

to ______________________________

under ______________________________

until ______________________________

unto ______________________________

up ______________________________

within ______________________________

without ______________________________

If you have spoken English most of your life, prepositions are easy. However, if you are an adult learning English for the first time, using prepositions is difficult. The best time to learn prepositions is during childhood; that's partly because it is easier for children to pick up subtle meaning in language usage than it is for adults who are learning a new language. The shade of difference between *in, on,* or *into* is sometimes negligible, with any one of the three words being acceptable. For example, any one of the following would be correct:

I'm getting *in* the bus.

I'm getting *on* the bus.

I'm getting *into* the bus.

Often when more than one answer can be correct, learners think that whatever they say will be wrong. Instead, realize there are many "right ways" to say a phrase; when you have a question, ask someone who is helpful. Then practice the phrases over and over again until you feel confident.

PRACTICE

Instructions: Select five of the prepositional phrases you wrote above and create a sentence for each of them. **For example:**

Phrase: about an hour

Sentence: The task will take about an hour.

Phrase: at the meeting

Sentence: Maria presented information at the meeting.

1.

2.

3.

4.

5.

CONJUNCTIONS

Conjunctions make connections, showing relationships and building bridges between ideas. In Chapter 3, "Punctuation," you will learn much about how conjunctions work in a sentence, but you need to learn the information here *before* you work on Chapter 3.

You need to learn the three categories of conjunctions, but do not let their titles become a stumbling block. Learn the terms quickly so that they don't become "bigger" than they really are. Here are the three categories of conjunctions: *coordinating, subordinating,* and *adverbial.*

Each of these types of conjunctions plays a major role in punctuation and in writing style.

- **Coordinating conjunctions**: *and, but, or, for, nor, so, yet.* These are the seven coordinating conjunctions, and you should memorize them.

Coordinating conjunctions imply equality, at least in structure, among the items they connect.

- **Subordinating conjunctions:** *if, when, as, although, because, as soon as, before, while, after, since, even though, unless, whereas,* and so on. This list is a sampling of subordinating conjunctions. There are too many subordinating conjunctions to memorize; however, you can tell whether a word is a subordinating conjunction by placing it at the beginning of a complete sentence. If the sentence no longer sounds complete, then the word is probably a subordinating conjunction. (You will cover more information about this in Section C of this chapter.) For example:

Complete: Bob arrived at the meeting.

Incomplete: *If* Bob arrived at the meeting . . . what?

Incomplete: *When* Bob arrived at the meeting . . . what?

Incomplete: *Although* Bob arrived at the meeting . . . what?

Subordinating conjunctions show how ideas relate to one another, aiding the reader in understanding what the writer is stating.

- **Adverbial conjunctions:** *however, therefore, for example, thus,* and so on. Since there are so many adverbial conjunctions, here is a more detailed list:

therefore	hence	in summary	that is	furthermore
however	thus	moreover	in contrast	on the contrary
for example	in addition	of course	as usual	in general
fortunately	in conclusion	otherwise	unfortunately	consequently

Adverbial conjunctions build bridges between ideas and help the reader understand the writer's intention; they provide **transitions.** If you place an adverbial conjunction at the beginning of a complete sentence, the sentence will still be complete. For example:

George was offered the job of his choice.

Fortunately, George was offered the job of his choice.

Of course, George was offered the job of his choice.

PRACTICE

Instructions: In the following sentences, identify each conjunction and its category (coordinating, subordinating, or adverbial).

1. Since we arrived on time, we were able to hear the keynote speaker.

   ____

2. However, the speech was not very interesting.

   ____

3. While the president spoke, lunch was served.

   ____

4. The participants listened carefully, but they missed a lot of information.

   ____

SPEAKING BUSINESS

Adverbs and Modifiers: Business English and local languages can differ in the way adverbs are used. A common local-language pattern is to leave off the *ly;* for example, "Drive safely" would be spoken as "Drive safe."

In Chapter 6, "Modifiers," you will work on adjectives and adverbs in depth, identifying other ways that Business English and local language may differ.

Ask Yourself: *What are other examples of how I use adverbs differently when speaking in informal situations as compared to formal situations?*

5. I plan to go to the conference next year, and my supervisor will go with me.

____

6. For example, Martha insisted on leaving the meeting early.

____

7. The decision was made, but I wasn't involved.

____

8. Make your travel arrangements, or you may not be able to attend.

____

9. After Janet arrived, the meeting got on the right track.

____

10. Therefore, you are the best candidate for the job.

____

ADJECTIVES AND ADVERBS

Adjectives and adverbs are both modifiers, which means they describe other words. Neither adjectives nor adverbs are as important in business writing as they are in creative writing. Whereas they can be overused in business writing, other forms of writing do not come to life without adjectives and adverbs. Can you imagine reading a novel or poem without the vivid details that adjectives and adverbs paint in your mind?

- **Adjectives** modify nouns and pronouns, adding color, taste, feel, and other dimensions to the words they describe. Effective use of adjectives gives readers a strong visual of that which is being described. Here are a few examples: *bright, new, slow, yellow, tall, warm, fuzzy, clear, little,* and *great.*
- **Adverbs** modify adjectives, verbs, and other adverbs, providing the same sort of element to writing that adjectives do by adding more depth, color, or intensity. Adverbs answer the questions *how, when, where,* and *why.* Here are a few examples of adverbs: *quickly, quietly, friendly, very, more, most, less,* and *least.*

Some adverbs are formed by adding *ly* to an adjective:

Adjective	Adverb
rapid	rapidly
bright	brightly
loud	loudly

A *bright* light is shining. (adjective)

The light is shining *brightly.* (adverb)

Here are a few words that can be used as adjectives or adverbs:

deep late slow quick

Even though some adverbs do not need the *ly* ending, writing and speaking generally flow better when the *ly* ending is used.

VOCABULARY: WORD USAGE

Word Choices: Have you ever used the word *thru?* You know what it means, right? Well, think again. The word *thru* is not a Business English word, and you will not find it in an abridged dictionary. Use the word *through* instead, as in "She walked through the doorway."

Of course, you could also confuse the meaning with the word *threw,* which is the past tense form of the verb *throw,* as in "Bob threw the ball."

From now on, only use *thru* when it is used as part of "drive-thru." And remember, just because a word is common and you see it written everywhere doesn't mean it is a word that is considered "legal" in Business English.

PRACTICE

Instructions: In the following sentences, identify the adjectives and adverbs.

1. The bright new sign lights up the highway beautifully.

2. The green folder was on Mikala's messy desk.

3. They set low standards but barely met them.

4. Mike egregiously avoided the unwanted task.

5. Be sure you speak loudly enough to be heard.

ARTICLES: DEFINITE AND INDEFINITE

A, an, and *the* are three articles that modify nouns. *A* and *an* refer to a thing or person in general and thus are called *indefinite articles.* Sometimes it is difficult to choose between *a* and *an.* Here are simple guidelines:

- Use *a* before a word that begins with a consonant sound or a long *u* sound:

  George wears *a* unique tie every day.

- Use *an* before a word that begins with a vowel sound even if that word begins with a consonant (such as the sound "en" or "em"):

  Stephanie prefers *an* apple.

  An NBC reporter provided the information.

The refers to a specific thing or person and is thus called a *definite article.*

Jose would like to go to *the* movie that you suggested.

Mr. Pappas would prefer *the* black tie.

PRACTICE

Instructions: For the following nouns and adjectives, decide whether to use the article *a* or *an:*

_____ unusual	_____ elementary	_____ FDA
_____ nation	_____ brilliant	_____ membership
_____ uniform	_____ opening	_____ eminent
_____ principle	_____ NBC	_____ yellow

VOCABULARY: WORD USAGE

However: *However* is an adverb, but it can also function as a conjunction; as a conjunction, *however* can be either a subordinating conjunction or an adverbial conjunction. In the following examples, note the different functions of *however.*

However you decide to proceed, we will support you.

Mr. Houston should respond to the report *however* he chooses.

However, the employees will also respond as they choose.

• Internet Exercise 2.2

Word Fun: The Internet offers lots of opportunities to have fun with words. For links to activities and games that will build your word power while you play, visit the Web site at **www.mhhe.com/youngBE**.

At the home page, select "Student Activities," and then click on the "Chapter 2" link to find instructions for getting started.

SECTION B CONCEPT CHECK

1. What are the four major pronoun cases? Give an example of each.

2. What is a nominal? Give an example of a verb and its nominal form.

3. What are the three types of conjunctions? Give two examples of each.

SECTION C: WHAT IS A SENTENCE?

What is a sentence? The simple answer is that a **sentence** consists of a verb and its subject and expresses a complete thought. A more complex answer is that a sentence is an independent clause. Let's do some work with clauses so that you gain control over complicated sentence structures.

CLAUSES AS FRAGMENTS

A **clause** is a group of words that contains a subject and verb. A clause is an important grammatical unit.

Two basic types of clauses are **independent clauses** and **dependent clauses.** Their names describe their functions: an independent clause can stand alone; a dependent clause cannot stand alone (and needs support from an independent clause).

- *An independent clause is a sentence:* it has a subject and verb and expresses a complete thought.

  The meeting was delayed.

- *A dependent clause is a fragment:* it has a subject and verb but does not express a complete thought; it cannot stand alone. Dependent clauses often begin with subordinating conjunctions, such as *when, if, although,* and *because.*

  When the meeting was delayed . . .

Because it is a fragment**,** a dependent clause needs to connect with an independent clause to be complete.

When the meeting was delayed, we decided to go to lunch.

An independent clause becomes a dependent clause if a subordinating conjunction is added to it, as you can see in the following examples:

because the meeting was delayed

although we decided to go to lunch

even though we decided to go to lunch

while the meeting was delayed

A major grammatical mistake is ending a dependent clause (which is a fragment) with a terminal mark of punctuation such as a period, a question mark, or an exclamation point. (For more information on terminal marks of punctuation, see the *The Gregg Reference Manual,* Section 1.)

If you place a period at the end of a dependent clause, you create a fragment.

Incorrect: *Because* the meeting was delayed**.**

Incorrect: *Even though* we decided to go to lunch.

The example below is a simple sentence; it has a subject and verb and expresses a complete thought.

Sentence: Adam advised our committee to disband.

Here are the fragments that result when a subordinating conjunction is added to the beginning of the independent clause:

Fragment: *Although* Adam advised our committee to disband

Fragment: *After* Adam advised our committee to disband

Fragment: *Because* Adam advised our committee to disband . . . what happened?

When you read a fragment, the question that may pop into your mind is "What next?" That's because a fragment leaves the reader wondering where the sentence is going.

Here are ways to correct these types of fragments:

1. Turn the dependent clause into an independent clause. You may be able to do this simply by removing the subordinating conjunction.
2. Attach the dependent clause to an independent clause. Often the sentence before or after the dependent clause completes it nicely.

Incorrect: March was suggested as a good month for our annual meeting. *Even though this is the month that we also have our charity gala dinner.* Many managers supported the idea.

By connecting the dependent clause with the sentence that precedes or follows it, the correction is made:

Correct: March was suggested as a good month for our annual meeting even though this is the month that we also have our charity gala dinner. Many managers supported the idea.

Or:

Correct: March was suggested as a good month for our annual meeting. Even though this is the month that we also have our charity gala dinner, many managers supported the idea.

Of course, you could have removed *even though,* which would have turned the dependent clause into an independent clause. However, the sentences sound choppy without a transitional word, as shown below:

Weak: March was suggested as a good month for our annual meeting. This is the month that we also have our charity gala dinner. Many managers supported the idea.

PRACTICE

Instructions: Identify whether each of the following is a dependent clause (a fragment) or a complete sentence.

1. Since an analysis of the data would provide the information for a new report.
2. I already analyzed the data for the new report that George needs.
3. If you give the new report to George before noon on Friday.
4. Try to predict the outcome of the proposed merger.
5. Because the new merger will affect our corporate structure at all levels.

PHRASES AS FRAGMENTS

Fragments can also be formed when a **phrase** is punctuated as a sentence. Unlike a clause, a phrase does not have a subject and a verb. Here are long, involved phrases that could be mistaken for sentences:

Incorrect: *To present* yourself objectively in all situations so that you remain professional.

Incorrect: *Communicating* with several of the managers to get their opinion about the situation.

To avoid fragments, punctuate only independent clauses as complete sentences. You can correct the above phrases by making sure each has a subject and a verb:

Correct: (You) Present yourself objectively in all situations so that you remain professional.

Correct: You should communicate with several of the managers to get their opinion about the situation.

Here are two common types of phrases that are mistaken as clauses:

- **Infinitive phrase.** An *infinitive* is formed by adding *to* to the base form of the verb. An infinitive can act as a noun, adjective, or adverb. The following are examples of infinitives: *to speak, to read, to listen, to arrive,* and *to create.* An infinitive phrase is formed when a group of words follows the infinitive. Here are some long infinitive phrases that could be mistaken for sentences:

  To speak slowly and clearly so that your audience understands every word

  To read all sorts of journals and magazines in your field of study

  To listen carefully to every step of the instructions

  To arrive at the meeting fully prepared to give a presentation

  To create a list of all the activities that pertain to the project

- **Gerund phrase.** A gerund is formed by adding *ing* to the base form of the verb. Gerunds function as nouns. The following are gerunds: *going, seeing, being, following, communicating, speaking,* and so on. Here are the infinitive phrases shown above presented as gerund phrases:

  Speaking slowly and clearly so that your audience understands every word

  Reading all sorts of journals and magazines in your field of study

  Listening carefully to every step of the instructions

  Arriving at the meeting fully prepared to give a presentation

  Creating a list of all the activities that pertain to the project

WRITER'S TOOLKIT

Editing vs. Composing

Effective writing is more an issue of *editing* than it is of *composing.* As soon as you stop fixing individual sentences as you are composing, part of the difficulty with writing disappears immediately.

Though composing has its own challenges, only when you compose freely will you realize the difference; writing becomes much easier when you put your insights on the page without editing them.

Once you separate composing from editing, you gain control of your writing.

VOCABULARY: NEW WORDS

Added to the *American Heritage Dictionary* in 2000:

earwitness, noun: An individual who hears an incident occur and who later gives a report on what he or she heard.*

* *American Heritage Dictionary of the English Language,* 4th ed., copyright © 2000 by Houghton-Mifflin, updated 2003. All rights reserved.

An infinitive or gerund phrase can also function as the subject of a sentence. Using some of the infinitive and gerund phrases above, here's how they would appear as subjects:

> To speak slowly and clearly so that your audience understands every word is advice that you will hear often.
>
> To read all sorts of journals and magazines in your field of study keeps you up to date even in the midst of a busy schedule.
>
> Listening carefully to every step of the instructions ensures efficient use of time.
>
> Arriving at the meeting fully prepared to give a presentation is your only option.
>
> Creating a list of all the activities that pertain to the project would be a good starting point.

PRACTICE

Instructions: Identify whether each of the following is a complete sentence or is a gerund or an infinitive phrase (a fragment).

1. An analysis of the data would provide the information for a new report.
2. Analyzing the data for information for the new report that George needs.
3. Give the new report to George before noon on Friday.
4. To predict the outcome of the proposed merger affecting our jobs.
5. The new merger will affect our corporate structure at all levels.

SECTION C CONCEPT CHECK

1. What are the differences between a dependent and an independent clause?
2. What is the difference between an infinitive and a gerund? Give an example of each.
3. A dependent clause usually starts with what kind of conjunction?

Internet Exercise 2.3

Worksheets: For additional exercises on the topics discussed in this section, visit the Web site at **www.mhhe.com/youngBE.**

At the home page, select "Student Activities," and then click on the "Chapter 2" link to find instructions for getting started.

CHAPTER 2 SUMMARY

You now have a clear idea of what a sentence is—and what a sentence isn't. You understand how to turn fragments into complete sentences, making your writing grammatically correct. You also understand the various parts of speech and the role they play in sentences; you can recognize the difference between subjective and objective pronouns and identify coordinating, subordinating, and adverbial conjunctions. But most importantly, you understand how to identify the sentence core.

Before reading this chapter, you may not have used the term *sentence core;* now you realize that it is one of the most important terms in your writing vocabulary. As you move through later chapters, you will learn how to control the sentence core. As you become more adept at controlling the core of sentences, your writing will become clearer and more powerful.

Even if you have not yet mastered every concept in this chapter, don't worry—you will review the important principles again in later chapters. However, before moving on to Chapter 3, make sure that you understand how to recognize the three types of conjunctions: *coordinating, subordinating,* and *adverbial.* If you do, you are ready to begin your work with punctuation in Chapter 3.

CHAPTER 2 CHECKLIST

As you work with the sentence core:

____ Have you identified the verb first?

____ Have you underlined the verb two times so that it stands out visually?

____ To identify the subject, have you looked for a word or words that precede the verb?

____ Can you identify the real subject when it is different from the grammatical subject?

____ Can you identify subordinating conjunctions?

____ Can you identify adverbial conjunctions?

____ Can you list the seven coordinating conjunctions?

____ What is a complete sentence?

____ What is a fragment?

____ What is a clause?

____ What is a dependent clause?

____ What is an independent clause?

CHAPTER 2 END-OF-CHAPTER ACTIVITIES

Before starting these activities, realize that you must use the tools from Chapter 1 (mind mapping, freewriting, and focused writing) to compose freely. When you do writing exercises throughout this book, do not stop to correct your errors as you compose. Instead, leave corrections and changes for the editing phase of your writing.

ACTIVITY 1: PROCESS MEMO

INSTRUCTIONS: Write your instructor a short message describing some of the principles you learned in this chapter; focus on ideas that seemed to surprise you or make a difference. What did you learn that you can apply? Is sentence structure beginning to make more sense? As part of your message, explain the sentence core and identify the three types of conjunctions, giving two or three examples of each conjunction. If you have Internet access, you can complete this exercise online at www.mhhe.com/youngBE and then send an e-mail to your instructor.

ACTIVITY 2: IDENTIFYING CORE ELEMENTS

A. THE SENTENCE CORE

INSTRUCTIONS: In the following sentences, identify the verb by underlining it twice, and then identify the subject by underlining it once.

1. The report does not indicate new procedures for the accounting department.
2. Our director of finance will determine the meeting location.
3. Bob Simms flew to Boston on Friday after the meeting.
4. My associate informed me of the merger.
5. Charlie spoke about our expanding budget.
6. Malcolm's article appeared in five different journals.
7. The second speaker entertained everyone in the audience.
8. Indicate your new address on the enclosed form.
9. The only good excuse for not going to the meeting would be illness.
10. Find the answer quickly.

B. THE SENTENCE CORE

INSTRUCTIONS: In the following sentences, identify the verb by underlining it twice, and then identify the subject by underlining it once. (Watch for *you*- and *I*-understood subjects and for compound subjects and verbs.)

1. Inform the committee of your decision and request an extension.
2. The committee chair and members will understand your dilemma and grant your request.
3. Advise me later in the day about your decision.

4. Thank you for your fast response to my request.

5. Michael Jones and Rupert Alessandro arrived early and indicated their preferences.

6. Take the initiative and listen to their recommendations.

7. The vice president attended the conference yesterday but will return tomorrow.

8. Please indicate your preferences and make your request in writing.

9. My supervisor asked me about the problem and told me that I needed to solve it.

10. Reggie and Giorgi completed the work and left early.

C. VERBS

INSTRUCTIONS: In the following sentences, identify the verb by underlining it twice, and then identify the subject by underlining it once. (Watch for *you* understood, compound subjects and verbs, and gerund and infinitive phrases as subjects.)

1. To get a new job is Bob's main objective.

2. Jan and Bob will complete the assignment and present the information in the meeting.

3. The price and locale are good selling features for the building.

4. Planning the meeting to coincide with our annual sales conference was a good idea.

5. Informing everyone about the change in plans occurred at the beginning of the meeting.

6. Apply for the job before deciding you cannot get it.

7. Fill out the forms completely.

8. Asking for a raise is not always the wisest approach.

9. To arrive on time and prepared shows your interest.

10. Arriving late and disrupting the meeting are two sure ways to lose their interest.

D. CLAUSES AND PHRASES

INSTRUCTIONS: Identify which of the following are complete sentences, which are infinitive or gerund phrases, and which are dependent clauses.

1. To understand the situation they are in at this time of the year.
2. You can make the change if you put your mind to it.
3. Working on the same project together for several years now.
4. Only if you would like me to assist you with the team project that is due next week.
5. Jack has proved himself as the best project leader.
6. Since the request came from the president of the corporation, not your supervisor.
7. Pay special attention to your client's requests.
8. You are successful and should be proud of your accomplishments.
9. Going to every team meeting and arriving on time.
10. Summarize your goals at the beginning of every new quarter.

E. PRONOUNS

INSTRUCTIONS: In the following sentences, identify each pronoun and its case.

1. Susan left herself a message so that she would not forget.
2. If we attend the meeting, they will give the contract to you and me.
3. The supervisor and her team will do their best on the project.
4. If you assign the report to Jim and me, I will work with him.
5. The job was mine before it was yours, so please ask me for assistance.

F. CONJUNCTIONS

INSTRUCTIONS: In the following sentences, identify the conjunctions and indicate whether they are coordinating, subordinating, or adverbial.

1. Their interview went well, but they still did not get the assignment.
2. However, the team can request additional information if they need it.
3. When you arrive at my office, have the front desk call me.
4. Therefore, you should not need to wait for any length of time.
5. While you wait, you can check your e-mail messages.

G. PRONOUNS

INSTRUCTIONS: In the following sentences, identify the modifiers and indicate whether they are adjectives or adverbs.

1. The situation is nearly under control.
2. Adam requested that the very interesting data be presented at the board meeting.
3. Speak slowly and you will be understood well.
4. You did a good job on your monthly report.
5. What did they finally agree to?

ACTIVITY 3: SPEAKING BUSINESS

INSTRUCTIONS: Do you ever have a problem with words ending in *ing?* In other words, do you have a tendency to say "in'" at the end of words ending in *ing,* such as *talkin', walkin', dancin', feelin',* and so on?

Pronounce each of the words below slowly and clearly. As you do, focus on the inside of your mouth, paying special attention to the ending of each word. For example, when you pronounce "talk*in',*" your tongue is flat and at the roof of your mouth as you end the word. When you pronounce "talk*ing,*" the tip of your tongue is at the bottom of your mouth and the top of your throat closes briefly.

talking	walking	speaking	making	staying	listening
arriving	writing	going	working	fixing	asking

Now make a list of ten words of your own. Work with a partner practicing the pronunciation. Give each other feedback as to whether you are doing a good job or need more practice.

ACTIVITY 4: DEFINING YOUR LOCAL LANGUAGE

Language is a system. That means you use language patterns consistently whether they are local language patterns or Business English patterns. Identify the language patterns you use for verbs, pronouns, and modifiers. Become conscious of whether you are using local language or Business English patterns. In Chapter 4, you will work on verbs; in Chapter 5, pronouns; and in Chapter 6, adjectives and adverbs. By raising your awareness now as to how your local language differs from Business English, you will find these chapters easier to master.

INSTRUCTIONS: With a partner, make a list of the ways your local language differs from Business English. Identify the part of speech for each type of error. In other words, does the difference relate to verbs, pronouns, or modifiers?

ACTIVITY 5: E-WRITING

INSTRUCTIONS: You have been asked to fill in for a sick coworker until a temp arrives. Using his PDA, your coworker has forwarded to you several messages he took before leaving the office and a copy of the "cheat sheet" he uses in taking messages. Here's the cheat sheet:

CF	=	Call from
NA	=	No answer
VMF	=	Voice mail from
LM	=	Left message
WCB	=	Will call back
RE	=	Regarding
WF	=	Waiting for

Rewrite the following telephone notes as clear and concise messages.

1. CF Morgan Hall RE chg mtg w/Megan Stern to Mon 11.15 LM 4 Megan.

2. CF Adam Wright 4 Wilmer Kaden RE Santo proposal: WF Sept financials.

3. VMF Kazer Corp 4 Audrey Horn. Wont process PO w/o signed auth. Pls advs.

4. LM All-Star Temps. WCB.

5. VMF J Rollins 4 Bob Barnes: LM w/Paul Jenkins RE policy cvrge. Plz provide Summ by Wed 8/12

6. CF All-Star Temps avail temp = nu badge + prkg key + instrctns h/t work kypd.

7. Per V.P. mrkting, plz ask Wilmer 2 bring Gelman fldr + env. impact rprts to Fri team vid conf.

8. CF Martin M. 4 Megan: no lunch 2day b/c of rain. Resched?

ACTIVITY 6: THESAURUS DRILL

INSTRUCTIONS: In order to develop variety in your writing, replace the boldface words and phrases below with substitutes that have the same meaning as the originals.

The Baker Company sent me a **job** application. Their **instructions** were **unclear,** so I waited until I could get my questions answered **before completing** it. That was a good **idea** because I would have jeopardized my **opportunity** for **being placed** at their **firm.**

ACTIVITY 7: THE "WRITER'S REFERENCE MANUAL" DRILL

BACKGROUND: In this chapter, you learned that the three major categories of conjunctions are coordinating conjunctions, subordinating conjunctions, and adverbial conjunctions. Conjunctions are transitional words. As transitions, conjunctions help the reader make connections between ideas. For example, some conjunctions help compare and contrast information *(yet, on the contrary, rather, instead);* other conjunctions show sequences *(afterward, finally);* and so on.

INSTRUCTIONS: Find the entry for conjunctions in the "Writer's Reference Manual." List five types of transitions that conjunctions perform. For each category, list two conjunctions. For example:

	Category	Examples
	showing consequence	as a result, consequently, therefore
	contrasting	although, even though, however
1.	______________	______________
2.	______________	______________
3.	______________	______________
4.	______________	______________
5.	______________	______________

ACTIVITY 8: VOCABULARY LIST

A. COMMONLY MISSPELLED WORDS

INSTRUCTIONS: The list below contains words taken from a compilation of the 500 most commonly misspelled words and from the chapter. Practice them until you can spell them automatically and use them correctly.

1. adverbial conjunction	(n) a type of connector that builds transitions, such as *however*
2. affirmative	(adj, n) positive, not negative
3. analyze	(v) study, explore, examine, evaluate
4. augment	(v) supplement, add to, expand
5. competent	(adj) capable, knowledgeable, experienced, skilled
6. coordinating conjunction	(n) a type of conjunction that connects equal parts, such as *and*
7. conjunction	(n) a word that connects or builds logical connections between words, phrases, or clauses (for example, coordinating, subordinating, and adverbial conjunctions)
8. exaggerate	(v) overstate, embellish, amplify, inflate
9. extraordinary	(adj) unusual, astonishing, unexpected, strange
10. fallible	(adj) capable of making a mistake; imperfect
11. facsimile	(n) exact copy, duplicate, reproduction (fax)
12. hors d'oeuvre	(adj) appetizer
13. misspelled	(v, adj) spelled incorrectly
14. nominal	(n) a noun derived from a verb (for example, *development*)
15. parallel	(adj) similar, equivalent, corresponding
16. permanent	(adj) enduring, lasting, stable, unending
17. subordinating conjunction	(n) a type of conjunction that shows relationships, such as *after*
18. rescind	(v) to take back, repeal, withdraw, cancel

B. SIMILAR WORDS

INSTRUCTIONS: The list below contains similar words, some of which are profiled in the Vocabulary Soundalike Sidebars in each chapter. Use these words in sentences until their meaning becomes clear.

assure/ensure/insure: These three verbs are similar in meaning but are used differently.

Assure means to give a person confidence that something will happen. Use *assure* when the object is a person:

Tom *assured* me that he would arrive on time.

Ensure means making certain that something happens. Use *ensure* when the object is a thing:

I will *ensure* that the meeting goes as planned.

Insure means to protect against loss, as in insurance. (The preferred usage for "to make sure" is *ensure,* not *insure.*) For *insure,* think of *insurance:*

The airline will *insure* your baggage for a small fee.

among/between: *Among* usually refers to more than two; *between* refers to two only. *Between* is always used when the reference is to individual items, even though an "item" might consist of more than one unit.

Among the three girls, Sylvia is the tallest.

That should remain *between* the two of them.

You can transfer money *between* all your accounts.

THE INBOX

COMPOSING

A Web log, or *blog,* is a type of Web site that resembles a journal or diary. Blogs are public documents, unlike private journals, although many blogs contain personal expressions and thoughts. Many students keep blogs as a record of their college experiences, and some college courses use blogs as a means of communication. In this exercise, you are going to look at a student blog and post a reply.

One of your classmates has started a blog about her English class. Your class has just finished studying Chapter 2. As Jane recorded her thoughts on the chapter, she remembered that the sentence core was very important, but she couldn't remember the method used to identify the core. Reply to her blog and explain how to find the sentence core. Make a sample sentence to demonstrate finding the sentence core.

Jane's blog:

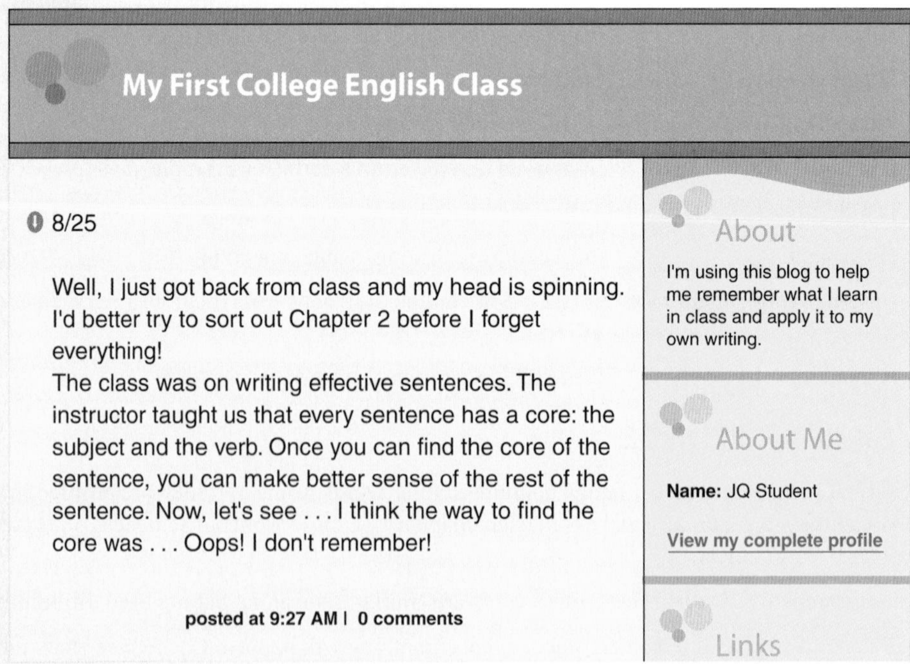

My First College English Class
8/25
Well, I just got back from class and my head is spinning. I'd better try to sort out Chapter 2 before I forget everything!
The class was on writing effective sentences. The instructor taught us that every sentence has a core: the subject and the verb. Once you can find the core of the sentence, you can make better sense of the rest of the sentence. Now, let's see . . . I think the way to find the core was . . . Oops! I don't remember!
posted at 9:27 AM | 0 comments
About
I'm using this blog to help me remember what I learn in class and apply it to my own writing.
About Me
Name: JQ Student
View my complete profile
Links

Your reply:

Post your reply here.

REFLECTING

Reread Jane's post and underline the subject of her sentences. Double underline the verbs.

In your journal, write about how blogging and journaling are similar, and then write about how they are different. Does recognizing the sentence core help you understand other people's writing, whether it is informal or formal? How so?

DISCUSSING

1. As you wrote your reply to Jane's blog, were you aware of your language choices? Is a blog a formal or casual writing situation, or do your writing choices for blogs depend on the topic and the intended audience?
2. In a small group, discuss the type of writing that best suits blogging. When you come to an agreement, present your thoughts to the other groups in the class.

EDITING

Lucas's journal entry, shown below, contains some errors in spelling and grammar. Use the knowledge you acquired from Chapter 2 to edit his writing. If you are not sure how to correct an error, find the core of the sentence as your starting point. You might work in groups to rewrite this journal entry.

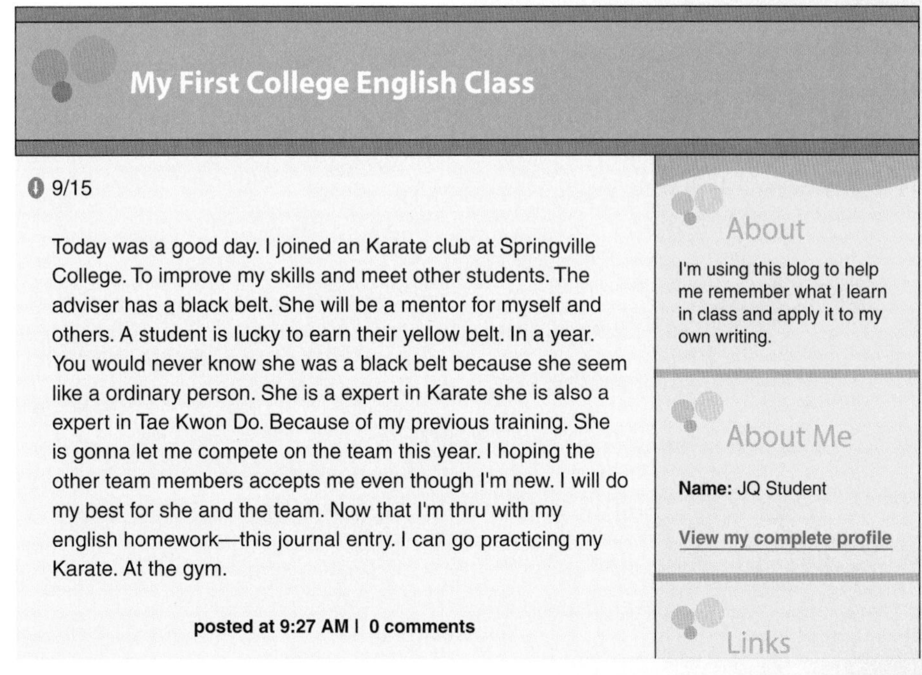

My First College English Class
9/15
Today was a good day. I joined an Karate club at Springville College. To improve my skills and meet other students. The adviser has a black belt. She will be a mentor for myself and others. A student is lucky to earn their yellow belt. In a year. You would never know she was a black belt because she seem like a ordinary person. She is a expert in Karate she is also a expert in Tae Kwon Do. Because of my previous training. She is gonna let me compete on the team this year. I hoping the other team members accepts me even though I'm new. I will do my best for she and the team. Now that I'm thru with my english homework—this journal entry. I can go practicing my Karate. At the gym.
posted at 9:27 AM | 0 comments
About
I'm using this blog to help me remember what I learn in class and apply it to my own writing.
About Me
Name: JQ Student
View my complete profile
Links

END CHAPTER 2 EOC ACTIVITIES

KEY TO LEARNING INVENTORY

1. subject and verb
2. subject complement
3. T
4. T
5. T
6. F
7. T
8. T
9. T
10. F

CHAPTER 2 ENDNOTES

1. Sidney Greenbaum, *A College Grammar of English,* Longman, New York, 1989, p. 27.
2. Ibid., p. 54.
3. Ibid., p. 33.
4. Karen Elizabeth Gordon, *The Deluxe Transitive Vampire,* Random House, New York, 1993, p. 3.
5. Joseph M. Williams, *Style: Toward Grace and Clarity,* University of Chicago Press, Chicago, 1990, p. 27.
6. Greenbaum, p. 53.
7. Jim Corder and John Ruszkiewicz, *Handbook of Current English,* HarperCollins, 1989, p. 28.

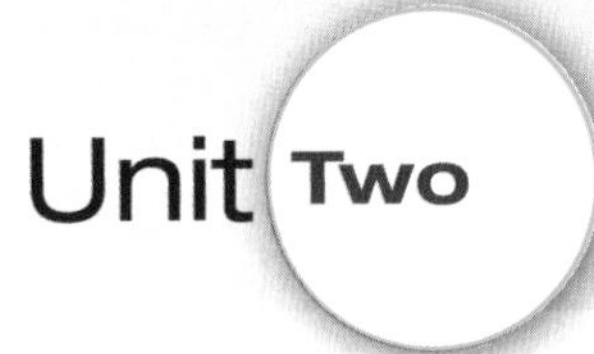

English in Action

Get ready to work on your skills: each chapter in this unit is an intense skill builder. You will start by working with punctuation, further refining your ability to control the sentence core. Then you will work with the three parts of speech that give writers and speakers the most challenges: verbs, pronouns, and modifiers. Chapters 3 through 6 are sequenced so that you will build a strong foundation. Give each chapter your best, and your efforts will make your success in the following chapter that much easier.

Always keep in mind your purpose for improving your Business English skills: flexible career options. For example, just about every job in the business world includes e-mail. When you begin to interview, one of the first questions recruiters will ask will be about your communication skills. After you get on the job, your ability to write with confidence will save you time and earn you credibility on a daily basis.

Unit 2 English in Action

MEMO AND E-MEMO ESSENTIALS

Communicating With Memos and E-Memos

Organizations use memos to communicate information internally. If your communication is going to an external client, send a letter instead.

Today most memos are sent electronically as *e-memos,* with customized software providing a template. E-memos are sent in-house through a company's intranet system (most corporations give employees access to the Internet; however, memos are not sent to outside clients). As with e-mail, you can create special mailing lists for e-memos or reports that you send to specific groups.

Though hard-copy memos are still a valuable tool, fewer hard copies are being sent through interoffice mail. Why take a day to send information when you can send it immediately via electronic mail? Electronic mail cuts down on paper and clutter. You can file e-memos and retrieve them when you need to print copies for use in meetings or other purposes.

FIGURE U2.1 Sample Memo

To: Board of Directors
From: Darlene Richards
Date: August 15, 2007
Subject: Literary Circle Strategy

As you requested, here is information about our Literary Circle and what we need to implement it next year.[1]

The Literary Circle currently meets monthly and employees from both our New York and Chicago offices participate. Participants from the Chicago office join the meeting via NetMeeting. The average meeting consists of 15 employees, representing all divisions within the company. Evaluations show that participants rate the program highly.

Our objectives for next year include:

1. Maintaining a high level of participation.
2. Selecting material that will generate interest.

To achieve these objectives, we are requesting continued support from the human resources department.

DR

Basic Parts of Memos

Memos have a standard format from which there is little deviation. (See Figure U2.1.) The heading can be in all caps or in lowercase with initial cap.

1. **Heading:** The necessary elements for a memo heading are the following: *To, From, Date,* and *Subject* (or *Re*), along with a *cc* notation if appropriate. You can vary the order in which you place these elements. If you are addressing two or three people, try to fit the names on the same line. For longer lists, you can type the names one under the other. For extremely long lists, you can type "See Distribution List Below" after the *To* prompt. Provide the distribution list at the end of the memo under the other reference notations.
2. **Body:** Start the body of the memo 2 or 3 lines below the end of the heading. Single-space and block paragraphs at the left: put a double space between them. For long memos, use a heading for second pages, which your software will provide.
3. **Salutation and Closing:** Memos do not require a salutation or a signature; however, many writers prefer to add both. By adding a salutation, such as "Dear Marge:" or "Marge," you make a memo seem more personal. Adding your handwritten initials next to your name at the top (or at the bottom) also personalizes a memo.

If you are distributing a hard copy of a memo, put a check mark next to each recipient's name as you put each memo into an interoffice envelope or place it in a distribution bin.

E-Memo Templates

Most corporations now provide templates for memo headings; with customized software, you can use a template to create messages for different purposes. For example, the template heading for an e-memo announcing a phone conference could appear as "Phone Conference" instead of "Memo." This specific heading alerts the reader immediately to the content of the message.

If you need to make your own heading, you can use a template provided by your software. Microsoft Windows includes the template shown in Figure U2.2.

Memos Versus E-Mail

A great deal of overlap exists in the way hard-copy memos, e-memos, and e-mail are used.

E-mail is the least formal mode of written communication, and you can use e-mail for both internal and external clients.

Memos convey information to coworkers (but do not engage recipients in a dialogue, as e-mail does).

E-memos provide a more structured format than e-mail and are equivalent to standard, hard-copy memos.

FIGURE U2.2 Sample E-Memo

Memorandum

To: [Click **here** and type name]
CC: [Click **here** and type name]
From: [Click **here** and type name]
Date: current date will be inserted automatically
Re: [Click **here** and type subject]

The template shown in Figure U2.2 is only one among many provided by software companies; however, it contains the necessary elements for the heading: *To, From, Date, Re (Subject),* along with a *CC* notation. (You can delete the *CC* notation if you are not using it.)

The order in which these elements are placed can vary. Some companies now put *Subject* first because that information is more important to recipients than reading their own names. The entries following the guide words should be blocked at the left and should clear the last guide word by at least two spaces.

Chapter Three

Punctuation

A kiss can be a comma, a question mark, or an exclamation point. —Mistinguett, singer (1875–1956)

Do you feel confident about using commas? Right now, you may be guessing about comma placement every time you use one. If that's the case, you are no different from the majority of writers. Commas are only tiny little scratches on the page, yet they wield great power when you don't know the correct way to use them—now it is time to turn that situation around.

With a little practice, commas will make sense. Then you will be ready to master the semicolon. Commas and semicolons form a basic foundation for understanding other types of punctuation. Once you learn them, you will be ready to work on the dash, ellipsis marks, and the colon (which are presented in Chapter 7). Once you become adept at punctuation, you can use it to add variety and personal style to your writing.

Punctuation packages words into logical bundles for clarity, but punctuation itself also communicates subtle shades of meaning and even emotion. As you work through this chapter, realize that punctuation is also the key to solving many grammatical problems, such as fragments and run-ons. Learning how to use commas and semicolons correctly means that you can stop guessing and move forward with confidence.

To learn more about The Writing Process, please visit our Web site at **www.mhhe.com/youngBE**

Outline

Chapter 3: Punctuation

Section A: The Comma

Section B: The Semicolon

Objectives

When you have completed your study of Chapter 3, you will be able to:

1. Demonstrate correct use of the comma and semicolon.
2. Apply basic comma and semicolon rules in composition.
3. Understand the role of coordinating, subordinating, and adverbial conjunctions in punctuation.
4. Revise fragments and run-ons, turning them into complete sentences.

Learning Inventory

1. The most common way writers determine comma placement is to look for "pauses." T/F
2. Looking for pauses is the best way to place commas in a sentence. T/F
3. One way to find out if you could use a semicolon is to substitute a period. T/F
4. When the first word of a sentence is an adverbial conjunction, a semicolon will follow. T/F
5. Place a semicolon before *but* when it separates two independent clauses. T/F
6. Place a comma after *but* when you place a semicolon before it. T/F
7. When the subject of a sentence is a person's name, place a comma after the name. T/F
8. Do not place only one comma between the subject and the verb of a sentence. T/F
9. Meaning is clearer when you place a comma before *and* in a series. T/F
10. A run-on sentence results when a comma is placed between two clauses but a semicolon is needed. T/F

Goal-Setting Exercises

Think for a moment about the kinds of mistakes you make using punctuation marks such as commas and semicolons. What confuses you, or what questions do you have? What kinds of comments do teachers write on your papers: does your writing contain run-ons or fragments? Write three goals about the changes you want to make in your writing when it comes to punctuation.

1. ____________________
2. ____________________
3. ____________________

Before reading further, take a moment to answer a question: What is your current "system" for placing commas? In other words, what is your main reason for placing a comma in a sentence? Right now take a moment to jot down the word or words that popped into your mind.

____

____

SECTION A: THE COMMA

If you place commas based on "pauses," you are not alone. That's what most people say. Another common response is "to take a breath." You may be surprised to learn that neither of these responses is a valid reason for using a comma.

Based on this misunderstanding, have you ever reread the same sentence, pausing in different places each time? If you place commas on the basis of pauses, punctuation turns into a guessing game. Actually, there should be no guessing about punctuation—sometimes educated choices, but no guessing.

Punctuation is based on sentence structure or **syntax.** Syntax is another word for *grammar* and refers to "the orderly arrangement of words." Syntax creates natural breaks at the end of clauses, and comma rules provide guidance on where to look for these separations or natural breaks.

So here is the important point: Readers do pause at a comma, but that is not why the comma was placed there. Comma placement is based on rules (or theory). The rule came first, the comma came second, and the pause came third. That brings us to our starting point.

BASIC COMMA RULES

This section presents 12 basic comma rules. The first 2 rules stress when *not* to use a comma; the remaining 10 stress when to use a comma. Be aware that there are more comma rules than those listed in this section, and some rules have exceptions. The purpose of this section is to teach you the basics; this simplified approach will increase your understanding of the structure and rhythm of the language.

Once you learn the basic rules, you will be ready to learn exceptions to the rules as well as to learn about other punctuation marks. When you are ready to learn about exceptions to the comma rules, refer to *The Gregg Reference Manual.*

Comma Rule 1: The Golden Rule

When in doubt, leave it out.

Comma Rule 1 tells you to stop putting in commas unless you have a valid reason, and *pausing* is not a valid reason to use a comma. If you don't know a reason based on a rule, you have choices:

Don't use the comma.

Do additional research. (Refer to *The Gregg Reference Manual.*)

Rewrite the sentence so that you know you are correct. (This works with your own writing but not when you are proofreading someone else's work.)

This first rule tells you when *not* to use a comma as does Comma Rule 2. By using commas only when you are sure, you will avoid making many serious grammatical errors.

Comma Rule 2: The Cardinal Rule

Do not separate a subject and verb with just one comma.

In Chapter 2, you learned about **independent** and **dependent** clauses. A clause is formed when a subject and verb come together. The clause is an important grammatical unit and should not be interrupted by only one comma. Regardless of whether the clause is independent or dependent, do not insert a comma between the subject and the verb. For example:

Incorrect: Bob's manager, spoke about the issue at length.

Corrected: Bob's manager spoke about the issue at length.

VOCABULARY: SOUNDALIKES

To/Too/Two: These words are frequently used incorrectly.

To is a preposition and part of an infinitive.

Mark went *to* the store.

To whom it may concern . . .

Tell them *to go* to the meeting.

Too is an adverb relating to quantity.

We have *too much* work.

This has happened *too many* times.

They have given us the wrong order *too often.*

Two is a number.

Please provide *two* packets of materials.

I would like *two* cheeseburgers.

It is *too late* for the *two* of us *to* argue.

To avoid confusion:

Follow *to* with a noun or a verb

Follow *too* with an adverb

Two is a number; can you substitute the number *2?*

Below is a more complicated example because the subject and verb are interrupted by a "*who* clause." (You will learn more about this type of clause later in the chapter when you learn Comma Rule 5.)

Incorrect: The man, who gave us the information is no longer on duty.

Correct: The man who gave us the information is no longer on duty.

To recap Comma Rule 2: This rule says that one comma should *not* be placed between the subject and the verb in any clause, independent or dependent. When commas are used between a subject and its verb, it is most likely a **set of commas** (you will work with your first set of commas when you learn Comma Rule 5, which relates to nonessential elements).

PRACTICE

Instructions: Correct the punctuation in the following sentences. Also identify the sentence core of each main clause: first identify the verb and underline it twice; then work backward in the sentence to identify the subject and underline it once. If you have difficulty finding the subject, ask yourself if it is "*you* understood" (you) or "*I* understood" (I). **For example:**

Incorrect: The package arrived early in the day.

Corrected: The package arrived early in the day.

1. Mary, wrote a detailed report for the Chief Financial Officer.
2. Recruiting new employees, occurs through the human resources department.
3. When my assistant, researched and compiled the data, she achieved good results.
4. Mergers, and acquisitions, accelerate a company's growth.
5. Our director, and placement counselors, created a strategy for new hires.

MORE COMMA RULES (RULE 3 THROUGH RULE 12)

The remaining comma rules are more specific than the first two rules. Each comma rule names the reason for the comma's use and has an abbreviation. For example, the next rule is *Comma Conjunction,* with the abbreviation *CONJ.*

By applying a name to each comma rule, you can analyze the reason for using the comma. If you don't know the reason for using a comma, you may *not* need a comma.When you are unsure about the reason, either do more research or leave out the comma.

As you work through the comma rules, you will identify the core elements of main clauses (not minor clauses, such as *who* or *which* clauses). Identifying core elements is different from diagramming sentences. The core consists of the simple subject and simple verb, and it directly influences structure and style. Once you can easily identify core elements, you are one step closer to gaining control over your writing style. Consider the following points:

You will be tempted to place the comma and not bother to put the reason. Forcing yourself to identify the reason ensures that you are applying theory correctly, which ensures that you use commas correctly rather than haphazardly.

Once you understand punctuation, you will also understand structure. You will then be able to manipulate sentence elements and gain control over your writing style.

• Internet Exercise 3.1

Punctuation References: For information on punctuation resources—both online and on the bookshelf—go to the Web site at www.mhhe.com/youngBE. Select "Student Activities," and then click on the "Chapter 3" link to get started.

Comma Rule 3: Comma Conjunction (CONJ)

Use a comma to separate independent clauses joined by a coordinating conjunction.

By placing a comma before the conjunction, you are showing the *separation* between the independent clauses. There are only seven **coordinating conjunctions:** *and, but, or, for, nor, so, yet.* You may use the abbreviation *CC* to refer to coordinating conjunctions.

In the following examples, the subjects are underlined once, the verbs are underlined twice, and the coordinating conjunctions (CCs) are italicized. The name of the comma rule, or reason, is shown in parentheses after the sentence.

Bob went to the meeting, *but* he arrived late. (CONJ)

Mary summarized the report, *and* she did a good job. (CONJ)

Apply the comma conjunction (CONJ) rule in the practice exercise that follows.

PRACTICE

Instructions: Correct the sentences below by applying the comma conjunction (CONJ) rule. For each sentence, do the following: (1) Insert any missing commas. (2) In each main clause, underline the verb twice and the subject once. (3) Circle each coordinating conjunction (CC) that joins two independent clauses. (4) Even though it may seem redundant, write the reason *(CONJ)* after the sentence. **For example:**

Incorrect: Lester Jones encouraged me to manage the project and I told him that I would.

Corrected: Lester Jones encouraged me to manage the project, *and* I told him that I would. (CONJ)

1. Eight scientists were on the panel and six of them agreed about the issue.

2. Bill and I intend to meet with their comptroller but he has not had time for us.

3. Your subscription will be canceled next month so you must return your renewal today.

4. The speech captivated the audience and inspired them to participate in the study.

5. Our company joined the alliance yet we were not included in the conference.

APPLY

Instructions: Write three sentences below to demonstrate comma conjunction; use three different conjunctions. (Coordinating conjunctions: *and, but, or, nor, for, yet, so*)

EXAMPLE My plans include more education, and I am saving money for that purpose.

1. ______________________________

2. ______________________________

3. ______________________________

Comma Rule 4: Comma Introductory (INTRO)

Place a comma after a word, phrase, or dependent clause that introduces a main clause.

The comma introductory (INTRO) rule assumes that you are familiar with subordinating conjunctions (SCs) and adverbial conjunctions (ACs). If you did not learn them well enough in Chapter 2, you may want to go back and review them. Below is a brief summary.

Subordinating conjunctions are words or phrases that introduce dependent clauses; for example, *if, when, as, although, because, as soon as, before, while, after, since, even though, unless,* and *whereas.* Subordinating conjunctions show relationships between ideas related to time (such as *when, after,* and *while*) and also help compare and contrast ideas (such as *although, because,* and *even though*). You can tell whether a word is a subordinating conjunction by placing it at the beginning of an independent clause. If the independent clause becomes dependent, then the word is a subordinating conjunction.

Complete sentence: Bob chaired the committee.

Dependent clause: *Although* Bob chaired the committee,

Adverbial conjunctions are words or phrases that introduce or interrupt independent clauses; for example, *however, therefore, for example,* and *thus.* Adverbial conjunctions build bridges between ideas and help the reader understand the writer's intention; they provide **transitions.** For example, the word *however* indicates that a statement that follows it will contrast or contradict the statement that comes before it.

Bob chaired the committee. *However,* he did not bring the agenda to the meeting.

If you place an adverbial conjunction at the beginning of an independent clause, the clause will still be complete.

George was offered the job of his choice.

Fortunately, George was offered the job of his choice.

When placed at the beginning of a sentence, an adverbial conjunction or a subordinating conjunction signals that a comma is needed.

As the first word of a sentence, an adverbial conjunction (AC) is usually followed by a comma.

Therefore, we were late.

When a subordinating conjunction (SC) is the first word of a sentence, a comma is placed at the end of the subordinating clause. (Note: Do *not* place a comma immediately after the subordinating conjunction.)

Incorrect: Although, we were late, we did not miss anything important.

Correct: Although we were late, we did not miss anything important.

> **WRITER'S TOOLKIT**
>
> **Conjunction Functions**
>
> The three types of conjunctions function as comma signals, indicating where to put a comma or semicolon.
>
> **A.** *Subordinating conjunctions* are words and phrases that introduce dependent clauses and phrases. (Subordinating conjunctions show relationships.)
>
> Examples: *as, after, since, unless, because, although, until, whereas, if, even though, while, as soon as, when, though, so that, before.*
>
> **B.** *Adverbial conjunctions* introduce or interrupt independent clauses. (Adverbial conjunctions build bridges, helping the reader infer the writer's intent.)
>
> Examples: *however, in addition, furthermore, consequently, therefore, accordingly, in conclusion, as usual, in general, usually, for example, unfortunately, of course.*
>
> **C.** *Coordinating conjunctions* connect independent clauses or items in a series. *When needed,* put a comma *before* a coordinating conjunction, not after.
>
> The Seven CCs: *and, but, or, for, nor, so, yet.*

PRACTICE

Instructions: Correct the sentences below by applying the comma introductory (INTRO) rule. For each sentence, do the following: (1) Insert any missing commas. (2) In each introductory and main clause, underline the verb twice and the subject once. (3) Circle each adverbial conjunction (AC) and subordinating conjunction (SC) that introduces an independent clause. (4) Write the reason *(INTRO)* after the sentence. **For example:**

Incorrect: Once John assists you with the report things will run more smoothly.

Corrected: *Once* John assists you with the report, things will run more smoothly. (INTRO)

Incorrect: However do not depend totally on his support. (You)

Corrected: *However,* do not depend totally on his support. (INTRO)

1. Even though the director requested the information they did not provide it.

2. Therefore we obtained software that was outdated.

3. In addition the new software was incompatible with our computers.

4. Because the results do not match our efforts we will try a new approach.

5. Therefore we must develop fresh ideas for the next production cycle.

APPLY

Instructions: Write three sentences below to demonstrate comma introductory; use both subordinate and adverbial conjunctions.

EXAMPLE If I had known about the hard work, I still would have signed up for the class.

1. ____________________

2. ____________________

3. ____________________

Comma Rule 5: Comma Nonessential Element (NE)

Use commas to set off nonessential (nonrestrictive) explanations.

Though nonessential words or explanations add value, a sentence does not need them to be clear and complete. When nonessential explanations are taken out of a sentence, the sentence will still make sense.

A word of caution: This rule primarily pertains to *who* and *which* clauses that are not essential for clarity; do *not* set off prepositional phrases.

In the example below, the sentence will still be *clear and complete* if the *who* clause is removed.

> **Clear:** Alex George, who does my taxes every year, completed the audit. (NE)

Without the *who* clause, the sentence still makes sense:

> **Clear:** Alex George completed the audit.

Some sentences need the *who* clause to remain clear: the clause is essential to the meaning. (With grammar, the word *essential* is equivalent to *restrictive*.) **Essential elements** are not set off with commas. Here's a sentence with an essential *who* clause:

> **Clear:** The customer service representative who is in our New York office has your information.

Taking out the *who* clause leaves the sentence unclear:

> **Unclear:** The customer service representative has your information. (*Which representative?* The meaning sounds clear but is not complete without the *who* clause.)

The comma nonessential element (NE) is one of the few comma rules that call for a decision based on meaning rather than structure, making this rule trickier than some of the other rules.

PRACTICE

Instructions: Correct the sentences below by applying the comma nonessential (NE) rule. For each sentence, do the following: (1) Insert any missing commas. (2) In each main clause, underline the verb twice and the subject once. (3) Write the reason *(NE)* after the sentence.

For example:

Incorrect: The person who handles customer complaints is out to lunch.

Corrected: The person who handles customer complaints is out to lunch.

Incorrect: Would you assist Jorge who is in the fifth-floor conference room with inventory?

Corrected: Would you assist Jorge, who is in the fifth-floor conference room, with inventory? (NE)

1. Robert MacNeil who wrote *Do You Speak American?* worked as a newscaster.

2. Your client service representative who spoke with me on the phone was rude.

3. Carol Glasco who manages the consumer relations department is your liaison.

4. Any cashier who arrives late to work consistently will be docked.

5. The quarterly report which is always completed on time will be sent to your new address.

APPLY

Instructions: Write three sentences below to demonstrate comma nonessential element.

EXAMPLE My sister Jean, who works at J-Mark, attends Best College part-time.

1. ______________________________

2. ______________________________

3. ______________________________

Comma Rule 6: Comma Independent Comment (IC)

Use commas to set off a word or phrase that interrupts an independent clause.

This rule primarily relates to *adverbial conjunctions* that are interjected into an independent clause, expressing the writer's attitude and slightly interrupting the flow of the sentence. These independent comments can often be removed without affecting the sentence.

Joyce asked, *however,* if Carol could call her about the situation. (IC)

Margaret, *therefore,* will be able to assist Wally with the committee. (IC)

Our department would, *of course,* prefer to have Saturday off. (IC)

There are times when you must determine whether the adverbial conjunction plays a *vital, restrictive role* in the sentence *or* whether it is a *nonessential independent comment.* For example, in the following, the word *however* would not be set off with commas:

You indicated that *however* I got the job done would be satisfactory.

In this example, *however* is restrictive (essential): the sentence would not make sense if *however* were removed. For example: *You indicated that . . . I got the job done would be satisfactory.*

Adverbial conjunctions can sound out of place in the middle of a sentence. When you edit, try moving the adverbial conjunction to the beginning, and your sentence may sound better and be easier to understand. For example:

However, Joyce asked if Carol could call her about the situation.

Therefore, Margaret will be able to assist Wally with the committee.

Of course, the department would prefer to have Saturday off.

According to *The Gregg Reference Manual*, sometimes you must say a sentence out loud to know whether an adverbial conjunction is essential or nonessential. If your voice rises as you say the sentence, leave it in; if your voice drops, leave it out.

PRACTICE

Instructions: Correct the sentences below by applying the comma independent comment (IC) rule. For each sentence, do the following: (1) Insert any missing commas. (2) In each main clause, underline the verb twice and the subject once. (3) Write the reason *(IC)* after the sentence. **For example:**

Incorrect: The regional manager however requests that you maintain this account.

Corrected: The regional manager, however, requests that you maintain this account. (IC)

1. The writer of the document however forgot to sign it.

2. Simpson's quarterly report therefore reflects increased earnings.

3. Roger wanted to implement the program however possible.

4. My manager furthermore suggested that I complete the report within the deadline.

5. Their actions fortunately did not impair our negotiations.

SPEAKING BUSINESS

Vowel Sounds: Did you realize that whenever you pronounce a vowel sound your tongue is down and flat? Vowel sounds vary according to how much the lips and teeth are parted.

If you want to work on a particular vowel sound, first make a list of words that have similar and contrasting sounds.

For example, if you want to work on the way you pronounce the word *been,* make a list of words that rhyme with the traditional pronunciation of *been,* such as *then, ten, men*, and *hen.* Next, make a list of words that sound similar to your current pronunciation, which may sound like "bin"; for example, *spin, chin, Quinn,* and *pin.*

As you say each word out loud, notice how your tongue flattens and also notice how far you open your mouth and lips. For more practice, see EOC Activity 4 on page 92.

Ask Yourself: *Which vowel sounds do I want to work on?*

Comma Rule 7: Comma Direct Address (DA)

Use commas to set off the name or title of a person addressed directly.

When you see a person's name or formal title, you may need a comma; but first, distinguish whether the person is being *spoken to* or *spoken about.*

Alice, could you please inform the consultant that we need additional time? (DA)

(I) Thank you, Melanie, for allowing Mr. Grey to attend the conference in my place. (DA)

Simon expected that you, Kenneth, would complete the proposal. (DA)

Sir, (you) please allow ten days for a response to your questions. (DA)

Note the following:

- The direct address can occur anywhere in the sentence: beginning, middle, or end. The direct address is not the subject of the sentence. In fact, it cannot be the subject because it is set off with commas. (Remember Comma Rule 2?)
- If you have difficulty finding the subject in a direct-address sentence, consider whether the subject is "*I* understood" (I) or "*you* understood" (you).

Commas are *not* used to set off the name of a person being spoken about or referred to indirectly.

Alice informed the consultant that we needed additional time.

Melanie allowed Mr. Grey to attend the conference in my place.

Kenneth completed the proposal.

PRACTICE

Instructions: Correct the sentences below by applying the comma direct address (DA) rule. For each sentence, do the following: (1) Insert any missing commas. (2) In each main clause, underline the verb twice and the subject once. (3) Write the reason *(DA)* after the sentence. **For example:**

Incorrect: Josef can I count on you to help me with the quarterly budget?

Corrected: Josef, can I count on you to help me with the quarterly budget? (DA)

With direct-address commas, often the subject is implied ("*you* understood" or "*I* understood").

Incorrect: Doctor thank you for seeing me in this emergency.

Corrected: Doctor, (I) thank you for seeing me in this emergency. (DA)

1. Victoria have you completed the year-end report?

2. Victoria has completed the year-end report.

3. Silvio please reconsider your decision to apply for the Tampa assignment.

4. Thank you Franklin for conveying the information to the D.C. office.

5. Yumiko inform the task force that the issue should be discussed.

Comma Rule 8: Comma Appositive (AP)

Use commas to set off words or phrases that describe or identify a preceding noun or pronoun.

When a brief explanation follows a noun or pronoun, it is considered a restatement. This restatement is usually a nonessential appositive. Here are some examples:

Charles, my brother, attended university on a basketball scholarship. (AP)

Ms. Abrams, vice president of finance, speaks highly of you. (AP)

(You) Please indicate to Andrew, my associate, your time frame. (AP)

Some appositives are essential, which means that they are restrictive and should *not* be set off with commas. An **essential appositive** occurs with names when two or more people fit the category and the meaning would not be clear if the appositive—the name—were removed. In the following example, John is an essential appositive because Angelica has more than one coworker:

Angelica's coworker John selected the menu.

If Angelica's only coworker were John, his name would be set off with commas because the meaning would be clear *with* or *without* his name. In the following example, Trisha has only one brother, so his name can be set off with commas:

Trisha's brother, Randy, became CEO of the family business.

PRACTICE

Instructions: Correct the sentences below by applying the comma appositive (AP) rule. For each sentence, do the following: (1) Insert any missing commas. (2) In each main clause, underline the verb twice and the subject once. (3) Write the reason *(AP)* after the sentence. **For example:**

Incorrect: Mr. Flaherty my professor selected the location of the summit.

Corrected: Mr. Flaherty, my professor, selected the location of the summit. (AP)

1. Ana my administrative assistant mentioned the account.

2. Robert my personal trainer gave the information to Rosie my assistant.

3. Your consultant should confer with our financial adviser George Roth.

4. My cross-training activities met the requirements of Lisa Ramos my boss.

5. My sister Elaine always shares her knowledge about finance.

Comma Rule 9: Comma Address/Date (AD)

Use commas to set off addresses and dates.

Writers make many mistakes with this rule, especially when an address or date occurs in the middle of a sentence.

When a complete date occurs within a sentence, use commas to set off the month, day, and year:

Della insisted that February 11, 2009, would be the only date to choose.

When a date includes only a month and year, do not separate the month and year with a comma:

The target date for our merger is July 2008.

When an address occurs in a sentence, use commas to set off the city, state, and country:

Jeffers announced that our branch in Houston, Texas, would host the on-site training.

Here are a few more examples:

> Cooper said that Monday, March 20, 2006, was his first day on the job. (AD)
>
> Tuesday, April 19, 2007, arrived, and the project still did not begin. (AD)
>
> Alex decided that Jacksonville, Florida, offered the best facilities. (AD)
>
> The meeting was scheduled in Springfield, Massachusetts, not Springfield, Illinois. (AD)
>
> Rome, Italy, is known as the eternal city. (AD)

Do *not,* under any circumstances, put a comma between the month and the day. For example, the following would *never* occur: *August,* 15, 2006. It stands corrected as follows: *August 15,* 2006.

PRACTICE

Instructions: Correct the sentences below by applying the comma address/date (AD) rule. For each sentence, do the following: (1) Insert any missing commas. (2) In each main clause, underline the verb twice and the subject once. (3) Write the reason *(AD)* after the sentence. **For example:**

> **Incorrect:** The summit is in Irvine California on March 22 2007.
>
> **Corrected:** The summit is in Irvine, California, on March 22, 2007. (AD)

1. Does Conrad live in Springfield Massachusetts or Springfield Illinois?
2. Nichols said that Tuesday May 7 was the date for the meeting.
3. Would you be available on Wednesday December 8 2009 to speak at the conference?
4. Joanne has resided in Arlington Texas for several years now.
5. The November 2006 convention was relocated from New Orleans Louisiana to Tampa Florida.

Comma Rule 10: Comma Series (SER)

When three or more items occur in a series, put a comma after each item.

Some sources indicate that the comma before the *and* optional. However, at times the meaning of a series can be misinterpreted without the comma. Since one purpose of punctuation is to achieve clarity, this text recommends that you place the comma before *and.* For example:

> Marcia completed Sections A, B, and C of the report. (SER)
>
> (You) Please prepare potatoes, peas, and carrots for the company outing. (SER)
>
> Mr. Grey instructed that his assets be divided among Bob, Rose, Chuck, and Sophie. (SER)

Here are some questions to ponder:

- In the second example above, how will the peas and carrots be prepared? If the instructions had read "potatoes, peas and carrots," how do you think they would have been prepared?

- In the third example, what if Mr. Grey had omitted a comma and the instructions read "divided among Bob, Rose, Chuck and Sophie"? Should each get an equal share, or should Chuck and Sophie split one share? (With the comma before *and,* there is no question.)

PRACTICE

Instructions: Correct the sentences below by applying the comma series (SER) rule. For each sentence, do the following: (1) Insert any missing commas. (2) In each introductory and main clause, underline the verb twice and the subject once. (3) Write the reason *(SER)* after the sentence. **For example:**

Incorrect: The list of supplies included flip charts laptops and notebooks.

Corrected: The list of supplies included flip charts, laptops, and notebooks. (SER)

1. The Detroit office faxed us the cover letter contract and processing fee.

2. Milton's goals are to finish college find a great job and travel overseas.

3. Because Rick ordered supplies we now have printers cell phones and laptops for all.

4. After investigators entered the office, they collected hard drives cell phones and laptops from everyone.

5. Wilson speaks French Russian Chinese and Arabic.

▸Language Diversity

Boston English: Best known for its habit of dropping the *r* and using a broad *A*, Boston English is the dialect not only of Boston but also of much of eastern Massachusetts. Boston English has much in common with the accents of Rhode Island, New Hampshire, and southern Maine, and it is frequently grouped with New York–New Jersey English, though there are subtle differences between the accents of Boston and New York.

Below is a list of words written as they are pronounced in the Boston English dialect. How many can you identify?

1. pahk
2. bah
3. wiid
4. lahge
5. wicked
6. sqwea
7. byd
8. da tuneriz
9. stahtid
10. gidadaheah

Boston English: Wudja pahk da cah and gimmeah hand with dis hammah?

Standard: Would you park the car and give me a hand with this hammer?

Comma Rule 11: Comma Words Omitted (WO)

Use a comma for the omission of a word or words that play a structural role in a sentence.

At times, words that are omitted in sentences still play a structural role, such as the "*you* understood" subject. Although omitting words can be grammatically correct, some omitted words can also create a *gap*. When a gap occurs, use the "words omitted comma" to fill the gap. Here are some instances when you should use the words-omitted (WO) comma:

***And* Omitted.** When two adjectives modify the same noun, they should be separated by *and;* if the word *and* is omitted, separate the adjectives with a comma. For example:

The *new and innovative* idea drew a positive response.

The *new, innovative* idea drew a positive response.

***That* Omitted.** The word *that* sometimes functions as a conjunction. When the omission of *that* breaks the flow of a sentence, use a comma to fill in the gap. (Most often, omitting the word *that* does not create a break in the flow, and a comma would not be placed in its absence.) Here's an example of *that* removed with a comma added to take its place:

The point remains, they never sent us the contract.

The point remains (that) they never sent us the contract.

Here's an example of *that* removed without a comma added:

Jolene insisted the participants receive all materials prior to the meeting.

Jolene insisted (that) the participants receive all materials prior to the meeting.

Repetitive Words Omitted. Sometimes words are omitted when their restatement would be obvious:

The wrong information was given to Stephan; the correct information, to Doug.

The wrong information was given to Stephan; the correct information (was sent) to Doug.

Comma Rule 12: Comma Contrasting Expression or Afterthought (CEA)

Use a comma to separate a contrasting expression (often beginning with* but, not, *or* rather than*) or an afterthought that is added to the end of a sentence.

This rule takes many different forms and is thus more complicated than the other basic rules. As you become a more experienced writer, you may find yourself referring to this rule. Here are some examples:

My manager asked me to go to the seminar, not the luncheon. (CEA)

I encourage you to bring Tom to the event, but only if you wish. (CEA)

The CEO announced the merger, creating chaos in the audience. (CEA)

The leader informed the group that we would reconvene at noon, not at 1 p.m. (CEA)

PRACTICE

Instructions: Correct the sentences below by applying the comma words-omitted (WO) and comma contrasting expression or afterthought (CEA) rules. For each sentence, do the following: (1) Insert any missing commas. (2) In each main clause, underline the verb twice and the subject once. (3) Write the reason *(WO)* or *(CEA)* after the sentence. **For example:**

Incorrect: The restaurant was selected by Mr. Johnston not Mr. Kaper.

Corrected: The restaurant was selected by Mr. Johnston, not Mr. Kaper. (CEA)

1. Alicia finished the project on Friday not on Wednesday.

2. Their office has been closed for months creating a gap in the market.

3. You should apply for the Boston position but only if you are interested.

4. The old dilapidated building still stands on the corner of State and Lake.

5. Sue sends the report every Tuesday not every Wednesday.

In Box 3.1, review the original e-mail and determine the kinds of changes you would make to improve it before examining the revised version.

BOX 3.1 The Editing Process

BEFORE

To: Joe Chipman
CC:
Subject: Nominate

My purpose in writing this message is to nominate Mary Jo O'Malley as the person for the month for next month which is September. Mary's main duties consist of maintaining account transactions processing night-drop transactions and balancing deposits and withdrawals in addition to her daily duties, Mary is a great team player. Encouraging others to succeed and being supportive of our departments needs. Her attitude work ethics and motivation serve as a model for others to follow and Mary possesses a grat deal of knowledge about customer service and she shares her knowled with her coworkers also mary knows how to manage time to produce positive results. Finally, I would like to point out that Mary has a great respect for others and has a terrific sense of humor . It is an honor for me to nominiate this gifted employee.

Dana Whitman
Assistant Manager
312-555-1212

AFTER

To: Joe Chipman
CC:
Subject: Person of the Month Nomination

Joe,

I would like to nominate Mary Jo O'Malley as the person for the month for September.

Mary's main duties consist of maintaining account transactions, processing night-drop transactions, and balancing deposits and withdrawals. In addition to performing her daily duties, Mary is a great team player. She encourages others to succeed and is supportive of our department's needs. Mary's attitude, work ethic, and motivation serve as a model for others to follow. Mary possesses a great deal of knowledge about customer service, and she shares her knowledge with her coworkers. Also, Mary knows how to manage time to produce positive results.

Finally, I would like to point out that Mary has a great respect for others and has a terrific sense of humor. It is an honor for me to nominate this gifted employee.

Best regards,

Dana

Dana Whitman
Assistant Manager
312-555-1212

SECTION A CONCEPT CHECK

1. Describe the comma rules designated by the following abbreviations: CONJ, INTRO, IC, DA, and AP.

2. Describe the comma rules designated by the following abbreviations: AD, SER, CEA, and WO.

SECTION B: THE SEMICOLON

Do you use semicolons in your writing? Writers commonly insert a comma in places that need a semicolon (or period). When a comma is used where a semicolon belongs, the result is a *run-on sentence,* which is a serious grammatical error.

Semicolons add variety and keep your writing from getting choppy when sentences are short. Semicolons also communicate to readers that ideas are related or close in meaning. Once you learn the semicolon rules, experiment using them. If you still don't like semicolons, you need never use one. However, after you know how to use them correctly, you may actually like semicolons!

BASIC SEMICOLON RULES

Semicolon Rule 1: Semicolon No Conjunction (NC)

Use a semicolon to separate two independent clauses that are joined* without *a conjunction.

Have you ever heard of the saying, "semicolon in place of period"? Most of the time, you can tell that you are using a semicolon correctly if you can substitute a period for it. A semicolon is not as strong as a period, which is a terminal mark of punctuation. Use a semicolon when one or both statements are short and related in meaning; the semicolon helps the reader infer the connection between the ideas. For example:

Suni attended the marketing seminar; William refused to go. (NC)

PRACTICE

Instructions: Correct the sentences below by applying the semicolon no conjunction (NC) rule or the comma conjunction (CONJ) rule. For each sentence, do the following: (1) Insert any missing punctuation. (2) In each main clause, underline the verb twice and the subject once. (3) Write the reason *(NC)* or *(CONJ)* after the sentence. **For example:**

Incorrect: The company surveyed its employees many issues were identified.

Corrected: The company surveyed its employees; many issues were identified. (NC)

1. The agenda was followed exactly all members of the committee were pleased.

2. The repairman did not arrive yet and I am concerned about our deadline.

3. My mistake was offering Bill the job his mistake was accepting it.

4. Every question has an answer sometimes it is not what you want to hear.

5. Find the auditor and give him the report.

APPLY

Instructions: Write three sentences to show the use of semicolon NC.

EXAMPLE My manager received a promotion; she is transferring to a new department. (NC)

1. ______________________________

2. ______________________________

3. ______________________________

Semicolon Rule 2: Semicolon Transition (TRANS)

Place a semicolon before and a comma after an adverbial conjunction when it acts as a transition between independent clauses.

Adverbial conjunctions provide transitions between independent clauses; these transitions help the reader infer the writer's intention. Here are some examples:

> Bradshaw agreed that we were right; *however,* he refused to sign the contract.
>
> We asked for more time; *fortunately,* they were able to grant our request.
>
> Our representative followed their instructions; *therefore,* he alleviated their concerns.
>
> Your participation is critical; *for example,* you convinced them to adopt our proposal.

PRACTICE

Instructions: Correct the sentences below by applying the semicolon transition (TRANS) rule. For each sentence, do the following: (1) Insert any missing punctuation. (2) In each main clause, underline the verb twice and the subject once. (3) Write the reason *(TRANS)* after the sentence. **For example:**

Incorrect: Our company does not offer that product however we have a better one.

Corrected: Our company does not offer that product; however, we have a better one. (TRANS)

1. The meeting began on time however several key people were late.

2. My name was missing from the agenda therefore please add it to the list.

3. Jones Company resigned from our task force contact them about this.

4. Our company offers an excellent tuition reimbursement policy unfortunately most employees do not take advantage of it.

5. Large companies provide excellent benefit packages of course many small companies have great benefits also.

VOCABULARY: KEY TERMS

Antonyms, Synonyms, and Homonyms: Words that end with the suffix *nym* (from the Greek word *onoma,* for "name") often describe classes of words and the relationships between words. For example, the word *pseudonym* refers to an assumed, or false, name. The following are among the most commonly used *nym* words.

Antonyms are pairs of words that have opposite meanings, such as *early* and *late*, *accidental* and *intentional*, and *attack* and *defend.* Words can have more than one antonym; for example, *wise* and *clever* are antonyms of *foolish.* Can you identify antonyms of the following words?

absent ________
forget ________
question ________
abundant ________
quick ________
exit ________

Synonyms are two or more words that have the same, or similar, meanings, such as *occupation*, *vocation,* and *profession*. Business writers use synonyms to add interest to their writing and to avoid repetitive phrasing. Can you identify synonyms of the following words?

qualified ________
hinder ________
question ________
lost ________
commence ________
hearty ________

Homonyms are two or more words that sound the same but are (usually) spelled differently and mean different things, such as *bases*, *basis,* and *basses* and *sights*, *sites,* and *cites.* Here are a few more examples of homonyms:

flew	flue	flu
peak	peek	pique
rain	reign	rein
weather	wether	whether

APPLY

Instructions: Write three sentences to show the use of semicolon TRANS.

EXAMPLE I left for lunch early; however, I still did not have enough time. (TRANS)

1. ______________________________

2. ______________________________

3. ______________________________

Semicolon Rule 3: Semicolon Because of Commas (BC)

When a clause needs major and minor separations, use semicolons for major breaks and commas for minor breaks.

Major and minor breaks don't occur very often when the writer keeps sentences simple, clear, and concise. Often this rule applies when several cities and states or names and titles are listed, as in the following examples:

> Baxter Foods opened new franchises in San Francisco, California; Tucson, Arizona; Chicago, Illinois; and Houston, Texas.
>
> Several employees will be honored at our annual meeting, and they are Dennis Spisek, vice president of communications; Ben Johnston, director of sales; and Kathleen Sutterlin, marketing specialist.

This rule also applies when sentences are long and complex, containing independent clauses with subordinate clauses that require a comma or commas. For example:

> Michael Janulewicz offered Cathy Dugan the job; but because Cathy has a conflict with her other position, she cannot start working for us until the end of May.
>
> Our new marketing campaign begins in May; and since that does not meet your objectives, I suggest that you develop your own campaign.

The semicolons in the following example are needed because of the commas, which relate to Comma Rule 11 (repetitive words omitted):

> The training sessions will occur throughout the day. Employees from the fifth floor will meet at 10 a.m.; from the seventh, at 1 p.m.; and from the ninth, at 3 p.m.

This example could be simplified by removing the semicolons and using only commas:

> **Revised:** Employees from the fifth floor will meet at 10 a.m., from the seventh at 1 p.m., and from the ninth at 3 p.m.

PRACTICE

Instructions: Correct the sentences below by applying the semicolon because of comma (BC) rule. For each sentence, do the following: (1) Insert any missing punctuation. (2) In each main and introductory clause, underline the verb twice and the subject once. (3) Write the reason *(BC)* after the sentence. **For example:**

> **Incorrect:** We were expecting complaints errors and problems from our customer survey but we were pleasantly surprised when Mica Grady who is our new market research team leader gave a presentation showing an upward turn in customer satisfaction and quality control.
>
> **Corrected:** We were expecting complaints, errors, and problems from our customer survey; but we were pleasantly surprised when Mica Grady, who is our new market research team leader, gave a presentation showing an upward turn in customer satisfaction and quality control. (BC)

1. Our new faculty are Francesca DuSole professor of linguistics Peter Czyneki professor of physics Simone Blanca professor of British literature and Jim Starzek professor of computer science.

2. Our presentations will follow a specific order. The sales department will present at 1 p.m. in Boardroom A the accounting department at 2 p.m. in Boardroom B the operations department at 3 p.m. in Boardroom A and the marketing department at 4 p.m. in Boardroom B.

3. The growth of Village Pizza has been phenomenal over the past two years. We are pleased to announce the opening of four new locations: Madison Wisconsin Chicago Illinois Lansing Michigan and Topeka Kansas.

4. You handled the conflict with that customer very well but if I were you I would still let Ms. Sanderson know what occurred by sending her a memo.

5. You certainly meet the qualifications for this position but since you cannot start until after August and since you indicated that the salary range does not meet your expectations we are not able to offer you the position.

SECTION B CONCEPT CHECK

1. Describe the semicolon rules referred to by the following abbreviations: NC, TRANS, and BC.

2. If periods and commas serve just as well, why use semicolons at all in your writing?

3. What is the difference between commas and semicolons?

Internet Exercise 3.2

Practice Sheets: Need more punctuation practice on the topics covered in this chapter? Go to the Web site at **www.mhhe.com/youngBE.** Select "Student Activities," and then click on the "Chapter 3" link to get started.

CHAPTER 3 SUMMARY

You may have discovered that by improving your punctuation skills, you also improve your grammar skills and writing style. The exercises in this chapter have given you not only practice with punctuation but also more practice with the sentence core. Once you can control the sentence core—the subject and verb—you are on your way to controlling your writing.

Remember, if a "sentence" does not have a complete sentence core, it isn't a sentence: it is likely to be a fragment. In chapters to come, you will rely on the skills that you have developed in this chapter. Because you worked hard to develop your new skills, using verbs and pronouns correctly will make sense to you in a short time.

Review Table 3.1 periodically to make sure that you do not fall back into your old habit of basing punctuation on *pauses*!

CHAPTER 3 CHECKLIST

To check your understanding of commas and semicolons, review the rules in Table 3.1.

TABLE 3.1 | Basic Comma and Semicolon Rules

BASIC COMMA RULES
1. **The Golden Rule:** When in doubt, leave it out. *If you don't know the reason* why *you are putting in a comma, don't use one.*
2. **The Cardinal Rule:** Never separate a subject and verb *with only one comma.* **Incorrect:** Mr. Jones, asked that the meeting begin on time. **Correct:** Mr. Jones asked that the meeting begin on time.
3. **Conjunction (CONJ):** Use a comma to separate independent clauses when they are joined by a coordinating conjunction *(and, but, or, for, nor, so, yet).* Mary would like to go to the meeting, but she has a conflict.
4. **Introductory (INTRO):** Place a comma after a word (an adverbial conjunction), phrase, or dependent clause that introduces a main clause. *Furthermore,* their discount reduced our cost. *After the meeting,* George offered to chair the committee. *When your client arrived,* you both began working on the project.
5. **Nonessential Elements (NE):** Use commas to set off nonessential (nonrestrictive) elements. *When nonessential elements are removed, the sentence remains complete and clear in meaning. Nonessential elements often come in the form of* who *or* which *clauses.* Phyllis Smith, who ran for office last year, attended the meeting. The woman who ran for office last year attended the meeting.
6. **Independent Comment (IC):** Use commas to set off a word or phrase that interrupts an independent clause. *An independent comment often comes in the form of an* adverbial conjunction *such as* however *or* therefore. Our team will, however, need more time to complete the report.
7. **Direct Address (DA):** Use commas to set off the *name* or *title* of a person addressed directly. Our company, *Mrs. Roberts,* appreciates your business. *Mr. Franco,* our mission supports your cause. Please, *sir,* (you) take a seat in front. When you cannot easily identify the grammatical subject, consider whether "*you* understood" is the subject. *You understood* is an implied subject represented by *(you).*

TABLE 3.1 | Basic Comma and Semicolon Rules *(continued)*

BASIC COMMA RULES

8. Appositive (AP): Use commas to set off words or phrases that describe or identify a preceding noun or pronoun.

Charles, my associate, will join us at 8 o'clock.

The president, Mr. Sims, prefers that meetings begin on time.

9. Addresses and Dates (AD): Use commas to set off addresses and dates.

Notice that a comma is placed before and after the year and the state names.

John listed January 5, 2000, as his start date.

She has lived in San Francisco, California, for the past six years.

Boston, Massachusetts, is a great city for a conference.

10. Series (SER): When three or more items occur in a series, use a comma after each item.

Putting a comma after the word and *makes the meaning clearer for the reader.*

George would like potatoes, peas, and carrots for dinner.

The estate was left to George, Alice, Bob, and Rose.

11. Words Omitted (WO): Use a comma for the omission of a word or words that play a structural role in a sentence.

The long, involved report arrived on my desk today.

12. Contrasting Expression or Afterthought (CEA): Use a comma to separate a contrasting expression or an afterthought that is added to the end of a sentence, often beginning with *but, not,* or *rather than.*

We will meet in New York on Tuesday, not on Wednesday.

BASIC SEMICOLON RULES

1. No Conjunction (NC): Use a semicolon to separate two independent clauses that are joined without a conjunction.

This rule is sometimes referred to as "semicolon in place of period."

They invited me to join the board; I decided that I would.

If *and* were added to the sentence, you would use a comma instead of a semicolon:

They invited me to join the board, *and* I decided that I would.

A general rule of thumb: You can use a semicolon where you could use a period.

Semicolons are used when one or both sentences are short and closely related in meaning.

2. Transition (TRANS): Place a semicolon before and a comma after an adverbial conjunction (such as *however, therefore, consequently,* and *nevertheless*) when it acts as a transition between independent clauses.

Jane invited Tom to the meeting; however, he was not able to attend.

3. Because of Commas (BC): When a sentence needs major and minor separations, use semicolons for major breaks and commas for minor breaks.

The president sent the report to Bob, Charley, Rose, and me; but I didn't have time to read it.

CHAPTER 3 END-OF-CHAPTER ACTIVITIES

ACTIVITY 1: PROCESS MEMO

INSTRUCTIONS: Write your instructor a short message indicating how your use of commas and semicolons has changed. Are you more confident using punctuation? What questions or problems do you still have? What about fragments and run-ons: do you now know how to correct these grammatical errors?

If you have Internet access, you can complete this exercise online at **www.mhhe.com/youngBE** and then send an e-mail to your instructor.

ACTIVITY 2: PUNCTUATION WORKSHEETS

WORKSHEET A: COMMA RULES—INTRO, AP, DA, AD

INSTRUCTIONS: In each main clause, underline the verb twice and then underline the subject once; insert any missing commas, and write the reason for each at the end of the sentence: introductory *(INTRO),* apposition *(AP),* direct address *(DA),* or address and date *(AD).*

Incorrect: When Isaac has time he will contact you.

Corrected: When Isaac has time, he will contact you. (INTRO)

1. Before Erik came to work for us we outsourced all of our human resources needs.

2. The office on the left the one with the glass door is your new office.

3. As I mentioned before we do not allow our employees to bring their children to work with them.

4. Our new client is based in Spokane Washington and is our largest account.

5. We are grateful Ms. Lazlo that you have chosen Midland Communications as your cellular service.

6. Please communicate directly with George Burns our human resource director to request the correct form.

7. Your letter dated November 17 2006 has certainly clarified your position.

8. After the conference call would you care to join me for lunch at Alexi's?

9. Lily you are the best computer graphics expert we have ever had!

10. Katy Ramirez our human resources manager will help you choose the appropriate health care plan.

11. Our attorney said that July 22 2006 was our next court date.

12. By the way did you notice the new couch in the lobby?

13. Ms. Akton please believe that we are doing our best to resolve this issue.

14. The new convention center will be located in Arlington Heights Illinois.

15. My new accountant Sheila Savarise earned her degrees at Harvard.

WORKSHEET B: COMMA RULES—CONJ AND IC; SEMICOLON RULES—NC AND TRANS

INSTRUCTIONS: In each main clause, underline the verb twice and then underline the subject once; insert any missing commas and semicolons, and write the reason for each at the end of the sentence: comma conjunction *(CONJ),* comma independent comment *(IC),* semicolon no conjunction *(NC),* or semicolon transition *(TRANS).*

Incorrect: The invoice was incorrect we paid it before we noticed the error.

Corrected: The invoice was incorrect; we paid it before we noticed the error. (NC)

1. Do you send most of your messages through e-mail or do you prefer the traditional method of "snail mail"?

2. Our vice president was a computer science major in college consequently he rarely calls the help desk.

3. We are however quite pleased with your service.

4. My assistant prefers a MacIntosh computer I prefer a PC.

5. Computers as a rule work only as fast as the person operating them can work.

6. Before the personal computer or PC, businesses used word processors and typewriters accordingly many typists and data entry clerks had to learn new computer skills to keep their jobs.

7. Any computer can be a server but ideally it should be made for that purpose.

8. Servers are usually large-capacity computers that manage a network's resources some servers have specific resources to manage.

9. Some servers however are dedicated to data and are called "file servers."

10. All our client information was stored on the file server but it crashed yesterday afternoon.

11. We worked on the file server until 2 a.m. this morning unfortunately we couldn't save all the data.

12. My office hours are from 9 a.m. until 5 p.m. my husband's hours are from 8 a.m. until 4 p.m.

13. We will not under any circumstances lower our bid.

14. The research team was late with its report nevertheless we managed to make our presentation on time.

15. We need the Rodriguez account updated by noon and we need to make sure it's accurate.

ACTIVITY 3: COMMA RULE REVIEW

A. COMMA CONJ AND COMMA INTRO

INSTRUCTIONS: In each main clause, underline the verb twice and then underline the subject once; insert any missing commas, and write the reason for each at the end of the sentence: comma conjunction *(CONJ)* or comma introductory *(INTRO)*.

Incorrect: If Jake scheduled the meeting how could Jesse have canceled it?

Corrected: If Jake scheduled the meeting, how could Jesse have canceled it? (INTRO)

1. Many types of office productivity suites exist but some are more expensive than others.

2. Unfortunately many people buy the most expensive software because they think it is the best available.

3. Many excellent office suites exist and the price does not predict their usability.

4. Look for versatility in an office suite yet make sure the software components integrate with each other.

5. For example the word processing software should be able to insert spreadsheet data as an object in a document.

6. At the same time the word processing software and the spreadsheet program should be able to stand alone as highly functioning applications.

7. Many people download shareware or trial versions of office suites and then they can try many brands before making a purchase.

8. By the way many of these shareware and trial downloads are available at www.cnet.com.

9. ZDNet also offers many shareware and trial download but its address is different from its name: www.hotfiles.com.

10. Finally many people prefer the interface of www.tucows.com for their shareware downloads.

B. COMMA NE, AP, DA, AND AD

INSTRUCTIONS: In each main clause, underline the verb twice and then underline the subject once; add any missing commas, and write the reason for each at the end of the sentence: nonessential element *(NE)*, appositive *(AP)*, direct address *(DA)*, or address and date *(AD)*.

Incorrect: Please complete the enclosed form which is printed on bright yellow paper and return it in the enclosed stamped envelope.

Corrected:

1. The convention will begin on Friday May 26 2006 and will end on Friday June 6 2006.

2. My neighbor a famous baseball player gave me free World Series tickets.

3. Your new client is located in the Helmsley Building 333 West Walker Street Valparaiso Indiana.

4. Marta who has been with the company for eight years works in accounting.

5. The secretary who arrives first will be given his or her choice of desks.

6. And so Dr. Griffin we are sure you will choose our travel agency for its high quality of service and unbeatable value.

7. Will someone who has used this copy machine before help me fix this paper jam?

8. Yes Maribel you will receive a raise this year.

9. Boston which is my favorite city will host next year's convention.

10. My assistant Henry Bellwood will take notes during our meeting.

11. Hello Katherine it is nice to finally meet you.

12. Jan Hendressen our international liaison has earned a doctorate in international relations.

13. The hot-dog stand on the corner which has great hot dogs has been a part of our downtown culture since 1923.

14. Please believe that we intend to follow through on this issue Mr. Padilla.

15. The customers who received the erroneous flyers must nevertheless have the sale terms honored.

ACTIVITY 4: SPEAKING BUSINESS

INSTRUCTIONS: Are there vowel sounds that you want to work on? Earlier in the chapter, you may have worked on vowel sounds contrasting the words *been* and *bin*. Let's do a brief review:

1. Whenever you pronounce a vowel sound, your tongue is down and flat.
2. Vowel sounds vary depending on how much the lips and teeth are parted.
3. If you want to work on a particular vowel sound, first make a list of words that have similar and contrasting sounds.
4. For example, if you want to work on the way you pronounce the word *sit,* make a list of words that rhyme with the traditional pronunciation of *sit,* such as *fit, lit, mit, kit,* and *hit.*

5. Next, make a list of words that sound similar to your current pronunciation, which may sound like the *e* in *set*; for example, *let, bet, pet,* and *vest.*
6. As you say each word out loud, notice how your tongue flattens and also notice how far you open your mouth and lips.
7. Are there other vowel sounds you want to work on?

ACTIVITY 5: COMMA AND SEMICOLON RULE REVIEW

A. COMMA CONJ AND COMMA WO; SEMICOLON NC

INSTRUCTIONS: In each main clause, underline the verb twice and then underline the subject once; insert any missing commas and semicolons, and write the reason for each at the end of the sentence: comma conjunction *(CONJ),* comma words omitted *(WO),* or semicolon no conjunction *(NC).* For example:

Incorrect: Our CEO arrived at our office unexpectedly everyone suddenly became serious and focused.

Corrected: Our CEO arrived at our office unexpectedly; everyone suddenly became serious and focused. (NC)

1. The fact is you have not worked here long enough to ask for a promotion.
2. I have worked here for two years yet I have not been promoted.
3. At first we were nervous about the merger now we are excited about the many new opportunities it's created.
4. Salespeople who have reached the $100,000 level will receive an extra week of vacation those who have reached the $50,000 level two extra personal days.
5. Please inventory the office's computers and please include all peripherals.
6. The negotiations will be held from 10 a.m. to 2 p.m. Monday through Wednesday.
7. You may choose our executive package or you may choose one of our many value packages.
8. Brenda often brought her own lunch to our meetings the rest of us preferred to eat at the local coffee shop.

9. Shelly would not accept the offer nor would she explain why.

10. The new laptops have caused quite a stir everyone who has a PC is now requesting an upgrade.

11. Remember we will always be happy to serve your technology needs.

12. Danica spent countless hours on the Benson account but she was not fairly compensated for her time.

13. The truth is I've never used this software application before today.

14. Please spend some time reading the instruction manual for you will find many answers to your questions.

15. We will continue to provide the best service available please continue to voice your concerns.

B. COMMA IC AND CEA; SEMICOLON TRANS

INSTRUCTIONS: In each main clause, underline the verb twice and then underline the subject once; insert any missing commas and semicolons, and write the reason for each at the end of the sentence: comma independent comment *(IC),* comma contrasting expression or afterthought *(CEA),* or semicolon transition *(TRANS).*

Incorrect: You are welcome to add a new section to the report if you wish.

Corrected: You are welcome to add a new section to the report, if you wish. (CEA)

1. Dr. Sonders rather than Dr. Jeffries will see you today.

2. We are willing to negotiate a new price but only if you grant us exclusive rights.

3. Our dealings with our major competitor moreover have been quite civil.

4. Selena indicated that she would not accept a promotion on the contrary she stated that she needs more time for her family and would like to reduce her hours.

5. Our largest Canadian distributor not our European partner has requested a change in teleconference dates.

6. Rosa needs to finish the invitations to our open house before tomorrow morning otherwise no one will know about this event until it is over.

7. Sylvia was willing to reenlist in the service but not without a sign-on bonus.

8. We have therefore decided to sponsor a different product.

9. Many employees have been taking home office supplies for their personal use therefore we have decided that each department will inventory and budget its own supplies.

10. Heavy bond paper rather than copy paper is appropriate for résumés.

11. Juana has as you may well know a degree in engineering.

12. You have not answered our many phone calls and letters therefore we must close your account.

13. Everson & Watts, Inc., will continue to serve as our primary supplier otherwise we might have to consider the European market.

14. A master of science not a bachelor's degree is required for the position.

15. In our most recent opinion poll, most customers preferred our original product furthermore nearly 80 percent indicated that they did not like the new product.

ACTIVITY 6: CUMULATIVE CHAPTER REVIEW

INSTRUCTIONS: Insert commas and semicolons as necessary in the following text.

Dear Ms. Munez:

Thank you for your résumé and cover letter. You are certainly qualified to become a member of our marketing department unfortunately, we have no full-time positions available at the present time. Your grades are excellent, and your list of college activities is impressive; I do not want to lose you to another company.

We will I believe, have openings in approximately six months. I will certainly hold your résumé until that time; however, I would like you to consider two other ways to join our company in the meantime. I can offer you a position as a marketing intern or as a part-time "floater." A "floater " in case you are wondering, is a person who is able to shift from task to task quickly and adapt to different environments. Our floaters or part-timers, help out on various projects where temporary staff is needed. This position might be perfect for a new college graduate you will be able to sample the many types of projects we undertake. If on the other hand you would prefer to work with only one team perhaps you would prefer the marketing internship program. The experience you'll gain as an intern is invaluable however it is not a paid position. Currently we have an intern slot available on our graphic design team which is most likely to have a full-time opening in February.

There are advantages to both positions and if you would like to discuss these options further please call me at the number indicated on my enclosed business card. I hope Ms. Munez that you will consider one of these positions for the immediate future. We are sure to have full-time positions open within the next six months.

ACTIVITY 7: "WRITER'S REFERENCE MANUAL" DRILL

INSTRUCTIONS: Use the "Writer's Reference Manual" at the end of this book to learn about URL addresses.

1. What is the user name of an e-mail address?

2. What symbol follows a user name?
3. What are the final two elements of an e-mail address?

4. The following are top-level domains (TLDs). What does each TLD signify?

.com ____________________

.org ____________________

.edu ____________________

.net ____________________

.gov ____________________

ACTIVITY 8: VOCABULARY LIST

A. COMMONLY MISSPELLED WORDS

INSTRUCTIONS: The list below contains words taken from a compilation of the 500 most commonly misspelled words and from the chapter. Practice them until you can spell them automatically and use them correctly.

1. accessible (adj) easy to get to, approachable
2. adolescent (n) teenager, young person; (adj.) teenage
2. bulletin (n) official statement, news report, periodical
4. cohesive (adj) unified, consistent, organized, interconnected
5. coherent (adj) logical, rational, consistent
6. committee (n) working group; team
7. concession (n) the act of yielding; special consideration; compromise
8. conscientious (adj) careful, thorough, meticulous, diligent
9. emphatic (n) a word that stresses or emphasizes another word; such as, *very.*
10. enunciation (n) articulation, elocution, pronunciation
11. knowledgeable (adj) well informed; familiar; erudite; expert
12. necessary (adj) essential; required; indispensable; crucial; vital
13. leisure (n) freedom from work; relaxation; free time
14. maneuver (n, v) a strategic movement; a physical movement requiring skill; to perform maneuvers
15. omission (n) exclusion; oversight; error

B. SIMILAR WORDS

INSTRUCTIONS: The list below contains similar words, some of which are profiled in the Vocabulary Builders in each chapter. Use these words in sentences until their meaning becomes clear.

supposed to /used to: These are both regular verbs in past tense; don't forget to end them in *ed.*

You are *supposed to* attend the meeting. (Not: You are suppose to . . .)

I *used to* go to work at that company. (Not: I use to work . . .)

sit/set: The verb *sit* (as in sitting in a chair) is intransitive, not taking an object: *Sit* down. The verb *set* (as in setting something down) is transitive, and it requires an object: *Set* the plants on the balcony.

Sit anywhere in the room that you prefer.

You may *set* your coat on the chair.

ad/add: *Ad* is a short form for the noun *advertisement. Add* is a verb meaning "to combine into one sum or to attach."

She placed an *ad* in the paper.

Add her name to the list.

than/then: The conjunction *than* is used in comparisons; the adverb *then* relates to time.

I would rather get up early *than* sleep late.

When you agree to the new schedule, *then* I will have more time.

to/too/two: *To* is a preposition and is used in prepositional phrases or before the base form of a verb to create an infinitive, as in *to go* or *to see; too* is an adverb relating to quantity, as in *too much* or *too soon; two* is a number.

Jeremy went *to* the meeting and then asked us *to go* with him *to* dinner.

They have given us the wrong order *too* late and *too* often.

Please provide *two* packets of materials.

THE INBOX

COMPOSING

Many colleges offer peer tutoring in their writing centers. For this exercise, pretend that you volunteer as a peer tutor in your college's writing center. Angela Wu, the director of the center, is developing a punctuation manual as a tutoring aid and has asked for your help. Your assignment is to write a paragraph explaining Basic Comma Rules 1 and 2. Alternatively, if you prefer, you may write a paragraph explaining one of the semicolon rules. Angela has asked you to write the paragraph in a simple, easy-to-understand style and to include a sample of each rule.

REFLECTING

Do you like the idea of numbering the basic comma rules? What is good about such an approach? Are there any drawbacks?

What did you believe about punctuation and grammar before you began studying this book? Have your beliefs and attitudes changed, and, if so, how?

DISCUSSING

Which punctuation rules are the most difficult to remember? The class should break into small groups. In your group, decide which rules pose the greatest difficulties. Why do these particular rules stand out? Examine what makes them difficult, and discuss ways to understand and retain them.

Your instructor will give each group a piece of paper with two punctuation rules written on it. Each group should keep its rules secret from the other groups. In your group, create a sentence for each rule; write the sentence twice, once with the punctuation and once without. After the groups have completed their sentences, they should take turns writing the sentences with punctuation omitted on the board. The other groups should confer to place the punctuation in the correct place and to name the rule. Repeat this process until all the rules have been discussed and all the sentences correctly punctuated. Students should write these examples in their journals for future reference.

EDITING

Please edit the following excerpt from the *Peer Tutoring Manual,* Chapter 2. Look for punctuation and spelling errors.

First it is extremely important to establish an atmosphere of trust and security. Students, will stop coming in for tutoring if they feel embarrassed, or uncomfortable. For this reason; we do not use red pens, in fact, we encourage you to help the student mark her own paper as you talk her through the issues. Take a friendly approach introducing yourself and asking the student her name. Spare a few minutes, to ask questions, about the student's major; weather she likes her classes or not; and feelings about writing, in general. From there you, can segue into her concerns about her current writing assignment. If the student, is unsure of where she needs help ask her some open-ended questions like:

What is the assignment?
How much have you completed so far?
What are the strengths, of the paper?
What are the weaknesses?
Are there particular parts of the paper that are troubling you?

Keep in mind that our tutoring sessions last only 20 minutes each. Whlie it is important to spend time developing rapport and geting the student to express her concerns about her paper you still have to keep an eye on the clock. However the student, should never be aware that you are mindful of time be discrete, in your gauging of time.

After, establishing a comfortable environment move on to examining the paper itself. Spend the bulk of your time on this phase of the tutoring process. Examine the parts of the paper which most trouble the student and than look at the overall organization of the paper. Form your suggestions in the shape of questions so that the student doesn't feel she is being told how to "correct" her paper rather, she should feel that she herself has the knowledge to improve the paper and you are merely helping her recognize that fact.

Finally wrap up the session, by reiterating, for the student the issues she needs to work on. Ask her, if she has any questions and provide encouraging comments about your belief in her abilities to complete the assignment. Don't forget to encourage her to come back to the writing center to.

KEY TO LEARNING INVENTORY

1. T
2. F
3. T
4. F
5. F
6. F
7. F
8. T
9. T
10. T

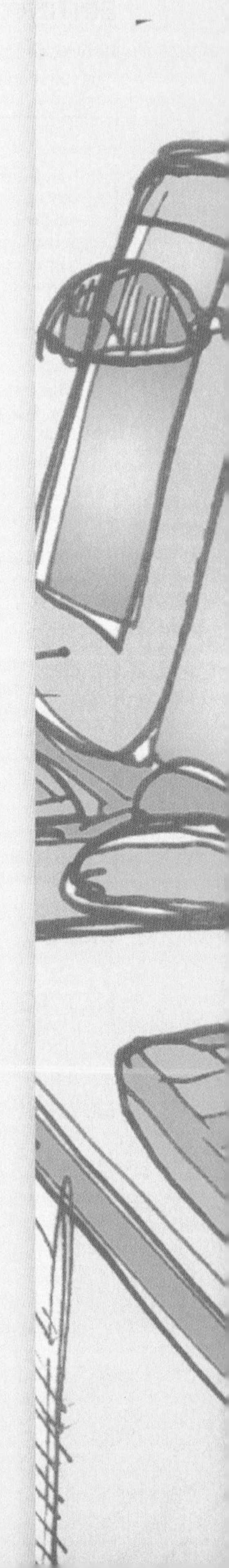

Chapter Four

Verbs at Work

"When I make a word do a lot of work like that," said Humpty Dumpty, "I always pay it extra."
—Lewis Carroll, mathematician and writer (1832–1898)

One could argue that verbs "work harder" than other parts of speech. The verb is the only part of speech that changes form, and in doing so, it tells time. Based on the tense of the verb, you know whether an event *happened* in the past, *is happening* in the present, or *will happen* in the future.

As you have already learned, the verb is the powerhouse of the sentence, determining its other core parts: the subject and, when applicable, the object. Verbs express action. Verbs develop power behind your message and help you get right to the point. Verbs exude energy and can even provoke your reader to take desired action. Verbs are vital, but they can also seem complicated because they change form. As a result, many speakers and writers fumble with the way they use some troublesome verbs.

Did you know that not all verbs express action? A handful of verbs express *state of being* rather than action. You will learn subtle differences in the way these two types of verbs function so that you can use modifiers correctly.

You will want to identify how verb use in your local language differs from that in Business English and then practice the verbs that differ until you master them. Every exercise in this chapter is designed to help you with a different kind of verb issue.

To learn more about The Writing Process, please visit our Web site at **www.mhhe.com/youngBE**

Outline

Chapter 4: Verbs at Work

Section A: The Basics About Verbs
Section B: Mood and Tense
Section C: Active Voice
Section D: Parallel Structure

Objectives

When you have completed your study of Chapter 4, you will be able to:

1. Apply past and past participle forms of irregular verbs correctly.
2. Form verbs in past time: include *ed* endings in speech and writing.
3. Use the *s* form of verbs correctly (third-person singular, present tense).
4. Apply the subjunctive mood in speech and writing.
5. Write without shifting tense unnecessarily.
6. Translate passive voice into active voice.
7. Use context to determine when passive voice is appropriate.
8. Demonstrate parallel structure with verbs and verb phrases.

Learning Inventory

1. The subject and verb are the core of a sentence. T/F
2. Some verbs have both a past tense form and a past participle form. T/F
3. A helper verb (such as *is*, *has*, or *do*) must be used with a past tense form. T/F
4. The past tense and past participle of all regular verbs end in *ed.* T/F
5. The verb in a sentence determines its grammatical subject. T/F
6. For irregular verbs, add *ed* to form both the past tense and the past participle. T/F
7. The base form of a verb is called an *infinitive.* T/F
8. All third-person singular verbs in present tense end in *s*. T/F
9. In the subjunctive mood, use *were* (rather than *was*) with *I*, *he*, and *she*. T/F
10. Use a helper with the past tense form of irregular verbs. T/F

Goal-Setting Exercises

Do you use verbs differently in your local language than you do in Business English? Are you unsure of the correct form of some irregular verbs? Do you sometimes leave off endings of verbs, such as the *s* in present tense verbs or the *ed* in past tense? What about your writing: what kinds of comments do teachers write on your papers? (For example, do you shift tense or voice?) Now write three goals that you want to achieve with verbs in your writing and speaking.

1. ______________________________

2. ______________________________

3. ______________________________

SECTION A: THE BASICS ABOUT VERBS

You probably use verbs the same way in your writing as you do in your speaking. In other words, if you write a certain way, it's probably because you speak that way too. In this section, you will focus on the difference between the way you use verbs in your local language and the way you use them in Business English. Your goal will be to add the Business English pattern to the way you use certain verbs.

ACTION VERBS AND LINKING VERBS

When you think of verbs, you probably think of *action*. That's because almost all verbs in the English language are action verbs, transferring action from the subject to the object. However, a few select verbs do not transfer action but instead express *state of being.*

1. **State-of-being verbs** are also called **linking verbs** because they *link* the subject to a word or words that follow the linking verb. (Similarly, action verbs are tagged "action" because they transfer action from the subject to the object: Reggie threw the ball.)
2. Common linking verbs are *to be (am, is, are, was, were), appear, become, seem*, and at times *smell, taste, feel, sound, look, act*, and *grow*.
3. Since linking verbs do not transfer action, they are considered weak verbs and should not be overused.

The difference between action verbs and linking verbs becomes more important when you are working with modifiers. (In Chapter 6, where you will work with modifiers, you will see how action verbs can be modified by adverbs but linking verbs cannot.) For now, let's see how to use verbs correctly.

Verb Parts

When people have problems with verbs, it is most often because they are using verb parts incorrectly. So, for the moment, stop focusing on verb tense and start focusing on verb parts. By doing so, you will solve most of your problems with verbs.

Verb parts (or *verb forms*) are developed from the **base form** of the verb, often referred to as the **infinitive.** Here is a foundation for understanding verbs:

1. Verbs are either *regular* or *irregular.*
2. For past time, the two principle parts are the *past tense* and *past participle.*
3. **Regular** verbs form their past tense and past participle by adding *ed* to the base (that's why they are "regular"). For example, *walk* is a regular verb; its past tense form is *walked*, and its past participle is also *walked.*
4. **Irregular** verbs *vary* in the way the past tense and past participle are formed. For example, *write* is an irregular verb; its past tense form is *wrote*, and its past participle is *written.*
5. Past participles need a **helper** or **auxiliary** verb. Common helping verbs are the forms of *be (is, are, was, were)* and *have (has, have, had).*
6. In present time, all verbs have an ***s* form,** which is constructed by adding *s* to the base of the verb. The *s* form is also known as **third-person singular** (in simple present tense); for example, *listens, speaks, has, does.*

Common Errors

With the above points in mind, here are the kinds of mistakes that occur with Business English:

- Using the past tense and past participle of verbs incorrectly.

Incorrect: The manager *had ask* for the form the other day.

Correct: The manager *had asked* for the form the other day.

> **VOCABULARY: WORD USAGE**
>
> **Loan/Lend:** Can you figure out what is wrong with the following?
>
> I can loan you lunch money.
>
> Alberto loaned me his notebook.
>
> If you said using the word *loan* as a verb, you are correct. The word *loan* is a noun, and nouns cannot be used as verbs. Thus, you cannot "loan" anything to anyone. The correct word to use is *lend*. The past tense form of *lend* is *lent,* and so is the past participle.
>
> I can lend you lunch money.
>
> Alberto lent me his notebook.
>
> To improve your use of *loan* and *lend,* write three or four sentences using each word correctly and then practice reading them aloud a few times.

Incorrect: An associate *would've went* to the meeting if asked.

Correct: An associate *would've gone* to the meeting if asked.

- Leaving off the *s* for *s*-form verbs.

Incorrect: Bill Snyder *maintain* all equipment in our department.

Correct: Bill Snyder *maintains* all equipment in our department.

- Shifting tense inappropriately within a sentence or paragraph.

Incorrect: The coordinator *says* that the meeting *was canceled.*

Correct: The coordinator *said* that the meeting *was canceled.*

The remainder of this section goes into detail about each principle related to common verb errors.

Regular Verbs in Past Time

Verb Principle 1: *When using regular verbs in past time, add* ed *to the base to form the past tense and past participle.*

Leaving off the *ed* with regular past-time verbs relates as much to speaking as it does to writing. If you have a habit of leaving off the *ed* when speaking, you will most definitely leave off the *ed* when writing.

Here are some examples of past-time usage:

Incorrect: The Commerce Committee *assist* me with the information.

Correct: The Commerce Committee *assisted* me with the information.

Incorrect: Alexander said that he *incorporate* his business last year.

Correct: Alexander said that he *incorporated* his business last year.

PRACTICE

Instructions: Correct the following sentences by using the past-time form for each verb.
For example:

Incorrect: My assistant help me with the project.

Corrected: My assistant *helped* me with the project.

1. Bob finally indicate that the information was wrong.

2. The dean encourage me to apply for graduate school.

3. My interview result in a job offer at another company.

4. Ms. Fielding told me that their company merge with a larger one last year.

5. Have you plan for the interview?

For more practice using regular verbs in past time, complete EOC Activity 3 on page 125.

Verbs in Past Time: Helper Verbs

Verb Principle 2: *When using verbs in past time, do* not *use a helper verb with the past tense form; however, you must use a helper verb with the past participle.*

With *regular verbs,* the past tense and past participle are the same; they both end in *ed.* As a result, with regular verbs in past time you cannot make an error based on using or not using a helper verb. However, with irregular verbs, this kind of error is common.

- When using the past participle form of an irregular verb, you *must* use a helper.
- When using the past tense form of an irregular verb, you *cannot* use a helper.

Listed below are a few irregular verbs that are used in the examples that follow. (The helper verbs were randomly chosen.) For a more complete list of irregular verbs, see Table 4.1.

Base	Past Tense	Past Participle
choose	chose	(has) chosen
do	did	(have) done
freeze	froze	(had) frozen
go	went	(is) gone
see	saw	(are) seen
speak	spoke	(was) spoken
write	wrote	(were) written

For *irregular verbs,* here are the two most common errors:

1. *Type 1 error:* Using an irregular past tense form with a helper.

    Incorrect: Your budget *is froze* until next year. (*is frozen*)

    Incorrect: The director *has spoke* about that problem. (*spoke* or *has spoken*)

    Incorrect: Marty *has* finally *did* the paperwork for the proposal. (*did* or *has done*)

    Incorrect: The report *had went* out yesterday. (*went* or *had gone*)

2. *Type 2 error:* Using an irregular past participle without a helper.

    Incorrect: Margaret *seen* Bob at the conference. (*saw* or *had seen*)

    Incorrect: They *done* the work last week. (*did* or *had done*)

    Incorrect: Barbra *chosen* the décor for the new office. (*chose* or *has chosen*)

    Incorrect: Alice *been* the director for a year now. (*has been*)

Here is how to stop making errors with irregular verbs:

1. Know the correct past tense and past participle form of each irregular verb.
2. When using the past tense form, *do not use* a helper or auxiliary verb.
3. When using the past participle, *use* a helper.

If you do not have a problem with the verbs presented here, diagnose your own language pattern to know which verbs give you problems.

EXPLORE

Instructions: Observe speech patterns in a public place (in a restaurant or an elevator, on a bus or train, on the street). Listen until you hear five local-language statements involving verbs. Make a list of the verbs or of the statements and bring them to class for discussion.

TABLE 4.1 | Irregular Verb Chart

Your best bet with these irregular verbs is to memorize their past tense and past participle forms.

Base Form	Past Tense	Past Participle
be (am, is, are)	was, were	been
become	became	become
break	broke	broken
bring	brought	brought
build	built	built
buy	bought	bought
catch	caught	caught
choose	chose	chosen
cost	cost	cost
dive	dived, dove	dived
do	did	done
draw	drew	drawn
drink	drank	drunk
drive	drove	driven
eat	ate	eaten
fall	fell	fallen
find	found	found
fly	flew	flown
forget	forgot	forgot, forgotten
forgive	forgave	forgiven
freeze	froze	frozen
get	got	got, gotten
give	gave	given
go	went	gone
grow	grew	grown
hold	held	held
know	knew	known
lay* *(to place)*	laid	laid
lie *(to recline)*	lay	lain
lie *(to speak untruth)*	lied	lied
lend	lent	lent
lose	lost	lost
prove	proved	proved, proven
ride	rode	ridden
say	said	said
see	saw	seen
sell	sold	sold
set*	set	set
sink	sank	sunk
sit	sat	sat
shake	shook	shaken
shine	shone	shone
shine*	shined	shined
shrink	shrank	shrunk
show	showed	showed, shown
speak	spoke	spoken
stand	stood	stood
steal	stole	stolen
swim	swam	swum
take	took	taken
teach	taught	taught
throw	threw	thrown
understand	understood	understood
wear	wore	worn
write	wrote	written

Note: Past tense does not take a helper verb, but past participle must have a helper verb. Helper verbs consist of the various forms of *to be* and *to have (is, was, were; has, have, had).*

* Transitive verbs that need an object to be complete.

PRACTICE

A. Instructions: In the following partial list of irregular verbs, see if you know the correct past tense and past participle of each. Select a helper verb for each past participle. Remember, any form of be (*is, are, was, were*) or have (*has, have, had*) can function as a helper.

	Base		Past Tense	Past Participle
EXAMPLE	break	(no helper)	broke	have broken

Choose any helper for the remainder:

Base	Past Tense	Past Participle
1. become	________	________
2. bring	________	________
3. buy	________	________
4. catch	________	________
5. dive	________	________
6. do	________	________
7. draw	________	________
8. forget	________	________
9. freeze	________	________
10. go	________	________
11. get	________	________
12. grow	________	________
13. lend	________	________
14. pay	________	________
15. speak	________	________
16. spend	________	________
17. stand	________	________
18. think	________	________
19. throw	________	________
20. write	________	________
21. wear	________	________

B. Instructions: Circle the correct verb in each of the sentences below.

EXAMPLE Andersen had (flew, flown) to New York last week.

1. Joanne had finally (did, done) the report.
2. Who has (choose, chose, chosen) the menu fo r the banquet?
3. If you had not (went, gone) to the meeting, you would not be ready.
4. The accountants (brang, brought) the audit to the board meeting.
5. My manager (loaned, lent) me his car for two weeks.

For more practice using irregular verbs in past time, complete EOC Activity 2 on page 123.

Communication Challenges

Business English vs. Local Language: When you use a verb differently from its prescribed usage in Business English, you are using your local language.

Identify where your local-language verb patterns differ from those in Business English, and then practice the Business English pattern until you feel comfortable.

To some degree or another, everyone speaks a local language. Grammar is only one aspect of how languages differ; another aspect is pronunciation. For example, do you say things such as "*Wa jeet* for lunch?" "*Howja* do on the test?" "*Whoja* go to the meeting with?"

Ask Yourself: *What local-language patterns have I noticed in my speech or writing?*

APPLY

Instructions: Select five verbs that you use differently in your local language than you do in Business English. For each verb, compose three sentences in local language and then translate your sentences into Business English. Try to use both the past tense and the past participle forms.

Verbs in Present Tense: The *S* Form

Verb Principle 3: *In simple present tense, apply the* s *form correctly to third-person singular verbs.*

Third-person singular verbs are also known as the ***s* form** because they *all* end in *s*. Many people consistently make errors with the *s* form. For example:

Incorrect: The service department *have* the right attitude about business.

Correct: The service department *has* the right attitude about business.

Incorrect: Wilson *don't have* the information we need.

Correct: Wilson *does not (doesn't) have* the information we need.

VOCABULARY: KEY TERMS

Transitive and Intransitive Verbs: Have you ever wondered about the difference between the verbs *lay* and *lie?* These verbs are confusing and rarely used correctly.

The verb *lay,* which means "to place," is transitive and needs an object. The verb *lie,* which means "to recline," is intransitive and cannot be followed by an object.

- Transitive verbs need a direct object.
- Intransitive verbs cannot have a direct object.

Most verbs can be used with or without a direct object, but a few verbs are *only* transitive or *only* intransitive. The verbs that are especially tricky are the ones that seem to come in pairs, such as *lay* and *lie* or *sit* and *set*. Here are some examples of transitive and intransitive verbs.

	Base	Past Tense	Past Participle
Intransitive	lie	lay	lain

Marcus felt ill so he had lain *down.*

	Base	Past Tense	Past Participle
Transitive	lay	laid	laid

Sue laid the *book* on the table.

	Base	Past Tense	Past Participle
Intransitive	sit	sat	sat

Izzy sat *down.*

	Base	Past Tense	Past Participle
Transitive	set	set	set

Fred set the *book* on the table.

In these examples, the adverb *(down)* modifies the intransitive verbs, but the direct object *(book)* follows the transitive verbs.

PRACTICE

A. Instructions: Correct the simple present tense sentences below. **For example:**

Incorrect: Their accountant have all of the information.

Corrected: Their accountant *has* all of the information.

1. Our sales representative don't always complete the reports on time.
2. While Jolie work on a solution, Peter wait for an answer.
3. The training director always follow the guidelines for the course.
4. The director haven't analyzed the data from their department.
5. Meredith say that my expense account have not been turned in yet.

B. Instructions: Make corrections in present or past time where errors occur. **For example:**

Incorrect: After Melanie spoke at the meeting, she ask her supervisor for feedback.

Corrected: After Melanie spoke at the meeting, she *asked* her supervisor for feedback.

1. Every week Milton discuss current issues in a group e-mail.
2. At last month's meeting, our manager present the team awards.
3. Our team prepare the last quarterly report within the deadline.
4. For every meeting, Alice write the agenda.
5. At the last conference, a vendor display our product.

C. Instructions:

1. Select a topic and write a paragraph or two about your topic in present time. Focus on using the third-person singular. You can write about your favorite activity. For example, "This year my favorite activity is running. Running helps me . . ."
2. Now "translate" your present tense paragraph into past time. For example, "Last year my favorite activity was running. Running helped me . . ."

SUBJECT-VERB AGREEMENT

While the *s* form is a specific area of subject-verb agreement that gives writers problems, you also need to focus on subject-verb agreement in general. Here are some tips to help you with subject-verb agreement:

1. The simple present time takes the base form of the verb for all persons other than third-person singular (which is the *s* form). Both regular and irregular third-person singular verbs end in an *s*. (For example, *walk* becomes *walks* and *do* becomes *does*.)
2. Past tense for regular verbs is formed by adding *ed* to the base form (*walk* becomes *walked*).
3. The past tense for irregular verbs is formed in various ways; however, all persons use the same form. (For example, I *took*, you *took*, she *took*, and so on.)
4. The past participle of irregular verbs is formed in various ways; though all persons use the same past participle form, the helper verb changes. (For example, I *have taken,* she *has taken.*)

Language Diversity

Portmanteau Words: A *portmanteau word* is a word that fuses two words; for example, *Spanglish* (fusing *Spanish* and *English*), *brunch* (*breakfast* and *lunch*), and *telecommunications* (*telephone* and *communications*).

The original French word *portemanteau* refers to a large leather suitcase that opens into two hinged compartments (*porte* = carry and *manteau* = coat or cloak), but Lewis Carroll coined a new spelling and meaning in *Through the Looking Glass and What Alice Found There.* While explaining to Alice the words to the poem Jabberwocky, Humpty Dumpty says, "Well, *slithy* means *lithe* and *slimy* . . . . You see it's like a *portmanteau*—there are two meanings packed up in one word."

A portmanteau word is now often referred to simply as a portmanteau. And the word *portmanteau* has gradually taken on even broader meaning, describing the fusing of more than words. For example, as mentioned above, *Spanglish* is a portmanteau *word;* Spanglish is also sometimes referred to as a portmanteau *language* (rather than a dialect) because the language arises from the mixing of English and Spanish languages.

Below is a list of portmanteau words. Can you identify the original words that were fused together?

Swatch

____

animatronics

____

spork

____

Konglish

____

telethon

____

moped

____

cyborg

____

infomercial

____

smog

____

Ask Yourself: *Can I think of any portmanteau words that I use in my daily communications?*

Since *to have* can be a troublesome verb, let's use it as an example:

Present Tense		Past Tense	
Singular	Plural	Singular	Plural
I have	We have	I had	We had
You have	You have	You had	You had
He, she, it has	They have	He, she, it had	They had

The main exception to this pattern is the verb *to be,* which breaks all the rules for present tense and past tense. Here is how *to be* is conjugated:

Present Tense		Past Tense	
Singular	Plural	Singular	Plural
I am	We are	I was	We were
You are	You are	You were	You were
He, she, it is	They are	He, she, it was	They were

Your biggest challenge in ensuring subject-verb agreement is determining whether your subject is singular or plural. If you have a singular third-person subject, make sure that you apply the *s* form of the verb. Sometimes subject-verb agreement gets tricky when you are working with a compound subject or choosing a helper verb. The following exercise will give you practice with subject-verb agreement.

VOCABULARY: KEY TERMS

Progressive Tenses: Refer to the present perfect progressive tense as the *recent past*. The recent past uses a present tense helper such as *has* or *have* and implies that action happened in the past but is ongoing.

I have been answering calls every day this month.

Refer to the past perfect progressive as the *distant past*. The distant past uses the past participle *had* as the helper. This implies that the action happened in the past and was completed in the past.

I had been attending meetings about the product every day last fall.

However, try *not* to focus on tenses. Most of the time you use tenses correctly; when you make mistakes with verbs, your mistakes probably involve irregular verbs in past time. Focus on the following to improve your language patterns:

1. Use the past tense form of irregular verbs without a helper.
2. Use the past participle form of irregular verbs with a helper.
3. Make sure regular verbs in past time end in *ed.*
4. Keep verb tense consistent within the same sentence and paragraph.

PRACTICE

Instructions: Correct the following sentences for subject-verb agreement. Keep verbs in the same time as shown; in other words, keep present tense verbs in present time; keep past tense verbs in past time. Underline the subject of each sentence one time and the verb two times.

Incorrect: Sue and her manager has not yet given the latest report to the commissioner.

Corrected: Sue and her manager *have* not yet given the latest report to the commissioner.

1. The reporter and his source was not available for additional questioning.

2. Your department and mine has a significant amount of work to complete.

3. My interest in conducting an investigation of the two audits were made clear at the last meeting.

4. Completing monthly reports and attending team meetings has been two of my main duties.

5. A box with seminar supplies have arrived in the mailroom for you.

SECTION A CONCEPT CHECK

1. When using irregular verbs in past time, which past tense form requires a helper and which does not?

2. For regular verbs, describe how to form the past tense and past participle forms.

3. In simple present tense, the *s* form describes what person and tense?

SECTION B: MOOD AND TENSE

Mood is a grammatical term used to describe a writer's attitude toward a subject as it is expressed by the form of the verb. The mood that is most often overlooked is the subjunctive mood; using the subjunctive correctly adds sophistication to your speaking and ensures that your writing is correct.

Another kind of error that speakers and writers make is shifting tense unnecessarily. Using verbs consistently gives your writing flow and, once again, ensures that it is correct.

THE SUBJUNCTIVE MOOD

English has three moods: the indicative, the imperative, and the subjunctive.

1. The **indicative mood** states a fact or asks a question; most sentences are written in the indicative mood, including this one.
2. The **imperative mood** expresses a command or makes a request, such as "Stop!" or "Don't go there!"
3. The **subjunctive mood** expresses improbability, such as "If I *were* you . . ."

Many people do not use the subjunctive mood correctly. That's because the verb *to be* changes form in the subjunctive mood. Use the subjunctive mood when you convey a *wish* or *improbability*. Also use the subjunctive mood with certain requests, demands, recommendations, and set phrases.

- For the past subjunctive, *to be* is always expressed as *were*.

  ("If I *were* you, I would not give them advice.")

- For the present subjunctive, the verb is expressed in its *infinitive* form.

  ("It is imperative that Bob *attend* the conference.")

The subjunctive mood sounds professional; if you don't already use it, you may enjoy adding it to your speech pattern. Once you know the subjunctive mood well, you can choose where and when you use it. Read the examples below and then decide how you plan to incorporate the subjunctive mood into your speech and writing.

Statements Following *Wish* or *If*

If something is a *wish*, it is a possibility rather than a statement of fact. Since a *wish* is a possibility, the subjunctive mood applies. Use *were* in a subjunctive statement (even when you would normally use *was*).

Incorrect	Correct
I wish that I *was* at the seminar.	I wish that I *were* at the seminar.
Mitchell wishes the offer *was* true.	Mitchell wishes the offer *were* true.
My manager wishes she *was* able to help.	My manager wishes she *were* able to help.

When a sentence begins with the word *if,* often the statement that follows is an impossible or improbable *condition,* not a fact. Use the subjunctive mood for statements containing improbable conditions following *if.*

Incorrect:	Correct:
If I *was* you, I would choose a new plan.	If I *were* you, I would choose a new plan.
If he *was* the chairperson, he would agree.	If he *were* the chairperson, he would agree.
If I *was* in Boston, I would assist you.	If I *were* in Boston, I would assist you.

PRACTICE

Instructions: The following sentences are written in the subjunctive mood, past time; circle the correct form of the verb.

EXAMPLE: If Jeremy (was, were) your new manager, he would implement your suggestions,

1. Our entire department wishes Friday (was, were) a holiday.
2. Tyler wishes he (was, were) in your department.
3. If Jeren (was, were) your sister, would you support her in running for office?
4. I wish Boston (was, were) the location for our next conference.
5. If Alessandro (was, were) younger, (would, will) you hire him for the job?

The Present Subjunctive

The present subjunctive takes the *infinitive* or *base* form of the verb, regardless of the person or number of the subject. The present subjunctive occurs in *that* clauses after verbs expressing wishes, commands, requests, or recommendations. For example:

The president said *that* it is imperative that *we be* at the meeting.

My office assistant suggested (that) the *information be* included.

Reginald requested (that) the *speaker repeat* the Web address.

I insisted (that) *Bob answer* my question.

Note: The word *that* is implied even when it is removed. Do not remove the word *that* if a misreading of the sentence can occur without it.

PRACTICE

A. Instructions: The following sentences contain errors in present and past subjunctive mood. Circle the correct form of the verb.

EXAMPLE: The auditor required that my manager (compile, compiles) the tax information.

1. The CEO requested that the president (attend, attends) the company picnic.
2. It is imperative that your department (facilitate, facilitates) the sales meeting.
3. If Danuta (was, were) to offer you the position, would you take it?

4. My boss said that it was urgent that I (be, am) available to answer calls immediately.
5. If Alessandro (was, were) your manager, (would, will) you apply for the job?

B. Instructions: Write a short paragraph about a wish you have. Focus on using the subjunctive mood. **For example:**

> I wish I were able to go to New York on a short vacation. If I were in New York, I would make sure to visit . . .

For more practice with the subjunctive, complete EOC Activity 5 on page 126.

VERB TENSE AND CONSISTENCY

Verb Principle 4: *Within the same sentence and paragraph, do not shift tense unnecessarily.*

Inconsistency in verb tense relates to shifting between past tense and present tense without just cause. Even experienced writers make this common error because they cannot always see the logic behind the rule. In addition, this error is more difficult to find; verbs may be conjugated correctly, but their inconsistent use creates the problem. Consider these examples:

Incorrect: We *accepted* the terms of the contract because they *give* us no other options.

Correct: We *accepted* the terms of the contract because they *gave* us no other options.

PRACTICE

A. Instructions: The following examples contain errors in tense; correct the errors. **For example:**

Incorrect: I *explained* that we *are* behind schedule and that we *needed* more time.

Corrected: I *explained* that we *were* behind schedule and that we *needed* more time.

1. In your note, you say that the report was late.
2. Alex gives me the report today and then told me he was leaving.
3. Employees complain about that policy and wanted a change.
4. Human resources told me that my application is not filled out correctly.
5. The decision was difficult, and I need more time to give you an answer.

SPEAKING BUSINESS

***ed* Endings:** Even though a word ends in *ed,* the word can end in one of three possible sounds: "d," "t," or "ted."

The following verbs end with the "d" or "duh" sound. At the end of each word, your tongue should land behind your teeth, at the roof of your mouth.

learned	exchanged
filled	pledged
finalized	listened
exchanged	planned
formed	adjourned
resigned	applied

The following verbs end with the "t" or "tah" sound. At the end of each word, the tip of your tongue should land on the roof of your mouth, behind your teeth.

walked	picked
marked	clipped
skipped	focused
mixed	barked
laughed	asked

The following verbs end with the "ted" sound:

acted	excited
limited	united
amounted	counted
restricted	planted
encrypted	lifted

Coaching Tip: Be careful not to add an extra syllable at the end of verbs. For example, for the word *watched* some people mistakenly say "watch-ed" instead of "watch-t."

▸Language Diversity

Spanglish: A portmanteau (see Language Diversity sidebar on page 109) of the words *Spanish* and *English*, the term *Spanglish* refers to a dialect that has arisen primarily in the speech of the Hispanic population of the United States. Speakers can be found in large bilingual (Spanish and English) communities along the United States–Mexico border; throughout southern California, northern New Mexico, Texas, and Florida; and in New York City.

Beyond the mainland United States, Spanglish is also spoken in Panama (where the United States had control of the Panama Canal) and in Puerto Rico, long a U.S. territory. Through movies, television, and music, Spanglish has also spread across borders.

While in some cases, new words have been created, Spanglish has also changed the meanings of old words. *Carpeta*, for example, used to refer to a folder in Spanish; the word now refers to an American word, *carpet*. *Chequear*, another word with Spanglish origins, arose from the English verb *to check,* replacing the Spanish word for "to check," *verificar*. *Chequear* is now an accepted Spanish word.

Below is a list of Spanglish words. How many can you identify?

1. pan dulce
2. Staceys
3. aplicacion
4. èse
5. Cali
6. muy suave
7. Y-Que?
8. simón
9. wilo
10. open the radio

Spanglish speakers commonly mix English and Spanish words in conversation:

Spanglish:	Hola, buenos tardes, how are you?
	Well, y tu?
Business English:	Hello, good afternoon, how are you?
	Well, and you?

B. Instructions: In the following paragraph, identify where verbs shift tense unnecessarily and make corrections.

My manager says that my work was not good enough, so I decide that I need to make changes in the way I get my job done. After I try for a few days, I find that I could improve. When my manager sees my progress, she told me that I would get a better review. I say to her, "That's good news because I tried to improve and succeeded."

For more practice with verb tense and consistency, complete EOC Activity 6 on page 127.

LANGUAGE AS A SYSTEM

The way you use verbs is systematic. To adapt your use of verbs—using Business English in formal environments and local language in informal environments—work on changing patterns of your speech.

To make real improvement, you also need to change the way you think about language. Instead of feeling bad about not speaking or writing perfectly, use your energy to become more proficient. Translate local language into Business English, building a wall between the two language systems.

Also remember, *no one writes or speaks English perfectly: do your best and then let go of the rest.* Here's some advice: the next time you identify a specific verb pattern that you need to work on, compose a sentence in local language, translate it into Business English, and repeat it until you feel comfortable and confident. Then you will have more choices in every situation, formal and informal.

SECTION B CONCEPT CHECK

1. Give an example of using inconsistent verb tense within a sentence and then correct it.

2. What are the three moods, and what does mood express?

3. When is the subjunctive mood used?

SECTION C: ACTIVE VOICE

Now that you have spent time working on using verbs *correctly,* you can put power in your writing by using action verbs *effectively*.

VOICE: ACTIVE AND PASSIVE

Another quality of verbs is *voice:* voice tells whether the subject performs action or receives action.[1] In the **active voice,** the subject performs action; in the **passive voice,** the subject receives action. Experts agree that the active voice is easier to understand than the passive voice; with the active voice, the *subject, verb,* and *object* perform their prescribed grammatical functions. Here is an example:

Active

Jim threw the ball.	The subject *(Jim)* is transferring action to the object through the verb *(threw). Jim* is the **grammatical subject** based on position: in English, the grammatical subject generally precedes the verb. *Jim* is also the **real subject**. The real subject is the "who" or "what" that performs the action of the verb.

Passive—Version 1

The ball was thrown by Jim.	In passive voice, the subject is acted upon. In this example, the subject *(ball)* is not performing an action. Jim is still performing the action, but he is in the object position. In other words, the verb does not transfer action from the subject to the object. The grammatical subject *(ball)* is different from the real subject *(Jim).*

Passive—Version 2

The ball was thrown.	In this passive construction, the grammatical subject is *ball,* and it performs no action. Because the real subject is not in the sentence, even this simple construction is somewhat abstract.

- In the active voice, the grammatical subject performs the action of the verb: *the grammatical subject and real subject are the same.* Active voice is clear, direct, and concise.
- In the passive voice, the grammatical subject does not perform action: *the real subject is not the grammatical subject*. The passive verb *describes*, but it does not *act*. The passive structure is abstract and wordy.

Revising passive sentences into the active voice is one of the most important editing techniques you will learn. Active voice makes your writing easier for readers to understand and respond to. In the process of turning passive sentences into active ones, you may be able to cut other words and phrases that are unnecessary.

• Internet Exercise 4.1

Verbs Sell It: Witness verbs online and in action—see how they sell! Log on to the Web site at **www.mhhe.com/youngBE** and select the "Chapter 4" link to get started.

Communication Challenges

It's like correcting people's grammar. I don't do it to be popular. —Frasier Crane (Kelsey Grammer)

Challenge: One of the stores on your delivery route, a customer for 10 years, has various signs posted inside that contain spelling errors ("Thank you for you're patronage," "Sweat relish available," "Minimum Charge of $10"). You are on good speaking terms with the owner and the head clerk. Should you mention the errors? Why or why not? If your answer is yes, how would you approach the owner?

PRACTICE

Instructions: Change the following sentences from passive to active voice. **For example:**

Weak: A new project was given to us by Matthew.

Revised: Matthew gave us a new project.

1. Flexibility in part-time positions is considered a bonus by our human resource department.

2. Their outstanding performance was acknowledged by the CEO.

3. Any assistance that you need will be provided by our Guest Services Department.

4. The contract was not approved by the union representatives.

5. The promotion plan was not created by the vice president of marketing.

Even though the active voice is usually the preferred voice, passive voice is a grammatically correct construction. In fact, passive voice is more effective when you do not know who performed an action or do not want to call attention to that person.

For example, it is more tactful to say "My phone call was not answered" than to say "You never answered my call." At times, you may choose to write or speak in the passive voice to avoid hurt feelings. In your writing, you should use passive voice only when you don't know the real subject or don't want to point a finger at the real subject.

When you are composing, don't think about active or passive voice: just get your words onto the page. When you edit, check to make sure that you are using the best voice for your purpose. In other words, use the active voice unless you cannot identify the real subject or choose not to do so. Passive voice is indirect, but it is better to sound vague than to sound accusatory.

WRITER'S TOOLKIT

Active Voice

To change a sentence from passive to active voice, follow these steps:

1. Identify the verb.
2. Identify the real subject (not the grammatical subject). You can find the real subject by asking, "Who or what performed the action?"
3. Place the real subject at the beginning of the sentence. Follow it with the verb (correct tense, of course).

In the active voice, each part of the sentence performs its prescribed function:

	did	
Who	does	what.
	will do	
S	**V**	**O**

In English,

- The subject answers the question, "Who or what performed the action?"
- The verb performs action or expresses state of being.
- The object answers the question, "What?"

PRACTICE

Instructions: Change the following sentences from passive to active voice. Then indicate whether the best choice is the passive or active version. (Note: In some sentences, the actor or agent performing the action, the real subject, is shown within parentheses.) **For example:**

Passive: You have been given a poor recommendation (by me) because of late work.

Revised: I gave you a poor recommendation because you turned in your work late.

Choice: Use the passive version; it is more tactful and has a better tone.

1. An error was made (by Rob) and the work needed to be redone (by our team).

2. Your deposit should have been made yesterday to avoid late charges.

3. If payment is not received, a late penalty will be assessed on your account.

4. The food was not ordered on time (by you), and the delay didn't go unnoticed by guests.

5. A break is needed by everyone at times, and one should be taken (by you) now.

For more practice with the active voice, complete EOC Activity 7 on page 127.

REAL SUBJECTS AND STRONG VERBS

The subject and verb are critical elements of every sentence. Focus on using real subjects followed by strong verbs. See Table 4.2 for examples of action verbs. Here is how to keep your subjects real and verbs strong:

- Avoid starting sentences with *it is* or *there are.* (These are called **expletive forms**.)
- Use action verbs rather than state-of-being verbs *(is, are, seem)* and weak verbs (such as *make, give, take*).
- Turn nominals back into action verbs. (A *nominal* is the noun form of a verb, at times constructed by adding *tion* or *ment* to the base form of the verb; see Chapter 2, page 41, if you need a review.)

In each example below, the main subject is underlined once and the verb is underlined twice. Compare the subjects and verbs between the two groups:

We will make an investigation about the problem.	We will investigate the problem.
There are many people waiting to see you.	Many people are waiting to see you.
It is her request that we assist her.	She requests that we assist her.
He made everyone aware of the information.	He informed everyone.

SPEAKING BUSINESS

Pronouncing Difficult Words: Sometimes simple words can be difficult to pronounce. For example, the word *ask* is difficult because it ends in a **consonant cluster** (two or more consonants coming together form a cluster).

Consonants (such as *d, k, r, s, t*) are as easy to pronounce as vowels *(a, e, i, o,* and *u)* until they form a cluster, such as *st, sts, sks,* or *rd.* With consonant clusters, the tongue and mouth have to work very hard to pronounce all the distinct sounds. Sometimes speakers drop the last consonant or two; this practice should be avoided in business situations.

Here are some words with consonant cluster word endings that can be difficult to pronounce:

st /sts *test, tests, list, lists*

sk/sks *mask, masks, flask, flasks, ask, asks*

sp/sps *lisp, lisps*

To improve pronunciation, don't focus on the consonants—instead, extend the sound of the vowel that precedes them.

For example, when pronouncing the word *asks,* focus on the *a.* Say the *a* very slowly. Then gradually feel yourself pushing air through your front teeth as they come together to form the "s" sound. Finally, feel the *k* being formed in the back of your throat. Practice each part until you get it right. (You might prefer to practice in a quiet spot with a mirror.)

Ask Yourself: *Which words do I have difficulty pronouncing?* (Make a list.)

PRACTICE

Instructions: Revise the following sentences so that they have real subjects followed by strong verbs. **For example:**

Weak: It was the consultant's recommendation that we adopt the new policy.

Revised: The consultant recommended that we adopt the new policy.

1. It was the vice president's decision that he would chair the committee himself.

TABLE 4.2 | Action Verbs
Using strong action verbs can add power to your writing.

accelerate	demonstrate	help	monitor	rearrange
accept	describe	hypothesize	motivate	recognize
adapt	design	ignite	negotiate	reconcile
aid	develop	illustrate	observe	reconstruct
amplify	devise	implement	operate	reinforce
analyze	devote	incorporate	orchestrate	relate
apply	direct	increase	organize	reorganize
appraise	edit	influence	orient	report
arrange	empower	initiate	originate	restore
assemble	encourage	inspect	outline	review
assist	energize	inspire	participate	revise
awaken	enhance	install	perform	rewrite
break down	enlist	institute	persuade	score
build	establish	instruct	pinpoint	seek
challenge	estimate	interpret	plan	serve
change	evaluate	introduce	point out	simplify
choose	examine	invent	predict	solve
compile	expand	inventory	prepare	stimulate
complete	explain	launch	present	summarize
compose	extend	lead	preserve	support
compute	focus	learn	process	synthesize
construct	formulate	judge	produce	teach
consult	fortify	justify	promote	train
convert	generalize	listen	propose	unify
coordinate	generate	maintain	provide	use
counsel	guide	modify	rank	widen
create	heal	mold	rate	write

WRITER'S TOOLKIT

Subjects, Verbs, and End Stress

The core of a sentence is its subject and verb. Real subjects and strong verbs create a clear meaning. After the reader understands the actors and action, information at the end of a sentence stands out. The end becomes the stress point. Thus, you can emphasize important information by putting it at the end of a sentence following a real subject and strong verb.

Weak: At the conference, the certificates were presented *by the president.*

Revised: At the conference, the president presented *the certificates.*

Weak: Their creative solution was appreciated *by our entire staff.*

Revised: Our entire staff appreciated *their creative solution.*

When you revise a sentence from passive to active, you may also be moving the new information to the end so that it stands out for the reader.

2. It is George's delay in completing the paperwork that is blocking my advancement.

3. There may be new representatives added to our sales staff.

4. It is important that you complete your report on time.

5. There are many clients in the reception area waiting to see you.

SECTION C CONCEPT CHECK

1. What does voice (active or passive) tell you about the subject of a sentence?

2. When might it be more effective to use passive voice?

3. Describe steps you can take to keep your subjects real and verbs strong.

SECTION D: PARALLEL STRUCTURE

Using **parallel structure** means putting similar sentence elements in the same form. Parallel structure creates flow and consistency as it makes your ideas stand out. Writing that lacks parallel structure sounds choppy and disjointed and is difficult to understand.

In this section, you start with verbs as they appear in small units: words and phrases. Then you will work with sentences that shift from active to passive. Parallel structure is an important topic, and you will do more work with it in Chapter 8. For now, let's begin with a review of how to put similar elements in the same form by using gerunds and infinitives.

PARALLEL STRUCTURE WITH INFINITIVES AND GERUNDS

In Chapter 2, you learned that verbs could become nouns by changing form. Here's a brief review of two common ways that verbs become nouns:

- An **infinitive** is formed by adding the word *to* to the base form of a verb, as in *to go, to see, to be, to follow*.
- A **gerund** is formed by adding *ing* to the base form of a verb, as in *going, seeing, being,* and *following*.

One way writing can lack parallel structure is by presenting a list of items as a mixture of gerunds and infinitives. Here's an example:

Incorrect: Charley's favorite activities are *golfing, to fish,* and *swimming.*

Correct: Charley's favorite activities are *golfing, fishing,* and *swimming.*

Or: Charley's favorite activities are *to golf, fish,* and *swim.*

Present lists of items in the same grammatical form. In the above example, the list was made parallel by presenting the items as *gerunds* and then as *infinitives.* Gerunds and infinitives develop into phrases when an object and/or modifiers follow. For example:

Gerund Phrases	Infinitive Phrases
asking for a raise	to insist on the facts
talking to the right person	to find the best reason

When you have a list of words or phrases, make sure that you present them in the same form.

PRACTICE

Instructions: Edit the following sentences for parallel structure.

Incorrect: The new intern's duties include leading tours, to call customers, and stock deliveries.

Corrected: The new intern's duties include leading tours, *calling* customers, and *stocking* deliveries.

VOCABULARY: NEW WORDS

Added to the *Oxford Dictionary of English* in 2005:

wiki, noun: A Web site or database developed collaboratively by a community of users, allowing any user to add and edit content.

podcast, noun: A digital recording, of a radio broadcast or similar program, that is made available on the Internet for downloading to a personal audio player.

Added to the *American Heritage Dictionary* in 2005:

yoctosecond, noun: One septillionth (10^{-24}) of a second.

• Internet Exercise 4.2

Verb Worksheets: For more practice with the topics reviewed in this chapter, visit the Web site at **www.mhhe.com/youngBE** and select the "Chapter 4" link to get started.

1. You should focus on getting the job done and to call customers.

2. I will plan to attending the meeting and answering their questions.

3. Your enthusiasm will go a long way toward improving customer relations and get people involved.

4. The building foreman has requested that all residents keep up with changes and making an effort to notify management about their plans.

5. Ask your team to spend more time calling clients and to inform them of the changes.

Review the original memo and determine the kinds of changes you would make to improve it before examining the revised version.

BOX 4.1 The Editing Process

BEFORE

TO: Human Resources Department
CC:
FROM: Marjorie Allen

To Whom It May Concern:

An announcement was made by my manager that human resource has a position opening for a sales representative position. The opportunity is a great match for my background and qualifications, I am just finishing my degree in communication which allow me to bring good skills to the position. Being a part-time employee of the bank for over three years; I have gain a valuable knowledge of the policies and programs that make the bank the workplace that it is. The training classes and work experience has been a valuable asset that makes me better able to face the challenges of the sales position you are seeking to fill.

My skills and abilities are summarized in the attached resume. I look forward to hearing from you so tht we can this opportunity further.

Marjorie Allen

AFTER

TO: Mark Miller, Human Resources Manager
CC:
FROM: Marjorie Allen

Dear Mr. Miller:

My manager recently announced that you have an opening for a sales representative. I would like to apply for that position, and my résumé is attached.

My background and qualifications would be a great match for the position. I am just finishing my degree in communication, which has prepared me to speak and write effectively on the job. In addition, I have been a part-time employee of the bank for over three years. During that time, I have gained valuable experience and training that will make me a success in the position of sales representative.

Please let me know if you have time to meet with me to discuss this exciting position. I will call you in a day or two to see if there is a time for us to meet. In the meantime, you can reach me at 312-555-1212.

Marjorie

Marjorie Allen
Administrative Assistant
Accounts Receivable
Mailcode 0042

PARALLEL STRUCTURE WITH ACTIVE AND PASSIVE VOICE

As you learned in Section C of this chapter, active voice is often the voice of choice because it is direct, clear, and concise. Writers sometimes shift unnecessarily between active and passive voice within the same sentence. The result is writing that sounds choppy and lacks flow.

Here are a few examples:

Weak: I assigned sales territories last week, and all managers were informed.

Revised: I assigned sales territories last week and informed all managers.

Weak: A message was left for Mark, but I didn't receive a call back.

Revised: I left a message for Mark but didn't receive a call back.

PRACTICE

Instructions: Edit the following sentences for parallel structure with active and passive voice. **For example:**

Weak: Adam completed the report, and it was given to the chair of the department.

Revised: Adam completed the report and *gave* it to the chair of the department.

1. We have received mail all week, and now it must be sorted.
2. An invoice was sent to you last week, and we are expecting payment by the 10th of this month.
3. Projects have been assigned, but I will consider changes if made in writing.
4. An invitation was not sent to them, so I do not expect a reply from them.
5. Hotel reservations were made, but I need to change them.

For more practice with parallel structure, complete EOC Activity 8 on page 128.

SECTION D CONCEPT CHECK

1. How does a verb become an infinitive? A gerund? Give an example of each.
2. What is the effect when writing lacks parallel structure?

CHAPTER 4 SUMMARY

If you have mastered the principles in this chapter, you have gone a long way toward developing a foundation for powerful, credible writing. Here is a review of the principles you need to understand:

- **Verb Principle 1:** When using regular verbs in past time, add *ed* to the base to form the past tense and past participle.
- **Verb Principle 2:** When using verbs in past time, do *not* use a helper verb with the past tense form; however, you must use a helper verb with the past participle.
- **Verb Principle 3:** In simple present tense, apply the *s* form correctly to third-person singular verbs.
- **Verb Principle No. 4:** Within the same sentence and paragraph, do not shift tense unnecessarily.

Your issues with verbs won't go away on their own. Review the summary of verb tenses in Table 4.3, and do serious work on the end-of-chapter activities. If you still feel uneasy about some concepts, do the additional exercises on the Web. Invest the time and attention needed for you to become proficient with this most important part of speech.

CHAPTER 4 CHECKLIST

When composing business messages, consider the following:

____ Use helper verbs with irregular past participles.

____ Do not use helper verbs for irregular past tense.

____ Ensure that verb tense is consistent.

____ Check for parallel structure.

____ Check word endings (regular past tense verbs, *s* form).

____ Write in the active voice.

____ Apply subjunctive mood in speech and writing to wishes, commands, requests, or recommendations.

____ Apply subjunctive mood to improbable statements.

____ Pronounce word endings clearly, focusing on *s*-form and *ed* endings.

TABLE 4.3 | Verb Tenses

	Past	Present	Future
Simple tense	wrote *(an action that ended at a point in the past)*	write, writes *(an action that exists, is usual, or is repeated)*	will write *(an action that will happen in the future)*
Progressive *(be + main verb + ing)*	was writing *(an action was happening in the past)*	am/is/are writing *(an action that is happening now)*	will be writing *(an action that will be happening over time, in the future)*
Perfect (*have* + main verb)	had written *(an action that ended before another action or time in the past)*	has/have written *(an action that started in the past and was recently completed or is still ongoing)*	will have written *(an action that will end before another action or time in the future)*
Perfect Progressive *(have + be + main verb + ing)*	had been writing *(an action that happened over time, in the past, before another time or action in the past)*	has/have been writing *(an action occurring over time that started in the past and continues into the present)*	will have been writing *(an action occurring over time, in the future, before another action or time in the future)*

CHAPTER 4 END-OF-CHAPTER ACTIVITIES

ACTIVITY 1: PROCESS MEMO

INSTRUCTIONS: What kinds of insights have you had about the way you use verbs? Do you use verbs differently in your local language than you do in Business English? Review the goals that you wrote at the beginning of this chapter and then write your instructor a process memo describing your learning experiences, what you have achieved, and what you are currently working on. Have your skills improved? Do you feel more confident now?

If you have Internet access, you can complete this exercise online at **www.mhhe.com/youngBE** and then send an e-mail to your instructor.

ACTIVITY 2: IRREGULAR VERBS

PART A

INSTRUCTIONS: For each of the following verbs, write the past tense and past participle forms in the lines provided.

Base Form	Past Tense	Past Participle
be (am, is, are)	___________	___________
break	___________	___________
bring	___________	___________
buy	___________	___________
choose	___________	___________
cost	___________	___________
do	___________	___________
drink	___________	___________
drive	___________	___________
eat	___________	___________
fall	___________	___________
find	___________	___________
fly	___________	___________
forgive	___________	___________
freeze	___________	___________
get	___________	___________
give	___________	___________

go	___________	___________
hold	___________	___________
know	___________	___________
lay (to place)	___________	___________
lie (to recline)	___________	___________
lie (to speak untruth)	___________	___________
lend	___________	___________
lose	___________	___________
prove	___________	___________
ride	___________	___________
say	___________	___________
see	___________	___________
sell	___________	___________
set	___________	___________
sink	___________	___________
sit	___________	___________
show	___________	___________
swim	___________	___________
take	___________	___________
teach	___________	___________
throw	___________	___________
understand	___________	___________

PART B

INSTRUCTIONS: Circle the correct verb in each of the sentences below.

1. Mr. Juarez (threw, thrown) his briefcase on his desk.
2. The papers were (took, taken) out of the briefcase and put in a folder.
3. Jeff, Mr. Juarez's assistant, usually (keeped, kept) important contract papers in sealed folders.
4. Obviously, Jeff had (forgot, forgotten) to use the correct folders for the contract.

5. Mr. Juarez was surprised that Jeff had not (did, done) the task that he had asked him to do earlier in the day.
6. Nevertheless, because Jeff had (gone, went) to great lengths to prepare the contract, Mr. Juarez was not angry.

PART C

INSTRUCTIONS: In the following paragraph, you will find six incorrect irregular verbs in past time. Cross out the incorrect verb and write the correct form above it.

We had wore uniforms in the past, but our manager changed the regulations last month. I'm glad we don't have to wear uniforms anymore, because mine shrinked in the wash. I was so upset when I done it that I kicked the washing machine. After that, I throwed the ruined uniform in the garbage. Also, I had gave my other uniform to my sister, who also works here. I didn't know what to say when she asked me where my other uniform had went.

ACTIVITY 3: REGULAR VERBS

PART A

INSTRUCTIONS: To complete the sentences below, fill in each blank with the correct form of the verb shown in parentheses.

1. Last year when I (work) __________ at the bank, I received lots of training.
2. Also, my manager (permit) ____________ me to attend seminars at the university.
3. My manager, Shelly, (rely) _________ on me to keep my skills updated.
4. I (study) __________ many computer applications.
5. Unfortunately, when Shelly (relocate) ___________ to another office, the training budget was reallocated.
6. Lack of funds has not (stop) __________ my learning, however. Now I take courses at my community college.

PART B

INSTRUCTIONS: In the following paragraph, you will find six incorrect regular verbs in past time. Cross out the incorrect verb and write the correct form above it.

The Springdale Police Department offers citizen safety training last summer. I hope they will offer it again. I had so much fun and learnt a lot. When I arrive at the class last summer, something very interesting occurred. One of the students had recently been rob of his backpack and had use a technique call "using your environment." The student pulled off one of his rollerblades and threw it at the robber's ankles causing him to trip and drop the backpack!

ACTIVITY 4: SPEAKING BUSINESS—VERBS WITH *ed* ENDINGS

INSTRUCTIONS: A verb with the *ed* ending can end in one of three possible sounds: "d," "t," or "ted." Practice each of these sounds by doing the following:

1. *Verbs ending with the "d" or "duh" sound:* At the end of each word, your tongue should land behind your teeth, at the roof of your mouth. Practice pronouncing the following words: *learned, exchanged, filled, pledged, finalized, listened.*
2. *Verbs ending with the "t" or "tah" sound:* At the end of each word, the tip of your tongue should land on the roof of your mouth, behind your teeth. Practice pronouncing the following words: *walked, marked, clipped, focused.*
3. *Verbs ending with the "ted" sound:* Practice pronouncing the following words: *acted, limited, united, amounted.*

INSTRUCTIONS: Develop a list that contains three verbs from each of the three categories described above. Write a sentence using each verb in the past tense. (See the Speaking Business sidebar on page 113.)

ACTIVITY 5: SUBJUNCTIVE MOOD

PART A

INSTRUCTIONS: The following sentences are written in the subjunctive mood. Complete each sentence by writing the correct present or past verb form in the blank.

1. It is essential that you __________ early for our meetings.
2. He acts as if he __________ the boss!
3. I suggest that you __________ available for your clients.
4. I wish I __________ better prepared for the presentation.
5. If this meeting __________ any longer, I couldn't stay awake.
6. Ms. Deem asks that the receptionist _________ particular attention to new clients.

PART B

INSTRUCTIONS: In the following paragraph, you will find incorrect subjunctive verbs. Cross out the incorrect verb and write the correct form above it.

Danica, the director of operations, asked that my department joins her in the weekly meetings. She demanded that all employees are responsible for knowing the agenda ahead of time. If I was the director, I would send a hard copy of the agenda as well as an e-mail. It is essential that every employee understands what will be discussed. If I was Danica, I would send out the agendas well in advance of the meetings.

ACTIVITY 6: VERB CONSISTENCY

PART A

INSTRUCTIONS: The following sentences contain errors in tense; make corrections where necessary.

1. We were on our way to the movie when our car breaks down.

2. We all agree on the new procedure and signed off on it.

3. After examining how we handled the problem, we should use a different approach.

4. At the board meeting, Olivia announces her engagement and resigned from her position.

5. We will hire a new attorney, and she handles all future cases.

6. The client complained about poor phone support and requests a different product.

PART B

INSTRUCTIONS: Correct the unnecessary verb shifts in the paragraph below.

On my business trip, I flew on American Airlines and rent a car from Johnson Car Rental. They give me a minivan even though I request a sports car. At the convention center, I parked next to my rival salesperson, and she drives up in a rented Jaguar. I ask her which rental company she used, and she tells me that I always should use Budget Rentals. I am surprised and told her so.

ACTIVITY 7: ACTIVE VOICE

PART A

INSTRUCTIONS: Change the following sentences from passive to active voice. For example:

Weak: The report was given to me by my supervisor.

Revised: My supervisor gave me the report.

1. The meeting was scheduled by Jordan.

2. A full report will be given to you by our accounting department.

3. An effective solution was offered by the consulting firm from Dallas.

4. Major considerations about the proposal were brought up by my executive vice president.

5. The new patent attorney was hired by our human resources department at our Detroit branch.

PART B

INSTRUCTIONS: Revise the following paragraph so that sentences are written in the active voice.

The three-mile walk was announced by our human resources director. However, the purpose of the event was not explained clearly. As a result, the event was not attended by many people from my department. More funds would have been raised by our employees if they had known that the walk was a fundraiser for one of our employees.

ACTIVITY 8: PARALLEL STRUCTURE

INSTRUCTIONS: Revise the following sentences to achieve parallel structure. For example:

Incorrect: William encouraged us to join the task force and that recommendations be given to the team leader.

Corrected: William encouraged us to join the task force and give recommendations to the team leader.

1. The rules of the office are never take longer than a one-hour lunch break, never gossip about fellow employees, and not to smoke in the building.

2. I asked, was begging, and finally demanding a raise.

3. During my review, Mr. Chandler told me that I performed well, was meeting his expectations, and had been doing a good job.

4. Don't forget to read the report, to review the suggested revisions, and writing down your ideas.

5. LaShandra was told that she would be promoted, receive a raise, and to move into the bigger office.

6. Lee will have signed the agreement, make photocopies of it, and was mailing it back today.

7. Please read the proposed contract, put your signature on the last page, and returning it to us promptly.

8. When we first started our restaurant, we watched every penny and lots of long hours were worked.

9. Sophie told us she had written the report and had been distributing it for the meeting as well.

10. Your driving directions were confusing to me and caused me to miss the meeting.

11. We spent the last of our paychecks betting on horses, bought lottery tickets, and eating at a nice restaurant.

12. After the merger, we will work closely with our new counterparts, learning new procedures, and will have to compromise on many issues.

ACTIVITY 9: PUNCTUATION REVIEW— COMMA AND SEMICOLON RULES

INSTRUCTIONS: Correct the punctuation errors in the following sentences.

1. The VIP arrived late to the reception however we were still not prepared.

2. When you go on an interview make sure you bring an updated résumé.

3. We did not write the proposal within their guidelines yet they accepted it.

4. They requested us to bring the quarterly reports to the meeting not the weekly reports.

5. Brandon my sales representative gave me samples of the new product.

6. Our bank needs to issue a check to Barbra Krandall she has been expecting it for a week.

7. Team building can strengthen your team however training will not correct character flaws.

8. Find the time to do the report and stop making excuses.

9. A mission statement will bring focus to your group but everyone needs to believe in it.

10. When the UPS shipment arrives Jeremy let me know.

ACTIVITY 10: CUMULATIVE CHAPTER REVIEW

INSTRUCTIONS: Correct the errors in the following sentences.

1. The decision is political, and it was not made with everyone's interests in mind.

2. Human Resources had finally wrote a policy to alleviate hiring complaints.

3. Our department would've went to the conference, but corporate doesn't ask us.

4. The comptroller had request that the updated financials be sent out, but I forgot.

5. Their recommendations were to improve employee benefits, making provision for internal advancement, and the sick-day policy be changed.

6. Ramond is nervous, but he presented the information with eloquence.

7. If Margaret still don't know the answer, send an e-mail to Della.

8. The annual budget was officially froze because of the changes in the economy.

9. To correct the problem, they issued a report, are speaking to the press, and plan to hire a public relations firm.

10. Our corporate office has never went to outside sources for input to major decisions.

ACTIVITY 11: "WRITER'S REFERENCE MANUAL" DRILL

INSTRUCTIONS: In the "Writer's Reference Manual" at the end of this text, read the entry "affixes" and then answer the following questions.

1. What is an affix?

____

2. A word can be made up of three parts; what are they?

____

3. Indicate the meaning of the following prefixes and suffixes.

Prefix/Suffix	Meaning
-able	__________
bi-	__________
de-	__________
dis-	__________
-er	__________
-ful	__________
im-	__________
-ly or -y	__________
-ment	__________
mis-	__________
-ness	__________
-ous	__________
pre-	__________
re-	__________
un-	__________

ACTIVITY 12: VOCABULARY LIST

A. COMMONLY MISSPELLED WORDS

INSTRUCTIONS: The list below contains words taken from a compilation of the 500 most commonly misspelled words and from the chapter. Practice them until you can spell them automatically and use them correctly.

1. accrual — (n) accumulation, increase (an *accrual* of funds)
2. appearance — (n) looks, outward show, emergence
3. argument — (n) quarrel; a formal analysis or comparison
4. conscience — (n) sense of right and wrong
5. description — (n) narrative, depiction, explanation
6. domain — (n) the part of a Web address that follows the "dot" (e.g., *.com, .org, .net*)
7. gauche — (adj) uncouth, awkward
8. inedible — (adj) not to be eaten, indigestible
9. interference — (n) intervention, obstruction
10. mediocre — (adj) average, ordinary, second rate
11. occurrence — (n) incident, happening
12. preferred — (adj) favored (or past tense form of *to prefer*)
13. miscellaneous — (adj) various, diverse
14. presumptuous — (adj) presuming, arrogant
15. receipt — (n) acknowledgment, receiving, acceptance

B. SIMILAR WORDS

INSTRUCTIONS: The list below contains similar words, some of which are profiled in the Vocabulary Builders in each chapter. Use these words in sentences until their meaning becomes clear.

imply/infer: These two words are easily confused even though they mean the opposite of each other: *imply* means to suggest a meaning; *infer* means to conclude or interpret a meaning.

When the chairperson *implied* that the spending was out of line, the committee members *inferred* that there was a budget problem.

personal/personnel: *Personal* refers to a particular person. *Personnel* refers to a body of persons employed by an organization; *personnel* is also an administrative division of an organization.

Do not let *personal* problems affect your work.

There are many *personnel* issues to discuss at our next meeting.

may be/maybe: *May be* is a verb phrase suggesting possibility; *maybe* is an adverb meaning "perhaps."

He *may be* the next mayor.

Maybe it will rain tomorrow.

reason that/because: Use *that*, not *because,* after *reason.*

The *reason* she took the job was *that* she considered it a challenge.

She took the job *because* she considered it a challenge.

THE INBOX

COMPOSING

Compose a brief description of yourself using the prompts below. Each response should be at least five sentences, but you are certainly free to write more. Remember, this is not a graded exercise but an opportunity to integrate your critical-thinking skills with your newly refreshed knowledge of verb tense.

"I Was, I Am, I Will Be, I Wish I Were"

1. At one time in my life, I was . . .
2. At this time in my life, I am . . .
3. In five years, I will be . . .
4. I wish I were . . .

REFLECTING

Reread your "I Was . . . " composition. If you randomly changed the verb tenses, what effect would this have?

Can you identify the verbs and verb phrases in your composition and identify their tenses? Try to find one example of each verb tense in your "I Was . . . " piece. (Don't mark up your paper; keep a separate list because you will use your paper in the exercise below.)

DISCUSSING

1. Some languages have only one verb tense. Imagine a conversation in English using only the present tense. For example, instead of saying "I played basketball yesterday," the speaker of such a language would say, "I play basketball yesterday." Try to discuss what you did yesterday or the day before with another student using only the present tense. What difficulties arise?
2. Using a clean copy of your "I Was . . . " composition, exchange papers with another student. Identify examples of the verb tenses.
3. In a small group, create a paragraph using as many of your vocabulary words as possible (pages 132). See which group can use the most words in their paragraph and still have it make sense. Of course, pay special attention to verb tense.

EDITING

You are the editor of the college's career advice column in the student newspaper. This week your columnist has submitted an article on interview tips. Edit the article so that it is ready to go to print; look for punctuation, verb use, and spelling and word choice errors.

Interview Savvy: Part 1
By Randi Patal

This column will present a series on job interview skills over the next three issue. Part 1 covered interview preperation.

Weather you are interviewing for your dream job or to look for a part-time position to offset your college expenses; interview savvy will help you obtain your gole. many people who are qualify for positions they are seeking eliminate themselves from the competition within the first few minutes of their interview.

The first point to consider, is that first impressions does make a difference. A manager, at a local sports facility told me, "I don't care if our work environment is informal. An interview is an interview. Don't show up in flip-flops and shorts. That's a sign of disrespect. On the other hand, a person who shows up in neat, conservative clothing shows that he or she cares about detail and how he or she appears to others." Along these lines keep in mind, that the nature of the job do not excuse sloppy dressing. You are at the interview to proved that you are someone who are; reliable, mature, and dependable. A sloppy appearance will contradicts that image.

Another point, you should keeping in mind, is that it your responsibility to research the commpany before attend the interview. I recently watch a sitcom in which one of the characters was about to leave home for an interview. "What does this company do?" asked another character. "That's the first thing I'm going to ask when I get there," reply the first character. While such an attitude is amusing on a television show it will not be amusing to the person interviews you. Take time to look up the company's Web site for information about the company's mission statement products or services history locations, and organizational structure. You knowledge of the company will show your interviewer that you be truly interest in working for the company.

Another way to prepare for the interview is practicing to answer anticipated questions. Write down a list of questions that an employer might be ask, and then have a friend to help you practice. Actually responding aloud will help prepare you by give you confidence and experience. Springville's Career Advising Center offer mock interviews for students free of charge. Just stop in the center, which be located in Building C, Room 2114, to make an appointment. The Career Advising Center have lots of experience helping students understand what companies want from their personal.

The final point in today's segment is punctuality. One reason to arriving between ten to fifteen minutes early is because you can stop in the restroom to freshen up and checking your appearance in the mirror. You can also use this time to rehearse your responses and reviewing the commpany information in your mind. Finally if you, checks in with the receptionist approximately five minutes earlier than you scheduled appointment time; your interviewer will have time to finish what he or she is doing and prepare to focus on time with you. You will also demonstrated that you are dependable and respectful of other people's time. If you was the one give the interview, you would want the candidate to be on time. The receptionist will probably alert the interviewer that you were here, ask you to set down for a few minutes.

In next month's issue looked for Part 2 of this series which will address body language, specific questions you should ask during the interview, and how to end the interview on a positive note.

KEY TO LEARNING INVENTORY

1. T
2. F
3. F
4. T
5. T
6. F
7. T
8. T
9. T
10. F

CHAPTER 4 ENDNOTE

1. Melinda G. Kramer et al., *Prentice Hall Handbook for Writers,* New Jersey, 1991, p. 57.

Chapter Five

Pronouns

As far as I'm concerned, whom *is a word that was invented to make everyone sound like a butler.*
—Calvin Trillin, writer (1935–)

Do you use pronouns correctly? Does figuring out the difference between *I* and *me* or *who* and *whom* seem to get your head spinning? If so, you are not alone. Many of the problems you have with pronouns may have started when you were very young. Every time you made a comment such as "Me and my friend are leaving," you may have been corrected.

As a result of being corrected for misusing the pronoun *me,* many people avoid its use. Instead, they do what some call "hypercorrecting," which is selecting a word that sounds more sophisticated or professional than the correct choice. As a result, many people use the pronoun *I* when *me* would be correct. Another pronoun that people misuse for *me* is the pronoun *myself.*

Smart, professional people can make serious and obvious mistakes with pronouns, so you can't model your use of pronouns on the way others use them. Otherwise, if you hear someone in authority using pronouns incorrectly, your insecurity would cause you to pick up the error—it's sort of like catching a virus. To avoid making other people's mistakes your own, you must base your decisions on basic principles.

Knowing when to use *who* and *whom* can be challenging, but so can achieving pronoun-antecedent agreement and a consistent point of view. Within a short time, you will use pronouns correctly, and you will master them by learning a few basic principles.

To learn more about The Writing Process, please visit our Web site at **www.mhhe.com/youngBE**

Outline

Chapter 5: Pronouns

Section A: Pronoun Case

Section B: More on Subjects and Objects

Section C: Agreement and Point of View

Section D: Collective Nouns and Indefinite Pronouns

Objectives

When you have completed your study of Chapter 5, you will be able to:

1. Demonstrate correct use of subjective and objective pronouns.
2. Use possessive and reflexive pronouns correctly.
3. Apply consistent point of view with pronouns in writing.
4. Compare and contrast local-language patterns of using pronouns and Business English patterns.
5. Use pronouns correctly in speech and writing.
6. Be aware of the correct use of pronouns to avoid gender bias.
7. Identify singular and plural indefinite pronouns, and use them accordingly.

Learning Inventory

1. The pronoun *I* can be used as an object if it comes at the end of a sentence. T/F
2. Pronouns are categorized by cases. T/F
3. One way to find out if you can use *I* is to substitute *we.* T/F
4. When you don't know whether to use *who* or *whom,* use *that.* T/F
5. Pronouns sometimes need to agree with their antecedents. T/F
6. After the conjunction *than,* use a subjective pronoun when the verb is implied. T/F
7. The possessive pronoun *mine* is never made plural by adding an *s.* T/F
8. The pronoun *her's* shows possession. T/F
9. Only use the reflexive pronoun *myself* if it refers back to *I.* T/F
10. A common mistake with pronouns is using *I* when *me* is correct. T/F

Goal-Setting Exercises

Are pronouns challenging? What kinds of remarks do you receive on your papers about pronouns? Are there pronouns that you sometimes are unsure about, such as *me, myself, whom,* or *I?* Write three goals about the changes you want to make in your writing and speaking when it comes to using pronouns.

1. ______________________________

2. ______________________________

3. ______________________________

SECTION A: PRONOUN CASE

Pronouns are challenging partly because most people aren't even aware of the kinds of mistakes that they make: sometimes when *they think* that they sound their best, they are making obvious errors. If you aren't sure of pronoun use, learning the basic principles in this chapter will help you quickly become more proficient.

A **pronoun** is a word that is used in place of a noun or another pronoun. Words such as *I, you,* and *me* are personal pronouns because they indicate the person who is speaking, spoken to, or spoken about. Personal pronouns are categorized by **case,** and errors occur when pronoun case is used incorrectly. Here are the basic pronoun cases:

- Subjective
- Objective
- Possessive
- Reflexive

Now let's review each case and how to use it correctly.

HOW PRONOUN CASES WORK

When you write or speak, select a pronoun on the basis of the pronoun's function in the sentence. Here are the types of pronouns and the roles they play:

- *Subjective* pronouns are used as *subjects* of verbs.
- *Objective* pronouns are used as *objects* (usually of verbs or prepositions).
- *Possessive* pronouns *show possession* (of nouns or other pronouns).
- *Reflexive* pronouns reflect back to *subjective pronouns.*

Table 5.1 displays the singular and plural forms of the four basic cases in the first, second, and third person.

Let's review each pronoun case and see a few examples.

TABLE 5.1 | Pronouns: Four Basic Cases

This table displays the singular and plural forms of the four basic cases in the first, second, and third persons. You can determine the appropriate pronoun on the basis of the pronoun's function in the sentence.

	Subjective	Objective	Possessive	Reflexive
Singular:				
First person	I	me	my, mine	myself
Second person	you	you	your, yours	yourself
Third person	he, she, it who	him, her, it whom	his, hers, its whose	himself, herself, itself
Plural:				
First person	we	us	our, ours	ourselves
Second person	you	you	your, yours	yourselves
Third person	they	them	their, theirs	themselves

WRITER'S TOOLKIT

Rule-of-Thumb Substitution

If *we* can be substituted for the pair, use *I.* If *us* can be substituted for the pair, use *me.*

Incorrect: *Joe and me* are going to the meeting.

You would never say "*Us* are going to the meeting." Since you can't substitute the objective pronoun *us,* you can't use the objective pronoun *me* in the sentence above.

Incorrect: You can give *Joe and I* the details.

You would never say: "You can give *we* the details." Since you can't use the subjective pronoun *we,* you also can't use the subjective pronoun *I* in the sentence above.

If you still can't figure out whether to use *I* or *me,* take "Joe" out of the sentence. The correct pronoun will be obvious:

Correct: *I* am going to the meeting.

You can give *me* the details.

So remember, the next time you have difficulty deciding between the pronouns *I* and *me,* substitute *we* or *us* or remove the other person's name from the sentence.

VOCABULARY: SOUNDALIKES

Your/You're: These words are both pronouns; however, they have distinctly different functions. *Your* is a possessive pronoun and is always followed by a noun. (Nouns are underscored in the examples below.)

Your coffee spilled on the table.

Your assignments are organized by due date.

You gave us *your* direct phone number.

You're is a contraction of *you are.*

You're late for the Koller seminar.

Mr. Simms said that *you're* not interested in programming.

You're doing just fine without us.

SUBJECTIVE AND OBJECTIVE CASE PRONOUNS

Subjective, or *nominative,* pronouns are subjects of verbs. "Subject" pronouns must be followed by a verb (either real or implied), as shown in the following examples:

Marchand and *I* will prepare the report.

He and *I* became friends in college.

Jose has less time than *I* (have).

Simon sings better than *I* (do).

Can you think of a few examples using subjective pronouns? One of your examples should demonstrate how to use a subjective pronoun after the conjunction *than.*

1. ______

2. ______

3. ______

Objective pronouns are objects (and cannot be used as subjects). "Object" pronouns can be objects of verbs, infinitives, prepositions, or other types of phrases.

You can bring *him* with you to the annual sales event.

The manager included Alfonse and *me* in the team meeting.

(You) Please keep this information between *you* and *me.*

Can you think of a few examples using the objective pronouns *me, him,* and *her?* One of your examples should demonstrate how to use objective pronouns after the preposition *between.*

1. ______

2. ______

3. ______

PRACTICE

Instructions: Revise the sentences below by correcting pronoun case. **For example:**

Incorrect: Make sure you give your proposal to Margie and I before May 29.

Corrected: Make sure you give your proposal to Margie and *me* before May 29.

1. Dr. Soto replied that her and her husband will attend the charity ball.

2. Noel and me will also attend.

Noel & I

3. Either him or I will arrive early to greet the guests.

either he or I

4. The foundation called to ask both she and I to make a donation.

her and I

5. Gianna and her can also arrive early to set out the place cards.

gianna and she

POSSESSIVE AND REFLEXIVE CASE PRONOUNS

Possessive pronouns show possession. Notice that possessive pronouns such as *its, hers,* and *mine* do not have an apostrophe to show possession.

The book is *hers.*

You can't judge a book by *its cover.*

Their comments were unjustified.

Jonathan said that the books were on the counter, but I didn't see *mine.*

I looked in the stack of folders, but *mine*'s (mine is) not there.

Now think of a few examples of your own using the possessive pronouns. Make sure that one of your sentences contains *mine* or *mine*'s *(mine is).*

1. ____

2. ____

3. ____

Reflexive case pronouns are used when their corresponding noun or subjective case pronoun is already in the sentence. Reflexive case is often called the *intensive case* because it places attention or intensifies its **antecedent** (the word it refers to).

If you prefer, *I* will assist you *myself.*

Tricia said that *she* would complete the project *herself.*

Lucas rewarded *himself* for doing a fine job on the presentation.

Paulo and *Bill* helped *themselves* to the appetizers.

Local languages sometimes use different forms for the reflexive pronouns *himself* and *themselves,* such as "hisself" for *himself* and "theyselves" or "theirselves" for *themselves.*

Can you think of a few examples of your own using reflexive pronouns? Make sure one of your sentences includes *myself.*

1. ____

2. ____

3. ____

PRACTICE

Instructions: Revise the sentences below by correcting pronoun case. **For example:**

Incorrect: You can call Joe or myself to get the latest information.

Corrected: You can call Joe or *me* to get the latest information.

1. These boxes belong in Mr. Menendez's office; the other boxes belong in our's.

2. I have seen both proposals, but I still don't see the difference between you and her's.

3. Has yourself created these slides and visual aids?

4. The presenters wrote the script for the presentation theirselves.

5. The next presentation will be given by Roberto, Angelique, and myself.

SPEAKING BUSINESS

Mine Is/Mine Are: The pronoun *mine* creates problems for many. That's because when several items are involved, speakers often think that the pronoun *mine* should become plural. However, when *mine* is used as a pronoun, it is always singular and should never end in *s.*

When an *s* is added to the pronoun *mine,* it is preceded by an apostrophe and creates the contraction *mine's,* meaning "mine is." For example,

Where is your book? *Mine's* in my car.

If the speaker is referring to multiple items, the contraction cannot be formed:

Where are your books? *Mine are* in my car.

Of course, the word *mine* can be a noun, as in *coal mine* or *diamond mine.* As a noun, *mine* can become plural; for example, many *coal mines* are located in West Virginia.

Ask Yourself: *Do I have a tendency to add an* s *to* mine *when I am referring to plural items?*

SECTION A CONCEPT CHECK

1. Pronouns can be categorized into what major cases?

2. Can the pronoun *myself* be used in a sentence *without* referring to another pronoun?

3. Explain the difference between *I* and *me.*

SECTION B: MORE ON SUBJECTS AND OBJECTS

Speakers and writers alike have challenges deciding between *who* and *whom.* Other challenges relate to whether a subject or an object follows words such as *than* or *between.* This section gives you a bit more practice on correctly placing pronouns as subjects and objects in sentences.

Language Diversity

The Pronoun *Yous:* In Ireland,[1] *yous* is a plural form of *you.* In fact, the English language used to have a plural form of *you,* but that was back in the fourteenth and fifteenth centuries and was eventually dropped. Then, in the seventeenth and eighteenth centuries, some people tried to distinguish between singular and plural by making changes to the verb: *you is* and *you are* were used but then abandoned. Eventually, Irish speakers of English decided to distinguish between the singular and plural by adding an *s* to *you,* and thus the birth of *yous.* At times, the word *yis* or *yiz* is used in place of *yous.*

So if you are wondering why some New Yorkers or Chicagoans use the plural form of *you,* as in "yous guys," they come by it honestly. Irish immigrants brought the form over to the states probably about the turn of the last century.

Other forms of *yous* are "y'all," "all y'all," or "you'ins." *What form of* yous *do you use?*

PRONOUNS FOLLOWING THE PREPOSITION *BETWEEN*

Many speakers make mistakes with pronouns following the preposition *between.* Since *between* is a preposition, an object would normally follow it. Here are some examples:

Incorrect: Donald divided the project between Chuck and *I.*

Correct: Donald divided the project between Chuck and *me.*

Or: Donald divided the project between *us.*

Incorrect: Arlene suggested that the work be split between *she* and Elaine.

Correct: Arlene suggested that the work be split between *her* and Elaine.

Arlene suggested that the work be split between *them.*

Incorrect: Rosalie is the person *that* offered to help us.

Correct: Rosalie is the person *who* offered to help us.

Incorrect: Charlie is the one *that* spoke up at the meeting.

Correct: Charlie is the one *who* spoke up at the meeting.

When you are referring to a "class or category," you may use the word *that.*

Suzie is *the kind of* employee *that* works diligently.

Bart is *the type of* football player *that* wins games.

In each of the above examples, *kind of* or *type of* is part of the antecedent, making the use of *that* acceptable. However, even in these cases, *who* would have also been acceptable; for example, "Suzie is the kind of student who works diligently."

Your speech and writing will sound more sophisticated if you use *who* instead of *that* when referring to people. Another way to improve speech is to pronounce *who* correctly:

Incorrect: Whoja go to the ball game with?

Acceptable: Who did you go to the ball game with?

Formal: With whom did you go to the ball game?

VOCABULARY WORD USAGE

Who/Whom: Tips for deciding whether to use *who* or *whom:*

1. If you need a subject, the obvious answer is *who.*
2. If the word does not function as a subject, use *whom.*
3. When in doubt, use *who* and do not worry about it. (It sounds much worse to use *whom* incorrectly; *whom* used incorrectly sounds bad to everyone, even people who do not know the correct use of *who/whom.*)
4. Another tip is to substitute *he* for *who* and *him* for *whom.* (This will work in most, but not all, situations.)

Incorrect: Whom (him) goes there?

Whom (him) did that?

Correct: Who (he) goes there?

Who (he) did that?

PRACTICE

Circle the correct pronoun in the following sentences. **For example:**

(Who, Whom) presented the information to Alice's team?

Michael is the person (who, that) operates the machinery.

1. Please tell me (who, whom) created this presentation.
2. The person (who, whom) I saw presenting the material was quite professional.
3. Were you the speaker (who, that) presented in the Green Room this morning?
4. I didn't recognize (who, whom) I was speaking to
5. If I had known it was you (who, that) gave the presentation, I would have complimented you directly.

SECTION B CONCEPT CHECK

1. The word *between* is a preposition. Would a subjective or an objective pronoun follow it? Give an example of the kind of pronoun that would follow *between.*
2. The word *than* is a conjunction. Should a subjective or an objective pronoun follow it? Why?
3. When you use the pronouns *who, whom,* and *that,* which pronoun should *not* be used to refer to a person?

SECTION C: AGREEMENT AND POINT OF VIEW

Selecting the correct pronoun case is only part of the puzzle. When you use pronouns, they must agree with the words they represent and be used consistently. This section contains the information and practice you need to become proficient with this aspect of pronoun use.

PRONOUNS AND THEIR ANTECEDENTS

A pronoun must agree in number and gender with its antecedents; an **antecedent** is a word to which a pronoun refers. In the following example, *participants* is the antecedent of *they* and *their.*

> All *participants* must submit *their* applications immediately if *they* plan to attend the seminar.

Lack of agreement between pronouns and their antecedents creates an error. Here are some examples:

Incorrect: When *a person* listens, *they* need to stay focused.

When *one* listens, *he/she* needs to stay focused.

When *we* listen, *you* need to stay focused.

Correct: When a *person* listens, *he or she* needs to stay focused.

When *people* listen, *they* need to stay focused.

When *one* listens, *one* needs to stay focused.

When *we* listen, *we* need to stay focused.

A Pronoun Dilemma

Since pronouns must agree in number and gender with their antecedents, pronoun combinations such as *he or she* and *him or her* sometimes become necessary for correctness. However, these constructions are awkward.

In the past, a problem didn't seem to exist because people accepted the built-in gender bias of using *he, him,* or *his* for singular constructions. In the 1970s and 1980s this trend began to change. People started to become aware of the effect language can have on social and professional opportunities. As a result, the current pronoun dilemma came into the spotlight; but, unfortunately, this situation has no simple answer. One effective solution is using plural nouns as antecedents because plural pronouns are gender-neutral (*they, them*).

Your writing can be correct and flow smoothly by using plural nouns as antecedents, as in the following examples:

Awkward	Revised
A *person* must watch *his or her* diet.	*People* must watch *their* diets.
A *manager* listens to *his or her* employees.	*Managers* listen to *their* employees.
When a *friend* asks for help, *he or she* . . .	When *friends* ask for help, *they* . . .

You will learn more about this topic later in this chapter when you review gender-neutral writing.

PRACTICE

Instructions: Correct the following sentences for pronoun-antecedent agreement. **For example:**

Incorrect: When a manager gets promoted, they need to organize their responsibilities.

Corrected: When *managers* get promoted, they need to organize their responsibilities.

1. Each employee who wants their photo retaken for their ID card should see Marta tomorrow before 2 p.m.

2. When you arrive, one needs to have the old ID card to exchange for a new card.

3. The sales department will have their national convention in July this year.

4. Nobody should take more than their allotted share of free tickets to the concert.

5. Employees needing extra tickets should see his/her supervisor at least two days prior to the concert.

PRONOUN VIEWPOINT

Pronouns must have a consistent point of view (or viewpoint). By using a point of view to describe or narrate, a writer can be more direct and personal. Here are the various *viewpoints:*

	Singular	Plural
First person:	I	we
Second person:	you	you
Third person:	he, she, it	they
	a person	people
	one	

Here is the same sentence shown in the various viewpoints:

When *I* write, *I* must pay attention to every detail.

When *you* write, *you* must pay attention to every detail.

When a *person* writes, *he or she* must pay attention to every detail.

When *we* write, *we* must pay attention to every detail.

When *people* write, *they* must pay attention to every detail.

The only appropriate antecedent for *one* is *one; he or she* is *not* an antecedent for *one.* Though the viewpoint "one" is not used much in the United States, Great Britain and other English-speaking countries still use the one viewpoint in their speaking and writing. Here is the same example in the one viewpoint:

When *one* writes, *one* must pay attention to every detail.

Writers make mistakes by shifting viewpoints within the same sentence or among a group of sentences, as shown in the following examples:

Shifting Viewpoint

Incorrect: Listening is a skill that *we* should all improve. When *you* listen, *I* sometimes hear things that change *my* life.

Correct: Listening is a skill that *I* would like to improve. When *I* listen, *I* sometimes hear things that change *my* life.

VOCABULARY SOUNDALIKES

There/Their/They're: These three words are all pronouns; however, they have distinctly different functions.

- *There* is an *anticipating subject,* also known as an expletive form.

  There are too many questions to answer.

  There is an interesting play at the Goodman.

  There does not seem to be a problem.

- *Their* is a *possessive pronoun* and is always followed by a noun.

  Their dog ran into our yard.

  Their reports fell out of the file.

  They gave us *their* answer too late.

- *They're* is a contraction of *they are.*

  They're giving free cholesterol screenings at the clinic.

  George and Sue said that *they're* not interested in the antique clock.

  They're doing just fine without us.

To avoid confusion:

- With *there,* make sure a verb follows it (unless it is used as an adverb).
- With *their,* make sure a noun follows it.
- With *they're,* stop using the contraction and spell out *they are.*

Or: Listening is a skill that *we* should all improve. When *we* listen, *we* sometimes hear things that change *our* lives.

Or: Listening is a skill that *all* can improve. When *people* listen, *they* sometimes hear things that change *their* lives.

When a writer establishes a point of view, that point of view should remain consistent within sentences and paragraphs and at times throughout entire documents.

PRACTICE

Instructions: In the following paragraph, correct the pronouns and their antecedents so that you have a consistent point of view.

A new employee must understand that you will experience a period of adjustment at their new place of employment. Unfortunately, many new employees think that one's new supervisor and coworkers should adjust to you instead of the other way around. When you begin a new job, one should "lay low" for the first few months to learn the way this particular work environment functions. After one has held a position for three or four months, you can begin making appropriate suggestions and changes.

Pronouns and Gender Bias

When speaking from a point of view, keep your writing **gender-neutral.**

As mentioned, a few decades ago people commonly used language that was gender-biased, as did books, magazines, and newspapers. That is, when speaking from the third-person singular viewpoint, most speakers and writers defaulted to the masculine viewpoint: *he, him,* and *his.*

Gender bias is a form of discrimination. For example, think about speaking to an audience. You may quickly realize that you will disenfranchise half of it by speaking in *only* one viewpoint, masculine *or* feminine. To some degree, as language changes, so does thinking. Today, women enter professions that they were once blocked from solely because of their gender. Some people still discriminate on the basis of gender, and that's unfortunate.

Language has helped pave the path of gender equality. You can achieve gender-neutral language by adjusting the way you use pronouns, thereby respecting and reaching 100 percent of your audience. As a writer and speaker, use language in a conscious and an unbiased way. You will not only show respect but also be more respected. Here are some ways to remain gender-neutral:

1. Take out pronoun references when writing from a singular perspective:

   Weak: A manager should give *his or her* employees opportunities to share responsibility.

   Revised: A manager should give employees opportunities to share responsibility.

2. When possible, write from a plural perspective:

   First-person plural *(we, our, us):* *We* should give *our* employees opportunities to share responsibility.

   Third-person plural *(they, their, them, people):* *Managers* should give *their* employees opportunities to share responsibility.

3. Use the "you" point of view:

   Give *your* employees opportunities to share responsibility.

BOX 5.1 The Editing Process

BEFORE

Dear Sir and Madam;

When you think about it, everyone offers the traditional 3-year warranty; All-Pro Builders is the only one in the Construction industry that offers an additional 2years. That's 5 years total coverage on labor and material. That represents confidence, in both the workmanship and the material used.

Your potential customer recognizes this confidence when they hear of the 5- year expanded warrantee, and appreciated the added value at no addition cost!

My focas is servicing accounts thru marketing and developing. We will have booths at the Home and Garden Show, and Home Improvement Show this spring, and also a both at the Parade of Homes this summer. 5,000 brochures will be handed out introducing the expanded warranties program.

I'm looking forward to meeting you to show you examples of advertising that you would benefit from. Feel free to contact me at your earliest convenience. Thank you in advance for your time.

James Jones
Sales Representative

AFTER

Dear Home Builder:

Although everyone in the construction industry offers the traditional 3-year warranty, All-Pro Builders is the only one that offers an additional 2 years. That's 5 years' total coverage on labor and material. We can do this because we are confident in both our workmanship and our materials. When your customers hear of the 5-year expanded warranty, they appreciate the added value at no additional cost!

If you became our client, you would receive the best marketing and developing assistance in the business. Here are some benefits to using our program:

- Our expanded warranty program is one of a kind.
- We will have booths at the Home and Garden Show, Home Improvement Show, and Parade of Homes.
- Our representatives will hand out 5,000 brochures to introduce our expanded warranty program.

I'm looking forward to meeting you to show you examples of how you will benefit from our program and advertising. I will contact you within a few days to find a time that is convenient for you. In the meantime, please feel free to call me at 630-555-1212.

Sincerely,

ALL-PRO BUILDERS

James Jones
Sales Representative

Viewpoint in Professional Writing

The "You" Point of View

With professional writing, avoid overusing the pronoun *I*. By using the **"you" viewpoint,** you connect with readers and focus on their needs. For example:

Weak: I hope you respond to our questionnaire.

Revised: *(You)* Please respond to our questionnaire by Friday, April 14.

Weak: I appreciated your assistance with the Bakerfield project.

Revised: *Your* assistance with the Bakerfield project contributed to its success.

Weak: I think that you are a wonderful asset to our department.

Revised: *You* are a wonderful asset to our department.

Weak: I am hoping that you will join the committee to select new hires.

Revised: *(You)* Please consider joining the committee to select new hires.

Communication Challenges

Pronoun Mistakes or Hypercorrections: Pronouns may create more problems for speakers and writers than verbs create. Most people who make mistakes with pronouns are not even aware of their mistakes.

There is widespread confusion between the use of *I* and *me.* As children, many people were corrected when they used *me* as a subject: "*Me and John* are going to the store." A correction might have followed immediately, "No, that should be '*John and I* are going to the store.'"

As a result, many people default to the more professional-sounding subjective case pronoun *I* at times when *me* is the only correct choice. This kind of response is called *hypercorrecting.* To a trained ear, using *I* in place of *me* can sound like nails scratching a blackboard. Using *myself* in place of *me* sounds even worse.

The improper use of *I* and *myself* in the object position may have reached epidemic proportions, and this erroneous construction is contagious.

Challenge: With a partner, develop several examples using *I, me,* and *myself* incorrectly, and then revise your examples so that they are correct.

The "We" Point of View The **"we" viewpoint** is another frequently used point of view in business today. When writing business communications, you may find yourself expressing a view that also reflects your company's view. When that is the case, use the "we" viewpoint. For example:

Weak: The situation will be discussed at our next board meeting.

Revised: *We* will discuss the situation at our next board meeting.

Weak: I will address your complaint to our customer service department.

Revised: *We* apologize for problems you had with your account, and our customer service department will address your complaint immediately.

PRACTICE

Instructions: Correct the following paragraphs by putting them in a consistent point of view. Consider putting the first paragraph in the "I" point of view and the second paragraph in the "you" or "we" point of view. Just for fun, you may also want to put one of the paragraphs in the "one" point of view.

1. The purpose of writing from my perspective is to communicate ideas. It allows one to express ideas in a structured manner for others to review. To become a person that writes well, one must practice. In order to have good structure, I first identify my topic and do a mind map or brainstorm. Then you should write a draft and leave your rough copy until the next day. Finally, review for content, clarity, and information. Writing can be rewarding if a person knows what they are doing. I plan to write more so that I can improve my skills.

2. Listening is an important skill that I would like to improve. When a person listens, they show respect to the person to whom they are listening. When you listen, you must hear with your ears as well as one's heart. I find that listening makes you a better person because you develop more empathy for the other person. One feels validated when others listen to them. Thus, if a person wants to be a better communicator, they should spend time improving his or her listening skills.

VOCABULARY: SOUNDALIKES

It's/Its: *It's* and *its* cause serious problems for many well-educated writers.

- *It's: It* is a pronoun, and *it's* is a contraction of *it is.*

  It's a great day.

  It's too early to be this dark.

  They said that *it's* too late to submit the proposal.

- *Its: Its* is the possessive form of the pronoun *it.* Though possessive, *its* takes no apostrophe.

  The dog chased *its* tail.

  The baby lost *its* bottle.

  You cannot judge a book by *its* cover.

To avoid confusion:

- Stop contracting it is.
- Make sure *its* is followed by a noun.

SECTION C CONCEPT CHECK

1. Should pronouns always agree with their antecedents?

2. Why is it important to remain gender-neutral in your business writing?

Internet Exercise 5.1

World of Pronouns: For a look at the quirkier (believe it or not) side of pronouns, log on to the Web site at **www.mhhe.com/youngBE** and select the "Chapter 5" link.

SECTION D: COLLECTIVE NOUNS AND INDEFINITE PRONOUNS

Collective nouns and indefinite pronouns create difficulty for writers. Because writers may be unsure whether these words are singular or plural, subject-verb agreement becomes a challenge.

COLLECTIVE NOUNS

A **collective noun** is a word that is singular in form but represents a group, such as *team, committee,* or *board.* Difficulty arises because the writer or speaker must sometimes determine how to view the group: *Is the group acting together as a unit or separately as individuals?*

- When members of the group act as a unit, use singular pronouns and verbs. For example:

  The committee *has met* twice already this month.

  Our team *is finished* with the project.

- When members of the group act as individuals, use plural pronouns and verbs. In the examples below, the members of the group are acting as individuals because they are expressing disagreement or lack of consensus.

  The board *were* not in agreement about the merger.

  The committee *disagree* about hiring a consultant.

Since these sentences sound awkward as written, consider using *members of:*

The *members of the board* were not in agreement about the merger.

The *members of the committee* disagree about hiring a consultant.

Here is a list of common collective nouns:

administration	crew	group
army	crowd	herd
audience	department	jury
board	enemy	majority
cabinet	faculty	minority
class	family	nation
committee	firm	public
company	gang	staff
council	government	team

PRACTICE

Instructions: In the following sentences, identify the collective noun and determine whether it should be singular or plural. Correct verb and pronoun use so that the sentences have agreement and consistency. **For example:**

Incorrect: The staff does not agree on a location for the retreat.

Corrected: The *staff do* not agree on a location for the retreat.

Or: Members of the *staff do* not agree on a location for the retreat.

1. Our team wore its new t-shirts to the game.
2. The faculty voiced its diverse opinions about the new policy.
3. After hearing that the concert was canceled, the crowd slowly made their way to the parking lot.
4. The staff cast its votes yesterday; we should know the results today.
5. Your group of coworkers are certainly unusual.

▸Language Diversity

Janus Words: The term *Janus words* derives from Janus, the two-faced character of Roman mythology (from which the word *January* also derives). As the name implies, a *Janus word* is a word that has opposite meanings. Janus words are also known as **autoantonyms.**

The following are examples of Janus words:

bolt (verb):	to secure in place
	to dash away suddenly
cleave (verb)	to adhere, stick together
	to cut apart, divide
dust (verb)	to remove fine particles from (i.e., cleaning)
	to sprinkle fine particles onto
oversight (noun)	supervision
	omission
skin (verb)	to cover with a skin
	to remove a skin
strike (verb)	to miss (baseball)
	to hit, collide with
trim (verb)	to cut pieces off
	to add to, ornament

Can you identify the opposite meanings of the following autoantonyms?

rent	1.
	2.
sanction	1.
	2.
splice	1.
	2.

Can you think of any autoantonyms that you use in your daily conversations?

INDEFINITE PRONOUNS

Indefinite pronouns are words such as *one, anybody, both, each,* or *several.* The challenge in using an indefinite pronoun is determining whether it is singular or plural.

Singular Indefinite Pronouns: The pronouns *each, every, either, neither, one, another,* and *much* are always singular. When they are used as subjects, they take a singular verb.

Neither of the applicants *is* qualified for the job.

Much is expected of new employees.

Plural Indefinite Pronouns: The pronouns *both, few, many, others,* and *several* are always plural. When you use them, always use a plural verb.

A *few* (of the items) *were* left unfinished.

Several (contracts) *are* ready to send out.

Indefinite Pronouns Singular or Plural: The pronouns *all, none, any, some, more,* and *most* may be singular or plural, depending on the nouns that they refer to. The noun often occurs in a prepositional phrase (which begins with *to*) immediately following the pronoun.

None of the project is done correctly.	*None* of the coordinators are listed.
All of the space is filled.	*All* of the speakers are ready to present.

PRACTICE

Instructions: In the following sentences, identify the indefinite pronoun and determine whether it should be singular or plural. Correct verb and pronoun use so that there is agreement and consistency. **For example:**

Incorrect: Any of the participants who has a question should see me personally.

Corrected: Any of the *participants* who *have* a question should see me personally.

1. Only a few people checked his or her voice mail today.

2. Anyone who checked their voice mail today would have heard about the meeting.

3. Each employee check their voice mail and e-mail daily.

4. Much need to be done about this problem.

5. Everything run much better when we all communicate.

SECTION D CONCEPT CHECK

1. Give an example of a collective noun. Use it in a sentence as a singular noun and then as a plural noun.

2. Name three indefinite pronouns that can be either singular or plural.

3. Is the pronoun *neither* singular, plural, or both? Use *neither* in a sentence.

VOCABULARY NEW WORDS

New definitions added to the *Oxford English Dictionary* in 2006:[2]

phish, verb: To attempt to gather sensitive personal information fraudulently by masquerading as an honorable person or business in an apparently official electronic communication. (***phishing,*** noun)

iconize, verb: To use an image as an alias or as a fake icon on a desktop screen.

wizard, noun: An interactive computer program that acts as an interface to lead a user through a complex task by means of step-by-step dialogues.

wizard, adjective: the level of expertise of someone who is exceptionally skilled at a particular computing process.

Internet Exercise 5.2

Pronoun Worksheets: Need more practice with the topics covered in this chapter? Go to the Web site at **www.mhhe.com/youngBE**. Select "Student Activities," and then click on the "Chapter 5" link to get started.

CHAPTER 5 SUMMARY

Pronouns are challenging—maybe more challenging than you first realized when you began this chapter. However, through diligent practice, you have now made another major stride in your skill growth.

By continuing to observe how you use pronouns in your local language, you can build a wall between the way you use pronouns in Business English and the way you use them in your local language. Table 5.2 summarizes the critical aspects of pronoun use. Review it now, and use it in the future as a quick reference about pronouns.

TABLE 5.2 | Pronouns: Case

Subjective	Objective	Possessive	Reflexive
I	me	my mine	myself
you	you	your yours	yourself yourselves
he	him	his	himself
she	her	her, hers	herself
it	it	its	itself
we	us	our ours	ourselves
they	them	their theirs	themselves
one	one	one's	oneself
who whoever	whom whomever	whose	

- **Subjective case** pronouns are always followed by a verb. When two or more people are involved, you can substitute *we* or *they:* "*Jim and he (they)* will complete the report."
- **Objective case** pronouns can be objects of prepositions, infinitives, or verbs. When two or more people are involved, you can substitute *us* or *them:* "Send the report to *Ali and me (us).*"
- **Possessive case** pronouns show possession without an apostrophe: *its, hers, theirs.*
- **Reflexive case** pronouns correspond with subjective pronouns, intensifying the effect: "*I* will do the work *myself.*" If *I* is not in the sentence, do not use *myself.*
- ***Who/whom/that:*** *Who* is a subject; *whom* is an object. When referring to a person, use *who;* do not use *that* when referring to a person.
- ***Than*** is a conjunction: A subject and verb follow it, but often the verb is implied, leading writers to think they should follow *than* with an object. Use the subject and verb after *than* so that your speech doesn't sound stilted: "Martin is taller than *I am.*"
- Pronouns must agree with their antecedents in *number* and *gender.*
- Stay within the same *point of view* in sentences, paragraphs, and even, at times, entire documents.
- Use *gender-neutral pronouns* by writing in third-person plural rather than third-person singular.
- **Singular indefinite pronouns** are *each, every, either, neither, one, another,* and *much.*
- **Plural indefinite pronouns** are *both, few, many, others,* and *several.*
- **Singular or plural indefinite pronouns** are *all, none, any, some, more,* and *most,* depending on the nouns that they refer to.

CHAPTER 5 CHECKLIST

When reviewing your use of pronouns, pay attention to the following:

___ Subjective pronouns are functioning as subjects

___ Objective pronouns are functioning as objects

___ Reflexive pronouns refer to subject pronouns

___ Point of view (I, you, we, they) is consistent

___ Pronouns agree with their antecedents

___ Collective nouns have correct agreement with their verbs

___ Indefinite pronouns have correct agreement with their verbs

___ Writing is gender neutral

CHAPTER 5 END-OF-CHAPTER ACTIVITIES

ACTIVITY 1: PROCESS MEMO

INSTRUCTIONS: Write your instructor a short message indicating the kinds of changes you are now making with pronouns in your speaking and writing. Are you more confident using pronouns? What questions or problems do you still have?

If you have Internet access, you can complete this exercise online at www.mhhe.com/youngBE and then send an e-mail to your instructor.

ACTIVITY 2: PRONOUN WORKSHEETS

WORKSHEET A: USING CASE CORRECTLY

INSTRUCTIONS: In the following sentences, correct any errors in pronoun case. For example:

Incorrect: Allison gave the report to Lou and I this morning.

Corrected: Allison gave the report to Lou and *me* this morning.

1. Yesenia and me met with two prospective clients yesterday.

2. Both prospective clients decided that they would like to work with Yesenia and I.

3. Either her or I will write the contracts by Wednesday.

4. When I told my supervisor that these new accounts were mine's, Yesenia corrected me and said that the accounts were our's.

5. Yesenia and myself will share the responsibilities of the account equally.

6. I think that Yesenia is a better writer than me.

7. However, I am much better at talking with clients than her.

8. Between Yesenia and I, we will make these clients the happiest they have ever been with a marketing firm.

9. The last time our firm landed such important clients was last year when Bill, Yesenia, and myself obtained the Johnson Sporting Goods account.

10. I persuaded Yesenia to work with Bill and myself again on these new accounts.

11. I thought working together would alleviate some of the competitive tension between she and I.

12. We both have our talents: Yesenia is better at creating contracts and proposals than me; I am better communicating directly with the clients than her.

13. Because these accounts are so important, I will probably ask Bill to work with Yesensia and I.

14. Yesenia and him can draft contracts more quickly than anyone I know.

15. Bill, Yesenia, and me make a great team.

WORKSHEET B: PRONOUN-ANTECEDENT AGREEMENT

INSTRUCTIONS: In the following sentences, correct any errors in pronoun-antecedent agreement and point of view. Even though the sentences seem to relate to each other, consider each sentence individually. In other words, you don't need to develop a consistent point of view; but each sentence needs to be correct. (Your answers may vary.) For example:

Incorrect: One should be wary of credit card offers when they do not require that you have a job, a cosignature, or a credit history.

Corrected: *You* should be wary of credit card offers when they do not require that *you* have a job, a cosignature, or a credit history.

Or: One should be wary of credit card offers when they do not require that *one* have a job, a cosignature, or a credit history.

1. When one graduates from college, your first worry usually is finding a job.

2. For many graduates, however, his or her first worry is credit card debt.

3. Many banks offer credit cards to college students knowing that you are least likely to pay off all your debt.

4. In this way, creditors can make quite a bit of money off the interest it charges them.

5. College students are hurt in many ways by his or her credit card debt.

6. College students should consider the postgraduation monthly cost of their student loans before you accept a credit card offer.

7. As you sort through one's mail, avoid the temptation to open enticing credit card offers.

8. You might see a table for a credit card company set up in their student center at your college.

9. Keep in mind that such tables are there to make money for the credit card companies, not to help one out.

10. Often these tables are serviced by a fellow student who is paid according to how many completed applications they obtain.

11. But consider this: Will one be able to avoid the temptation of using that credit for things you don't need?

12. Many students begin the road to excessive debt by applying for your own "emergency" credit card.

13. As the emergency credit card becomes maxed out, students apply for another card to take their place.

14. Your credit card debt will not disappear on their own.

15. As one begins your first job, graduate school, or internship, the debt follows you.

16. According to the most recent Nellie Mae report, more college undergrads are carrying credit cards, and you are using them more often too.[3]

ACTIVITY 3: PRONOUN PRACTICE

INSTRUCTIONS: Correct any pronoun errors in the following sentences. For example:

Incorrect: My boss and me had lunch together today.

Corrected: My boss and *I* had lunch together today.

1. Jen was worried that Rob was more prepared for the meeting than her.

2. However, Jen knew the responsibility of writing the agenda was her.

3. Just between you and I, Jen is great at writing clear, concise agendas.

4. During the meeting, the agenda was used by Rob, Jen, and myself to lead the discussion.

5. Although Jen didn't speak much during the meeting, Rob and myself had to admit the agenda helped the meeting to run quite smoothly.

6. Jen and me have never worked together much in the past.

7. With this new project, however, her and me will be partners.

8. Rob asked we graphic designers to design the next client presentation.

9. Rather than divide the work between we two, Jen and I have decided to work together step-by-step.

10. Jen and me can work closely together because we have similar work styles.

11. For example, both her and me have messy desks, but we know how to find anything we need.

12. Her and I don't like to break our creative flow while we're working; rather, we work through our first draft, let it incubate overnight, and then start fresh the next day.

13. Other graphic designers in our office prefer they're work proofread one small piece at a time.

14. Rob, Jen, and myself will present our new concept designs in ten days.

15. Jen and I had better hurry; I always get nervous about deadlines, but Jen seems to be less nervous than me.

ACTIVITY 4: SPEAKING BUSINESS

INSTRUCTIONS: Make a list of the pronouns and categories of pronouns that you need to work on. For example:

1. Subjects and objects, such as *I* and *me.*
2. Possessives, such as *mine, yours,* and *hers.*
3. Reflexives, such as *myself, himself,* and *themselves.*
4. The various forms of *you:* "yous," "ya'll," "all y'all," "you'ins."

Next, write five sentences in local language for each specific pronoun or category on your list. Then translate the sentences into Business English. Here are a few examples:

Local Language	Business English
The issue should remain between you and I.	The issue should remain between you and me.
Those books are mines.	Those books are mine.
How are yous doing?	How are you doing?
Are all y'all going to the meeting?	Are you all going to the meeting?

Finally, share your local-language sentences with a partner, and have your partner translate your local-language sentences into Business English.

ACTIVITY 5: PRONOUN AND ANTECEDENT AGREEMENT

PART A

INSTRUCTIONS: Correct the pronoun errors in the following sentences. For example:

Incorrect: I always think a project is hard until you do some work on it.

Corrected: I always think a project is hard until *I* do some work on it.

1. Many people expect to be hired after your first job interview.

2. An experienced job seeker will tell you that one should expect several interviews before he or she begins receiving job offers.

3. On the other hand, there is that rare perfect fit, where both interviewer and interviewee know immediately that one has a good match.

4. In those uncommon situations, an interviewer might make an offer to you during the interview. You need to consider one's offer carefully.

5. It is never a good idea for one to accept a job offer during an interview, and it is not considered discourteous for you to ask for a week to consider the offer.

6. More than likely, job seekers will have to wait days or even weeks before hearing back from his or her interviewers.

7. Do not become discouraged: one might not immediately hear from a company because they had so many candidates.

8. One thing you can do to help one's cause is send a thank-you note.

9. A person should send a handwritten thank-you note immediately after their interview.

10. One's thank-you note can make the difference between you and another similarly qualified candidate.

PART B

INSTRUCTIONS: Write three pairs of sentences below to demonstrate pronoun-antecedent agreement. First, write a sentence that shows lack of agreement; second, correct your sentence to show pronoun-antecedent agreement. For example:

Incorrect: I am excited about the many job opportunities available to you today.

Corrected: *I* am excited about the many job opportunities available to *me* today.

1. ______________________________

____

2. ______________________________

____

3. ______________________________

____

ACTIVITY 6: CUMULATIVE PROGRAM REVIEW

INSTRUCTIONS: Correct the pronouns in the following sentences.

1. Natalia and me will attend the conference.
2. The first presentation will be given by Jose, Linda, and myself.
3. The second presentation will be divided between she and I.
4. Jonah is better at public speaking than me.
5. If a person arrives at the conference early, they can find a good seat.
6. One should arrive on time or early to show consideration for your fellow participants.
7. A person that arrives late can cause a distraction.

8. With too many distractions, you will have a difficult time listening to whomever is speaking.

9. You will further annoy people if you ask whom is speaking.

10. Yourself and everyone else will be happier if you arrive on time.

ACTIVITY 7: CORRECTING PRONOUN ERRORS

INSTRUCTIONS: Correct the pronoun errors and any other errors you find in the following text.

Set Yourself Apart: The After-Interview Thank-You Note

Your interview went well, and you are confident that yourself made a good impression. Now one just wants to relax and enjoy a stress-free day. Why should anyone bother with an after-interview thank-you note? First of all, taking the time to write that thank-you note shows that you are a candidate whom is different from other candidates—you care. It's also proof that your really interested in the position. Finally, it's a way to keep one's name in front. Make sure you send it within 24 hours of your interview, or the person that interviewed you might feel that they wasn't a priority for you.

If you had multiple interviews at one company, take the time to write a note to each person that interviewed you. If possible, mention something you and them discussed during the interview; this will help the interviewer remember yourself and also show that one was paying attention. The thank-you note is also a good place to reiterate the reasons that you are a good candidate for this position.

The format of the note is also important, and they should be written with care. Handwritten notes on plain paper or half-fold thank-you cards are still favored, and it doesn't take long to write. Before one sends the note, though, write a quick first draft on scratch paper, check their spelling, and neatly recopy the note on the card. Mail the thank-you note immediately, and make sure that they have adequate postage. Include a return address on the envelope. Use the business card that the interviewer gave yourself to address the envelope: a wrong name, title, or address will do much harm to the impression you made.

Just between you and I, the thank-you note will set you apart from all the other candidates: currently, only about 5 percent of job candidates send thank-you notes to his or her interviewers.

ACTIVITY 8: THESAURUS DRILL

INSTRUCTIONS: In order to develop variety in your writing, replace the boldface words and phrases below with substitutes that have the same meaning as the originals. Consider using indefinite pronouns. In places where you make substitutions, make sure that you still have correct subject-verb agreement.

We are offering a new training program through our human resources department. **All the employees** in our department look forward to taking the training, even though **not one of** our suggestions was part of the main program. **A lot of the** information in the training manual came from **three or four** people who took the program last year. After the training, if **a representative** from our department contacts you, feel free to give your honest feedback about the training.

ACTIVITY 9: "WRITER'S REFERENCE MANUAL" DRILL

BACKGROUND: **Text messaging** is a popular form of informal communication that people use with friends and family as well as close business associates. As instant messaging and text messaging have increased in use, a new language has emerged tailored to the immediacy and compactness of these new communication media.

INSTRUCTIONS: The following is a list of text-messaging abbreviations. Use the "Writer's Reference Manual" to decipher their meaning. (Note: Do not use these abbreviations in e-mail or any other type of professional business correspondence.)

BRB	EOD
SIG2R	TTTT
TA	OOH
UKTR	F2T
WAM	ILBL8
SSDD	KWIM
PTMM	TMOT
TPTB	HTCUS
LTNS	BTW
IYSS	EOM

ACTIVITY 10: VOCABULARY LIST

A. COMMONLY MISSPELLED WORDS

INSTRUCTIONS: The list below contains words taken from a compilation of the 500 most commonly misspelled words and from the chapter. Practice them until you can spell them automatically and use them correctly.

1. antecedent (n) a word that a pronoun refers to
2. assumption (n) supposition, guess, theory, conjecture
3. bias (n) prejudice, preconceived notion, favoritism, partiality
4. clients (n) customers, patrons, and at times coworkers
5. resistance (n) opposition; conscious and unconscious reasons that cause challenges
6. superfluous (adj) redundant, unnecessary, excessive in detail
7. thorough (adj) complete, meticulous, comprehensive

8. tomorrow (n) the day following today; the near future (the world of tomorrow)
9. transferred (v) to have carried or caused to pass from one place to another
10. unconscious (adj) not accessible to the conscious part of the mind; not aware
11. usually (adv) more often than not
12. unnecessary (adj) needless, redundant, uncalled for
13. vague (adj) unclear, indistinct, fuzzy
14. reiterate (v) restate, repeat, say again
15. veracity (n) truthfulness, accuracy, something that is true

B. SIMILAR WORDS

INSTRUCTIONS: The list below contains similar words, some of which are profiled in the Vocabulary Builders in each chapter. Use these words in sentences until their meaning becomes clear.

its/it's: These two words are often confused. *Its* is the possessive form of the pronoun *it* (everything in its place). *It's* is the contraction for *it is* or *it has.* (It's raining. It's begun.) There is no such form as "its'."

It's a great day for a celebration.

The car lost *its* appeal after we learned the price.

their/there/they're: Confusion of these three words is a spelling problem. *Their* is the possessive form of *they* (their house, their problems). *There* is used most often as an adverb (over there) or an anticipating subject (there are). *They're* is the contracted form of *they are.* (They're happy. They're certain.)

Their house is next to mine.

There are ten minutes before the meeting.

They're all attending the same conference.

They're over *there* in *their* car.

your/you're: These words are both pronouns; however, they have distinctly different functions. *Your* is a possessive pronoun and is always followed by a noun. *You're* is a contraction of *you are.*

Your assignments are organized by due date.

You're late for the Kollier seminar.

convince/persuade: To *convince* means to get someone to think the way you do. To *persuade* means to get the other person to take action.

Margaret *convinced* me that I was right about the decision to join the committee.

I *persuaded* her to attend the first meeting with me.

THE INBOX

COMPOSING

In a magazine or newspaper, find a photograph that has people in it. Write a paragraph describing the activity taking place in the photo. Try to write the paragraph without using *any* pronouns.

REFLECTING

Consider the paragraph you wrote about the photo. How difficult was it to avoid using pronouns? What is the effect of writing without pronouns?

Rewrite the paragraph using pronouns where you feel they would be appropriate. How has your paragraph changed? Do you like one paragraph better than the other? Why or why not?

DISCUSSING

1. Some writing experts think that the overuse of pronouns weakens writing. The theory is that writers should insert noun phrases in place of some pronouns to break up the monotony of repetitious and vague pronouns. Here's an example:

   The writer spent several years on *her* first novel. *She* was finally happy with *it* after endless hours of revising.

   The writer spent several years on *her* first novel. *She* was finally happy with *the final edition* after endless hours of revising.

   Do you think inserting a noun phrase in place of a pronoun makes a difference? Have your group discuss this question, and then present three examples supporting your view.

2. The Preamble to the United States Constitution states:

   > We the People of the United States, in Order to form a more perfect Union, establish Justice, insure domestic Tranquility, provide for the common defence, promote the general Welfare, and secure the Blessings of Liberty to ourselves and our Posterity, do ordain and establish this Constitution for the United States of America.

   As you read through this famous proclamation, notice the use of pronouns. Think about the historical setting against which the Preamble was written. Think about the Preamble as it applies to citizens today. Who are the "we" in "We the people"? For whom are the "Blessings of Liberty" being secured ("us")? Discuss how the use of pronouns can hinder or aid legal documents by the nature of their vagueness. Would the United States be a different country today if the Preamble had actually avoided the use of pronouns and stated the antecedents to which *we* and *our* refer?

EDITING

INSTRUCTIONS: Correct the agenda of this student activity meeting. Look for pronoun use.

Springville Community College Art Club
Fall Fundraiser Meeting Agenda
September 18, 2007
Chaired by Javaid Kaval

Its very important that we begin planning for the fall fundraiser early so we don't find ourself putting an event together at the last minute. Me and Casey Webster, the co-chair, have decided to appoint each person to their own area of responsibility. That's why this meeting was called by we to. When one put off these responsibilities, they have only theirself to blame. Therefore you should start working on you're area right away. The list will be distributed by myself and Casey but for now will read it ourself.

1. Shannon: Your responsible for contacting the banquet hall's owner. You and him will discuss the details of the timing, the food, and the seating arrangements.

2. Enrico: Please ask your dad if his company will donate the flyers again. Them flyers were really effective. Last year more people came to the banquet than ever, thanks him advertising it.

3. Jin-Lu: Me and Casey would like you to coordinate the raffle. One should keep a list of prizes so you can make thank-you notes later. Paula will help with the contacts for donations.

4. Paula: Your going to have to read thru last year's list of donators, and try to get theirselves to donate again. We can also spend some time at the end of the meeting brainstorming ideas for new donators, who we'll have to contact right away. The donators have to receive letters for tax purposes. Whom will help you, we don't know yet. The person whom was responsible last year has graduated and they didn't leave any contact information. We'll have to get help from our adviser, Mr. Brachton, whom is always willing to help us.

5. Peter: Me and you will work with Enrico and Casey on advertising. An ad in the school paper as well as the local paper would be good. You can talk with myself and them after the meeting today.

6. Shiriah: All of we club members decided that your the best one to select the art pieces for the predinner gallery show. Mr. Brachton will help you, and between you and he, the gallery is sure to be a success.

We'll finish the meeting now and start working on individual tasks. Any of them that need to meet with others should do so now or at least very soon. Time is flying: they're only six weeks before the fundraiser!

KEY TO LEARNING INVENTORY

1. F
2. T
3. T
4. F
5. F
6. T
7. T
8. F
9. T
10. T

CHAPTER 5 ENDNOTES

1. "Re: Yous (Youse?), Ireland and New York," May 9, 2003, **http://www.phrases.org.uk/bulletin_board/20/messages/1127.html**, accessed on June 8, 2006.
2. *Oxford English Dictionary,* quarterly updates; **http://oed.com/help/updates/philanthropal-pimento.html**, accessed on July 7, 2006.
3. Marie O'Malley, *Educating Undergraduates on Using Credit Cards,* **http://www.nelliemae.com/library/cc_use.html**, accessed on October 14, 2006.

Chapter Six

Modifiers

Time changes all things: there is no reason why language should escape this universal law.
—Ferdinand de Saussure, linguist (1857–1913)

A **modifier** is a word or group of words that describes another part of speech or even a complete sentence. A modifier is not a main element of a sentence because it is not a core element, such as the subject, verb, or object; but a modifier can be an important element.

Traditionally, when you think of modifiers, you think of adjectives and adverbs. Other types of modifiers include possessive and demonstrative pronouns as well as compound modifiers requiring a hyphen. Beautifully written prose riddled with descriptors occurs more often in poems, novels, or other sorts of fiction. While modifiers add richness and depth to meaning if they are used correctly, they are just as often overused or misused in business writing. In business writing, keep your writing simple, clear, and concise. Use only modifiers that are necessary; and when you use modifiers, make sure that you are using them correctly.

Because business writing is crisp and concise, modifying words or phrases are often among the first to be cut during editing. Try to eliminate excessive modifiers: those are words that you use to intensify meaning but that instead often have the opposite effect.

To learn more about The Writing Process, please visit our Web site at www.mhhe.com/youngBE

Outline

Chapter 6: Modifiers

Section A: The Basics—Adjectives and Adverbs

Section B: Position of Modifiers

Section C: Other Modifiers—Pronouns and Compound Adjectives

Section D: Hedges, Emphatics, Fillers, and Tag-Ons

Objectives

When you have completed your study of Chapter 6, you will be able to:

1. Modify active verbs with adverbs.
2. Ensure that adjectives are used as subject complements following linking verbs.
3. Use comparative and superlative adjectives correctly.
4. Place modifiers close to the word or words they modify.
5. Eliminate unnecessary hedges and emphatics in writing.
6. Avoid tag-ons and fillers such as *like* in speech.
7. Apply possessive pronouns correctly.
8. Use hyphens in compound modifiers.

Learning Inventory

1. Adjectives modify nouns and pronouns. T/F
2. Adverbs modify verbs, adjectives, other adverbs, and even entire sentences. T/F
3. A gerund phrase takes as its subject the closest noun following it. T/F
4. Using *more* or *less* with a suffix such as *er* expresses a higher comparative degree. T/F
5. An infinitive phrase can modify the entire rest of its sentence. T/F
6. The word *perfect* can be modified by *more than* but not by *less than.* T/F
7. Emphatics such as *very* and *totally* should be used often to make your point stand out. T/F
8. Modifiers make business writing more colorful, and "the more, the better." T/F
9. A hedge is a word or phrase, such as *kind* of *or usually,* that qualifies. T/F
10. The verb *feel* is a linking verb, and an adverb, not an adjective, should follow it. T/F

Goal-Setting Exercises

Think for a moment about how you use adjectives and adverbs in your speech and writing. Think about the words *like, very,* and *totally;* also consider phrases such as *much more better* or *more than perfect.* Write three goals about the changes you want to make in your speech and writing when it comes to adjectives, adverbs, and other types of modifiers.

1. ______________________________

2. ______________________________

3. ______________________________

SECTION A: THE BASICS—ADJECTIVES AND ADVERBS

Adjectives and adverbs are the most basic kinds of modifiers. A starting point to understanding adjectives and adverbs is identifying the kinds of words each modifies:

- **Adjectives** modify nouns and pronouns, adding color, taste, feel, and other dimensions to the words they describe. Adjectives give readers visual cues to the words they describe. Here are a few examples: *bright, dull, old, pink, short, warm, frizzy, outstanding,* and *great.*
- **Adverbs** modify adjectives, verbs, other adverbs, and at times even entire sentences, adding depth, color, or intensity. Adverbs answer the questions *how, when, where,* and *why.* Here are a few examples of adverbs: *friendly, actively, rarely, quick, quickly, recently, slow, slowly, more, most, less,* and *least.*

Writers and speakers make specific types of errors with adjectives and adverbs. Common errors include:

- Modifying action verbs with adjectives (action verbs should be modified with adverbs).

  Incorrect: Martin speaks *good.*

  Correct: Martin speaks *well.*

- Modifying state-of-being verbs with adverbs (linking verbs should be followed by adjectives).

  Incorrect: Della felt *badly* about the miscommunication.

  Correct: Della felt *bad* about the miscommunication.

- Using *more, most, less,* or *least* with a comparative or superlative *and* adding a suffix such as *er* or *est.*

  Incorrect: We were *more busier* yesterday than today.

  Correct: We were *busier* yesterday than today.

- Placing modifiers incorrectly (they should be placed close to the word or words they modify).

  Incorrect: Bob drove the car with the poor brakes *recklessly.*

  Correct: Bob *recklessly* drove the car with the poor brakes.

Now let's take a look at the principles you need to know to use adjectives and adverbs correctly in your business writing.

MODIFYING ACTION VERBS WITH ADVERBS

Modify action verbs with adverbs. The modifier following a linking verb is a subject complement; use an adjective to modify or describe the subject.

- An *action verb* is modified by an *adverb:*

  Incorrect: The computer runs *good.*

  Correct: The computer runs *well.*

- A *linking verb* is usually followed by a *subject complement;* use an *adjective* as a subject complement. (Of the 11 state-of-being or linking verbs, only 1 seems to give speakers and writers problems with modifiers: *to feel.*)

  Incorrect: I feel *badly* about the situation. (adverb used as subject complement)

  Correct: I feel *bad* about the situation.

VOCABULARY NEW WORDS

Added to *Merriam-Webster's Collegiate Dictionary* in 2006.[1]

cybrarian, noun: A person whose job is to find, collect, and manage information that is available on the World Wide Web.

steganography, noun: The art or practice of concealing a message, image, or file within another message, image, or file.

metadata, noun: Data that provide information about other data.

SPEAKING BUSINESS

Controversial Adverbs: *Hopeful* is an adjective; *hopefully* is an adverb. Using *hopefully* as an introductory word to modify an entire sentence has met with some controversy. However, *hopefully* has now joined the ranks of other adverbial conjunctions used to express the writer's attitude by modifying the entire sentence. The following are both correct:

I am *hopeful* that I will see you next week.

Hopefully, I will see you next week.

Most adverbs are formed by adding *ly* to adjectives, but another way to form adverbs is to add the suffix *wise* to a noun, as in *lengthwise* and *clockwise.* However, don't go overboard adding *wise* to nouns to form adverbs. Words such as *budgetwise* or *economywise* sound clumsy.[2]

One more reminder: *irregardless* has a built-in double negative—make sure that you use *regardless.*

- Adverbs commonly end in *ly;* however, many speakers and writers bobtail the adverb by leaving off the *ly* ending, giving the effect that an adjective, rather than an adverb, modifies an action verb. Adverbs to watch out for are *considerably, seriously, differently, really, badly,* and *surely.*[3]

Incorrect: Alice reacted *different* about the problem than I did.

Correct: Alice reacted *differently* about the problem than I did.

Though many adverbs can take either form, using the *ly* ending after action verbs has a smoother flow and sounds more professional to many ears.

Correct: Drive *slow.* **Preferred:** Drive *slowly.*

Correct: Speak *loud.* **Preferred:** Speak *loudly.*

Even though some adverbs can be used with or without the *ly* ending, adverbs such as *slow, quick,* and *deep* usually sound better with it.

PRACTICE

Instructions: Correct the errors in the following sentences. **For example:**

Incorrect: Jason feels *badly* about the mistake.

Corrected: Jason feels *bad* about the mistake.

1. I reminded Bob to drive safe on his road trip to Denver.
2. Our CEO felt badly about making staff changes.
3. The assistant did the job satisfactory.
4. I don't feel well about George getting the promotion.
5. The board felt badly about disintegrating the corporation.

EXPLORE

1. Identify five adjectives and adverbs.
2. Use each in a sentence.

USING COMPARATIVE AND SUPERLATIVE DEGREES

When using adjectives or adverbs to compare, either use more, most, less, *or* least *or use* er *or* est *to show the degree of comparison (but do not use both).*

Follow these rules:

1. When you compare *two items,* use the **comparative form** of the modifier. Form the comparative by adding *more* or *less* or the suffix *er.*
2. When you compare *three or more items,* use the **superlative form.** Form the superlative by adding *most* or *least* or the suffix *est.*

TABLE 6.1 | Adjectives and Adverbs
This table provides a partial list of adjectives and adverbs.

Adjective	Adverb (with long forms only)	
amicable	amicably	
attentive	attentively	
bad	badly	
beautiful	beautifully	
cautious	cautiously	
cheerful	cheerfully	
considerable	considerably	
current	currently	
different	differently	
eloquent	eloquently	
erratic	erratically	
extreme	extremely	
frequent	frequently	
implicit	implicitly	
initial	initially	
near	nearly	
ominous	ominously	
prompt	promptly	
real	really	
serious	seriously	
significant	significantly	
sincere	sincerely	
subtle	subtly	
sure	surely	
unilateral	unilaterally	
Adjective	**Adverbs (with long and short forms)**	
bright	bright, brightly	
cheap	cheap, cheaply	
direct	direct, directly	
even	even, evenly	
fair	fair, fairly	
first	first, firstly	
loose	loose, loosely	
quick	quick, quickly	
rough	rough, roughly	
second	second, secondly	
sharp	sharp, sharply	
slow	slow, slowly	
smooth	smooth, smoothly	
third	third, thirdly	
tight	tight, tightly	
wrong	wrong, wrongly	
IRREGULAR MODIFIERS		
bad	worse	worst
good, well	better	best
far	farther, further	farthest, furthest
little	less, lesser, littler	least, littlest
many, some, much	more	most

3. To determine whether to use *more, most, less,* or *least* or add a suffix, consider the following:

- If a word has only *one syllable,* use a suffix; for example: less*er*, great*est.*
- If a word has *three syllables,* use *more, most, less,* or *least;* for example: *most* interesting, *less* intriguing.
- If a word has *two syllables,* use either form; for example: *more* simple or simpl*er.*

Speakers make the following kinds of mistakes more often than writers do:

Incorrect: We need to use the *most latest* report when we make our decision.

Correct: We need to use the *latest* report when we make our decision.

Incorrect: As the participants became *more hungrier,* they also became more irritated.

Correct: As the participants became *more hungry,* they also became more irritated.

Incorrect: The solution became *less clearer* as we examined it more closely.

Correct: The solution became *less clear* as we examined it more closely.

Words such as *perfect, correct,* and *unique* are already in their ultimate state; avoid putting comparative degrees with these words, as in "more than perfect" or "the most unique."

Incorrect: Yesterday was the *most perfect day* I've ever had.

Correct: Yesterday was *perfect.*

Or: Yesterday was *the best day* I've ever had.

PRACTICE

Instructions: Correct the modifiers in the following sentences.

Incorrect: Everyone seemed more crankier after today's meeting than yesterday's.

Corrected: Everyone seemed *more cranky* (or *crankier*) after today's meeting than yesterday's.

1. The office manager upgraded our printers, selecting the most fastest model.

2. Their award went to the candidate who was more humbler than the other.

3. The job offer was more than perfect.

4. Jason will go more further in this company than anyone now imagines.

5. Our committee has asked for more better facilities than we had last year.

USING ADJECTIVES TO COMPARE

Objects must be of the same kind to be comparable. Often statements include incomparable items.

		Implied Elements
Incorrect:	Our products are better than our *competitor.*	
Correct:	Our products are better than our *competitor's products.*	*(are)*
	Or: Our products are better than our *competitor's.*	*(products are)*
Incorrect:	This production line runs faster than *anyone else.*	
Correct:	This production line runs faster than *any other.*	*(production line runs)*
	Or: This production line runs faster than anyone else's production line.	*(runs)*

This principle bridges what you learned about pronouns in Chapter 5. In other words, notice how incomparable items are made comparable by placing a subject and verb (which is often implied) after the conjunction *than.*

PRACTICE

Instructions: In the following sentences, make corrections in adjectives and adverbs. **For example:**

Incorrect: Jones Company introduced their line of clothing faster than us.

Corrected: Jones Company introduced their line of clothing faster than *we introduced ours.*

1. Xavier's office is bigger than our manager.
2. My office has more windows than the rest.
3. Jason learned to use the productivity software later than us.
4. The executives ordered their lunches before us.
5. However, our desserts were much tastier than them.

VOCABULARY SOUNDALIKES

Farther/Further: Use *farther* when you are speaking about distance that you can measure. Use *further* when you are indicating figurative distance, such as "to a greater or lesser degree."

In other words, if you can't measure actual distance with a yardstick, use the word *further.*

Jackson lives *farther* from work than you do.

Our project is much *further* along today than it was yesterday.

AVOIDING DOUBLE NEGATIVES

To negate a statement, use only one negative.

If you use a **double negative**—more than one negative in a sentence—your statement actually becomes positive. The word *not* is the most commonly used word for negating; less common words that negate a statement are *nothing, never, hardly, barely,* and *scarcely.*

Incorrect: I *can't hardly* get my work finished.

Correct: I *can hardly* get my work finished.

Or: I *can't* get my work finished.

Incorrect: The crew *wasn't barely* finished before it started to rain.

Corrected: The crew *was barely* finished before it started to rain.

Or: The crew *had just* finished when it started to rain.

The word *regard* has the negative form *regardless.* Speakers sometimes add the prefix *ir* to the negative form *regardless,* forming a word that has a built-in double negative: *ir-regard-less.* Avoid using the word *irregardless.*

PRACTICE

Instructions: Correct the double negatives or incorrect forms in the following sentences. **For example:**

Incorrect: Jim couldn't hardly believe what he heard from the contractor.

Corrected: Jim *could hardly* believe what he heard from the contractor.

Or: Jim *couldn't* believe what he heard from the contractor.

1. The receptionist wouldn't give us no information over the phone.

2. Martha didn't have no intention of helping us with the proposal.

3. Sylvestri couldn't barely wait to tell us his answer.

4. The contractors will not start construction irregardless of what we offer them.

5. The accountants won't give us nothing for the charity deduction.

SECTION A CONCEPT CHECK

1. If a word has only one syllable, how would you form its comparative form? How about a word that has three syllables?

2. What kind of verb is *to feel?* Is it likely to be followed by an adjective or an adverb? Why?

3. What error occurs when a sentence contains two or more negative words, such as *not,* that turn the statement positive? Give an example, along with its correction.

SECTION B: POSITION OF MODIFIERS

Another issue with modifiers occurs when they are not placed next to the word or words they modify. Often, the misplacement goes unnoticed; but when it is noticed, the meaning can be confusing or even comical. In this section, you will work with misplaced modifiers and dangling modifiers.

AVOID MISPLACED MODIFIERS

Place modifiers close to the word or words they modify to keep meaning clear.

Placing modifiers away from the words they modify can create not only a grammatical error but also an ambiguous meaning. With modifiers placed correctly, your writing has better flow and the meaning is clearer. Here are **some examples** of misplaced modifiers:

Incorrect: Ginther waited for Denise until the seminar started *outside the building.*

Correct: Ginther waited for Denise *outside the building* until the seminar started.

Incorrect: The computer shutdown resulted in our losing an entire day *this morning.*

Correct: The computer shutdown *this morning* resulted in our losing an entire day.

PRACTICE

Instructions: Place modifiers close to the words they modify.

1. The door on the first floor of Kinsey Hall which is red is hers.
2. The FedEx truck broke down by a bridge carrying our supplies on Route 83.
3. Kait kept the legal supplies in the supply cabinet that she had ordered.
4. We could smell the chili all the way up on the 24th floor that was for the fund-raiser.
5. There is a new scanner in the stockroom for your work area.

VOCABULARY NEW WORDS

Added to *Merriam-Webster's Collegiate Dictionary* in 2005:[4]

mouse potato, noun (slang): A person who spends a great deal of time using a computer.

big box, noun: A large chain store having a boxlike stucture.

soul patch, noun: A small growth of beard under a man's lower lip.

labelmate, noun: A singer or musician who records for the same company as another.

drama queen, noun: A person given to often excessively emotional performances or reactions.

CORRECT DANGLING MODIFIERS

A modifying phrase takes the noun closest to it as its subject. When the modifying phrase is separated from its real subject, the result is a **dangling modifier.** In fact, the subject of a dangling modifier may not even be in the sentence. And, once again, although the writer always knows the intended meaning, the reader can be confused, or even amused, by this grammatical mishap.

Here are two ways to correct dangling modifiers:

1. Move the subject next to its modifying phrase.
2. Turn the phrase into a clause by adding a subject and verb.

Incorrect: *Sitting in the hallway,* a last sip of my coffee comforted me.

Correct: *Sitting in the hallway, I* took a last and comforting sip of my coffee.

Or: As I sat in the hallway, a last sip of my coffee comforted me.

Incorrect: *Searching my cluttered desk,* the documents were located.

Corrected: *Searching my cluttered desk, I* located the documents.

Or: As I searched my cluttered desk, the documents were located.

Incorrect: *Entering the room,* Bryan's briefcase opened and confidential papers fell out.

Correct: *As Bryan entered* the room, his briefcase opened and confidential papers fell out.

▸Language Diversity

African American Vernacular English (AAVE): Also referred to as Black Vernacular English (BVE), Ebonics (a portmanteau of "ebony and phonics"), Ebo, or jive, AAVE shares many characteristics with various Creole English dialects spoken in many parts of the world.

AAVE has grammatical origins and pronunciation characteristics in common with various West African languages as well as with the English spoken in Great Britain and Ireland during the sixteenth and seventeenth centuries. AAVE developed from the need for multilingual populations of African captives to communicate among themselves and with their captors.

AAVE has contributed to Edited American English (EAE); words of African origins include *gumbo, yam, banjo,* and *bogus* as well as slang expressions such as *cool, hip,* and *hep.*

Below is a list of words written as they are pronounced in AAVE. How many can you identify?

1. finna
2. dig
3. hankty
4. cat
5. nufin
6. tole
7. jus
8. aks
9. tahm
10. gon

One of the more distinguishing features of AAVE is the use of forms of *be* in verb phrases. The use or lack of a form of *be* can indicate whether the performance of the verb is of a habitual nature. In EAE, this can be expressed only using adverbs such as *usually.*

AAVE	Edited American English
She workin'.	She is working right now.
She be workin' Mondays.	She frequently works on Monday.
She be steady workin'.	She is working steadily.
She been workin'.	She has been working.
She been had that job.	She has had that job for a long time and still has it.
She done worked.	She has worked. (action complete)
She fittin' go to work	She's about to go to work.

PRACTICE

Instructions: Reposition the modifiers as needed in the following sentences. **For example:**

Incorrect: Janine told me about the meeting this morning last night.

Corrected: Janine told me *last night* about the meeting this morning.

1. When only interns, Mr. Sims took us on service calls.
2. Filling out the forms, a mistake was made by the applicant.
3. After putting down the receiver, the phone rang again.
4. Traveling with her manager, her suitcases were left in Denver for two days before Alice realized it.

PLACE ADVERBS CORRECTLY

Whereas adjectives are generally placed before or after the word they modify, most adverbs can be placed in various positions, depending on the meaning the writer wishes to convey. However, place adverbs such as *only, nearly, almost, ever, scarcely, merely, too,* and *also* directly before or after the word they modify. When these adverbs are placed a distance from the word they modify, meaning can get distorted. Consider how the position of *only* changes the meaning of the following sentence:

Only I intend to assist you.	. . . no one else will.
I intend *only* to assist you.	. . . and do nothing else.
I intend to assist *only* you.	. . . and no one else.

PRACTICE

Instructions: Adjust the following sentences for adverb placement.

Incorrect: Bob only was trying to help you.

Correct: Bob was *only* trying to help you.

1. I only made three copies of the report.

2. Deanne almost bought all the new software in the catalog.

3. During the meeting, we nearly finished all the doughnuts and coffee cake.

4. Congratulations, Joanne, you almost have ten years on the job!

5. We will only need to purchase one computer for the research team.

• Internet Exercise 6.1

Fun With Adjectives: Visit the Web site at **www.mhhe.com/youngBE** and select the "Chapter 6" link.

SECTION B CONCEPT CHECK

1. How do you determine the subject of a modifying phrase?

2. How do you determine where to place the modifying word *only?*

3. What happens to a sentence when you place a modifying phrase away from its subject?

SECTION C: OTHER MODIFIERS—PRONOUNS AND COMPOUND ADJECTIVES

You probably don't think of pronouns as modifiers, but pronouns play an important role as modifiers. Let's examine how pronouns modify and what kinds of errors speakers and writers make with them.

POSSESSIVE PRONOUNS

There are two forms of possessive pronouns: one is used before a noun; the other is used to replace a noun.[5] The chart below lists the possessive pronouns in these two categories:

Subjective Case	Objective Case	Possessive Preceding a Noun	Possessive Replacing a Noun
I	me	my	mine
you	you	your	yours
he	him	his	his
she	her	her	hers
it	it	its	—
we	us	our	ours
they	them	their	theirs
who	whom	whose	whose

Some common errors occur with the two types of possessives. Here are the kinds of errors speakers and writers make with possessives:

1. Using the subjective or objective case instead of the possessive case preceding a noun.
2. Using a different form for the possessive case replacing a noun.

Here are some examples:

Local Language	Business English
The committee gave *they* answer already.	The committee gave *their* answer already.
Alice referred to *me* promotion.	Alice referred to *my* promotion.
You can take *you* time with the project.	You can take *your* time with the project.
Those pamphlets are *mines.*	Those pamphlets are *mine.*
The remark was *your'n* (or *you'n*).	The remark was *yours.*

PRACTICE

Instructions: In the following sentences, correct or replace the possessive case pronouns that precede nouns.

Incorrect: The employees took they lunch early.

Corrected: The employees took *their* lunch early.

1. Mr. Michaels gave he keys to the doorman.
2. When Alistar gets you'ns recommendation, he'll be pleased.
3. The department chair and the task force gave they recommendations last week.
4. The supplies at the front desk are yours; the ones that arrived yesterday are mines.
5. I'm going to take me time in sending the report.

VOCABULARY KEY TERMS

Homonyms, Oronyms, and Homophones: **Homonyms** are words that sound alike but are spelled differently and have different meanings *(need, knead, kneed).* Throughout this text, you have encountered many sets of homonyms in the Vocabulary: Soundalikes margin features. A **homophone** is one of two or more words that have the same sound. **Oronyms** are strings of words or phrases that sound alike.

Each of the following words is a homophone:

allowed, aloud

way, weigh, whey

nose, knows

The italicized words in the following sentences are examples of oronyms:

Some others I know prefer the frosted green color.

Some mothers I know prefer the frosted green color.

I don't know how *much your* people appreciate *a nice* show.

I don't know how *mature* people appreciate *an ice* show.

Whether I am wrong *or right.*

Weather eye am wrong *oar write.*

Finally, the following is a quote from a poem titled *Eye Halve a Spelling Chequer,* written almost entirely in **homophones.***

As soon as a mist ache is maid
It nose bee fore two long
And eye can put the error rite
Its rarely ever wrong

* Author unknown.

DEMONSTRATIVE PRONOUNS

Demonstrative pronouns modify nouns by "pointing to" them. Similar to possessive pronouns, demonstrative pronouns can be used in place of nouns. The four demonstrative pronouns are *this, that, these,* and *those.*

- *This* and *these* indicate something is nearby.
- *That* and *those* indicate something is away from the speaker.

Here are some of the kinds of errors speakers and writers make with demonstrative pronouns:

1. Using *the* instead of *this.*
2. Using *that there* instead of *that.*
3. Using *them* instead of *these* or *those* (depending on the meaning).

Here are some examples:

Local Language	Business English
That there Web site is good.	*That* Web site is good.
The paper is good.	*This* paper is good.
Some of *them* reports need updating.	Some of *those* reports need updating.
	Some of *these* reports need updating.

PRACTICE

Instructions: In the following sentences, correct the demonstrative pronouns.
For example:

Incorrect: I gave them reports to Sylvia.

Corrected: I gave *those* reports to Sylvia.

1. The manuals are on that there table in the corner.
2. Anderson asked for them pamphlets, not the ones you are sending.
3. Are them your clients you are referring to?
4. That there is a good reason to give them the project.
5. Jacob asked that we solve them problems before it's too late.

• WRITER'S TOOLKIT

Peer Editing

One of the best ways to improve the quality of your writing is to work with an editing buddy. By exchanging pieces of your writing with a peer on a regular basis, you and your buddy can give each other valuable feedback.

Corporations value cooperation. By regularly doing peer editing to improve your skills, you also develop excellent work values. You can use that experience on a job interview as an example of your dedication to improving your skills and being a good team member.

COMPOUND MODIFIERS

When two or more words come together as a unit to modify a noun, place a hyphen between them. When the modifiers follow the noun, the hyphen is needed only if the modifier remains as a unit. Here are some examples of these one-thought modifiers:

Modifiers Following a Noun	Group Modifier Preceding a Noun
The news is up to the minute.	up-to-the-minute news
The items are out of stock.	out-of-stock items
The report is two pages in length.	the two-page report
The meeting is for one or two days.	the one- or two-day meeting
A man who speaks quietly . . .	A man who is quiet-spoken
	Or: A quiet-spoken man
Buying products free of duty . . .	Buying duty-free products
	Or: Buying products duty-free

Writers often omit the hyphen in these compound modifiers. In fact, some modifier combinations have become very common and no longer need to be hyphenated. Some of the terms that used to be hyphenated may surprise you. For example:

data processing (procedures)	high school (diploma)
life insurance (policy)	income tax (returns)

Also, do not hyphenate the elements of a proper name used as an adjective. For example:

Supreme Court ruling

Fifth Avenue address

South American import

PRACTICE

Instructions: In the following sentences, correct the compound-adjective modifiers by placing a hyphen where needed. **For example:**

Incorrect: The out of date policy created problems for our agents.

Corrected: The *out-of-date* policy created problems for our agents.

1. Our store is located on a one way street.
2. We offer 24 hour a day service for your office product needs.
3. We provide high quality services at reasonable prices.
4. Check out our attention getting color brochures, which we can customize to your needs.
5. Also, make sure to read our flyer in the *Lehi Town Times.* You are sure to find some unheard of bargains on well known brands.

SECTION C CONCEPT CHECK

1. Under what circumstances do you add an apostrophe to possessive pronouns such as *mine, hers,* or *its?*
2. When would you place a hyphen between two words that modify another word jointly?
3. What should you use in place of *that there* or *this here?*

SECTION D: HEDGES, EMPHATICS, FILLERS, AND TAG-ONS

Writers often include extra information on the way to discovering their message. While editing, a writer needs to identify key points and evaluate the message from the reader's point of view. Information that is insignificant to the reader should be cut. In this section, you will examine some types of empty information to avoid in the business messages you craft: hedges, emphatics, fillers, and tag-ons.

BOX 6.1 The Editing Process

BEFORE	AFTER
May 24, 2006 To Whom It May Concern: I first met Lillie about 15 years ago at the First National Bank where Lillie was a employee at the bank and she voluntarily signed up for 2, 12 week training classes that were facilitated by myself. I am happy to report that Lillie did a excellent job, improving her skills dramatically. My reords also shows that Lillie had perfect attendance while attending the class and I found that Lillie was fully committed and excellent skill gains were made. If I had been required to give Lilli a grade it would have been A+ because of the quality of her work and her outstanding participation as well as other qualities that stand out in my mind about Lillie such as her warm, and compassionate way-of-being. I give Lillie my highest recommendation for whatever she may pursue. I look forward to hear from you should you need more information from me about Lilly. Very truely yours, Diana J. Gatto	May 24, 200624 Dr. Brad Johnson Best University 2323 West Chicago Avenue Oak Lawn, IL 60459 Dear Dr. Johnson: I first met Lillie about 15 years ago at the First National Bank. Lillie was an employee there and voluntarily signed up for two 12-week training classes that I facilitated. Lillie did an excellent job in the class: she had perfect attendance, participated fully, and supported other students with enthusiasm. Of course, Lillie was fully committed and made excellent skill gains. If the bank had required a grade, Lillie would have received an A+ because of the quality of her work and her outstanding participation. Another quality that Lillie possesses is her warm and compassionate way of being. Lillie deserves my highest recommendation. Please feel free to write me or call me for additional information. Sincerely, Diana J. Gatto Training Facilitator

HEDGES AND EMPHATICS

A **hedge** is a modifier that writers and speakers use to qualify a statement or express hesitation. An **emphatic** places emphasis on the word it describes in the attempt to create a stronger effect. According to Joseph Williams, author of *Style,* these types of modifiers often create weak, cluttered writing; he encourages writers to use hedges and emphatics sparingly.[6] Getting rid of hedges and emphatics puts more emphasis on your point. As Robert Browning said, *less is more.*

Here are some common hedges to avoid:

kind of	sort of	rarely
hardly	at times	tend
sometimes	maybe	may be
perhaps	rather	in my opinion
more or less	possibly	probably
seemingly	for all intents and purposes	to a certain extent
supposedly	usually	often
almost always	and so on	

Weak

For all intents and purposes, listening is an important part of communicating. Listening *may* help you connect with your audience by understanding *some of* their needs. By becoming a better listener, *to a certain extent* you become a better communicator, *at least in my opinion.*

Listed below are some common emphatics; *use them sparingly* or they will detract from the meaning:

very	most	many
often	literally	virtually
usually	certainly	inevitably
as you can plainly see	as everyone is aware	as you know
always	each and every time	totally
it is quite clear that	as you may already know	absolutely
undoubtedly	first and foremost	and so on

<u>Weak</u>

As everyone knows, listening is a *really* important part of communicating. Listening *certainly* helps you connect with your audience by understanding *most, if not all, of* their needs. By becoming a better listener, you *literally* become a better communicator, *as you may already know.*

Without the hedges and emphatics, here is the short paragraph:

<u>Revised</u>

Listening is an important part of communicating. Listening helps you connect with your audience by understanding their needs. By becoming a better listener, you become a better communicator.

PRACTICE

Instructions: Remove the hedges and fillers from the following paragraph.

As you may already know, our department is totally too busy now to even consider going to a seminar in June. To a certain extent, I am kind of disappointed that we will miss attending this very, very worthwhile event. It is quite clear that each and every time an opportunity such as this comes along, we should absolutely find a way to go because undoubtedly we will benefit from it. If things even kind of settle down, I will certainly call you to see if there is still room for us to participate.

▸Language Diversity

Pronouns: Sometimes the pronouns used in local language differ from those used in Business English. One pattern in local language is to use *me* instead of *myself.* For example, "I'll leave *myself* a message so I don't forget" could be spoken in local language as "I'll leave *me* a message so I don't forget."

Differences between local language and Business English occur with each of the pronoun cases. Chapter 5, "Pronouns," reviews pronouns in depth, comparing and contrasting Business English with your local language.

Ask Yourself: *What changes have I made in the way that I use pronouns when speaking in formal situations?*

FILLERS AND TAG-ONS

Fillers are not modifiers—they are empty words and add no value to your message. Two words that are often inserted as fillers in speech and writing are *just* and *like.*

Incorrect: My manager *like just* decided that I could *like* take the day off.

Correct: My manager decided that I could take the day off.

Incorrect: *So* I said that was cool and *just like* thanked her and everything.

Correct: I told her that was nice and thanked her.

In addition to eliminating fillers, pay attention to **tag-ons.** Though sentences *can* end in prepositions, often a preposition is added as an unnecessary tag-on. Tag-ons are grammatically incorrect. The word *at* is a common tag-on.

Incorrect: Where do you work *at?*

Correct: Where do you work?

Incorrect: Where do you plan to go to graduate school *at?*

Correct: Where do you plan to go to graduate school?

Here are some examples of sentences that end in prepositions that are now considered acceptable (in the past, these sentences would have been considered incorrect):

Correct: Please tell me what you are thinking *about.*

Formal: Please tell me *about* what you are thinking.

Correct: That's the meeting I want to be *at.*

Formal: That's the meeting *at which* I want to be.

Which unnecessary words do you repetitively put in your speech or writing? Do you repetitively insert words such as *like, just,* or *totally* in your speech? Do you have a tendency to use these words when you are feeling confident, or are you more likely to use them when you are unsure of yourself? Is this use an unconscious habit?

Some people refer to these speech qualities as "Valley girl talk"; however, they are common in all parts of the country. In social situations, using fillers and tag-ons is acceptable. However, if you use these types of expressions in a social situation, you are likely to carry over the habit into a business environment. Consistently using fillers and tag-ons in the business world can affect the way more sophisticated speakers judge your talent.

PRACTICE

Instructions: Edit the following sentences for fillers, tag-ons, hedges, and emphatics.

Incorrect: I just like sort of forgot to do the assignment.

Corrected: I forgot to do the assignment.

1. Would you like go with me to the meeting at like 4 P.M. today?

2. Please leave a message for the recruiter telling him where you live at.

3. Mike just like totally freaked out when Marge asked him where he had been at.

4. Tell the project manager where you would like to go to so he like considers your request.

5. Make this job like a priority so that you do like really, really well.

Internet Exercise 6.2

Adjective Worksheets: Need more practice on the topics covered in this chapter? Go to the Web site at **www.mhhe.com/youngBE**. Select "Student Activities," and then click on the "Chapter 6" link to get started.

SECTION D CONCEPT CHECK

1. Write a short paragraph about your career goals; fill the paragraph with emphatics and hedges.

2. Revise the paragraph so that you get right to the point.

3. Write a few sentences that contain fillers such as *like, just,* and *totally.* Now, edit out the empty words so that each sentence states its point concisely.

CHAPTER 6 SUMMARY

As you have seen, using modifiers in business writing is different from using modifiers in creative writing. Whereas your creative writing can be colorful, and even emotional, at times; business writing is clear, crisp, and to the point. However, even in creative writing, you should limit your use of hedges and emphatics and avoid the use of fillers and tag-ons. And placing modifiers close to the words they modify is just as important in creative writing as it is in business writing. The two genres bridge when it comes to using modifiers correctly. (See Table 6.2 for a review of the main points covered in this chapter.)

TABLE 6.2 | Adverb and Adjective Review

FUNCTIONS OF ADVERBS AND ADJECTIVES		
Adverbs modify verbs, adjectives, and other adverbs, as well as infinitives, gerunds, and participles. Adverbs answer questions such as: **Why? How? When? Where? To What Degree?**		
Adjectives modify nouns, including gerunds, and pronouns. Adjectives answer questions such as: **Whose? Which? How Much? How Many? What Kind?**		
Use adjectives after linking verbs such as *be (am, is, are, was, were)* and *feel* when the verb expresses the condition or state of being of the subject. For example: The report is *good.* She feels *bad* about the changes.		
COMPARISONS WITH ADJECTIVES AND ADVERBS		
Adjectives and adverbs have three forms to indicate degrees of comparison: positive, comparative, and superlative.		
• The **positive form** makes no comparison; it is the simple form of the modifier: *red, slow, seriously.*		
• The **comparative form** compares two things, indicating an increase or decrease over the positive form: *redder, slower, more seriously.*		
• The **superlative form** indicates the greatest or least degree among three or more objects: *reddest, slowest, most seriously.*		
COMPARATIVE: COMPARING TWO THINGS		
• Add *er* to words of one or two syllables.		
• Use *more* or *less* with words of two or more syllables.		
SUPERLATIVE: COMPARING THREE OR MORE THINGS		
• Add *est* to words of one or two syllables.		
• Use *most* or *least* with words of two or more syllables.		
IRREGULAR MODIFIERS		
Positive	**Comparative**	**Superlative**
bad	worse	worst
good, well	better	best
far	farther, further	farthest, furthest
little	less, lesser, littler	least, littlest
many, some, much	more	most
• Have you remembered to hyphenate compound modifiers? The report is *two pages long.* The *two-page report* is complete.		

CHAPTER 6 CHECKLIST

When composing business messages, consider the following:

___ Use comparative and superlative degrees correctly.

___ Place modifiers close to the word or words they modify.

___ Avoid double negatives.

___ Apply pronoun modifiers correctly.

___ Use hyphens in compound modifiers.

___ Eliminate fillers and tag-ons in speech.

___ Follow a linking verb such as *feel* with an adjective.

___ Apply an *ly* ending to adverbs that need it or sound better with it.

CHAPTER 6 END-OF-CHAPTER ACTIVITIES

ACTIVITY 1: PROCESS MEMO

INSTRUCTIONS: Write your instructor a short message describing some of the principles you learned in this chapter. How are you using modifiers differently? Are you focusing on your speech as well as your writing?

If you have Internet access, you can complete this exercise online at **www.mhhe.com/youngBE** and then send an e-mail to your instructor.

ACTIVITY 2: ADVERBS AND ADJECTIVES—THE BASICS

PART A

INSTRUCTIONS: Correct the sentences below for their use of adjectives and adverbs. For example:

Incorrect: If you feel badly about the situation, change it.

Corrected: If you feel *bad* about the situation, change it.

1. You did good on your latest report.

2. Her new computer crashes more frequently than you.

3. Riki felt badly about firing Sue.

4. You will be able to go further if you take the train than if you walk.

5. Our procurement officer finds the most latest technology available.

6. Your team works more diligently than anyone.

7. I can't hardly wait until summer break.

8. The lesser of your worries is how many vacation days you have left.

9. The middle managers have requested more better working conditions.

10. Why didn't the client have no way of getting to the open house?

11. Leaving the corporate world was one of the most hard decisions I've ever had to make.

12. The client seemed more happier after we waived the initial fees.

PART B

INSTRUCTIONS: In the paragraph below, correct errors in the use of comparative and superlative adverbs, as well as other common errors.

One of the most smartest lessons I learned when I was interviewing for jobs was never to say nothing negative about my previous employers. I wasn't hired for the most best job I could ever have hoped to find because they thought I felt too negatively about some tasks. After I wasn't never called, I phoned the person who had interviewed me to ask why they didn't offer me no job. She told me that they were looking for the most positivist person since the position required customer contact. I've learned my lesson good, and I'll never be negative during no interview again.

ACTIVITY 3: PLACING MODIFIERS CORRECTLY

PART A

INSTRUCTIONS: Correct the sentences below by placing modifiers close to the word or words they modify. For example:

Incorrect: Rushing to get the report finished, calls went unanswered.

Corrected: Rushing to get the report finished, *I did not answer calls.*

1. Buying my train pass, the turnstile tripped me.

2. The research team only spent 40 hours on the Davidson Project.

3. We bought more supplies for the project using the company credit card.

4. The manager left the note in a hurry.

5. I approached the lectern wearing my best suit.

6. Trying to avoid a crash, my car quickly turned to the right.

7. The client found evidence that she had been cheated in the investor report.

8. Arguing about the plan's integrity, the boardroom was noisy.

9. Clients should expect a period of adjustment who are switching suppliers.

10. Hurrying to the meeting, my coffee spilled all over my new jacket.

11. Will you bring these notes to my assistant in the manila folder?

12. The officer introduced himself to the group of citizens who recently graduated from the police academy.

PART B

INSTRUCTIONS: Correct the misplaced and dangling modifiers in the following memo; there may be other sorts of errors as well.

MEMO TO: Marketing Department Employees

FROM: Ginny DeLong, Marketing Vice President

SUBJECT: Employee Appreciation Outing

The employee appreciation outing will be held on June 8 which we have all been looking forward to. Our department only has to bring soft drinks and cups. Michael will provide details on the logistics of the soft drinks and cups who is my new assistant. Preparing for this outing, there will be one meeting this Wednesday. Please only come to the meeting if you plan on attending the outing. This year's outing will include games and prizes which will be held at Briarhill Park. All of you deserve this reward so please attend, relax and have fun, because you have worked hard this year.

ACTIVITY 4: SPEAKING BUSINESS

BACKGROUND: The following is a list of the most common errors that business speakers make with adjectives and adverbs:

1. Using an adverb after the linking verb *feel,* as in *I feel badly.*
2. Using *more, most, less,* or *least* and a suffix: "I'm more hungrier now than before."
3. Using the word *irregardless.*
4. Using double negatives, as in "That don't make no sense at all."
5. Adding tag-ons or using hedges and fillers, as in "He really, really like asked where you live at?"
6. Bobtailing adverbs by leaving off the *ly* ending, as in "Speak loud so I can understand."

INSTRUCTIONS: Identify which of the above you need to work on. For each topic, write at least five sentences in your local language and then translate them into Business English. Share your sentences with a partner. Read a sentence in local language aloud; in a spoken response, your partner will translate it into Business English. Though practicing your writing skills is important, so is practicing your speaking skills.

ACTIVITY 5: OTHER MODIFIERS—PRONOUNS AND COMPOUND ADJECTIVES

PART A

INSTRUCTIONS: The following sentences contain errors in modifying pronouns and compound adjectives. Make corrections as needed. For example:

Incorrect: All long term leases were offered and signed.

Corrected: All *long-term* leases were offered and signed.

1. Please place all written requests in that there box.
2. Do you have them reports that Julie needed?
3. The yellow folders are yours, and the blue ones are mines.
4. Please reconsider the numbers in your proposal; we need some down to earth estimates.
5. My research team will give you they report on Tuesday.
6. Hurry! Fields is having a going out of business sale today!
7. Ms. Jackson's office includes a made to order mahogany desk.
8. Alex bought he new car through an online auction.
9. The fifth floor receptionist is friendly.
10. That there presentation took me four hours to create.
11. The pilot announced that we would have a three to four hour delay.
12. Our financial consultant will help you decide whether you need a 6, 12, or 24 month certificate.

PART B

INSTRUCTIONS: The following paragraph contains errors in modifying pronouns and compound adjectives. Make corrections as needed.

Dear Mr. Nagella:

You have been a treasured client since our one year anniversary; therefore, we would like to offer you a one of a kind deal that is reserved for our best customers. Our senior sales representative, Kathy Wong, will contact you shortly with the details of this offer. After hearing the details, let me now if them terms are acceptable. Never before have we offered such an off the charts deal. Please look forward to hearing from Ms. Wong early next week.

Sincerely yours,

ACTIVITY 6: MISPLACED MODIFIERS

INSTRUCTIONS: In the following sentences, place modifiers correctly. For example:

Incorrect: Expecting conflict, the team formations were announced by the president.

Corrected: *Expecting conflict, the president* announced team formations.

1. Ed revealed the bid to a woman he thought was a coworker by mistake.

2. Braden first saw the Grand Canyon driving down a dirt road.

3. The reference desk is in the hallway which has a complete company directory.

4. A tree fell across the building which had been uprooted by the winds.

5. We leased a copier from a vendor that was broken.

ACTIVITY 7: EDITING AND REVISING

INSTRUCTIONS: Correct the following paragraphs for errors in punctuation, verbs, pronouns, hedges, and emphatics.

ELEMENTS OF A SIMPLE BUT SATISFYING ESSAY

The word *essay* come from the French *essai,* which means "attempt." The root of this word might indeed help you understand the nature of this genre: you be *attempting* to put forth, explain, to describe, or arguing a point. Many kinds of essays exist from like the visual type to the standard five paragraph theme however the elements below might really help simplify the process, for you.

First of all, an essay undoubtedly has *structure.* There is a clear beginning middle, and ending, the reader can pinpoint a turning point or "pivot" point in the essay.

Second, the essay has *style.* The writer sort of uses a specific voice (for example, sarcastic, nostalgic, or authoritatively). The writer also craft really elegant memorable sentences. After, hearing the essay reading aloud; the audience can totally remember specific lines and phrases.

Furthermore, the essay contains *evidence.* The writer provides completely vivid descriptions and cool images, using fresh and bold words, and includes somewhat figurative language such as, metaphor and simile. The writer uses complete and specific examples, to which the readers completely easily relate or envisioned.

Another important element is piquing the readers' interest with the *title,* and *introduction.* The writer should so totally avoid, mundane and nondescript, titles such as "Description Essay" or "Argument on the Death Penalty." The introduction should arouse anticipation in the readers so that them look forward to the rest of the essay.

Finally, the *conclusion* should really accomplish one of two things: leave the readers feeling *satisfied* or leave the readers *pondering.*

ACTIVITY 8: CUMULATIVE CHAPTER REVIEW

INSTRUCTIONS: The following sentences contain a variety of errors relating to modifiers; make corrections as needed.

1. Jen's new car is faster than you.
2. Billie felt badly about her consistent tardiness.
3. You will go farther in the company if you earn an M.B.A.
4. David gets the most earliest edition of the Sunday paper.
5. I can't hardly explain the discrepancies in the report.
6. We didn't have no answer for the accounting errors.
7. I noticed the new water cooler walking down the hallway.
8. David, Beth, and Donna took over the publishing company quickly by buying the majority of stocks.
9. Never throwing away leftovers, the lunchroom refrigerator was disgusting.
10. Customers will take advantage of the new discounts who like using our products.

11. Report to that there office when you return from lunch.

12. I gathered them account folders that you requested.

13. Should we waive the $200 a month fee?

14. The salespeople presented they quarterly reports at the board meeting.

15. Please reconsider leaving us; don't make a spur of the moment decision.

ACTIVITY 9: "WRITER'S REFERENCE MANUAL" DRILL

INSTRUCTIONS: In the "Writer's Reference Manual," read the entry "quantifiers" and then answer the following questions:

1. What is a quantifier?

2. Which quantifiers can you use in place of *a lot of* or *lots of?*

3. List four quantifiers that work with count nouns. (*Count nouns* represent items that can be tallied individually; for example, *tree, car,* and *dollar* are all count nouns.)

4. List four quantifiers that work with noncount nouns. (*Noncount nouns* represent items that come in mass and cannot be counted individually; for example, *honor, money,* and *luck.*)

5. List three quantifiers that work with either count or noncount nouns.

ACTIVITY 10: VOCABULARY LIST

A. COMMONLY MISSPELLED WORDS

INSTRUCTIONS: The list below contains words taken from a compilation of the 500 most commonly misspelled words and from the chapter. Practice them until you can spell them automatically and use them correctly.

1. apology (n) an act of contrition; an expression of regret
2. athlete (n) sportsperson, competitor

3. bidialectal (n) the ability to be fluent in two dialects
4. colloquial (adj) informal language, slang
5. clientele (n) customers, patrons, clients
6. conceive (v) imagine, envision, visualize
7. embarrass (v) to cause to feel self-conscious, ill at ease, or ashamed; impede
8. evaluation (n) assessment, appraisal, ranking, or rating
9. feedback (n) describing, giving facts and details
10. hackneyed (adj) lacking in freshness because of overuse; trite, banal
11. hedge (n) a word or phrase that qualifies a statement, such as "kind of"
12. lagniappe (n) Creole term, "throwing in a little something extra"
13. prevalent (adj) widely occurring, common, customary
14. privilege (n) benefit, opportunity, a right or advantage
15. verbatim (adj) word for word

B. SIMILAR WORDS

INSTRUCTIONS: The list below contains similar words, some of which are profiled in the Vocabulary Builders in each chapter. Use these words in sentences until their meaning becomes clear.

alot/a lot: *A lot* is always two words (and is sometimes considered colloquial).

We have *a lot* of things to discuss.

alright/all right: *All right* is the standard spelling; *alright* is a spelling error (according to an abridged dictionary).

Though it is *all right* to be a little late, try to be on time.

past/passed: *Past* is used as either a noun, an adjective, or a preposition meaning "time gone by" or "beyond." *Passed* is the past tense of the verb *pass* and means "moved along" or "transferred."

Katie John walked *past* the correct address. As she *passed* it, she noticed her mistake.

Bill *passed* the material to his friend.

In the *past,* we would not have *passed* so much time waiting.

regardless/irregardless: *Regardless* means "in spite of" or "despite." *Irregardless* is a redundancy, with the suffix *less* making the word negative; adding the prefix *ir* creates a built-in double negative. Use *regardless.*

Regardless of the situation, I will attend the event.

THE INBOX

COMPOSING

In your journal describe your favorite room or place. What does the room or place look like? How do you feel when you are there? What do you do when you are there?

Example:

A Cozy, Warm Escape
By Erin Vega

My room is my haven from the world. When I walk through the polished oak door, the coziness of my room envelops me. My color choices and lighting help maintain the cozy atmosphere. The carpet is a warm brown like freshly tilled earth. The walls are painted in a creamy light yellow that seems to glow like melting butter. My dresser and nightstand blend into the atmosphere with their warm earth tones. I have two lamps in my room that cast a subtle glow like an autumn sunset instead of glaring bright lights. My bed, in the center of the cozy little room, is covered with a dark chocolate fleece blanket that makes me think of a melting chocolate bar.

When I enter my room, I leave all the annoying, loud, and distracting sights and sounds behind. In my room I am at peace and can think and dream to my heart's content.

REFLECTING

Reread your paragraph describing your favorite room or place. How much sensory detail did you include? Make a quick list of the descriptive words and phrases you used. Would someone else be able to visualize this place if you took away those descriptive phrases? If you like, revise parts of the description that *tell* rather than *show* by replacing abstract words with concrete words.

DISCUSSING

1. Do you think that descriptive writing is important in the business world? Work in a group to create a list of jobs that require descriptive writing abilities. One example is the job of an attorney, who needs to describe events accurately. Another example is the job of an interior designer, who must describe design plans to clients. How many more examples can you think of?
2. In a small group, think of as many descriptive words as you can to describe your classroom. When you have a substantial list, work together to write a paragraph describing the classroom. The groups should take turns reading their descriptions.

EDITING

Please look for errors in modifiers, pronouns, verbs, punctuation, and spelling.

> Seneca Delivery Services Incident Report Form
>
> First and foremost, on the morning of January 22, 2007, I entered the supply room to take an inventory as I do every Friday. Coming into the room, the office supply shelf was empty. I couldn't hardly believe what I saw! All of the office supply was missing. This include 14 boxes of black pens, 12 box of blue pens, 65 notepads, 2 cases of sticky notes, 8 cases of photocopy paper, and a case of file folders, not too mention the box of miscellaneious supply that was on the top shelf. For all intents and purposes, I realize that someone had stole our supplies.
>
> Quickly checking each office, the supplies did not turn up anywheres. I feel very, very badly about this horable circumstance. I know that the responsibility is mines. I was really sure that I had lock the supply room on Thursday night. Whomever came in also has keys. I no now that I have to be more carefully considering the supply room.
>
> This loss come to about $870. This is a more bigger loss than last year when we left our reception area unlocked. But at least last year we knew it were not a employee of the companies'. Someone who work here had done this, I have come to fear. The outside doors was all lock and only a person with a key could let theirselves in. Its inevitably that we're need a new lock for the supply room.

END CHAPTER 6 EOC ACTIVITIES

KEY TO LEARNING INVENTORY

1. T
2. T
3. T
4. F
5. T
6. F
7. F
8. F
9. T
10. F

CHAPTER 6 ENDNOTES

1. Merriam-Webster Online, A sampling of new words from the new 2006 update of *Merriam-Webster's Collegiate Dictionary,* 11th ed., **http://www.m-w.com/info/new_words.htm**, accessed July 22, 2006.
2. Jim W. Corder and John J. Ruszkiewicz, *Handbook of Current English,* 8th ed., HarperCollins Publishers, 1989, p.181.
3. Corder, p. 180.
4. Merriam-Webster Online, accessed on July 22, 2006.
5. Constance Gefvert, Richard Raspa, and Amy Richards, *Keys to American English,* Harcourt, Brace, Jovanovich, Inc., New York, 1975, page 237.
6. Joseph M. Williams, *Style,* The University of Chicago Press, Chicago, 1990, page 126.

Practical Applications

In this unit, you move beyond the sentence core and the parts of speech: you will now cover advanced editing and revising principles. These principles will help you write sentences and paragraphs that are not only correct but also clear and concise. By the end of this unit, you will also move beyond writing e-mail, memos, and e-memos to writing business letters.

- Chapter 7 covers writing traps: possessives, capitalization, and number usage, as well as colons, dashes, and ellipsis marks.
- Chapter 8 prepares you to develop a powerful writing style at the sentence level by reviewing some principles you covered previously (such as the active voice) and presenting new principles as well.
- Chapter 9 prepares you to develop effective paragraphs, while also helping you to structure information in whole documents from beginning to middle to end.
- Chapter 10 pulls information together by giving you professional guidelines for office communication. You will even have an opportunity to work on your résumé and cover letter.

In this unit, you will start longer and more comprehensive projects. Everything that you learned in previous chapters will be put to use in this unit.

Unit 3 Practical Aplicatons

BUSINESS LETTER ESSENTIALS

Letters are used for formal communications when the topic demands more attention than a phone call or an e-mail message will provide. Below is information about the block-style letter (also referred to as the *full-block style*). Several additional styles exist (such as the modified-block style and simplified style); examples are posted on the Web site at www.mhhe.com/youngBE.

Basic Parts of Letters

Every letter, regardless of the style, contains basic elements or parts. With the block style, each part starts at the left margin. Thus, writers have no decisions to make about indenting lines or paragraphs. In Figure U3.1, review the Block-Style Business Letter. For a thorough explanation of letter parts and spacing, please go to the Web site at www.mhhe.com/youngBE.

FIGURE U3.1 Block-Style Business Letter

The Writing Institute
180 North Michigan Avenue
Chicago, IL 60611
www.writinginstitute.org
312-555-1212

February 14, 2007 — Start the **dateline** 3 lines below the letterhead or no more than 2 ½ inches from the top of the page

Mr. Bob Allison
GlobalCom Network
333 West Wacker Drive
Chicago, IL 60610

Start the **inside address** 4 to 5 lines below the date

Dear Mr. Allison: — Start the **salutation** 2 lines below the inside address

Thank you for asking us to help you improve your company's communication style and image. We'll start by covering the basics of a business letter, which includes three parts: the **introduction**, **body**, and **conclusion**.

The **introduction** of a business letter connects you to your reader and connects your reader to the purpose of your letter; for most letters, also state your main point in the introduction. In the **body** of your letter, include details, examples, and supporting points. The body should be as long as it takes to make your point, but no longer. For example, the body could be one paragraph for a short letter or any number of paragraphs for longer letters. Here are a couple more points:

1. Use visual persuasion, such as bullet points or numbering so that major points are instantly visible for your reader.

2. Apply correct formatting, such as double spacing between paragraphs, to achieve effective use of white space.

In your **conclusion**, define next steps: inform the reader of any action you will take or that you request the reader to take. Invite the reader to contact you for additional information, and give your contact information, if you choose.

Sincerely, — Start your closing 2 lines below the body

Reginald J. Grey
Instructional Designer

Start the **writer's typed signature** 3 to 5 lines below the closing
Include your **title**, if you choose

Enclosure — Use an **enclosure notation** for documents enclosed with the letter
Attachment — Use an **attachment notation** for documents stapled or paper-clipped
cc: Vincent Giorgio — *cc* stands for **courtesy copy**; start it a double space below the title

PS A **postscript** is an afterthought; include it a double space below the last of the other notations.

Chapter Seven

Writing Traps

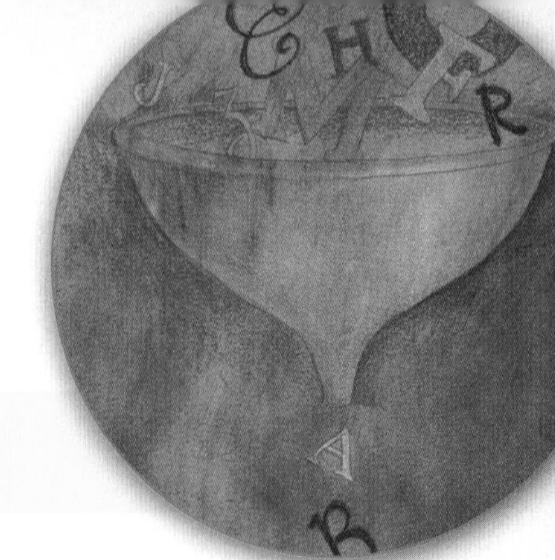

We can't solve problems by using the same kind of thinking we used when we created them.
—Albert Einstein, physicist, Nobel laureate (1879–1955)

This chapter covers a smorgasbord of topics that confuse writers. The chapter starts with plurals and possessives—topics that relate to the letter *s.* In English, the *s* causes more problems than any other letter. Along with learning more about the *s,* you will also learn how to use the apostrophe: should it be placed before or after the *s* with possessive nouns?

Capitalization is another writing trap. When writers are unsure of the rules, they have a tendency to capitalize too many words. And sometimes when they are "sure of the rules," they also capitalize too many words. In Section B, you will learn some basic guidelines so that you can make quick and easy decisions about capitalization; some of those rules may surprise you.

When you use numbers in a document, should they be written as words or numerals? When you learn the rules for numbers in Section C, you will be able to make clear, consistent decisions that keep your documents professional.

In Chapter 3, you learned punctuation rules for commas and semicolons, which gave you a sense of sentence structure. *Are you still paying attention to the difference between complete sentences and run-ons or fragments?* In Section D, you have an opportunity to reinforce your understanding of sentence structure as you review colons, dashes, and ellipses.

Colons, dashes, and ellipsis marks give your writing variety and flair, especially when you write e-mail. Just as using other elements of writing correctly gives you credibility, using these marks according to the rules also reinforces the credibility and professionalism of your writing. One more recommendation: With these marks, don't get carried away—use them sparingly.

To learn more about The Writing Process, please visit our Web site at **www.mhhe.com/youngBE**

Outline

Chapter 7: Writing Traps

Section A: Plurals and Possessives

Section B: Capitalization

Section C: Number Usage

Section D: Colons, Dashes, and Ellipses

Objectives

When you have completed your study of Chapter 7, you will be able to:

1. Punctuate singular and plural possessives correctly.
2. Apply capitalization rules in correspondence.
3. Distinguish between when to spell out numbers and when to use numerals.
4. Make informed decisions about using colons, dashes, and ellipsis marks.

Learning Inventory

1. Numbers below ten should always be spelled as words, not as numerals. T/F
2. When numbers above and below ten are in the same sentence, spell them in words. T/F
3. When a regular noun is plural and possessive, place the apostrophe after the *s*. T/F
4. Capitalize business titles only when they immediately precede a name. T/F
5. A dash can be used correctly in place of a comma, semicolon, period, or colon. T/F
6. A writer can use four or five periods for ellipsis marks. T/F
7. Use the term *percentage,* not *percent,* when no number appears with it. T/F
8. Proper nouns are always capitalized, but proper adjectives are not. T/F
9. For irregular plural possessives, add an apostrophe plus *s*. T/F
10. A person's official job title is always capitalized. T/F

Goal-Setting Exercises

What kinds of questions do you have about numbers, capitalization, or possessives? Do you use colons, dashes, or ellipsis marks correctly . . . or are you even sure what they are or what their purpose is? Write three goals stating what you would like to achieve in this chapter. Good luck!

1. ______________________________

2. ______________________________

3. ______________________________

SECTION A: PLURALS AND POSSESSIVES

Deciding where to place an apostrophe for a possessive is difficult enough when the noun is regular and singular, but what happens if the noun is irregular and plural? In this section, you will learn about singular and plural possessives as well as that "ever-elusive" apostrophe. Let's start by briefly reviewing nouns, as only nouns can be possessed or owned.

NOUNS AS POSSESSIONS

Nouns and pronouns can show possession or ownership of other nouns. At times, it can be tricky to identify a possessive because some nouns, such as *value* or *belief* or *hope,* are abstract; in other words, they are not concrete objects.

In Chapter 2, you learned that a noun can be a person, place, or thing, such as *brother, school,* or *CD player.* All of these words sound as if they can be owned or possessed by someone. You also learned that a noun can also be a quality, state, or action, such as *humor, thought,* or *arrival.*[1] At times, these abstract nouns—nouns other than persons, places, or things—can be challenging to identify.

The easiest way to determine whether a word is a noun is to place the word *the* in front of it. If the phrase sounds complete, the word is probably a noun. For example:

the idea the thought the color the glare

Whenever you see a noun ending in an *s,* ask yourself, *Is this noun plural or possessive or both?* When two nouns appear together, even when the first noun does not end in an *s,* check to see if the first noun possesses the second one. (The *s* may have been inadvertently left off the first noun.) Does the first noun need an apostrophe and *s* to show possession? For example:

Incorrect:	Bobs arrival	the windows display	the rooms color	Margies hope
Correct:	Bob's arrival	the window's display	the room's color	Margie's hope

SINGULAR POSSESSIVES

Singular Nouns Not Ending in *s*

To form the possessive of a singular noun that does not end in *s,* add an apostrophe and *s* (*'s*). This category is the easiest because you are taking a noun and adding to it in a logical way. Here are some examples:

Singular Noun	Singular Possessive
book	book's cover
manager	manager's responsibilities
friend	friend's advice
Mary	Mary's suggestion
brother	my brother's jacket

Sometimes it is difficult to determine whether a noun is showing possession; this is especially true with inanimate objects such as *wind* or *paper.* When in doubt, ask yourself if you can change the sentence around by using the word *of.* That is, *the paper of yesterday* becomes *yesterday's paper.* Here are more examples:

the end of the game	the game's end
the beginning of the movie	the movie's beginning
the force of the wind	the wind's force
the work of one day	a day's work
the color of the pen	the pen's color
the success of our team	our team's success
the heat of the sun	the sun's heat

At times, possessives can sound awkward, especially when a group of words string together to show possession, as in the following:

Awkward: an associate of mine's idea

my sister's accountant's advice

my manager's supervisor's request

When those constructions occur, show the possession by changing the word order, as shown below:

Preferred: an idea of an associate of mine

the advice of my sister's accountant

the request of my manager's supervisor

PRACTICE

Instructions: Change the following to the possessive form.

EXAMPLE the permission of the owner the owner's permission

1. the friends of my brother ________
2. the price of the book ________
3. the cover of the report ________
4. the influence of the team leader ________
5. the leaders of our nation ________
6. the advice of my professor ________
7. the reports of the agency ________

Singular Nouns Ending in *S*

To form the possessive of a singular noun that ends in *s,* add an apostrophe alone or add an apostrophe plus an *s ('s).* Follow these guidelines:

- If a new syllable is formed in the pronunciation of the possessive, add an apostrophe plus *s,* as in the following:

  the witness's answer

  Dallas's downtown area

  the hostess's guest list

  the actress's role

- If the addition of an extra syllable would make the word challenging to pronounce, add only the apostrophe, as in the following:

  Mr. Jones' (or Jones's) meeting

  Mark Phillips' briefcase

  for goodness' sake

PLURAL POSSESSIVES

Regular Plural Possessives

To form the possessive of a regular plural noun (a plural noun ending in *s* or *es*), add an apostrophe after the *s (s').* In other words, make the singular form of the noun plural *before* you make the noun possessive.

SPEAKING BUSINESS

***S* Endings:** You learned earlier in Chapter 4, "Verbs at Work," that the *s* form of the verb, or third-person singular, creates special problems for writers. Actually, other types of words ending in *s* create problems too.

In the plural form of common words, speakers often inadvertently leave off the *s;* for instance, "fifty cent." When writing or speaking in business, add an *s* when the Business English form demands it.

This chapter gives you practice with your writing skills, but also practice in pronouncing the *s.* Below is a list of singular nouns. Turn them into their plural forms, and then pronounce them out loud.

distributor	vendor
desk	dollar
artifact	DVD
apartment	executive
material	assistant
application	administrator

If you need more practice on this, do End-of-Chapter Activity 4.

Singular Possessive	Plural Possessive
the owner's address	a few owners' addresses
our manager's decision	all of the managers' decisions
an employee's question	many employees' questions
my shirt's collar	my shirts' collars
our mouse pad's design	our mouse pads' designs

When the singular form of a noun already ends in *s,* make the noun plural by adding *es* to the singular. Then form the possessive by adding an apostrophe. For example:

Singular	Plural	Singular Possessive	Plural Possessive
business	businesses	business's owner	businesses' owners
virus	viruses	virus's origination	viruses' originations

Notice in the above examples that when the possessive noun is plural, the object it modifies is also plural. That's because the objects being possessed are *count nouns,* nouns that can become plural.[2]

In contrast, some nouns come in mass and are considered *noncount nouns;* examples include *paint* or *cake* or *food.* Other examples of noncount nouns are *honor, integrity,* and *humor.*

Singular Possessive	Plural Possessive
a boy scout's honor	several boy scouts' honor
a person's integrity	many persons' integrity
a friend's help	our friends' help

For last names (surnames) that end in *s, x, ch, sh,* or *z,* add *es* to form the plural. Then form the plural by adding an apostrophe, as in the following:

Singular	Plural	Singular Possessive	Plural Possessive
Fox	the Foxes	Mr. Fox's car	the Foxes' family reunion
Banks	the Bankses	Mary Banks' schedule	the Bankses' get-together

Irregular Plural Possessives

To form the possessive of an irregular plural noun, change the singular form of the noun to the plural form and then add an apostrophe and *s (children's).*

Singular Possessive	Plural Possessive
a child's toy	the children's toys
one woman's hat	many women's hats
one man's idea	many men's ideas
a lady's suggestion	several ladies' suggestions
a woman's right	women's rights

PRACTICE

Instructions: Turn the following nouns into singular possessives and then plural possessives.

EXAMPLE contractor contractor's schedule contractors' schedules

	Singular Possessive	Plural Possessive
1. boss	my _____ office	both ______ offices
2. waitress	this ________ table	these _________ tables
3. year	this _____ schedule	both _____ schedules
4. secretary	my ________ laptop	our _________ laptops
5. director	the ________ speech	two ________ speeches
6. letter	a ______ format	these ______ formats
7. client	the ______ needs	all ______ needs
8. headquarters	the ___________ building	both ___________ buildings
9. salesperson	a ___________ commission	two ___________ commissions
10. vendor	our last _______ rate	three new _______ rates

VOCABULARY: SOUNDALIKES

Alright/All right: Though this might surprise you, "alright" is not a standard English spelling. The correct spelling is *all right.* To remember, think of something as being either *all right* or *all wrong.*

My manager said that it was *all right* for me to take Friday off, but she was not pleased about it.

GROUP WORDS

With group words or compound nouns, the apostrophe and the *s* are added to the last term. For example: Rule #7

the queen of England's duties

the attorney general's job

her mother-in-law's address

Though an awkward construction, plural group words occasionally occur. To make a compound noun plural, add the *s* to the *base word;* then add the possessive ending to the *last term.* With compound plurals, however, the preferred way is to show the possession by changing the word order. For example:

Awkward:	their mothers-in-law's addresses
	the attorney generals' statements
Preferred:	the addresses of their mothers-in-law
	the statements of the attorney generals

NOUNS IN SERIES

Rule #8

When two nouns joined by *and* share joint possession, add the apostrophe only to the last noun. When there is individual possession, add the apostrophe to both nouns. For example:

Joint Ownership	Individual Ownership
Mitch and Helen's mother	Mitch's and Helen's cars
Margaret and Bill's project	Margaret's and Bill's projects

ABBREVIATIONS

Rule #8

To make an abbreviation plural, simply add an *s.* For example:

three DVDs	blue, green, and yellow M&Ms
five VCRs	ten CDs

To make an abbreviation possessive, add an apostrophe and *s,* just as you would with regular possessive nouns. For example:

ABC's newscast	the ADA's guidelines for dental hygiene
CNN's reporters	the NBA's new season

POSSESSIVES STANDING ALONE

At times, a writer or speaker will make a comparison between two nouns that are showing possession but leave off the item being possessed after the second noun. Be careful in these constructions as the second noun also shows possession.

Barb's remark was similar to George's (remark).

We will meet in Alex's office, not Miko's (office).

Michele is working on her master's (degree).

PRACTICE

Instructions: Look for possessives and make corrections where necessary. Also correct any errors in spelling and grammar. **For example:**

Incorrect: Toby's input was more helpful than Dugan.

Corrected: Toby's input was more helpful than *Dugan's (input).*

1. Ambras and Lucias instructor refuse to let them work together.
2. Either Alexi's proposal or Basma will win the bid.
3. Milton suggested that we go to Ditkas for the holiday celebration.
4. My brother-in-laws attorneys opened their office last week.
5. Chandras and her roommate apartment need to be remodeled.

SECTION A CONCEPT CHECK

1. When a regular noun shows possession, where does the apostrophe go when the noun is singular? Where does the apostrophe go when the possessing noun is plural?
2. When an irregular noun is plural and possessive, where should the apostrophe be placed?
3. If two people, let's say Martha and George, have joint ownership of a cherry tree, how would that be displayed in possessive form? How would it be displayed if they owned separate cherry trees?

SECTION B: CAPITALIZATION

Capitalization creates special problems for writers. When writers feel unsure about capitalization, they sometimes write everything in lowercase—this practice is especially true in e-communication. Other times, writers seem to capitalize words randomly, possibly thinking that common nouns are actually proper nouns. For professional writing, follow the standard rules of capitalization so that your writing has credibility.

VOCABULARY KEY TERMS

Retronyms: A **retronym** is a new term coined for an old object or concept whose original name has come to refer to something else (or is no longer unique). *AM radio* is an example of a retronym; before the introduction of broadcast FM radio, the AM broadcast band radio was simply known as *radio.* Other examples of retronyms are *acoustic guitar, black-and-white television, regular coffee,* and *hard disk.*

In general, a retronym consists of the original noun that was used to describe something and an adjective that emphasizes the distinction to be made from the original form.

Here are more retronyms:

birth mother

brick-and-mortar store

classic Coca-Cola

real cream

field hockey

hot chocolate

mainframe computer

paper copy (hard copy)

rotary telephone

sit-down restaurant

snail mail (land mail, paper mail)

static electricity

vinyl record

World War I

Can you name three retronyms that you use in your everyday communications?

____

____

____

This section gives you basic rules that function as a good starting point. Because the rules are complex, keep an authoritative reference manual at your side, such as *The Gregg Reference Manual* (GRM). And even before getting started, please note that the personal pronoun *I* is always capitalized!

PROPER NOUNS VERSUS COMMON NOUNS

Before you work on individual rules of capitalization, the most basic place to start is identifying the difference between common nouns and proper nouns.

- A **proper noun** is the official name of a particular person, place, or thing.
- A **common noun** is a general term that refers to a class of things.

Proper Nouns	Common Nouns
Bill Smith	person
Janny Construction	company
Water Tower Place	shopping mall
Diet Pepsi	soda or pop or soda pop
Italy	country
Mediterranean Sea	ocean

Proper nouns are always capitalized; common nouns are not capitalized. However, sometimes it is difficult to identify whether a noun is proper or common. For example, imaginative names and nicknames that identify a particular person, place, or thing are also considered proper, such as Big Mac, Mr. Nice Guy, and Amber Alert.

Personal names are always considered proper nouns. Even so, some foreign spellings do not capitalize the first letter of the name. For example:

di Nicolo d'Angelo van Heus

When company names and personal names are involved, make sure you get the correct spelling directly from the source.

Here are some other categories of proper nouns, along with examples:

Titles of literary and artistic works	*The New York Times, Moby Dick*
Periods of time and historical events	the Civil War, the Middle Ages
Imaginative Names and Nicknames	the Founding Fathers, Mother Nature
Brand and trade names	Nabisco, IBM computers, Xerox copies
Points of the compass (when they refer to specific geographic regions)	the South, the East, the Northwest
Place names	Grant Park, Sears Tower
Organization names	LaSalle Bank, American Dental Association
Words derived from proper nouns	English, Spanish
Days of the week, months, and holidays	New Year's Eve, Mother's Day

PROPER ADJECTIVES

Proper adjective may be a new term to you, but the mystery will be gone once you know the definition: a **proper adjective** is an adjective derived from a proper noun, such as *American, Bostonian,* or *Machiavellian.* Proper adjectives are always capitalized, just as proper nouns are always capitalized.

ARTICLES AND PREPOSITIONS

In titles of organizations as well as literary and artistic works, capitalize the word *the* if it is the first word of the name, as in "The University of Chicago." However, if the word *the* is not the first word of the title, do not capitalize it; also do not capitalize the following:

Articles *(a, an)*

Conjunctions *(and, but, nor)*

Prepositions of three or fewer letters *(for, of, in, at)*

However, in titles you can capitalize prepositions that have four or more letters, such as *with, from, between,* and *among.*

In addition, some prepositions actually function as adverbs when they are part of verb phrases, such as *follow up, look forward,* or *come in.* As part of a verb phrase, these short words (which are usually considered prepositions) are capitalized when they are part of a title.

Make this your motto when it comes to capitalization decisions: *When in doubt, check it out.* Only a detailed reference manual can give you all the information you need for making specific capitalization decisions.

▸Language Diversity

Gullah: *Gullah* is a dialect spoken by the Gullah, an African-American population that traces its origins to African slave ancestry. Speakers of Gullah are predominantly found in the Sea Islands and in Georgia and South Carolina. Much of the vocabulary is English in origin, but the grammar and the pronunciation follow the patterns of several West African languages

Below is a list of words written as they are pronounced in the Gullah dialect. How many can you identify?

1. fiah
2. do'
3. eentruss
4. Augus'
5. eeduh
6. ax'me
7. ef
8. beritywell
9. do'step
10. eb'ryting

Gullah: Uh gwine gone day tomorrah.

Standard: I will go there tomorrow.

Gullah: Alltwo dem 'ooman done fuh smaa't.

Standard: Both of those women are smart.

FIRST WORDS

Another category of importance when it comes to capitalization is *first words,* such as the first word of a sentence. Capitalize the first word of each of the following:

Sentences

Poems

Direct quotations that are complete sentences

Independent questions within a sentence

Items displayed in a list or outline

Salutations and complimentary closings

Though these capitalization decisions may seem obvious to you, people make mistakes with these categories every day. For example, some unsure writers do not even capitalize the first word of a sentence, choosing instead to write entirely in lowercase. Writing entirely in lower- or uppercase significantly reduces the credibility of the writer and the document.

Some readers assume all uppercase implies shouting—but that isn't the case when a naïve writer makes an innocent mistake due to insecurity about capitalization rules. Here's the best response: Know the rules and follow them, but do not place judgment on colleagues who may not yet be as informed as you are.

PROFESSIONAL TITLES

Some people capitalize every title they see, thinking that a title is an official category or proper noun. However, a title is *not* a proper noun; here's the general rule to follow:

• Capitalize titles when they precede a name, but not when they are part of an appositive.

• Do not capitalize titles when they follow a name.

VOCABULARY
WORD USAGE

Latin Words and Abbreviations: Latin terms can interrupt the flow of reading and are frequently used incorrectly. Avoid using them (except for *a.m.* and *p.m.*) unless you are writing an academic paper or bibliography. Here is the correct meaning for a few common Latin terms and their substitutes:

per: *Per* is a Latin word meaning "through," "by," or "by means of." Use *per* correctly in common expressions such as *miles per hour* or *cost per day.* Also use it correctly in Latin phrases such as *per diem* ("by the day"). Avoid using *per* in general writing; for instance, instead of using *per our discussion,* substitute *as discussed.*

etc.: *Etc.* is the abbreviation for the Latin phrase *et cetera,* meaning "and other things of a like kind" or "and the rest." Avoid using *etc.* by substituting a description of the items you are leaving out.

Weak:

We will need to bring laptops, flip charts, etc., to the meeting.

Revised:

We will need to bring laptops, flip charts, and *other support materials* to the meeting.

Other substitutions for *etc.* include *and the like, and so forth,* or *and so on.* However, if you still choose to use *etc.* within a sentence, make sure you precede it and follow it with a comma. Also, do not precede *etc.* with the word *and* because *and* is part of its definition.

et al.: *Et al.,* from the Latin *et alia,* means "and others." Use it when you are writing a bibliography or citing a legal case, but avoid using it in sentences. Instead, write out *and others.*

i.e.: *Id est* means "that is."

e.g.: *Exempli gratia* means "for example."

a.m./p.m.: *Ante meridiem* means "before noon," and *post meridiem* means "after noon." For both *a.m.* and *p.m.,* use small letters and do not space between the letters.

Here are examples of how a professional title is displayed before a name, as part of an appositive, and after a name:

> You should have discussed that with *Vice President* Glen Eichelberger.
>
> We spoke to a *vice president,* Glen Eichelberger, about the problem.
>
> We asked Glen Eichelberger, *vice president,* about the matter.

Here are a few more examples:

> Dee Sims, *director of admissions,* will assist you.
>
> You can speak with *Professor* Ferretti at 3 p.m.
>
> They sent the letter to A. S. Ferretti, *professor,* at his Rome address.
>
> Mr. Shaun O'Brien, *president,* will arrive shortly.

The most common mistake with titles is to capitalize business titles that follow names. Overcapitalization of titles might be a carryover from the way titles are displayed on business cards and in the closings of letters and e-mail. However, within correspondence, titles of company officials are not capitalized when they follow or replace a personal name. Therefore, within a sentence, do not capitalize a title that follows the name of a person. Also, do not capitalize a title that is used as a substitute for a specific personal name. For example:

> Please send this to George Martinez, *president* of Martinez and Associates.
>
> The *president* will visit all our branch offices this spring.

Now that you know the rule, here's an exception to note: The titles of high-ranking government officials, foreign dignitaries, or international figures are routinely capitalized even when the title follows the name or stands alone.

> The *President* met with reporters at the White House.
>
> The *Vice President* asked the president of our company to help him with his campaign.

Titles Versus Occupations

It is easy to confuse a title with an occupation. Though titles are capitalized when they precede a name, occupations such as *lawyer, accountant,* or *financial analyst* are not capitalized. The term *doctor* can be either a title or an occupation; for this reason, capitalize *doctor* in a direct address. Note the differences in these examples:

> Thank you, *Doctor,* for responding.
>
> I asked the *doctor* for advice about nutrition and exercise.
>
> Please give the information to *Dr.* Raines before noon.

ORGANIZATIONAL TERMS

Capitalize common organizational terms in your own company, such as *advertising department, manufacturing division, finance committee,* and *board of directors.* Do not capitalize these terms when they refer to departments at another organization unless you want to show special importance.

> The Board of Directors meets on the first Friday of each month.
>
> The Finance Committee has not completed this year's budget.

We cannot proceed until their finance committee submits the information.

The Advertising Department will celebrate the announcement.

The advertising department of Smith and Ward will unveil its new campaign.

In each of the above examples, using lowercase for each organizational term would also have been acceptable.

HYPHENATED WORDS

Hyphenated words can be capitalized in a number of ways, depending on whether the words are at the beginning of a sentence, within a sentence, or in a title or heading.

- Within a sentence, capitalize only the parts of a hyphenated word that are proper nouns or proper adjectives.
- At the beginning of a sentence, capitalize the first part of the hyphenated word and other parts that are proper nouns or proper adjectives.
- In a heading or title, capitalize all the parts (except articles, short prepositions, and short conjunctions, as noted previously).

Within Sentences	Beginning Sentences	In Headings and Titles
e-mail	E-mail	E-Mail
up-to-date	Up-to-date	Up-to-Date
one-tenth	One-tenth	One-Tenth
mid-October	Mid-October	Mid-October

Regardless of the "official rule," capitalization practices vary somewhat from company to company and from country to country. Global and international corporations may have slightly different rules than the ones presented here. When you enter the business world, consult your company's in-house reference manual; while you work there, use the company manual as your final source for all writing decisions.

PRACTICE

Instructions: The following sentences contain errors in capitalization as well as a few other types of errors. Make corrections where necessary. **For example:**

Incorrect: i have only this to say, ms. chu: i have worked for You many year's and have learned a great deal.

Corrected: *I* have only this to say, *Ms. Chu: I* have worked for *you* many *years* and have learned a great deal.

1. I have personally never met executive vice president Meuhler.

2. Please address your concerns directly to your Attorney.

3. During the meeting, one of the Director's said, "we have far exceeded our Sales Goals for this Quarter: good job, Everyone!"

4. Would you prefer that i assist you with your Account's or that i assist George?

• Internet Exercise 7.1

Capitalization Resources: For additional information and practice with capitalization, visit the Web site at **www.mhhe.com/youngBE**. Select "Student Activities," and then click on the "Chapter 7" link to get started.

5. When i live on main street, I enjoyed walking to the Grocery store. Now that i live on a Street on the other side of town, I prefer taking the bus.

SECTION B CONCEPT CHECK

1. When should a business title be capitalized and when not?

2. How is the word *e-mail* displayed if it is part of a title or heading?

3. One category of words to capitalize is *first words*. Name a few items in which first words should be capitalized.

SECTION C: NUMBER USAGE

Deciding whether numbers should be written out as words or displayed as numerals can be confusing. In fact, there is no one definite set of number rules that are followed universally. There are two primary sets of rules: figure style and word style.

Figure style is the most commonly used set of rules. However, even within this one set of rules, exceptions abound. To add more confusion, different sources sometimes present the basics slightly differently. This text follows *The Gregg Reference Manual.*

This section first gives you basic number rules before going into more specialized number rules. After you have some practice, you will be prepared to use a detailed reference manual to select your best options at times when you are still unsure.

BASIC NUMBER RULES

The following ten rules give you the basics for number usage. Consider the first rule "the golden rule" of number usage. All rules after Rule 1 are exceptions to it, and even Rule 1 has a built-in exception. There's no way around the exceptions; however, once you learn the basics, you will have a consistent system for displaying numbers, making your writing decisions easier.

Rule 1: Numbers 1 Through 10

Spell out numbers 1 through 10; use numerals for numbers above 10. (However, you may use numerals for numbers 1 through 10 if you want them to stand out for quick reference, as displayed here.)

She asked for *eight* copies of the report.

Bob submitted *15* new accounts.

Rule 2: Numbers Beginning a Sentence

Spell out a number that begins a sentence. However, try to avoid starting a sentence with a number.

Fourteen guests are expected to attend, but only *six* responded.

Rule 3: Related Numbers

Use the same form for related numbers within a sentence. If some numbers should be written in words and others in figures, write all in figures; if the sentence starts with a number, spell out all numbers in the sentence.

Of the *15* members, *10* were associates and *5* were not.

Eleven of our employees use the car-share program; the other *twenty-two* do not.

Rule 4: Unrelated Numbers

When two unrelated numbers occur together and one of the numbers is a compound modifier, write one number in figures and the other in words. In most cases, spell out the number that will make the shorter word.

The clerk delivered eight 3-foot panels.

Rule No. 5: Fractions and Whole Numbers

When a fraction stands alone, write it in words. Use a hyphen between the numerator and the denominator unless either the numerator or denominator itself must be written with a hyphen (as in *twenty-one twenty-fifths).* Write a mixed number entirely in figures.

The boy ate *two-thirds* of the pie.

That stock now costs *3½* times its original value.

Rule 6: Indefinite Numbers

Write an indefinite number in words, not in figures.

She claims to have *hundreds* of friends.

They say *thousands* attended the rally.

Rule 7: Ordinal Numbers

Ordinal numbers end in *d, nd, rd, st,* or *th,* as in *first* or *second.* (In contrast, cardinal numbers do not have endings: *one, two, three,* and so on.) Write ordinal numbers in words if they can be expressed in one or two words.

Next year is Bob's *tenth* anniversary.

He works on the *fifth* floor.

This is the *twenty-fifth* time that happened.

Rule 8: Percentages

Express a percentage in figures with the word *percent.* Use the symbol % only in technical material and in tabulations. Use the term *percentage,* not *percent,* when no number appears with it.

Alice spends *10 percent* of her pay on travel.

The *percentage* is too high to be accurate.

Rule 9: Weights and Measurements

Use figures for weights, dimensions, and other measurements.

The room measures 15 feet by 20 feet.

She is 5 feet 6 inches tall.

Rule 10: Large Numbers

You can express a number in the millions or higher in a combination of figures and words if the number can be expressed as a whole number or as a whole number plus a simple fraction or a decimal amount.

We had over *$1.5 million* in sales last year.

PRACTICE

Instructions: Proofread the following sentences and make corrections where needed. **For example:**

Incorrect: Please send 12 copies of this report to New York, and two copies to Los Angeles.

Corrected: Please send 12 copies of this report to New York and 2 copies to Los Angeles.

1. Mary gave them fifteen copies of the report but only five copies of the letter.

2. She bought five pens, eight pads of paper and fourteen rulers.

3. 17 people are expected to attend the benefit.

4. The young man ordered one and a half gallons of paint.

5. You can retain 5% of the receipts from the event.

VOCABULARY: SOUNDALIKES

Every day/Everyday:
Every day means "each day," with *every* modifying *day.* As one word, *everyday* means "daily." If you can insert the word *single* between *every* and *day,* use the two-word form.

My *everyday* routine includes stopping for coffee at Mitch's.

Every (single) *day* Mr. Riley calls at the same time.

Do you have any everyday routines? What do you do every (single) day?

Review the letters in Box 7.1 on the next page to see the kinds of changes you can make to improve a document as you edit it.

WRITER'S TOOLKIT

Acronyms and Initialisms
Two commonly used types of abbreviations are initialisms and acronyms. **Initialisms** are pronounced letter by letter, such as *IBM* and *NYPD.* **Acronyms** are pronounced as words, such as *AIDS* and *SADD.* In most cases, both forms are written in capital letters, and the letters are not followed by periods.

When using an acronym or initialism for the first time in your writing, spell out the term and follow it with the abbreviation in parentheses:

Students Against Drunk Drivers (SADD) will hold its annual meeting in New York this year.

The *American Association of Retired Persons (AARP)* has lobbyists in Washington.

If you have a doubt about how to form a specific abbreviation, check its correct use in a dictionary or reference manual. *When in doubt, check it out.*

SPECIAL NUMBER RULES

Now that you have a base for dealing with numbers in general, review the following rules for specific uses of numbers. (For easy reference, the information in this part is numbered and lettered.)

1. Dates

a. When the day follows the month, write the day in figures without an ordinal ending (*d, nd, rd, st,* or *th*). Do not use figures for the month. For example:

The meeting is scheduled for *February 11.*

b. When the day precedes the month or stands alone, write it in figures with an ordinal ending or in words. For example:

We will meet on the *29th of May.*

c. Express complete dates in month, day, year sequence. For example:

The date we discussed was *August 3, 2007.*

d. The U.S. military and most countries other than the United States express dates in day-month-year sequence, without punctuation, as in the following:

We received the report on *7 September 2007.*

e. In formal invitations, spell out the day and year, as follows:

August fifteenth the fifteenth of August the fifteenth day of August

f. Avoid abbreviating dates in general correspondence (for example, *5/7/06*). However, you can abbreviate dates on business forms and in some informal business correspondence, such as e-mail (if other people at your company do it regularly). When you write to an outside client, spell out the date: *when in doubt, spell it out!*

BOX 7.1 The Editing Process

BEFORE	AFTER
Sept. 25, 2006 Mr. John Smith Senior Vice President First National Bank 151 North Michigan Ave. Chicago, Illinois 60610 Dear John, According to Dun & Bradstreet, over *90% of the small businesses fail within 5 years.* As a major lender in the small business market, your ability to maintain a profitable, consistent portfolio of business can be adversely effected by these large number of business failures. There are many documented reasons why these organizations fail; however it can almost always be attributed to the owner's lack of experience and expertise in essential facets of the business. In the best cases, business owners possess 50-60% of the skills necessary to effectively lead the organization. This gap of knowledge if not filled quickly will significantly increase the risk of business failure. As a lender, you will conduct periodic reviews on financials to determine if financial targets are being met; however other functions of the business are left to owner's expertise. To increase the success rate of small businesses, the owner needs to be educated on the key business functions while building an environment of flawless execution. Getting to this level of expertise can be a daunting task. As with any organization or person trying to quickly grow in a specific area, engaging a coach can help to ensure success. A coach is someone that will teach, instill accountability and provide support to the business owner. *Coaching Matters provides business performance coaching to the owners of small to medium size businesses! Our approach has been used in over 10,000 companies with amazing results! If you are not satisfied, we offer a 100% money back guarantee.* I would like the opportunity to meet with you to discuss how we could jointly work with your clients to ensure business success. I will give you a call the week of the 15th. Thank you in advance for your consideration. Sincerely, Kelly Jounell, Certified Coach	September 25, 2006 Mr. John Smith Senior Vice President First National Bank 151 North Michigan Avenue Chicago, IL 60610 Dear Mr. Smith: According to Dun & Bradstreet, over *90 percent of small businesses fail within five years.* As a major lender in the small business market, your ability to maintain a profitable, consistent portfolio can be adversely affected by this large number of business failures. As a lender, you conduct periodic reviews on financials to determine if a business meets its financial targets. However, other functions of the business are left to an owner's expertise, and sometimes an owner lacks experience and know-how in essential facets of the business. To increase the success rate of small businesses, *the owner needs to be educated on the key business functions while building an environment of flawless execution.* Getting to this level of expertise can be a daunting task; however, *engaging a coach helps ensure success.* A coach will teach, instill accountability, and support the business owner. Small to medium-size business owners can depend on the business performance coaching they get from *Coaching Matters:* • Our approach has been used in over 10,000 companies worldwide with amazing results. • As a result of our proven approach, we offer a 100 percent money-back guarantee. Would you have time to meet with me to discuss how we could work together with your clients to ensure business success? I will give you a call next week. I look forward to speaking with you—thank you for your time. Sincerely, Kelly Jounell Certified Coach

g. When you are responding to correspondence and refer to a date, give only the month and day. (The year should be obvious to the reader.) For example:

> Your letter of *August 9* provided the details I needed.

2. Time

a. Always use figures with the abbreviations *a.m.* and *p.m.* For example:

> Your *4:30 p.m.* flight to Denver has arrived on time.

b. For time on the hour, you do not need to include *:00* unless you want to emphasize the precise hour. For example:

> The messenger left the office at *11 a.m.*
>
> Our team will meet at *2:00 p.m.*

c. The term *o'clock* may be used with either figures or words to express time on the hour. Never use *o'clock* with either *a.m.* or *p.m.* For example:

Mr. Jones' *four o'clock* appointment has been canceled.

d. So that you are not redundant, do not use *a.m.* or *p.m.* with phrases such as *in the morning* or *in the afternoon;* however, you can use those phrases with *o'clock.* For example:

We will see you at *4 o'clock in the afternoon* on Friday.

3. Addresses and Phone Numbers

a. Use figures for all numbers in addresses except the numbered street names *One* through *Ten* and the house number *One.* For example:

Many dream of having the address *10 Downing Street.*

Donna's salon is at *One Astor Place.*

b. Do not abbreviate a compass point (*North, South, East, Northwest,* and so on) when it appears before a street name (unless space is very tight). For example:

My new address is *1244 West Pacific,* Apartment 1205.

She lives at *1200 East 62 Street,* not *1440 West 62d Avenue.*

c. For compass points that follow a street name, abbreviate compound directions that represent a section of the city, inserting a comma before them *(SW, NE)* but spell out *North, South, East,* and *West* following a street name.

59 Amber Lane, SW   111 Park West

d. Display phone numbers with periods or hyphens between parts.

You can call me at *312.555.0910.*

They faxed the information to *202-555-1423.*

4. Money

a. Use figures and the word *cents* for an amount under a dollar and figures with *$* for an amount of a dollar or more. For example:

The soda from the vending machine costs *75 cents.*

I spent *$3.55* at the dollar store.

b. Omit *.00* with even-dollar amounts except in a tabulation containing some amounts in cents only or in dollars and cents. For example:

The seminar now costs *$255,* so you should sign up soon.

c. When an amount under a dollar is related to other amounts of a dollar or more, express the numbers in a similar fashion:

The balance in my account should have been *$130,* but it was only *$.30.*

The folder costs *$3.60* at the supply store but only *$.80* at the drug store.

d. Use figures for periods of time related to loans and discounts.

By paying this invoice within *10 days,* you will receive a *5 percent* discount.

5. Age

a. Spell out an age given in years unless it is used as a statistic or in a news release.

Her brother is *twelve years old.*

J. R. Wilson, *43,* has been appointed vice president.

• WRITER'S TOOLKIT

Number Tidbits

Use numerals when you refer to chapter, page, and section numbers, as well as serial, style, model, part, or other similar numbers. Capitalize the word that precedes the number for all above except the word *page.*[3] For example:

Refer to Chapter 6, Section 2, for the information.

The quote was on page 10.

Unless it is the first word of a sentence, you may abbreviate *number* if it precedes a figure. Use the abbreviation *No.* (singular) or *Nos.* (plural). If a noun such as *invoice* or *check* precedes the number, do not include the abbreviation *No.* For example:

Refer to No. 10 on page 56.

They sent us Invoice 4567 last week.

The bank needs more information to process Check 5546.

b. Spell out ordinals referring to birthdays or anniversaries unless you want to place special emphasis on them. Use figures for ordinals that require more than two words (hyphenated numbers count as one word).

Jimmy's *twelfth* birthday is Friday.

You are invited to our *twenty-fifth* anniversary celebration.

Our company will celebrate its *125th* anniversary next year.

PRACTICE

Instructions: Correct any number errors in the sentences below. **For example:**

Incorrect: I received an eight percent discount on my purchase.

Corrected: I received an *8* percent discount on my purchase.

1. Your next payment is due July 15th.
2. The invoice did not arrive until August 14th.
3. Her new address is 1442 W. 14 Street.
4. Brown Company sent us an invoice for $150,000.00, but we owed them only $15.00.
5. The meeting will start at 4:00 p.m. this afternoon in the 5th-floor conference room.

SECTION C CONCEPT CHECK

1. What is the golden rule of number use, and what is the built-in exception?
2. What is the easiest way to display the following numbers? 1,500,000 and 10,750,000
3. For time on the hour, under what circumstance would you use the *:00,* as in *2:00?*

•Internet Exercise 7.2

More on Numbers: For additional information and practice with numbers visit the Web site at **www.mhhe.com/youngBE**. Select "Student Activities," and then click on the "Chapter 7" link to get started.

SECTION D: COLONS, DASHES, AND ELLIPSES

The comma and semicolon have been the traditional, basic punctuation marks of business writing. However, now that business depends on casual forms of writing such as e-mail, writers often use less traditional marks such as *dashes* and *ellipsis marks,* and these marks are often used incorrectly or overused.

If you use them correctly, the colon, dash, and ellipsis marks can add variety and flair to your writing. Using these marks correctly does not take much effort, but remember to use them sparingly.

THE COLON

The colon can add power to your writing: colons alert the reader that information will follow to explain or illuminate the information that preceded it.

a. *Use a colon to indicate a list.* Often the colon is preceded by one of the following terms: *these, the following,* or *as follows.*

> These are the items to add to the agenda: annual meeting schedule and draft report changes.

b. *Use a colon after the words* note *and* caution.

> Note: If a complete sentence follows the word *note* or *caution,* capitalize the first word of the sentence that follows it.

c. *Use a colon in business letters after the salutation.* Standard punctuation style calls for the placement of a colon after the salutation. In open punctuation style, no punctuation appears after the salutation or the greeting.

d. *Use a colon at the end of one sentence to introduce the next sentence.* The first word of the second sentence is normally not capitalized. However, you can capitalize the first word of the sentence after the colon if the sentence requires special emphasis. Use this rule sparingly: no more than one time for a short document.

> LaSalle Bank is a great place to have an account: it ranks number one in customer service.

e. *Use a colon after a complete sentence that introduces a list; however, do not use a colon after an incomplete sentence.*

Incorrect: The items include: a laptop, a cell phone, and an inventory list.

Correct: The items include a laptop, a cell phone, and an inventory list.

PRACTICE

Instructions: Insert a colon where needed. **For example:**

Incorrect: You have done well on your first review you received the highest scores of all our new employees.

Corrected: You have done well on your first *review:* you received the highest scores of all our new employees.

1. My assistant is remarkable, he can create a presentation in less than an hour.

2. My emergency breakdown kit includes these items, cables, flares, and a cell phone.

3. Caution. The coffee is very hot.

4. Remember my advice "You can catch more flies with honey than with vinegar."

5. There are only two appointment times left Thursday at 9 a.m. or Friday at 10:30 a.m.

ELLIPSIS MARKS

Ellipsis marks (also known by the plural form *ellipses*) consist of three periods with a space before, between, and after them (. . .).

- Ellipsis marks indicate an omission of a word or several words.
- When ellipses occur at the end of a quoted sentence, a fourth period is added.

Ellipsis marks are used formally in business and academic documents and informally in e-mail messages. For formal use, writers should familiarize themselves with the rules and stay within those boundaries. For informal writing, writers should be selective on the latitude they give themselves in straying from the rules.

In formal business and academic documents, ellipses are most often used with quoted material. When only selected parts of a quotation are relevant, the material that is left out is indicated by ellipses.

At all times—whether a document is formal or informal—ellipsis marks should be typed correctly. Ellipses can be found in the most unusual and incorrect forms: two, three, or four periods without spaces between the periods. Writers sometimes even vary the number of periods each time they use them. This is a clue to educated readers that the writer doesn't know how to use ellipses and has not taken the time to check a reference.

A FORMAL QUOTE

> Most people live, whether physically, intellectually or morally, in a very restricted circle of their potential being. They make use of a very small portion of their possible consciousness, and of their soul's resources in general, much like a man who, out of his whole bodily organism, should get into a habit of using and moving only his little finger. Great emergencies and crises show us how much greater our vital resources are than we had supposed. —*William James*

QUOTE SHORTENED USING ELLIPSES

> Most people live . . . in a very restricted circle of their potential being. . . . Great emergencies and crises show us how much greater our vital resources are than we had supposed. —*William James*

In informal documents, writers use ellipsis marks to indicate they are not completing their thoughts in writing. Used this way, writers assume the reader will infer what was omitted. Here's an example of using ellipses in an e-mail:

> Janet,
>
> The meeting will be on the 27th of this month, but I'm not sure they have our issue on the agenda. What do you think we should do . . . please advise.
>
> Talk to you later.
>
> D.J.

PRACTICE

A. Instructions: Write your own sentences modeled after the example provided.

EXAMPLE — I asked for your answer, and then I waited . . . and waited . . . and waited . . .

MODELED VERSION — I asked for a response, and then I asked again . . . and again . . . and again . . .

1. "Well, I was just asking . . ." said Drake.
2. I thought about your question . . . and thought . . . and thought . . .
3. We should probably finish the project by Wednesday . . . or perhaps by Friday.
4. After seeing the Palm Pilot cell phone for the first time, Kindra said, "What on earth . . . ?"

WRITER'S TOOLKIT

Periods, Exclamation Points, and Question Marks

With e-mail, writers often throw in exclamation points to express emotion; however, as you will see below, that is not how exclamation points should be used.

The Period—A Courteous Request: A period indicates the end of a statement. However, a period can also be used to indicate the end of a **courteous request.** That is, when a writer asks a question to prompt action rather than receive a response, the sentence ends in a period rather than a question mark.

> Could you stop by my desk this afternoon to pick up your report.

The recipient would not respond, "Yes, I could." The statement is phrased as a question because it may sound more polite that way. Therefore, if you do not expect a question to be answered, consider whether it might be a courteous request.

The Exclamation Point: Exclamation points indicate surprise. This mark is highly overused, especially in e-mail. When used correctly, an exclamation point can occur after a word, phrase, or complete sentence.

> Stop!
>
> Congratulations on your promotion!

Whenever you use an exclamation point, consider whether it adds value to your writing or, instead, makes your writing sound too casual or too full of emotion. To be safe, use the exclamation point sparingly.

The Question Mark: Question marks indicate a question the writer expects the reader to answer. Similar to exclamation points, under some circumstances, question marks can occur after individual words as well as complete sentences structured as statements or questions.

> What next?
>
> He said that he would do what?
>
> What did he say?

Questions, as well as statements, can end in prepositions as long as the preposition is not a "tag on," as in "Where do you live *at?*"

> Whom would you like to attend the meeting with?

B. Instructions: Complete the exercises below as described.

1. Find three pieces of writing that use ellipsis marks—an article from a newspaper or magazine, an e-mail, or a letter from a friend. Identify whether or not the ellipsis marks are used correctly. Ask yourself: *Is it always easy to figure out what has been left out and replaced with ellipses?*
2. On the Internet, locate a news article. Assume you are writing a paper on the topic covered in the article. Choose two paragraphs in the article to quote from, and then practice shortening the quotes by using ellipsis marks.

C. Instructions: Read the following paragraphs and create a quotation from them. Shorten the quote by using ellipsis marks.

The Gettysburg Address by Abraham Lincoln[4]

Gettysburg, Pennsylvania

November 19, 1863

Four score and seven years ago our fathers brought forth on this continent, a new nation, conceived in Liberty, and dedicated to the proposition that all men are created equal.

Now we are engaged in a great civil war, testing whether that nation, or any nation so conceived and so dedicated, can long endure. We are met on a great battle-field of that war. We have come to dedicate a portion of that field, as a final resting place for those who here gave their lives that that nation might live. It is altogether fitting and proper that we should do this.

But, in a larger sense, we can not dedicate—we can not consecrate—we can not hallow—this ground. The brave men, living and dead, who struggled here, have consecrated it, far above our poor power to add or detract. The world will little note, nor long remember what we say here, but it can never forget what they did here. It is for us the living, rather, to be dedicated here to the unfinished work which they who fought here have thus far so nobly advanced. It is rather for us to be here dedicated to the great task remaining before us—that from these honored dead we take increased devotion to that cause for which they gave the last full measure of devotion—that we here highly resolve that these dead shall not have died in vain—that this nation, under God, shall have a new birth of freedom—and that government of the people, by the people, for the people, shall not perish from the earth.

Student version: In his Gettysburg Address, Lincoln said,

"____

____

____

____"

THE DASH

The dash is the most versatile of all punctuation marks and can be used in both formal and informal documents.

- The dash is represented by two hyphens without a space before, between, or after them. Word processing software automatically produces an *em dash* when you type hyphens in this manner.
- The dash can be a substitute for the comma, semicolon, period, or colon.
- A single dash places emphasis on the information following it; a pair of dashes emphasize the information between them.

VOCABULARY: NEW WORDS

New definitions added to *Merriam-Webster's Collegiate Dictionary* in 2006:[5]

lurk, intransitive verb: To read messages on an Internet discussion forum (such as a newsgroup or a chat room) without contributing information (such as addresses, schedules, and notes).

bubble, noun: A state of booming economic activity (as in a stock or real estate market) that often ends in a sudden collapse.

killer application, noun: Commonly shortened to "killer app," a computer application of such great value or popularity that it ensures the success of the technology with which it is associated.

Here are some examples:

> Trisha hosted the charity gala dinner—it raised more money than any other event in the history of our organization.
>
> Charlie Richards—our new CEO—invited me to apply for the position of senior VP.

A word of caution: Use dashes sparingly. Though the dash is a traditional mark of punctuation, it is less conventional than the other marks it represents (the comma, semicolon, period, and colon). If you want to be a bit flamboyant, use some dashes. Just make sure you express your flamboyancy in a conservative way by restricting your dashes to no more than one or two per page.

PRACTICE

Instructions: Insert a dash where needed. **For example:**

Incorrect: We are more than pleased with the response we've had to our new product, sales have more than tripled.

Corrected: We are more than pleased with the response we've had to our new product—sales have more than tripled.

1. Anne Arrington, Julie Fast, and Sam King all were present to receive their awards.
2. My hometown team—the Chicago White Sox has a relatively new stadium.
3. Your expectation finishing the project by noon was difficult, but we managed to accomplish it.
4. My favorite day of the week is Sunday my day off.
5. The Parkinson deal in addition to the Levy account will help our team move ahead in the corporate competition.

• WRITER'S TOOLKIT

Common Symbols (Glyphs)

The following typographical symbols (also known as *glyphs*) are not true punctuation marks but are useful tools for any writer. Can you identify the meaning or use of each one?

ampersand	&
asterisk	*
at	@
caret	^
bullet	•
dagger	†
degree	°
double dagger	‡
pound sign	#
underscore	_
vertical bar	|
greater than	>
less than	<
pilcrow	¶

SECTION D CONCEPT CHECK

1. Identify the different uses of the colon.
2. Is it appropriate for business writing to include less formal punctuation, such as the dash and ellipses? Why or why not? Would your answer be different for messages written to coworkers than it would be for letters written to clients? To the president of the company?
3. Do you use punctuation to make your writing resemble your conversational style? How does using dashes and ellipses affect the tone of your writing?

CHAPTER 7 SUMMARY

Below is a quick guide to possessives and capitalization, and Table 7.1 is a quick guide to numbers. Though a short summary of rules is of no benefit without thorough study first, it can be a handy reference or study tool.

For plurals and possessives, pay attention to the following:

- When a singular noun not ending in *s* shows possession, add an apostrophe and *s ('s): book's cover.*
- When a singular noun ends in *s,* let the pronunciation guide you. If a new syllable is formed, add an apostrophe plus *s ('s): boss's advice.* If a new syllable is not formed, just add an apostrophe ('): *Ms. Jennings' proposal.*
- When a regular plural noun shows possession, add an apostrophe after the *s (s'): books' covers.*
- When an irregular plural noun shows possession, change the noun to the plural form and then add an apostrophe and *s: children's toys.*
- To avoid confusion, always make your noun plural *before* you change it to show possession.

For capitalization, remember to capitalize:

- Proper nouns but not common nouns.
- The personal pronoun *I.*
- Business titles when they precede a person's name but not when they follow it.
- The first word of sentences, direct quotations that are complete sentences, displayed items, and complimentary closings.
- Titles of literary and artistic works, periods of time and historical events, brand and trade names, points of the compass designating specific geographic regions, place names, organization names, and words derived from proper nouns.

TABLE 7.1 | Basic Number Rules

Rule
1. **Numbers 1 Through 10.** Spell out numbers 1 through 10 (unless you want them to stand out for quick reference). Use numerals for numbers above 10.
2. **Numbers Beginning a Sentence:** Spell out a number that begins a sentence.
3. **Related Numbers:** Use the same form for related numbers within a sentence. Figures trump words unless the sentence starts with a number.
4. **Unrelated Numbers:** When two unrelated numbers occur together and one of the numbers is a compound modifier, write one in figures and the other in words.
5. **Fractions and Whole Numbers:** When a fraction stands alone, write it in words, as in *one-half.* However, write a mixed number entirely in figures, as in *5 3/4.*
6. **Indefinite Numbers:** Write an indefinite number in words, not in figures.
7. **Ordinal Numbers:** Write ordinal numbers in words if they can be expressed in one or two words.
8. **Percentages:** Use figures with the word *percent.* Use the symbol % only in technical material and tabulations. Use the term *percentage,* not *percent,* when no number appears with it.
9. **Weights and Measurements:** Use figures for weights, dimensions, and other measurements.
10. **Large Numbers:** Express a number in the millions or higher in a combination of figures and words.

CHAPTER 7 CHECKLIST

When composing business messages, consider the following:

___ Have you made your nouns plural before making them possessive?

___ Have you checked to make sure your plural possessives are consistent with the words they modify?

___ Have you spelled out numbers under ten?

___ Have you used numerals for numbers 11 and above?

___ Have you used the same form for all numbers within a sentence, with numerals trumping words?

___ Have you capitalized all proper nouns?

CHAPTER 7 END-OF-CHAPTER ACTIVITIES

ACTIVITY 1: PROCESS MEMO

INSTRUCTIONS: Write your instructor a short message that demonstrates some of the principles you learned about possessives, number usage, and capitalization. Write a few examples showing your usage before you studied this chapter, and then show the corrections. Include a colon, a dash, or ellipses in your message. If you have Internet access, you can complete this exercise online at **www.mhhe.com/youngBE** and then send an e-mail to your instructor.

ACTIVITY 2: REVIEW OF PLURALS AND POSSESSIVES

A. PLURALS

INSTRUCTIONS: Look for plurals and possessives and make corrections where necessary. Also correct any errors in spelling and grammar.

1. Will all three attornies be present?

2. Those two company's will be our major competition in the contract bid.

3. I have never heard of anyone being allergic to potatos.

4. Several copys' of the report will be available after todays meeting.

5. I believe I have misplaced the portfolio's.

B. POSSESSIVES

INSTRUCTIONS: Look for errors in plurals and possessives and make corrections where necessary. Also correct any errors in spelling and grammar. For example:

Incorrect: The companies director will make her final decision after this mornings' meeting's.

Corrected: The *company's* director will make her final decision after this *morning's meetings.*

1. Most of our employee's are happy with our health benefit's package and the employees pension plan.

2. I need three inspector's certificates to proceed.

3. Have you met the new human resource's director? She is Mr.'s and Mrs. Smiths' daughter.

4. Two employee's cars were stolen from the lot last night.

5. Both Tom and Marta's desks are the new model. Have you saw them?

6. The Harris will have lunch with us to discuss a possible closing date.

7. Jenna was surprised to learn that she receives two week's vacation instead of one.

8. Last weeks' board meeting was out of control. Lets stick to the agenda this time.

9. The CPAs claims' that we didn't return all our receipts are untrue.

10. Are you attending Jake's and Marsha's wedding?

ACTIVITY 3: REVIEW OF CAPITALIZATION AND NUMBERS

A. CAPITALIZATION

INSTRUCTIONS: Make corrections where needed. For example:

Incorrect: When i requested the information, i assumed that they would send it.

Corrected: When I requested the information, I assumed that they would send it.

1. Do you speak polish or any slavic languages?

   Polish , Slavic

2. The memorial day weekend is a great time to get away.

   Memorial Day

3. Soon we will open factories in maine and boston.

   Maine and Boston

4. My brother works for the internal revenue service

   Internal Revenues Service

5. The offices will be closed on new year's day.

   New Year's Day

6. Vice president Sharon Patel will provide the latest data for your project.

   President

7. Have you ever seen lake michigan?

   Lake Michigan

8. We were stunned to hear the Receptionist say, "You must all have your ID's to enter."

9. The global technology corporation is our main partner.

   Technology

10. Leslie, a Human Resources Specialist, is working on her Doctorate.

B. NUMBERS

INSTRUCTIONS: Correct any number errors in the sentences below. For example:

Incorrect: Please call me at 4:00 o'clock p.m. tomorrow.

Corrected: Please call me at *4 p.m.* tomorrow.

1. When you were 18 years old, were you able to vote?

2. We are expecting $1,500,000.00 in revenues this year.

   1.5 million

3. The letter was sent to 166 West 14th Street.

   OK

4. Work hours are from 9 o'clock a.m. till 5:00 o'clock p.m.

5. We received the letter on the 21 of January.

   21st

6. This material costs $.80 cents per unit.

   No dollar

7. Please order 15 labels, 10 folders, and 7 envelopes.

   OK

8. We received 1000s of responses to our mailing.

   thousand

9. Delbert's franchise is now worth 1/2 its original value.

   half

10. When we receive the 5 coupons, we will send you a refund.

    OK

11. This is my 3rd request to receive a copy of the manual.

    OK

12. We have completed about 20% of the project, which is a higher percent than we expected.

    twenty-percent

ACTIVITY 4: SPEAKING BUSINESS—*S* ENDINGS

BACKGROUND: You learned in this chapter and in Chapter 4, "Verbs at Work," that the *s* form of the verb, or third-person singular, creates special problems for writers. Actually, other types of words ending in an *s* create problems too.

INSTRUCTIONS: Here's more practice with the *s* form. Make sure you pay special attention to the *s* sound when you pronounce words out loud. Below is a list of singular nouns and verbs. Turn the nouns into their plural form and the verbs into their *s* form; then pronounce each word out loud.

list	disk	frisk	ask
mask	bask	card	specific

Now make a list of words that you find challenging to pronounce. Work with a partner and practice them until they feel routine.

ACTIVITY 5: REVIEW OF COLONS, DASHES, AND ELLIPSES

INSTRUCTIONS: The following sentences contain errors with colons, dashes, and ellipsis marks. Make corrections where needed. For example:

Incorrect: Send the information to the following address; 1090 West Roosevelt Avenue.

Correct: Send the information to the following address: 1090 West Roosevelt Avenue.

1. My manager has proposed some changes to the report's design spiral binding, color charts, and a table of contents.
2. The suggestions you made replacing the lighting, buying new chairs, and painting the walls a bright color have made a positive change in the office's atmosphere.
3. There is only one trait I cannot tolerate a lack of punctuality.
4. Saying that we have spent enough time on the renovation project is an understatement we have spent over 200 hours writing the proposal alone.
5. Note the first paragraph of the employee handbook states: "All employees will become thoroughly familiar with company policy.

ACTIVITY 6: JABBERWOCKY

INSTRUCTIONS: Review Lewis Carroll's "Jabberwocky" poem from *Through the Looking Glass and What Alice Found There,* printed below. Read the poem aloud. Underline each nonsense noun, verb, and adjective, and mark each with the appropriate part-of-speech label. For example, the word *slithy* in the first line would be underlined and labeled an adjective. Circle nonsense clauses and prepositional phrases. Then, on a separate piece of paper, rewrite the poem, replacing the nonsense words you identified with standard words of your own. Without using nonsense words, see if you can achieve the same tone as Carroll.[6]

Jabberwocky

by Lewis Carroll

'Twas brillig, and the slithy toves
Did gyre and gimble in the wabe;
All mimsy were the borogoves,
And the mome raths outgrabe.

"Beware the Jabberwock, my son!
The jaws that bite, the claws that catch!
Beware the Jubjub bird, and shun
The frumious Bandersnatch!"

He took his vorpal sword in hand:
Long time the manxome foe he sought—
So rested he by the Tumtum tree,
And stood awhile in thought.

And as in uffish thought he stood,
The Jabberwock, with eyes of flame,
Came whiffling through the tulgey wood,
And burbled as it came!

One, two! One, two! And through and through
The vorpal blade went snicker-snack!
He left it dead, and with its head
He went galumphing back.

"And hast thou slain the Jabberwock?
Come to my arms, my beamish boy!
O frabjous day! Callooh! Callay!"
He chortled in his joy.

'Twas brillig, and the slithy toves
Did gyre and gimble in the wabe;
All mimsy were the borogoves,
And the mome raths outgrabe.

ACTIVITY 7: CUMULATIVE REVIEW

INSTRUCTIONS: Correct the following letter for errors in possession, capitalization, number usage, and punctuation. If you have questions about formatting, refer to Figure U3.1, "Block-Style Business Letter," in the Unit 3 opener.

Custom Fit Computers
2786 Lawndale Corp Dr
Chantilly, VA 20151
Phone 703-378-6475, Ext. 201
Fax 703-378-2687
www.Customfitcomputer.com

January 26, 2007

Pam Gains
Wilson Elementary School
5982 West Dunnough
DOWNERS GROVE, IL 60515

Re: E-rate Application

Dear Ms. Pam Gain,

The e-rate application process is rapidly drawing to a close for Funding Year 2007, the 471 submissions are due by February 6. If you have already selected your vendor congratulations! If you still need a vendor for internal connections equipment and/or service we can help!

every year hundreds of schools submit 470 applications but they never submit a 471 form. For many they were simply overcome by events and never solicited quotes for others they thought that submitting the 470 would result in quotes that they could use for the 471. For other schools it was simply a case of publishing their requirements but no vendor submitted a quote.

Whatever the reason if you're still without a vendor we can help. Custom Fit Computers is a national systems integrator experienced in computer voice and video applications and we provide "a custom fit from standard parts". we've been an E-Rate vendor since the first year of the program. If you need

* servers we can provide name brand or custom built
* PBX we are 3Com NBX– and Cisco-authorized
* videoconferencing equipment we are Polycom and Vcon partners
* video equipment we are partnered with Real Server, VBrick, Scala, MagicBox and many others

And, don't let our Virginia location confuse you we've installed and supported installations worldwide (in Iceland, cuba, Spain, Jordan, and Japan and throughout the United States) both directly and through local partners.

Every year we submit hundreds of last minute quotes for customers some literally "last minute." Phone, fax, or e-mail your requirements and we'll find a solution for you to submit. From now through february 6 we'll be operating 8 AM to 10 PM EST 7 days a week. Don't lose your chance at your share of E-Rate money call us today! We'll make the process as painless as possible.

Thanks for your time

Steve Jones VP Sales

ACTIVITY 8: READ/REFLECT/RESPOND

BACKGROUND: Time is critical when responding to e-mail. In the business world, you are expected to respond to many messages daily. This activity introduces a short process that allots 12 minutes in total for you to *read, reflect* on, and *respond* to a question that is somewhat familiar to you.

You will spend time planning, composing, and editing your message. While 12 minutes may seem short for this, the time is adequate for writing a brief and accurate message. Get used to moving from one stage of the process to the next; your confidence will grow as you get more practice.

INSTRUCTIONS: Select one of the situations below, and then follow these guidelines in writing your response:

1. Take 3 minutes to read the message and map your response.
2. Take 6 minutes to compose a brief response.
3. Spend 3 minutes editing and revising your message.

- You applied for a part-time position at a local business. The business owner, Malory Williams, sent you an e-mail asking for more information. She would like you to give details about your school or work experience that show you are responsible and motivated.
- You are chairing a committee to welcome new students to your college. Write a welcome letter that lets them know what they can expect during their first two weeks of classes and some pointers to help them be successful.

ACTIVITY 9: "WRITER'S REFERENCE MANUAL" DRILL

INSTRUCTIONS: Read the entry "abbreviations" in the "Writer's Reference Manual" and then answer the following questions:

1. In a business document, what is the appropriate way to use an abbreviation for a department named *Computer Technology and Design?*

2. Explain the difference between an acronym and an initialism.

3. What is the best way to abbreviate state names?

4. Explain what the following statement means when it comes to using abbreviations: *When in doubt, spell it out.*

ACTIVITY 10: VOCABULARY LIST

A. COMMONLY MISSPELLED WORDS

INSTRUCTIONS: Practice the words below until you can spell them automatically and use them correctly.

1. authenticity — (n) genuineness, legitimacy
2. colloquial — (n) an informal style of speech that includes clichés and slang
3. cliché — (n) an overused, worn-out phrase that has lost its meaning
4. culture — (n) the norms, beliefs, behavior, and ways of thinking of a group of people
5. ethnocentrism — (n) viewing (and judging) the world through the eyes of one's own culture
6. foreign — (adj) located away from one's own country; not natural; unrelated
7. global — (adj) local know-how with a multinational presence
8. idiom — (n) a word or phrase that has a different meaning from its literal meaning
9. international — (adj) across national boundaries; describing a company that sells goods or services in more than one country
10. multinational — (adj) describing a company that has business functions established in more than one country
11. per diem — (n, Latin phrase) by the day
12. perspective — (n) point of view, outlook
13. resilient — (adj) hardy, tough, durable, flexible, quick to recover
14. retrospect — (n) a review of past events
15. unequivocal — (adj) absolute, certain, decisive

B. SIMILAR WORDS

INSTRUCTIONS: Use the words below in sentences until their meaning becomes clear.

alright/all right: Though this might surprise you, "alright" is not a standard English spelling. The correct spelling is *all right.* To remember, think of something as being either *all right* or *all wrong.*

You should check to make sure that it is *all right* to leave early.

every day/everyday: *Every day* means "each day," with *every* modifying *day.* As one word, *everyday* means "daily." If you can insert the word *single* between *every* and *day,* use the two-word form.

I eat lunch *every day* at noon.

That is one of my *everyday* routines.

THE INBOX

TAKING A SOFT-SKILLS INVENTORY

The term **soft skills** refers to a set of skills that human resource managers look for in new employees. A Google search for *soft skills* will produce approximately 37,600,000 hits. So what are soft skills? If there are *soft* skills, are there also *hard* skills?

- *Hard skills* pertain to your ability to perform a specific job. Hard skills are easily measurable and quantifiable; for example, either you can operate a cash register or you can't.
- *Soft skills,* on the other hand, relate to the way you interact with others as you perform your hard skills. Soft skills are more difficult to measure, although they are every bit as important as hard skills in the job market. Often, soft skills are referred to as *transferable skills;* that is, they are applicable to many jobs.

Using the following list of soft skills, assess yourself by putting a star (☆) next to the skills you believe are your strongest. Next, put a checkmark (✓) next to the skills you have that you believe need a little improvement. Finally, put an *X* next to the skills you believe you need to improve the most.

___ Listening effectively

___ Recognizing positive traits in others

___ Willing to learn from your mistakes

___ Showing cultural sensitivity

___ Showing enthusiasm and positive attitude for your work

___ Being reliable and dependable

___ Embracing your company's vision and mission

___ Taking initiative when appropriate (leadership)

___ Stepping back when appropriate (followership)

___ Maintaining honesty in all situations

___ Behaving professionally, not emotionally

___ Practicing strong communication skills, including verbal, written, and electronic

___ Using time-management practices

___ Demonstrating self-control

___ Showing empathy for others while maintaining your own high standards

___ Being mindful of the feelings of others when giving direction (tact)

___ Showing courtesy to everyone regardless of position

___ Practicing loyalty

___ Applying ethics in your decision-making process

___ Helping others to get along when working in a group

COMPOSING

Pretend that you are the manager of Play Ball, a popular sporting goods store in the mall. You have been receiving some complaints from customers about your salespeople's attitudes and manners. In one case, an employee named Wendy told a customer who was trying to return a faulty item, "I don't want to hear your problems. If you don't have a receipt, that's your fault and I can't refund your money."

Write an electronic memo to your employees encouraging improvement of soft skills. Keep in mind that for some employees, your memo will be their first exposure to the concept of soft skills.

REFLECTING

Do you think certain careers require a stronger emphasis on soft skills than others? To what extent will soft skills factor into your performance in the career field of your choice?

DISCUSSING

The list of soft skills provided for you in this exercise is by no means comprehensive. Brainstorm in a small group to add more soft skills to the list. When you are satisfied with your list, work on developing the definition of soft skills. Finally, using a poster board or computer, create a one-page poster about soft skills. Can you create a graphic image to enhance the poster?

EDITING

Below is an employee evaluation written by a colleague. Your colleague has asked you to proofread the evaluation for errors in wordiness, grammar, punctuation, and spelling.

Employee Evaluation;
Micah Pazek, First level service Coordinator
Henson Technical enterprises

Micahs' overall performance has shown Vast Improvement since last year's Evaluation. Specifically, Micah, has improved in three areas' technical and Managerial knowledge of his job, customer service, and attendance. For improvement Micah need's to work on his Motivation and learn to take initiative.

First Micah has attended all mandatory training, for First Level Service Coordinators. Additionally: he volunteered for editional training in Cultural Diversity, Communications, and Customer Service. His soft skills' have greatly improved: making him a much more affective Supervisor. Micah has also completed an Online course to receive Software Certification in our database software and our scheduling software. Micah has became an resource to entry level Service Coordinators and is even viewed by some, as a mentor. This change in Micahs capability, is a vast improvement when compared to his' prufomance last year.

In the area of customer service. Micah has grown tremendously. The monthly Customer Satisfaction Reports has gone up thirty percent since Micahs last evaluation.

During, this evaluation period Micah, has had only 2 absences and was never tardy compared with the sixteen days of absence and 8 days' tardy he had last year. His improvement in this area is vital as he sets an example for the entry level service coordinators.

An area of concern is Micah motivation. While his attending training and earning certification do show some improvement in motivation he still lack enthusiasm for day to day tasks'. Micah requires constant direction from his first line supervisor even tho this is Micahs 3rd year in this position. Micah need to reevaluate the importance of daily tasks and realize that while the "big picture" is important he cannot pick and chose which daily tasks he deem interesting and forgot the rest.

CAREER-BUILDING PORTFOLIO

Over the next four chapters, you will have the opportunity to complete ten model documents for a career portfolio. Maintain this portfolio and add to it as you continue your education. Add samples of your best work from other writing classes, or add samples of other types of work such as spreadsheets, graphic art, or research papers. Use the portfolio to organize your career-related documents, such as résumés, letters of reference, contacts, and interview tips. Maintaining this "career kit" will help you keep all your career-related documents on hand. You can also use it as a demonstration portfolio to showcase your abilities and interests when applying for a job or a promotion or admission to graduate school.

PORTFOLIO DOCUMENT 1

Revise the memo you wrote for the composing exercise in this Inbox. When you are satisfied that it is the best document you can produce, make a final, clean copy to put in your career-building portfolio.

PORTFOLIO DOCUMENT 2

Write a letter of application for the type of job you would like to obtain either now or after you finish your degree. Highlight your soft skills in your cover letter, since your résumé will highlight your hard skills. Soft skills are often considered *transferable skills* because they can be applied on any job regardless of specialty. Keep in mind that having one good cover letter will benefit you in your job search, as you can tailor that one letter to the specifics of many different positions. Visit the Web site for a sample document and a template.

KEY TO LEARNING INVENTORY

1. F
2. F
3. T
4. T
5. T
6. F
7. T
8. F
9. T
10. F

CHAPTER 7 ENDNOTES

1. Sidney Greenbaum, *A College Grammar of English,* Longman, New York, 1989, p. 108.
2. Ibid., p. 108.
3. William Sabin, *The Gregg Reference Manual,* 10th ed., McGraw-Hill/Irwin, Boston, 2005, pp. 141–142.
4. Lincoln quote, Project Gutenburg, **http://www.gutenberg.org/etext/4**, accessed on September 7, 2006.
5. "New Words and Sense Sampler," *Merriam-Webster's Collegiate Dictionary,* 11th ed., **http://www.merriam-webstercollegiate.com/info/new_words.htm**, accessed on October 1, 2006.
6. **http://www76.pair.com/keithlim/jabberwocky/poem/jabberwocky.html**, accessed on November 1, 2006.

Chapter Eight

Writing Powerful Sentences

A man who uses a great many words to express his meaning is like a bad marksman who, instead of aiming a single stone at an object, takes up a handful and throws at it in hopes he may hit.
—Samuel Johnson, lexicographer (1709–1784)

So far you've worked on developing skills so that your writing is correct. Now you will work on editing and revising skills so that your writing is reader-friendly. To achieve that aim, this chapter reinforces the principle *less is more.*

Good business writing is crisp and concise. Time is precious, and writing that is complicated or wordy loses the reader quickly. Readers want to get to the point and know the actions they must take to respond. In Section A, you will work with principles for developing a sentence style that is simple, clear, and concise. Then, in Section B, you will apply some of those same principles to control the tone of your writing so that you connect with your audience.

This chapter provides the foundation for an **editing strategy.** Once you have clear principles on which to base your decisions, you will manage the writing process effectively. For now, your goal is to understand and apply the principles that lead to simple, clear, and concise writing.

To learn more about The Writing Process, please visit our Web site at **www.mhhe.com/youngBE**

Outline

Chapter 8: Writing Powerful Sentences

Section A: Sentence Style

Section B: Tone and Style

Objectives

When you have completed your study of Chapter 8, you will be able to:

1. Revise sentences from passive to active voice.
2. Use the active and passive voices effectively.
3. Apply an editing strategy to remove empty information, redundancy, and outdated expressions.
4. Correct sentences for parallel structure.
5. Build transitions with adverbial and subordinating conjunctions.
6. Apply principles of style to shape the tone of a business document.

Learning Inventory

1. A writing style is created by a series of writing decisions.	T/F
2. As a writer advances, editing and composing merge into one activity.	T/F
3. A good editing practice is getting rid of unnecessary nominals.	T/F
4. Using the active voice is one component of clear, concise writing.	T/F
5. A sentence can have a real subject even when it doesn't have a grammatical one.	T/F
6. In a passive sentence, the real subject precedes the verb.	T/F
7. Using complicated words makes a writer sound smarter.	T/F
8. In a sentence, new information is more important than old information.	T/F
9. Parallel structure gives writing flow by putting words in similar format.	T/F
10. In the active voice, the real subject and grammatical subject are the same.	T/F

Goal-Setting Exercises

Think for a moment about your writing style. What kinds of comments do you hear from teachers and friends about your writing? Are you too wordy or abrupt? Are your sentences difficult to understand? Write three goals about your writing: What would you like to achieve? What changes would you like to make?

1. ________________________________

2. ________________________________

3. ________________________________

SECTION A: SENTENCE STYLE

The topics in this section deal with style, specifically a style that is **simple, clear, and concise.** Before we start, think of **style** as *many individual writing decisions that add up to an overall effect.* Each writing decision—or aspect of style—produces a different result. The idea is to make decisions that simplify the message for your reader. Here are some topics that affect style:

- Controlling sentence structure, length, and content.
- Using the active voice.

- Being concise.
- Building old to new information flow.
- Using parallel structure.
- Using conjunctions to show relationships.
- Bridging ideas effectively.

As you work on each one of these concepts, you will be one step closer to developing a writing style that is simple, clear, and concise. However, please keep in mind that these are editing tools and that you must practice these principles a great deal before you build expertise. Let's get started.

CONTROL SENTENCE STRUCTURE

In punctuation and grammar exercises, you have already worked extensively with the sentence core, the **subject** and **verb.** Now you will connect how the sentence core helps determine your writing style.

Readers or listeners must hear both the subject and the verb of a sentence before they begin to understand its meaning. Putting too many words between the subject and the verb complicates the process. Thus, *keeping a subject close to its verb helps the reader understand the message more easily.* In each example below, the subject is underlined once and the verb is underlined twice. (Subjects and verbs of secondary clauses are not underlined.)

Weak — Jimmy Carter, the 39th President of the United States serving from 1976 until 1980 who has developed a reputation over the years for being a humanitarian due partly to his work in Africa curing a disease that caused blindness as well as his work with Habitat for Humanity, received the Nobel Peace Prize in 2002 for "his decades of untiring effort to find peaceful solutions to international conflicts, to advance democracy and human rights."[1]

Revised — Former President Jimmy Carter received the Nobel Peace Prize in 2002 for "his decades of untiring effort to find peaceful solutions to international conflicts, to advance democracy and human rights." As the 39th President of the United States, Jimmy Carter held office from 1976 until 1980. Over the years, he developed a reputation for being a humanitarian partly because of his work in Africa curing a disease that caused blindness and his work with Habitat for Humanity.

Putting the subject and verb closer together makes the sentence easier to read. However, breaking the longer sentence into three shorter sentences also makes it more manageable.

CONTROL SENTENCE LENGTH

Keep your sentences between 10 and 22 words in length; this principle is based on the amount of information the average reader retains. Beyond 22 words, a reader may find it necessary to reread the beginning of the sentence to understand its meaning. For example:

Weak — Writing experts suggest keeping sentences to fewer than 22 words in length because readers may have difficulty retaining information in longer sentences and may need to read the beginning of a sentence over again if the meaning of the beginning becomes lost by the time the end is reached. (49 words)

This is a bad sentence, but you get the idea. Sentences longer than 22 words can become unmanageable for the reader (as well as the writer). When you edit your writing, be on the alert for sentences that look long. When sentences take more than two full lines, take a moment to count the number of words. When writers stop to count words of long sentences, they sometimes find sentences that are more than 45 or even 55 words long.

If a sentence contains more than 22 words, either break the information into shorter sentences or cut unnecessary information. When you follow this principle, you will improve both the quality and the readability of your writing.

CONTROL SENTENCE CONTENT

Each sentence should have only one controlling idea. When a sentence contains more than one controlling idea, the meaning is not clear.

Weak — Several employees contacted human resources to complain about our new dress policy, *and* we have a meeting scheduled next Tuesday at 11 a.m.

What is this about? Are the dress policy and the meeting separate issues, or are they related? Based on the way the sentence is written, these ideas appear disjointed; that's because each is given equal weight. You can correct this by subordinating one of the ideas and showing how the ideas are related. If needed, you can add a bit of information to complete the information.

Revised — *Since* several employees contacted Human Resources to complain about our new dress policy, we will meet next Tuesday at 11 a.m. to discuss it.

Here's another example:

Weak — Kline Corporation canceled our construction project, *and* I met with Stone Construction.

Revised — *Because* Kline Corporation canceled our construction project, I met with Stone Construction to see if they were available.

At the end of this section, you will do more work using conjunctions to show relationships and bridge ideas.

USE THE ACTIVE VOICE

In Chapter 4, "Verbs at Work," you learned that the active voice is clear, direct, and concise. Since the active voice is one of the most important qualities of good business writing, here is a brief review:

- In the active voice, the grammatical subject performs the action of the verb: *the grammatical subject and real subject are the same.*

  Reggie borrowed my book.

In the above example, the grammatical subject is *Reggie,* and the real subject is also *Reggie,* who was doing the borrowing.

- In the passive voice, the grammatical subject does not perform the action of the verb: *the grammatical subject and real subject are not the same.*

  My book was borrowed by Reggie.

In this example, the grammatical subject is *book,* and the real subject is still *Reggie,* the one performing the action of borrowing.

▸Language Diversity

Malapropisms: Richard Brinsley Sheridan's 1775 play *The Rivals* debuted Mrs. Malaprop, a character with the habit of substituting a similar-sounding word for a word that she actually intended to use. In an example of Mrs. Malaprop's dialogue, "He is the very pine-apple of politeness!" she uses the word *pineapple* instead of *pinnacle.*

The word *malapropism* soon became attached to such slips in word selection. Today it refers to a similar-sounding word or phrase that has been used incorrectly in place of another, having a humorous or ridiculous result.

The sentences below contain malapropisms, some of them from well-known individuals. Underline the word or part of the sentence that has been used incorrectly, and then indicate the correction on the line that follows.

Malapropism: ". . . promise to forget this fellow—to illiterate him, I say, quite from your memory." *(The Rivals)*

Correction: obliterate

1. Flying saucers are just an optical conclusion.
2. Always go to other people's funerals, otherwise they won't come to yours. (Yogi Berra)
3. Well, that was a cliff-dweller. (Wes Westrum, about a close baseball game)
4. A rolling stone gathers no moths.
5. Let's get down to brass roots.
6. The three types of veins are arteries, vanities, and capillaries.
7. What a waste it is to lose one's mind. Or not to have a mind is being very wasteful. (Dan Quayle, former vice president)
8. Mother no's best.
9. Their father was some kind of civil serpent.
10. Shhh! I hear footprints. (Vernon Appoy)

Although you learned the difference between grammatical subjects and real subjects in Chapter 4, here's a brief review:

- The grammatical subject of a sentence *precedes* the verb.
- The real subject is the "actor" or "agent" performing the action of the verb.

In a passive sentence, the real subject appears in the object position, if it is in the sentence at all. Here are the steps to follow to change a sentence from passive to active voice:

1. Identify the verb of the sentence.
2. Identify the real subject. Ask yourself: *Who or what performed the action of the verb?*
3. Place the real subject at the beginning of the sentence.
4. Follow the real subject with the verb.
5. Adjust the tense of the verb to agree with the real subject.

Here's an example:

Passive: The situation was created by Alan.

What's the verb? *was created*

Who did the creating? *Alan*

Active: Alan created the situation.

In Section B, you'll do more work with the active and passive voices, seeing how they affect the tone of a document.

PRACTICE

Instructions: Change the following sentences from passive to active voice. **For example:**

Weak: The new idea was suggested by Matthew.

Revised: Matthew suggested the new idea.

1. An article about staff development was left on my desk by Frances.
2. Office equipment was purchased by my new assistant, Fred.
3. New reports are reviewed and summarized weekly by our financial analysts.
4. The call was made by Alyssa's developmental editor, not by Alyssa herself.
5. Our bid for the computer training was lost.

BE CONCISE

Due to the challenge of composing, writers often use too many words. At times, a writer may not even understand the key points of a message until thoroughly developing the topic. Once you understand your key points, cut the message so that you get right to the point.

Excessive words make your message more difficult to understand. When you edit, the fewer words you use, the more your message will stand out.

Communication Challenges

A *Thinker or Feeler* Approach: Some businesses use a test called the Myers-Briggs to determine personality tendencies that might affect how a person achieves a task. The Myers-Briggs is based on the psychology of Swiss psychiatrist Carl Jung.[2]

One of the major categories on the Myers-Briggs is the *thinking-feeling* category. Scoring high on either *thinking* or *feeling* will influence the tone of a person's writing.

Thinkers tend to base their decisions on hard facts without considering emotional factors. Thinkers get right to the point and make little or no effort to connect with the reader as one human to another.

Feelers, on the other hand, consider emotional factors a priority. They place more emphasis on connecting with the reader than on the information being conveyed.

Thinker message:
Our team meeting today is at 4 p.m.; arrive promptly.

Feeler message:
Hi, team. This is just a reminder that we are having our team meeting today at 4 p.m. I'd appreciate it if you would arrive on time because we have a lot to cover. If for some reason you need to be late, let me know. Hope your day is going well. I look forward to seeing you later today. Thanks.

While neither approach is right or wrong, a balanced approach is more effective.

Balanced message:
Hi, team. We will start our team meeting today promptly at 4 p.m. Let me know if you have any conflicts.

While thinkers take a straightforward approach, feelers have the urge to be social and friendly. Thinkers resist using fluff and niceties, but feelers search out ways to express things other than their direct message. Of course, everyone exhibits characteristics of each type; personality type is a matter of degree. Whether you're a thinker or a feeler, the key is to find a balance between the two.

Wordy	When you are writing any sort of business document, a critical principle of writing is using as few words as you possibly can to get your message across because the more words you use, the more challenging it is for readers to understand your key points: Less is more.
Concise	Use as few words as you possibly can to get your message across: Less is more.

Being concise also relates to eliminating *redundant phrases* and *outdated expressions.* Here are some examples:

The *final outcome* will be good.	The *outcome* will be good.
My insurance is *cheaper in cost* than his.	My insurance is *cheaper* than his.
Thank you in advance for your help.	*Thank you* for your help.
The training gadget was *round in shape.*	The training gadget was *round.*
We are *in receipt of* your letter.	We *received* your letter.
As *per* our discussion, I am . . .	*As we discussed,* I am . . .
Attached please find the requested form.	The form you requested is *attached.*
I wish to thank you for . . .	*Thank you* for . . .

PRACTICE

Instructions: Remove redundancy and outdated expressions from the following sentences (and change from passive to active, if needed):

Weak: Enclosed please find the amended proposal.

Revised: The amended proposal *is enclosed.*

1. As per our discussion, the meeting will take place on Tuesday.

2. At the present time, we have no openings available for interns.

3. One will note that much care has been given by us as to the presentation of these documents and their bindings.

4. We find that in the majority of instances promoting interns is quite beneficial to our company.

5. For the means and purposes of refreshing your knowledge of the *Green v. Holdenberg* case, we have created a brief case history.

BUILD OLD TO NEW INFORMATION FLOW

When a sentence starts with a familiar idea as a lead-in to an unfamiliar idea, readers have an easier time making connections. While composing, you may find yourself starting with new ideas (the unfamiliar) and then linking them to your topic (the familiar). When editing, move the familiar idea to the beginning of the sentence and move the unfamiliar idea to the end.

For example, suppose you are sending a message about an upcoming meeting. As you compose, you may start with the new information.

Weak — A budget concern that the finance committee recently discovered will be addressed during our April board meeting.

When you edit, switch the order so that the sentence begins with the familiar (meeting):

Revised — *During our April board meeting,* we will address a budget concern that the finance committee recently discovered.

By beginning the sentence with the familiar concept (meeting), you ease your readers into the unfamiliar information. Here's another example:

Weak — Membership in our company's newly developed wellness facility is a benefit of your new position.

Revised — *A benefit of your new position* is membership in our company's newly developed wellness facility.

• Internet Exercise 8.1

Personality Indicators: For more information on the Myers-Briggs Personality Type Indicator, visit the Web site at **www.mhhe.com/youngBE**.

At the home page, select "Student Activities," and then click on the "Chapter 8" link to find instructions for getting started.

PRACTICE

Instructions: In the following sentences, adjust the information flow so that old topics precede new information. **For example:**

Weak: Revising the quarterly budget is the first thing on our agenda.

Revised: *The first thing on our agenda* is revising the quarterly budget.

1. To merge with the most prestigious Fortune 100 brokerage firm is our goal.

2. Finding a locale that is near a train station is a major consideration for new space.

3. Wearing professional office attire every day except Friday is required because of the new dress policy.

4. Closing restrooms on the fifth floor for two weeks because of remodeling was a notice Joe placed on the bulletin board.

5. WordPerfect, PowerPoint, Excel, computer-assisted graphics, and other software-related training will be offered as part of our annual training in May.

USE PARALLEL STRUCTURE

In Chapter 4, "Verbs in Action," you learned that parallel structure creates balance and clarity by presenting related words in the same grammatical form. Make sure that you present related nouns, verbs, phrases, and clauses in a consistent form. Here are some examples:

Incorrect: Acquisitions are based on the *trends of the markets* and my *broker's advice.*

Correct: Acquisitions are based on *market trends* and my *broker's advice.*

Incorrect: Spend time today *answering the phones* and *the agenda must be prepared.*

Correct: Spend time today *answering the phones* and *preparing the agenda.*

Incorrect: The Baker project would have gone smoothly if *reports were prepared on time, we returned their calls,* and *would have included some sort of follow-up.*

Correct: The Baker project would have gone smoothly if *we had prepared reports on time, returned their calls,* and *included some follow-up.*

Parallel structure adds flow through consistency in form. When checking for parallel structure, look for consistent verb tense, word endings, and voice (active or passive). Correcting for parallel structure comes while you are editing your work, not composing it. (You will find more on parallel structure in Chapter 10, Section C.)

SPEAKING BUSINESS

Avoiding Slang, Slanted Language, and Sarcasm: Most people use slang on a daily basis. Phrases (or idioms) such as "biting the bullet," "hitting a home run," and "carved in stone" are taken for granted by many American speakers. However, even these common **colloquial** terms should be avoided in business writing and speaking, especially in formal situations.

In addition, word choices can present a neutral picture or a slanted one. To control the tone of a written document, choose words that have a neutral tone rather than those that create negative overtones.

Slanted: Amanda chastised me for not agreeing with her about which vendor to choose.

Neutral: On the basis of Amanda's feedback, we have different opinions about the choice of vendor.

Slanted: Harry has become notorious for his outrageous extravagance with client perks.

Neutral: Harry is known for providing perks to his clients.

If you use slanted language, your reader may think you are trying to manipulate information; and in the end, you will lose credibility.

Also avoid sarcasm in business writing, and limit the use of humor. You have no idea what your reader's mood will be when your message arrives. Always stay on the safe side, and leave out anything that can be misinterpreted.

Make a list of five slang terms that you use and then write their Business English equivalent. For example:

We struck out.	We lost the deal.
I put the cart before the horse.	I acted too soon.

PRACTICE

Instructions: Correct the following sentences for parallel structure. **For example:**

Incorrect: The desk had a leg that was broken and a scratch on the top of it.

Corrected: The desk had a broken leg and a scratched top.

1. My goals for this training session are (1) to ensure all field agents become familiar with our new tracking system and (2) the demonstration of our new handheld devices.

2. The field agents were advised to keep track of their daily expenses on their handheld devices and using their laptops to communicate with the home office.

   to use

3. The efficiency of the new handheld devices depends on their ease of use, their reliability, and whether or not they are tough and durable enough.

4. Our use of technology far exceeds your team.

5. To begin using your laptop, simply key in your user name and password, and then the Enter key should be hit.

USE CONJUNCTIONS TO SHOW RELATIONSHIPS

Good writing follows a logical flow of thought. One way to achieve a logical flow is to use connecting words, such as conjunctions, to show relationships between ideas. The two types of conjunctions that show relationships within a sentence are coordinating conjunctions and subordinating conjunctions. Adverbial conjunctions primarily act as bridges between sentences.

You worked with these conjunctions extensively in Chapter 3, "Punctuation," so you should be somewhat familiar with them. Here's a brief refresher on how they function, along with a few examples:

VOCABULARY: WORD USAGE

If/Whether: The word *if* is often used when the word *whether* would be the correct choice. Use *whether* when the statement that follows contains or implies the phrase *or not.* For example:

Incorrect: She isn't sure *if* she will go to the meeting.

Correct: She isn't sure *whether (or not)* she will go to the meeting.

For formal writing, use *whether* in expressions such as *learn whether, know whether,* and *doubt whether.* To get used to the change, add the implied *or not,* as in "whether *or not* I will go."

1. **Coordinating conjunctions** join items of equal grammatical structure: they connect independent clauses or items in a series. There are only seven coordinating conjunctions, and some people remember them because together they spell the acronym *FANBOYS: For, And, Nor, But, Or, Yet, So.*

   Here's an example of how a coordinating conjunction connects thoughts of equal value:

   Bill will host the upcoming retreat, *and* we are pleased that he is coordinating the event.

2. **Subordinating conjunctions** are words and phrases that introduce **dependent clauses.** Subordinating conjunctions show relationships between the ideas they connect. Here are a few common subordinating conjunctions:

after	because	unless	as soon as
although	before	until	while
as	even though	since	so that

   Here is an example of how a subordinating conjunction shows a relationship:

   Weak: Malcolm became the new office manager. He redesigned our office space.

   Revised: *Once* Malcolm became the new office manager, he redesigned our office space.

BRIDGE IDEAS EFFECTIVELY

Adverbial conjunctions build bridges between ideas and help the reader understand the writer's intention. Adverbial conjunctions are transition words. Here are a few common adverbial conjunctions:

therefore	in summary	that is	consequently
however	as usual	in conclusion	on the contrary
for example	in addition	of course	unfortunately
fortunately	hence	otherwise	as a result
furthermore	in general	thus	finally

Here is an example of how an adverbial conjunction shows a relationship between ideas to provide a transition:

Weak: They declined our invitation to dinner. They adopted our proposal. *(choppy, no bridge between the clauses)*

Revised: They declined our invitation to dinner; *however,* they adopted our proposal.
(*However* provides a transition between the two actions and shows the relationship between them.)

When ideas are connected effectively, readers are able to follow the line of thought. Adverbial conjunctions and subordinating conjunctions enhance the flow of your writing by bridging ideas and showing relationships. These conjunctions also help readers understand a writer's intent, giving readers a clue to the meaning of a sentence or paragraph *before* they read it; for example:

However
On the contrary — *The idea that follows will contrast with the one that came before it.*
Although
Even though

Fortunately — *Something good is about to happen.*
Unfortunately — *Something not so good is about to happen.*

Thus
Therefore
Consequently — *The writer is reaching a conclusion for the reader.*
As a result
Because

Finally
In summary — *You can relax; we've finally reached the end.*
In conclusion

The editing principles in this section assist you in making a document simple, clear, and concise and thus reader-friendly. Next, in Section B, you will see how to use these principles to affect the tone of a document, making it more or less formal.

PRACTICE

Instructions: Use adverbial, subordinating, or coordinating conjunctions to add transitions to the following sentences. (Experiment with different transitions to see how the meaning changes.) **For example:**

Weak: I knew about the position. I did not apply for it.

Revised: I knew about the position; *however,* I did not apply for it.

1. Frank arrived late. The meeting started on time.

2. Elizabeth chaired the committee. Luis would not participate.

3. Your ideas are good. We have a job opening.

4. My manager will not approve the expenses. I must cancel the training.

5. My attorney did not return my calls. I called five times.

SECTION A CONCEPT CHECK

1. List at least three principles that would be part of an editing strategy. Give an example of each.

2. Conjunctions play a major role in punctuation, but they also play a major role in writing style. What role do they play in writing? Give an example or two.

3. To remain reader-friendly, a sentence should contain a maximum of how many words?

SECTION B: TONE AND STYLE

This section shows you how writing style affects the tone of your documents. By adjusting your writing style, you can make your messages more inviting to readers: When you use a professional tone, rather than an overly formal tone, readers will connect with you and your ideas in a more personal way. When you use the "you" point of view, readers will feel as if you are focusing on their needs; as a result, they may be more open and receptive to your ideas. Here are the concepts you will cover in this section:

- Focusing on the "you" point of view.
- Turning nominals into active verbs.
- Using voice to control level of formality.
- Choosing simple language.
- Keeping a positive focus.
- Writing in the affirmative.

FOCUS ON THE "YOU" POINT OF VIEW

In Chapter 5, "Pronouns," you reviewed the concept of pronoun point of view. Since the "you" viewpoint is a critical aspect of good writing, it merits a review so that you can have a deeper understanding of it.

Have you ever had a conversation with someone and every other sentence began with the pronoun *I?* How did it make you feel? When people start many or most of their sentences from the "I" viewpoint, this doesn't mean that they don't care about others; they simply may not realize how to place their focus on the listener or receiver. Let's review the various viewpoints before focusing on the "you" viewpoint:

	Singular	Plural
First person	I	we
Second person	you	you
Third person	he, she, it	they

The "you" viewpoint connects your readers to your message because it speaks directly to them, allowing an easier understanding of your message. By keeping the highlight on your reader and your reader's needs, you may also become more client-oriented in your thinking.

As you compose, do not worry if you state things from the "I" point of view. When you edit, change appropriate sentences to the "you" point of view. For a self-check, count the number of times you use each pronoun (*I* or *you*) in your document. The numbers will give you insight into where you are placing your stress.

Here are some examples:

"I" viewpoint: *I* am happy to know someone as efficient as you are.

"You" viewpoint: *You* are one of the most efficient people I know.

"I" viewpoint: *I* would like to ask you if you could help me with the agenda.

"You" viewpoint: Could *you* please help me with the agenda?

"I" viewpoint: *I* appreciate your input.

"You" viewpoint: *Your* input is valuable.

Notice how starting with *I* puts emphasis on the writer, not the reader. At one time, business writers were discouraged from starting any sentences with *I*. As a result, writers overused the passive voice. Since active voice is usually more effective than passive, *I* once again became an appropriate viewpoint and is no longer a business writing taboo. For example:

Passive voice: The *report was completed* and sent to you last week.

Active voice/"I" viewpoint: *I completed* the report and sent it to you last week.

Though sentences are more effective when they highlight the reader's position, the "you" viewpoint is not always possible. To be effective, use the "I" viewpoint, but don't overuse it. In formal reports, neither the "I" nor the "you" viewpoint is stressed; writers often use the third-person singular *(he, she, it, the company)* and first-person plural *(we, our company).*

PRACTICE

Instructions: Adjust the tone of the following sentences to the "you" viewpoint. **For example:**

Weak: I am writing to let you know that I appreciate your outstanding work.

Revised: *Your* work is outstanding.

1. I think the best person for the job is you.

2. Never before have I witnessed such expertise as yours.

3. Although I hesitate to ask you, I must request that you return the supply cabinet keys.

4. Without causing too much trouble, I need to ask a favor.

5. I find that your clients tend to be lifelong customers.

Internet Exercise 8.2

Customer Service: For a closer look at the important role the "you" point of view plays on the Internet, visit the Web site at **www.mhhe.com/youngBE**. At the home page, select "Internet Exercises." Click on the "Chapter 8" link to find activities and links to explore.

TURN NOMINALS INTO ACTIVE VERBS

In Chapter 2, you learned that a **nominal** is a noun that originated as a verb. For example, the verb *appreciate* becomes *appreciation* in its nominalized form. As you will see, using a nominal often makes writing more complicated.

Nominalized: I want to express my *appreciation* for your help.

Active: I *appreciate* your help.

As in the example above, the nominal may displace an action verb, replacing it with a weak verb (such as *make, give, have*). In general, using nominals encourages complicated, passive writing.

Sometimes writers prefer to use nominals because they think using longer, more challenging words sounds smarter. However, in writing, *your* goal is to make complex messages as *simple* as you can. Here are more examples of nominals that were formed by adding *tion* or *ment* to the base of the verb:

Verb	Nominal	Verb	Nominal
transport	transportation	encourage	encouragement
develop	development	accomplish	accomplishment
dedicate	dedication	validate	validation
separate	separation	evaluate	evaluation

A few nominals form in other ways:

Verb	Nominal
analyze	analysis
criticize	criticism
believe	belief

At times, nominals are necessary; however, use them only when they improve the efficiency and quality of your writing. When nominals do not improve the writing, the reader has a more difficult time understanding the message.

Here is an example using *illustrate* and *illustration:*

Nominal: An *illustration* of the project was completed by a graphic artist.

Active: A graphic artist *illustrated* the project.

Below is an example using *revise.* The first sentence uses *revision,* which is the nominal form of *revise.* In the second sentence, the nominal is removed; however, the sentence is still passive. In the third sentence, *revise* is an active verb.

Nominal: The *revision* of the budget was accomplished by our team at our monthly meeting.

Passive: The budget *was revised* by our team at our monthly meeting.

Active: We *revised* the budget at our monthly team meeting.

PRACTICE

Instructions: Underline the nominals in the following sentences and then rewrite the sentences by changing the nominal into the active form of the verb. Some sentences may also need to be changed from passive to active. **For example:**

Incorrect: The analysis of the data was done by Nick.

Corrected: Nick *analyzed* the data.

1. Please provide clarification of your remarks.

2. The demonstration of the new product line will be presented by your team tomorrow.

3. The vice president's expectation was to raise the quarterly sales quota by 15 percent.

4. Please see to the distribution of those flyers during the sales presentation.

5. Our negotiations were successful.

USE VOICE TO CONTROL LEVEL OF FORMALITY

Just as writing can be too informal, it can also be too formal and complicated. The most informal style is the way people chat with their friends online. Most grammar and punctuation rules are thrown out; everything may be in lowercase; phrases take the place of sentences; there may be no beginning or ending; and so on. If you write informally to your friends, be mindful that *all* other situations are more formal and require that you follow the rules of Business English.

Some of the topics covered in Section A of this chapter help determine tone, such as using the active or passive voice and choosing simple or complicated words. Here is a brief reminder of how to identify voice:

- *Active voice:* The subject performs the action of the verb. *Jim planned the meeting.*
- *Passive voice:* The subject does not perform the action of the verb. *The meeting was planned by Jim.* (*Meeting* is the subject, and *meeting* is not performing the action of the verb.)

At times, the passive voice sounds more formal than the active voice. The passive voice can be abstract and indirect; it also encourages the use of complicated words such as nominals, which may give a pretentious effect. Other elements that affect the level of formality include the use of personal pronouns and contractions.

Business writing is neither highly informal nor highly formal: business writing falls in the category of *medium formality* and can be described as *professional.* In business writing, use the active voice and choose simple words. In addition, use pronouns (such as *I, you, us,* and *we*) so that you may refer to your reader and yourself in a direct and personal way.

- **Professional:** Active voice; simple words; personal pronouns (such as *I, you,* and *we*); and, at times, contractions, such as *can't* for *cannot* and *don't* for *do not.*
- **Highly formal:** Passive voice; complicated language; nominals; abstract references; no contractions; and Latin abbreviations.

BOX 8.1 The Editing Process

BEFORE

From: SystaProducts Customer Service
To: Della Reese
Cc:
Subject: Re: Your Order - Invoice # M778

Thank you for your recent inquiry.

Our return process is very simple. Please write the following code on the top of the box M778 this code is used to identify the package when it gets back to our warehouse, and please send it to the address below. We recommend shipping via UPS, FedEx or DHL because they supply tracking information automatically with their ground service (If you use USPS please request Delivery Confirmation and Tracking Service). Also please keep all shipping records and paperwork until your credit is fully processed. Please include a copy of your original packing slip with the M778 number as well as your full name and address on top. You will receive an e-mail notification once the package has been received by our warehouse system. Once the package has been received it takes approximately 14 business days for the credit to be fully processed but may still take 1 to 2 billing cycles to show on your card statement. We do not cover the cost of return shipping. Thank you for allowing us the opportunity to assist you.

SystaProducts
Attn: Returns A1835
4505 Wessley Pkwy
Boston, MA 2720

If you need further assistance, you may contact our Client Support Center by email at orders@systaproducts.net, by phone at 1-555-555-5353 or by visiting our web site at www.SystaProducts.net.
Thank you,

D.W.

AFTER

From: SystaProducts Customer Service
To: Della Reese
Cc:
Subject: Your Order—Invoice M778

Dear Della:

Our return process is very simple.

1. Send your package to the following address:

   SystaProducts
   Attn: Returns A1835
   4505 Wessley Parkway
   Boston, MA 27200

2. Send your package via UPS, FedEx, or DHL so that it will be tracked automatically; if you use the USPS, request delivery confirmation so that you can track your package.
3. Enclose a copy of your original packing slip in the box.
4. Write your full name and address as well as the return code, M778, on top of the box.
5. Keep all shipping records and paperwork until your credit is fully processed.

When we receive your package, we will send you an e-mail. Once we receive the package, it takes approximately 14 business days for the credit to be fully processed (but it may still take 1 to 2 billing cycles to show on your credit card statement). We do not cover the cost of return shipping.

If you need further assistance, you may contact our Client Support Center by e-mail at orders@systaproducts.net, by phone at 1-555-555-5343, or by visiting our Web site at www.SystaProducts.net.

Thank you for giving us the opportunity to assist you.

Dennis

Dennis Wilson
Customer Service Representative
SystaProducts
4505 Wessley Parkway
Boston, MA 27200
Phone: 555-555-5353

Here are examples of highly formal and professional writing:

Highly formal: An indication of their disinterest was evidenced by their lack of a response to our request.

Professional: They indicated their disinterest when they did not respond to our request.

Today most people consider highly formal writing stilted. Though in the past much academic and scientific writing was written in this highly formal, stilted style, the current trend is to write in a professional style for those genres as well.

CHOOSE SIMPLE LANGUAGE

Whether you choose simple words or more complicated ones also affects the tone of your document. When possible, use a simple word instead of a complicated one. Here are a few examples:

When we reach the *termination* of this project . . .	When we reach the *end* of this project . . .
Chuck is *contemplating* making a change.	Chuck is *thinking about* making a change.

▸Language Diversity

Hawaiian Pidgin: *Hawaii Pidgin English,* also known as *Hawaii Creole English (HCE)* and *pidgin,* finds its origins as a form of communication used between non-native and native English speakers in Hawaii. However, don't confuse Hawaiian English, the official English language used in the state of Hawaii, with Hawaiian pidgin. Locals use pidgin in everyday conversation and in advertising targeted toward Hawaiian residents.

Hawaiian pidgin has been influenced not only by English but also by the Portuguese, Cantonese, Korean, and Spanish languages. Characteristics of Hawaiian pidgin include dropping the *r* after a vowel (*car* might be pronounced *cah,* similar to the Boston English pronunciation), pronouncing the *l* sound at the end of a word as an *o* or an *ol* (*people* is often pronounced *peepo*), and using falling intonation at the end of questions.

In general, Hawaiin pidgin omits forms of *to be* when referring to inherent qualities of an object or person (*Da puppy cute* or *Cute, da puppy* as opposed to *The puppy is cute*) but uses the word *stay* in place of *to be* when referring to a temporary state or location (*Da book stay da counter* rather than *The book is on the counter*).

Below is a list of words written as they are pronounced in the Hawaiian pidgin dialect. If these words were used by a client who spoke in the Hawaiian pidgin dialect, would you be sure of their meanings?

1. eriding
2. An den
3. no can
4. planny
5. talk story
6. onolisicious
7. like beef?
8. haad rub
9. aznuts
10. bodda you?

Here are examples of Hawaiian pidgin:

I so hungry.	I'm famished.
I meet you in 10 minutes. K'DEN.	Ok, then, I'll meet you in 10 minutes.
Come on, we go moi moi.	Well, it's time to go to sleep.
Where your car stay?	Where is your car?

Hawaiian Pidgin:	Inside my house we get my gramma, my muddah, my two bruddahs, and my three sistahs.
Business English:	I have a large family living in the same household; Grandma, Mother, both of my brothers, and all of my three sisters.
Hawaiian Pidgin:	An den? Ho pretty good, how you?
Business English:	And how might you be doing this glorious day? Just fine. And how are you doing, my friend?

We *are desirous* of a good result.	We *want* a good result.
Their decision *is contingent upon his reaction.*	Their decision *depends on how he reacts.*
Prior to making a decision, . . .	*Before making their decision, . . .*

PRACTICE

Instructions: Simplify the following sentences. **For example:**

Weak: Subsequent to the meeting, we were able to make good progress.

Revised: *After* the meeting, we were able to make good progress.

1. It has been brought to my attention that the store has been accepting competitors' coupons.
2. It would be so appreciated if you would fill me in on the new manager's background.
3. Pursuant to your request, my assistant is sending you several brochures and flyers.
4. In the event of a power outage, the generator will keep our file server running.
5. On behalf of the marketing department, we would like to welcome you to the company.

KEEP A POSITIVE FOCUS

Everyone appreciates positive words, and even subtle comments add energy. In writing, you help set a positive tone by describing situations in affirmative language. In other words, rather than saying what will go wrong if procedures are *not* followed, *say what will go right if the procedures are followed.* Here are some examples:

Negative: If you *do not complete* the application by the deadline, you *will not be* considered for the project.

Positive: If you *complete* the application by the deadline, you *will be* considered for the project.

Negative: If you *do not respond* by Friday, I *will not be* able to use your input.

Positive: If you *respond* by Friday, I *will be* able to use your input.

To improve tone, focus on what will go right if things are done according to plan rather than what will go wrong if things are not. It sounds less threatening to the listener or the reader.

Think of a sentence or two that you have written (or received) in the negative, and then translate them into positive statements.

____

____

____

____

VOCABULARY SOUNDALIKES

Assure/Ensure/Insure: These verbs have similar meanings but are used in different ways.

Assure: to give a person confidence that something will happen. Use *assure* when the object is a person.

I assure *you* that the delivery will arrive on time.

Ensure: to make certain that some "thing" happens. Use *ensure* when the object is a thing.

Our accounting department ensures the *invoice is accurate.*

Insure: to protect against loss, as in *insurance.* (Use *ensure,* not *insure,* for "to make sure.") For *insure,* think of insurance.

You can insure your possessions to protect yourself from loss.

The key to using *assure* and *ensure* correctly relates to their objects:

- With *assure,* the object is always a person.
- With *ensure,* the object is a thing.

And remember, use *insure* only when you are discussing insurance.

WRITE IN THE AFFIRMATIVE

Writing in the affirmative is tied to keeping a positive focus, but from a slightly different bent. English is a language best understood in the affirmative. In other words, writing is a bit more difficult to understand when the word *not* is used. Writing in the affirmative takes fewer words and keeps information more simple and sometimes more positive, important qualities in business. Here are some examples:

Marc *cannot* help you.	Marc is *unable* to help you.
The meeting *will not start on time.*	The meeting *will start late.*
Tasha *does not have* the resources.	Tasha *lacks* the resources.
Jasmine's skills are *not the same* as Mel's.	Jasmine's skills are *different from* Mel's.

Writing in the affirmative also helps focus the message on positive results. For example:

Negative: If you *do not contact* the client today, you *will not meet* their deadline.

Positive: If you *contact* the client today, you *will meet* their deadline.

Negative: You *will not be offered* that position; you are *not qualified.*

Positive: You *should apply* for other positions that *better match your qualifications.*

Whenever you can, edit a sentence to state the same message without the word *not.* Your writing not only will be written in the affirmative but also may sound more positive.

PRACTICE

Instructions: Revise the following sentences so that they are written in the affirmative. **For example:**

Weak: The committee will not be able to consider your request.

Revised: The committee *is unable* to consider your request.

Weak: If you do not send your résumé by the deadline, you will not be considered.

Revised: If you *send* your résumé by the deadline, you *will be* considered.

1. If you do not have the receipt, we will not be able to give you a refund.
2. We are sorry that our 800 number was not working for the past 12 hours.
3. Your credentials do not meet our requirements for the position.
4. We cannot send you the replacement part for your carpet sweeper until you provide the serial number.
5. We are sorry that we cannot have your order completed by your requested date, July 15.

SECTION B CONCEPT CHECK

1. Why is the "you" point of view important in business writing?
2. What is the difference between the active voice and the passive voice? What is the preferred voice for business writing?
3. What is a nominal? Give three examples of nominals, and then turn them into verbs.

CHAPTER 8 SUMMARY

Section A covered aspects of style that make writing simple, clear, and concise and thus more readable.

• Keep subjects and verbs close.

• Limit sentences to 22 words.

• Use the active voice.

• Cut excess words.

• Build old to new information flow.

• Use parallel structure.

• Show relationships and bridge ideas by using conjunctions.

Section B showed how style affects tone.

• Write in the "you" point of view.

• Turn nominals into active verbs.

• Write in a professional tone, not too informal or too formal.

• Choose simple language.

• Use positive and affirmative language.

By incorporating these principles into your editing strategy, your writing will not only be simple, clear, and concise but also connect with your readers. However, *principles of style relate to editing, not composing.* Apply these principles when you edit, not when you compose. And remember, the more you compose and edit, the better your skills will become.

CHAPTER 8 CHECKLIST

For style, have you incorporated the following principles?

___ Keep sentence length to 10 to 22 words.

___ Structure subjects and verbs close together.

___ Keep sentence content to one main idea.

___ Use the active voice when possible.

___ Use the passive voice when appropriate.

___ Turn nominals into active verbs.

___ Use real subjects and strong verbs.

___ Cut empty and redundant words and phrases.

___ Focus on the positive; write in the affirmative.

___ Start with old information and lead to new information.

___ Use parallel structure.

___ Keep modifiers close to the word or words they modify.

___ Use conjunctions to show relationships.

___ Bridge ideas effectively.

For tone, have you considered the following?

- ___ Keep an appropriate level of formality.
- ___ Use the "you" viewpoint.
- ___ Balance the thinker and feeler approaches.
- ___ Give an objective response.
- ___ Use a positive attitude.
- ___ Keep language gender-neutral.
- ___ Avoid slanted language, slang, and sarcasm.

CHAPTER 8 END-OF-CHAPTER ACTIVITIES

ACTIVITY 1: PROCESS MEMO

INSTRUCTIONS: Write your instructor a short message describing some of the principles you learned in this chapter. Do you now have control of the tone and style of your sentences? What principles do you apply to achieve a simple, clear, and concise writing style?

If you have Internet access, you can complete this exercise online at **www.mhhe.com/youngBE** and then send an e-mail to your instructor.

ACTIVITY 2: TEAM EXERCISES

A. ACTIVE/PASSIVE VOICE

INSTRUCTIONS: With a partner, create a list of ten action verbs (such as *apply, revise, create,* and *develop*). Write a sentence in the active voice for each word on the list. Your partner will then rewrite each sentence using the passive voice. Both sentences for each verb should have the same meaning. For example, for the verb *apply,* the active sentence might read *Mark applied the information;* the passive sentence would read *The information was applied by Mark.*

B. COORDINATING, SUBORDINATING, AND ADVERBIAL CONJUNCTIONS

INSTRUCTIONS: With a partner, list several coordinating, subordinating, and adverbial conjunctions. Then use several of the conjunctions to connect two short sentences that would sound choppy without the conjunction as a connector. For example:

Weak:	We arrived on time. The meeting started late.
Revised:	We arrived on time, *but* the meeting started late.
	Or: We arrived on time; *however,* the meeting started late.

ACTIVITY 3: MORE MALAPROPISMS

INSTRUCTIONS: Underline the incorrect word in each malapropism below. Rewrite the sentence correctly in the space provided. For example:

Incorrect: Let's get down to brass roots.

Corrected: Let's get down to brass *tacks*.

1. The doctor felt the man's purse and said there was no hope.
2. I just want to thank everyone who made this day necessary. (Yogi Berra)
3. You can observe a lot by watching. (Yogi Berra)
4. The flood damage was so bad they had to evaporate the city.
5. You have to take the bad with the worse.
6. Marie Scott . . . has really plummeted to the top. (Alan Weeks)
7. The police are not here to create disorder; they're here to preserve disorder (former Chicago mayor Richard Daly)
8. I am mindful not only of preserving executive powers for myself, but for predecessors as well. (George W. Bush)

ACTIVITY 4: SPEAKING BUSINESS

PART A

INSTRUCTIONS: Edit the following statements to remove slang, slanted language, and sarcasm so that they could be used in professional business correspondence.

1. Thanks for your quick reply to my e-mail; I've only had to wait five days.
2. We didn't get to first base with our proposal to implement a team building program.

3. We should inform them that they need to stop looking for the pot at the end of the rainbow.

4. You are pushing the envelope; they may not even give us the bid.

5. Their representatives aren't the smartest crackers in the box, but they'll meet the bill.

6. So you say that my proposal isn't good enough—and why is that?

7. We are all glad that you decided to grace us with your presence.

PART B

Write five sentences using your informal patterns of speech, and then translate them into formal Business English.

____

____

____

____

ACTIVITY 5: BEING CONCISE

BACKGROUND: When Angles and Saxons came together in Europe centuries ago, redundant phrases were necessary. Each group had its own expressions; two words were needed so that everyone could understand the meaning. Although this habit has outlived its usefulness, the pattern of using redundant phrases lives on.

INSTRUCTIONS: Rewrite the following redundant phrases, leaving out the unnecessary words so that the meaning becomes clear. If it helps, add a word or place the redundant pair in a phrase. For example, *any and all situations* becomes *all situations; a full and complete report* becomes *a complete report.*

Paired Expressions

any and all	hope and trust
at this day and time	problems and issues
basic and fundamental	questions and problems
each and every	separate and distinct
facts and figures	true and accurate
first and foremost	true and honest
full and complete	various and sundry
goals and objectives	ways and means

Modifiers

completely eliminate
close together
close proximity
each individual
exactly alike
final outcome
final completion
final result
following after
free gift
important essentials
more perfect
most unique
new breakthrough
one hundred percent complete
one hundred fifty percent better
precisely accurate
totally accurate
two equal halves
true facts

Verb Add-Ons

add up
add together
cancel out
continue on
finish up
combine together
continue to remain
grouped together
plan ahead
refer back to
repeat again
send out
start out
still continue

ACTIVITY 6: INFORMATION FLOW—PROOFREADING AND EDITING

INSTRUCTIONS: You are planning to write an article that explains how high school students should choose a college. You've taken the notes below, but they are not in order. Reorganize the notes to show a correct flow of information.

Planning for College: An Overview

- After all your research and soul-searching, don't forget to stay on track with deadlines. Submit your applications and test scores, complete your Free Application for Federal Student Aid (FAFSA: **http://www.fafsa.ed.gov**); apply for college-specific scholarships, and begin the waiting game!
- In your planning binder, make a list of your career interests. Research these interests with your school guidance counselor or on the Internet. One good place to start is the federal government's *Occupational Outlook Handbook,* which provides useful information on most professions (**http://www.bls.gov/oco/home.htm**).
- At this point, you might want to consider using professional services to help you prepare for the college admission tests required by your selected colleges. Although college test preparation services tend to be costly, they are usually worth your time.
- Using the Internet or the school's guidance office, peruse college catalogs and consider the many features of a college that might appeal to you: size, location, expenses, types (coed, religious, private, public, etc.). Eliminate the colleges that do not have programs that grant degrees in your area of career choice. Make a list of the colleges that interest you.
- During your senior year, you will have many tasks to complete and decisions to make. Putting together a college planning binder is a good way to keep all your information in one place.

- Once you have narrowed down your choice of colleges, use a separate piece of paper in your binder to list their admission requirements. Put each requirement on a separate line so that your list resembles a checklist.
- Visit your school's guidance counselor. He or she will help you determine your interests, strengths, and financial options.
- After making a list of career choices that interest you, take an honest survey of your skills and abilities. Compare the education and career requirements with your own abilities and experience. Narrow down your list of career choices on the basis of your self-assessment. Your goal is to find a career that fits your interests *and* your abilities.
- One of the most important items to note is the deadline for applying to each college. List this information in a bold color on the top of each college checklist you have made.
- In addition to test preparation, one of the most daunting challenges you'll face is the admission essay. You simply must seek expertise in this area: read previously successful admission essays, seek help from advisers and teachers, and consider obtaining professional services.
- Most colleges have guided tours for prospective students. Schedule as many of these as you can; it is important to visit the campus to get an idea of its environment. Talk to current students, and ask questions about their experiences with the college.

ACTIVITY 7: ACTIVE AND PASSIVE VOICE

PART A

INSTRUCTIONS: Change the following sentences from passive to active voice. For example:

Weak: The meeting was canceled by my manager.

Revised: My manager *canceled* the meeting.

1. The audit was performed by a certified accountant.

2. The reports were delayed when new data had to be included.

3. The new interns are being trained by Chloe and Michael.

4. The slide show was presented by me.

5. The flights were delayed by the storm.

6. My flights are usually booked by my assistant.

7. The copyright rules were broken by the new intern.

8. My assistant was given the day off by my boss.

9. The instructions were read before we began assembling the desk.

10. The order was taken by the waitress.

11. Companies have been destroyed by changes in import and export law.

12. The software has been downloaded by the technician.

13. Your submission of the completed form is required to arrive in our office by November.

14. Refreshments will be provided by the support group.

15. Written instructions will be included in the package.

PART B

INSTRUCTIONS: Revise the following paragraph from passive voice to active voice. Look for other types of errors in grammar and punctuation, and correct them as well.

Our last annual sales meeting was facilitated by you. Now preparations are being made to meet on October 15th for this years' meeting. A facilitator will once again be needed, and you are being asked to consider returning for the facilitation of this years' meeting. A short warm-up activity would be a kick off piece that you would present. Leading a discussion on the pros and cons of our new product line would be facilitated by yourself in the afternoon. Your response is needed by September 15th.

ACTIVITY 8: ELIMINATING REDUNDANCY AND OUTDATED EXPRESSIONS

INSTRUCTIONS: Edit the following sentences to remove empty information, redundancy, and outdated expressions. For example:

Weak: Enclosed please find our latest report.

Revised: Our latest report is enclosed.

1. Attached please find the information you requested.

2. Per your request, we will ship the item by overnight express.

3. Please be informed that we no longer offer consulting services to the general public.

4. Your prior arrangement would best be served if you arrived in a timely fashion.

5. It is advisable for the purposes of this agreement that you retain a signed copy.

6. I am in receipt of your letter dated May 12.

7. Enclosed herewith you will find a variety of options from which to choose.

8. Should you require further guidance, please consult our administrative staff.

9. When will you initiate the new project?

10. It is fully expected that you will comply with the terms of our agreement.

ACTIVITY 9: EDITING STRATEGY

INSTRUCTIONS: Edit the following short paragraph so that the message is simple, clear, and concise. Try to make the following changes:

- Use active voice.
- Cut excess words.
- Use simple words.

Compensation for Completion of Training

All local employees endeavoring completion of company certified educational courses or training would be best served by their supervisors' focus on the recognition of their achievement. Furthermore, empowerment of cooperative teams will be facilitated by compensation for meritorious completion of said indicated training.

ACTIVITY 10: PARALLEL STRUCTURE

INSTRUCTIONS: The following sentences lack parallel structure. Make changes where appropriate. For example:

Incorrect:	Writing is a good way to express creativity, develops your critical thinking, and will make you feel relief from stress.
Corrected:	Writing is a good way to express creativity, *develop* critical thinking, and *relieve* stress.

1. Getting too many phone calls distracts me and are causing me to make mistakes.

2. During my first week on my new job, I arranged six meetings, typing two contracts, and got paid a bonus.

3. When the university changed its night program, several students were unable to finish their degrees and to transfer credits was impossible.

4. Have you considered earning an online degree? You can work when you are finding the hours convenient to you and where you find it comfortable to work.

5. Although online degrees can be expensive, many employers offer tuition reimbursement and sometimes giving promotions or raises for credits earned.

6. My wardrobe has changed a lot since college: now, instead of sweats, I wear suits; instead of sneakers, I will be wearing pumps; and instead of a ponytail, my hair is worn styled.

7. My friend spends too much time playing computer games, goes to rock concerts, and likes eating junk food.

8. You can eat lunch in the cafeteria, or we're going to the local coffee shop.

9. This seminar had begun two days ago and is continuing today.

10. During my lunch break, I enjoy visiting the sites of the city, to look at the shoreline, and shop for bargains.

ACTIVITY 11: "WRITER'S REFERENCE MANUAL" DRILL

INSTRUCTIONS: In the "Writer's Reference Manual," read the entry "addresses" and then answer the following questions:

1. For a business letter, where do you start the inside address?

____

2. What are the two styles for addressing envelopes?

____

3. Which style does the USPS prefer? Which style is the most commonly used?

____

4. When sending a package, where on the outside of the package can you tape an envelope?

____

5. Display the following address correctly: Brown Boxleightner Corporation, 2324 East End, Mr. Morgan Freeman, Winston, Arkansas, 45645, President, Suite 435.

____

ACTIVITY 12: VOCABULARY LIST

A. COMMONLY MISSPELLED WORDS

INSTRUCTIONS: The list below contains words taken from a compilation of the 500 most commonly misspelled words and from the chapter. Practice them until you can spell them automatically and use them correctly.

1. censure (v) criticize, scorn, show disapproval
2. congruence (n) equivalence, similarity, the quality or state of agreeing
3. core (n) center
4. camouflage (n) any means of concealment; dissimulation
5. charlatan (n) a person who deceives others, a quack, a fake
6. dogmatic (adj) rigid and inflexible due to an established opinion
7. facilitator (n) a person who leads a group discussion
8. interrupt (v) break continuity or uniformity, to stop action or speech
9. laissez-faire (adj) lenient and easy-going
10. nebulous (adj) indistinct, vague, misty
11. omniscient (adj) infinitely knowing
12. ostracize (v) exclude from a group, ignore, snub
13. prerogative (n) an exclusive right or privilege
14. rapport (n) the condition of mutual trust and understanding
15. saboteur (n) a person who sabotages the efforts of others

B. SIMILAR WORDS

INSTRUCTIONS: The list below contains similar words, some of which are profiled in the Vocabulary Builders in each chapter. Use these words in sentences until their meaning becomes clear.

assure/ensure/insure: These three verbs are similar in meaning but used differently.

Assure means to give a person confidence that something will happen. Use *assure* when the object is a person; for example: Tom *assured* me that he would arrive on time.

Ensure means to make certain that some "thing" happens. Use *ensure* when the object is a thing; for example: I will *ensure* that the meeting goes as planned.

Insure means to protect against loss, as in *insurance.* (Use *ensure,* not *insure,* when you mean "to make sure.") For *insure,* think of *insurance;* for example: The airline will *insure* your baggage for a small fee.

if/whether: The word *if* is often used when the word *whether* would be the correct choice. Use *whether* when the statement that follows contains or implies the phrase *or not.* Use *whether* in expressions such as *learn whether, know whether,* and *doubt whether.*

Incorrect: I'm not sure if I learned about that (or not).

Corrected: I'm not sure *whether* I learned about that or not.

THE INBOX

COMPOSING

You have been chosen by your instructor to be a group leader in an optional study group for this class. Draft a letter to your classmates convincing them to attend the biweekly study group. For example, you might say that your instructor will provide comprehensive study guides for all tests but that only students attending the study sessions will receive the guides. Use the techniques you have learned in this and all the previous chapters to make your letter friendly and positive.

REFLECTING

Look at the draft of your letter to your classmates. Did you take a "you-centered" approach? Using a word processing program, revise the letter to change it into a flyer. Is there a difference between persuasive letters and advertising?

Do you think that persuasive writing takes place often in the workplace? If so, how?

DISCUSSING

1. With a partner, revise your letter to your classmates. Help each other find passive sentences, redundant and outdated phrases, and nonparallel structure.
2. In small groups, discuss the last time you had to attend a function or complete a task that was mandatory. How was the information presented? Could the information have been presented in a more positive manner?

EDITING

The English professor who wrote this memo needs to take a class on clear writing. See if you can reduce this verbiage to one paragraph.

TO: English 326 Students
FROM: Professor MacGregor
DATE: October 12, 2007
RE: Attendance at Bi-Weekly Study Sessions

It has come to my attention that most students are not attending the bi-weekly study sessions. It is to the benefit of students that they should attend these worthwhile sessions. As per prior communications, said study sessions have not been declared mandatory; however, the final outcome of any given student's grade may very well be dependent upon his or her participation thereof.

One will note the various posting of notices and announcement to be found about the classroom, the dorms, and the student activity center. Whereas it seems to be the case that students have such free time as to engage in futile and inane goings-on which can be described only as puerile and inconsequential, it has not become apparent that these same students formerly mentioned have had occasion to comport themselves in a fashion suitable for intellectual and scholarly young people. Further, it must be noted that these same "scholars" prefer the delectations of the bawdy theatre and meretricious pool hall to the more stately and comely albeit rigorous atmosphere of the study hall.

While it cannot be proclaimed that a student's grades will necessarily plummet to the depths of Dante's *Inferno* sans study session; nevertheless, let it be said that should a student's grades suffer the martyrdom of a steep and sudden drop, there would be none to take the blame unless it were the student himself or herself who, having chosen the tawdry and mundane over the enlightened pathway, must then take upon themselves the burden of the blame therewith.

CAREER-BUILDING PORTFOLIO

Let's add another revision and a new document to your portfolio. Make these documents the best samples of your work. When you complete the portfolio, you will be able to proudly display your work.

PORTFOLIO DOCUMENT 3

Revise either the persuasive letter or the flyer you wrote for the composing activity in this Inbox. When you are satisfied with it, put a clean copy in your portfolio.

PORTFOLIO DOCUMENT 4

Visit the U.S. Department of Labor's *Occupational Outlook Handbook* (**http://www.bls.gov/oco/home.htm**) to research a career field in which you are interested. Find information on the average starting salary, working conditions, training, and the employment outlook. Write a *one-page report in memo format* describing the career of your choice.

KEY TO LEARNING INVENTORY

1. T	6. F
2. F	7. F
3. T	8. F
4. T	9. T
5. F	10. T

CHAPTER 8 ENDNOTES

1. **http://www.cartercenter.org/aboutus/bio2.htm**, accessed on July 27, 2006.
2. **http://www.myersbriggs.org/my_mbti_personality_type/mbti_basics/c_g_jungs_theory.asp**, accessed on October 30, 2006.

Chapter Nine

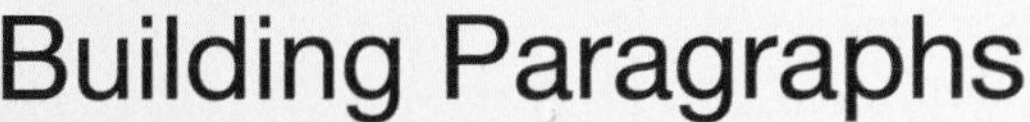

Building Paragraphs

Our admiration of fine writing will always be in proportion to its real difficulty and its apparent ease. —Charles Caleb Colton, author and clergyman (1780–1832)

So far you have focused on editing sentences to achieve simple, clear, and concise writing. Now you will examine how to edit and revise short messages, focusing specifically on effective paragraphs. The paragraph is the basic unit of all business correspondence, including e-mail, letters, and memos. Once you feel confident composing and revising paragraphs, you will have control over every business and academic document you write.

With paragraphs, you will apply principles of information flow, going from old to new information. Controlling information flow ensures that your messages are *cohesive* and *coherent.* You achieve a cohesive, coherent paragraph by constructing a *topic sentence* that builds into a *topic string.* In this chapter, you will be introduced to the *PEER model,* a guide to structuring information as you compose or revise.

In addition, you will review transitions as they relate to connecting larger chunks of information. To apply what you are learning, you will practice editing short messages so that they are cohesive, coherent, and reader-friendly. By the time you finish this chapter, you will have reached an important step in developing your skills as a business writer.

To learn more about The Writing Process, please visit our Web site at **www.mhhe.com/youngBE**

Outline

Chapter 9: Building Paragraphs

Section A: Cohesive Paragraphs and Coherent Paragraphs

Section B: The Process of Revising

Section C: Structure: Beginning, Middle, and End

Section D: Transitions and Connectors

Objectives

When you have completed your study of Chapter 9, you will be able to:

1. Develop cohesive and coherent paragraphs.
2. Build effective paragraphs by using a topic sentence and a topic string.
3. Eliminate empty information from sentences and paragraphs.
4. Identify transitional elements and apply them to paragraphing decisions.
5. Compose, edit, and revise paragraphs for effective information flow.

Learning Inventory

1. Coherent paragraphs consist of sentences that have differing topics. T/F
2. One principle in developing effective paragraphs is new to old information flow. T/F
3. When composing, you should try to put the topic sentence at the beginning of your paragraph. T/F
4. When editing, you should revise your paragraph for information flow. T/F
5. Which two of the following choices describe effective paragraphs?

   a. topical b. cohesive c. edited and revised d. coherent e. PEER
6. Information flow consists of a third category, which is empty information. T/F
7. Which of the following is true?

   a. A topic string leads to a topic sentence.

   b. A topic sentence develops into a topic string.
8. Conjunctions function as transitions between sentences and paragraphs. T/F
9. There is one best way to write information, and that's every writer's goal. T/F
10. Every document, no matter how short, has a beginning, middle, and end. T/F

Goal-Setting Exercises

Are you unsure of your paragraphing? Do you sometimes end up with a solid block of sentences without making a paragraph break? Do you ramble on, going from one idea to another, all in the same paragraph? Think for a moment about your goals as they relate to paragraphing, and then write three of them below.

1. ____

2. ____

3. ____

SECTION A: COHESIVE AND COHERENT PARAGRAPHS

Business documents of all types depend on well-written paragraphs. Readers are confused when writers jump from one idea to another without developing a line of thought. Whether you are writing an e-mail, a letter, or a research paper, you need to make good paragraphing decisions.

Readers assimilate information in chunks, and they have difficulty reading one long narrative with no breaks. If you do not insert paragraph breaks naturally as you compose, put them in when you edit and revise. Read your writing out loud or have someone read it to you. When you hear a new topic, start a new paragraph.

Once you have enough experience writing, you will make paragraph breaks as a natural part of composing. When you edit, you will structure the content to make your paragraphs cohesive and coherent.

- **Cohesive** paragraphs present *one main idea* or topic. All ideas in the paragraph connect to the main idea, having a common purpose. Adequate details support the main idea so that the reader understands the main point.
- **Coherent** paragraphs develop the main idea in a *logical way* through a *logical flow of ideas.* The writer develops the topic in a consistent, rational way. Readers can make sense of the content because one idea leads to another.

To assist you in gaining control over editing and revising paragraphs, this section develops each of these principles in more detail.

COHESIVE PARAGRAPHS

Cohesive paragraphs develop one main idea, and this idea controls the content of the paragraph. The sentence that presents the main idea or topic in the most effective way is called the *topic sentence.* Each sentence in the paragraph should relate to the topic sentence, thereby developing a *topic string.*

- *Topic sentence:* A **topic sentence** is a *broad, general sentence* that gives an overview of the paragraph. A topic sentence presents the main or controlling idea, and the rest of the paragraph radiates from that idea. Though the topic sentence can be placed anywhere in the paragraph, it is most effective as the first or second sentence.
- *Topic string:* A **topic string** is a *series of sentences* that develop the specific idea presented by the topic sentence. Each sentence extends what the readers know about the controlling idea, helping readers digest the topic before linking it to the next main idea.

By developing a topic string from a topic sentence, you are ensuring that your paragraph is cohesive. The topic sentence introduces the common thread, and the topic string pulls that common thread through every sentence in the paragraph.

Here is an example of a topic sentence followed by a topic string:

> Proofreading is checking a manuscript for errors in grammar and spelling and correcting them. When you proofread, look for errors in punctuation, capitalization, and number usage. Identify and correct all run-on sentences and incomplete thoughts. Proofreading makes a document correct and therefore makes it professional and credible.

What is the topic sentence in the paragraph above? Is it the first sentence? The paragraph above is *cohesive* because the topic string develops only

Communication Challenges

Pop Quiz 1: The job application for a sales position at a company that makes computer software asks you to answer the following question:

> On a routine sales call to an existing client (in your new territory), the client refuses to deal with you because he is so unhappy with the company's past service. How would you handle the situation?

Pop Quiz 2: The job application for a managerial position at a local bank includes this question:

> Can you think of an experience in which you had to exchange information with someone who was hard to understand? For example, the person may have been speaking very quickly and nervously and with an accent different from your own. Tell us about it. How did you deal with the situation? How did it turn out?

Challenge: In a timed exercise, take 10 minutes to prepare a paragraph-long response to one of these questions. Remember, you want to impress!

the aspect of proofreading that relates to the topic sentence: *Proofreading is checking a manuscript for errors in grammar and spelling and correcting them.* However, the paragraph above was originally written as follows:

> I believe proofreading is checking a manuscript for errors in grammar and spelling and correcting them. I used to know a proofreader, and I thought she must have been very smart. I never really found out. At least one would have to be very alert. I do occasionally find spelling errors in articles or books that I read, and I am always surprised when I do. I wonder how the error escaped the attention of the proofreader. Apparently proofreaders are human too and subject to errors. When I proofread, I also look for errors in punctuation, capitalization, and number usage. When you proofread, identify and correct run-on sentences and incomplete thoughts. Proofreading makes a document correct and therefore makes it professional and credible. The mistakes I find are usually understandable. They are usually small words and very similar to the correct word.

Though the entire paragraph above is about proofreading, it jumps to very different aspects of proofreading. For example, *checking a manuscript for errors* is a different aspect of proofreading than is *knowing a proofreader.* Hence, staying on the same broad topic is not necessarily the same as developing that topic through a cohesive and logical flow of ideas. (The paragraph also contains several grammatical mistakes.)

By focusing on the topic "proofreaders," the writer can also develop a cohesive paragraph:

> I occasionally find spelling errors in articles or books that I read, and I am always surprised when I do. The mistakes I find are usually small words and similar to the correct word. However, I still wonder how the error escaped the attention of the proofreader. Proofreaders must be smart or at least very alert. Apparently proofreaders are human too and subject to errors.

Identify your topic sentence by selecting the sentence that best captures the broader, more general topic that the rest of the paragraph develops through specifics. Every sentence in the paragraph should develop some element of the topic sentence; every sentence should also be directly related to the other sentences in the paragraph. Otherwise, you need to start a new paragraph to develop the new topic.

Though a topic string ensures a cohesive paragraph, it does not ensure a coherent paragraph. Staying on the same topic is not the same as developing that topic through a logical flow of ideas. Let's examine how to develop paragraphs that are coherent as well as cohesive.

PRACTICE

Instructions: Read the paragraph below about coaching, and then answer the following questions:

1. Which sentence is the topic sentence, capturing the topic in a broad and general way?
2. Which sentences develop the topic string, directly supporting the topic sentence while remaining related to each other?
3. Which sentence or sentences start to develop a new topic and should be removed so that the paragraph is cohesive?

> Coaching is one of the fastest-growing markets in the United States. Given the growth of the coaching market, it appears that society is beginning to understand how all aspects of business and life can be affected by coaching. Gaining confidence to make decisions without help will be your result from coaching. Removing obstacles, taking advantage of your talents, and moving forward in a positive direction are all things a professional coach can help you to do. To improve their skills in a particular area, for years athletes, entertainers, and politicians have worked closely with coaches. In the case of Tiger Woods, he has three separate

coaches depending on the expertise required. To teach clients how to fish, not to fish for them, is the mission of coaching.

SPEAKING BUSINESS

Correcting Quirks: Some words develop pronunciation peculiarities that cannot be explained by the way they are spelled. In fact, when words are pronounced with extra letters and syllables, those elements are added when the word is written. Here are some examples from Appendix B of *The Gregg Reference Manual:*

government	Say *GUH-vern-ment,* not *GUH-ver-ment.*
Illinois	Say *ill-lih-NOY,* not *ill-lih-NOYZ.*
library	Say *LIE-brer-ree,* not *LIE-ber-ree.*
nuclear	Say *NOO-klee-ur,* not *NOO-kyoo-lur.*
picture	Say *PIHK-chur,* not *PIT-chur.*
sandwich	Say *SAND-witch,* not *SAN-witch* or *SAM-witch.*

Remember, changing your patterns of speaking takes work. Practice until you feel comfortable with the preferred pronunciation. You will have more practice with these types of words in the End-of-Chapter Activities.

See *The Gregg Reference Manual,* Appendix B, for a more complete list of words.

COHERENT PARAGRAPHS

To achieve a coherent paragraph, aim for a logical flow of ideas; one idea leads logically to the next idea as it extends the reader's knowledge. Apply principles of information flow, developing ideas from the familiar (old) to the unfamiliar (new). (In Chapter 8, you worked with information flow at the sentence level.)

In each sentence, put old information first and follow it with new information. The old information relates to the main idea (topic) of the paragraph; the new information extends the reader's understanding of the topic. Building old to new information flow helps readers make connections; familiar ideas ease readers into the unfamiliar.

The paragraph about coaching in the Practice above sounds choppy and incoherent because new information is presented first and then attached to old information. That paragraph can become coherent by adjusting the information flow. Here's how to achieve effective information flow:

- Move the topic of *coaching* (old information) to the beginning of each sentence.
- Move information about *the benefits* (new information) to the end of each sentence.

The topic string then flows from the topic of *coaching* (which is a constant topic) to new information or *benefits* (which varies or expands). In the examples that follow, old information is in bold and new information is in italics.

ORIGINAL TOPIC SENTENCE ~~Given the growth of the coaching market, it appears that society is beginning to understand how~~ *all aspects of business and life can be affected* **by coaching.**

REVISED TOPIC SENTENCE **Coaching can affect** *all aspects of business and life.*

New to old: *Removing obstacles, taking advantage of your talents, and moving forward in a positive direction are all things* **a professional coach can help you to do.**

Old to new: **A professional coach** *can help you remove obstacles, take advantage of your talents, and move forward in a positive direction.*

New to old: *Gaining confidence to make decisions without help will be* **your result from coaching.**

Old to new: **As a result of coaching,** *you will gain confidence and learn to make independent decisions.*

Now, here is the Practice paragraph revised to have old to new information flow:

REVISED: **Coaching can affect** *all aspects of business and life.* **A professional coach** *can help you remove obstacles, take* *advantage of your talents, and move forward in a positive direction.* **As a result of coaching,** *you will gain confidence and learn to make independent decisions.*

You may notice that the topic "coaching" changes subtly in its form though not in its meaning. This variation in form adds creativity and keeps the writing from becoming monotonous.

PRACTICE

A. Instructions: Revise the information flow in the paragraph below by following these steps:

1. Identify the topic sentence and topic string.
2. If a sentence is not part of the topic string, remove it.
3. Adjust information flow so that old information (or the main topic) introduces new information.

> Our company piloted a coaching program for managers. Managers could take an active role in their own development through this intense program. A weekly meeting was scheduled between managers and their coaches for feedback sessions about employee relations. Assessments and inventories were also given by the coaches so that managers could define their management style. Advice was offered by these innovative professionals to help managers deal with resistance and difficult situations. Although some managers did not fully participate and they were disappointed when they saw the results. Employee morale had improved and so did the bottom line by the end of this innovative, intense coaching program.

B. Instructions: Write a two- or three-paragraph memo to your instructor about one of the following concepts:

1. *Editing sentences:* What principles do you apply to create simple, clear, and concise sentences?
2. *Today's news:* What interesting business developments have you recently read or heard about?
3. *Your objectives:* What are your career goals? What kind of job do you want to have two years from now?

Compose freely until you get your main ideas on the page. Then look for the sentence that best captures the essence of your paragraph (your topic sentence). Move your topic sentence to the beginning of the paragraph, and then edit each sentence so that it is simple, clear, and concise. Does each sentence relate to the topic sentence? If not, edit it out or use it to start a new paragraph.

• Internet Exercise 9.1

Proofreaders' Marks: A chart of the most frequently used marks appears in Figure 9.1 on the next page. For more information on proofreaders' marks, including practice exercises, log on to the Web site at **www.mhhe.com/youngBE**. Once you have accessed the home page, select "Student Activities" and then the "Chapter 9" link to get started.

COMPOSING AND EDITING: THE PROCESS OF WRITING PARAGRAPHS

When composing, do not concern yourself with writing cohesive, coherent paragraphs. Also, as you get your ideas on the page, don't be concerned about information flow; you may find yourself first capturing new information and then linking it to the old. You are still learning about your topic; organize and prioritize your ideas when you edit and revise.

FIGURE 9.1 Most Frequently Used Proofreaders' Marks

Mark It Up: *Using proofreaders' marks can shorten the time it takes to edit a document. These common marks and symbols—a form of editorial shorthand—reduce the need for writing out longer notes or instructions.*

REVISION SYMBOLS

Symbol meaning	Example
Insert a letter	May arive early
Insert a word	on computer (the)
Delete a letter	sales calll
Delete a letter and close up	miss pelled word
Change a letter or word	tgo new sights (w, sites)
Delete a word	sent two two copies
Transpose	hte most the of time
Add one space	at ourmeeting
Add two spaces	guest speaker He is
Delete space	in the spread sheet
Leave one space	for two days
Indent five spaces	The next step is
Capitalize a letter	detroit, Michigan
Lowercase a letter	This is
Lowercase a word	PROGRAM
All capitals	fortran
Initial capital only	PROGRAM
Stet (do not change)	price $15.99
Center	TITLE
Single-space	ss For complete directions, see the appendix.
Double-space	ds Our findings are based on three months of research and observation.
Align horizontally	We notified the staff.
Align vertically	Please notify all staff members of the change.
Insert an apostrophe	Chriss memo
Insert a comma	one, two and three
Insert a dash	months we are
Insert an exclamation point or question mark	No! Really?
Insert a hyphen	twenty five years
Insert a period	We reached the end
Insert a semicolon or a colon	before long; however, bring these items:
Insert parentheses	fact (see page 215)
Insert quotation marks	She said, "Yes."
Delete punctuation	Joe is, about fifty.
Bold	MEMO TO:
Italics	the book The Best (ital)
Underscore	the book The Best
Spell out	5 printers on Aug. 15
Change to figures	eighteen guests (18)
Move to the right	March 5, 2004
Move to the left	Sincerely,
Move as shown	c: Sherry Jones Enclosure
New page	The order was delivered today by express courier. pg We have all the parts needed for the job.
No new page	The order was delivered no pg Page 2 today by express courier.
New paragraph	The order was delivered today by express courier. ¶ We have all the parts needed for the job.
No new paragraph	The order was delivered today by express courier. no¶ We have all the parts

When composing, you may write several sentences before writing your topic sentence, the sentence that best captures the topic of your paragraph. You will know your topic sentence partly because it crystallizes your insight and acts as an umbrella for the details of your topic. When you edit, tag your topic sentence and move it to the beginning of your paragraph. Then work through the paragraph sentence by sentence to adjust the information flow and create a topic string. You may need to cut some sentences and move others. *Cutting is the painful part of editing!*

Even though your objective is cohesive and coherent paragraphs, you cannot follow a recipe. Good paragraphs relate more to art than to science. Each paragraph is unique, and its development depends on its content and the meaning you create and convey: a paragraph cannot be defined by a specific number of sentences or words and cannot be designed by a formula.

SECTION A CONCEPT CHECK

1. When revising a paragraph, where should you move the sentence that best captures the essence of your topic?

2. When evaluating the flow of your paragraph, should you arrange information from new to old or from old to new?

3. Two words to describe well-written paragraphs are *cohesive* and *coherent.* What does each quality entail?

SECTION B: THE PROCESS OF REVISING

Revising deals with *substance* as well as *structure.* You are reshaping content on the basis of meaning, putting the most important information first. With paragraphs, you are moving the best-written and most comprehensive sentence to the topic-sentence position. On a larger scale, you are moving your most relevant information to the beginning, clearly stating your purpose up front.

Revising is a *revisioning* process. According to Cathy Dees, revising is *reseeing, rethinking, questioning, rewriting, and re-creating. Revising is recursive; it is a cycle.*[1] Being a cyclical process, revising requires that you recycle your thinking; you must see your material with fresh eyes and an open mind and set new priorities to restructure the content.

Here are some qualities of the **revising process:**

- *Revisioning:* Step back and evaluate your document and its purpose. Has your vision shifted? Does your thesis or purpose statement still capture the essence of your document? What are your main points? Can your reader readily identify your main points? Rethink your content on the basis of what you now understand.

- *Questioning:* Questions are the doorways to answers; continue to probe and explore your content. Are there gaps in your thinking? Have you developed your thinking beyond first responses or superficial ones? Are you overly attached to an answer that may not be complete? Are you trying to make answers fit where they don't? Change is inherent in the thinking process, and answers will change as your thinking evolves.

- *Identifying critical issues:* When your content is familiar, you are ready to prioritize key points. Have you presented critical information first? Do you need to reorganize information or eliminate empty information? What is relevant to your readers and what adds clutter? Highlight the most important information by presenting it first.

- *Rewriting:* Now that you have a new perspective, you may need to rewrite parts of your document. First drafts are the most difficult because the content is unfamiliar. When the topic becomes familiar, ideas flow and writing becomes easier. Your deeper understanding will reflect your new vision.

Revising demands that you shed some of your original thinking, but revising also demands that you shed some well-constructed sentences and paragraphs that do not add value. Cutting is painful; you worked hard to sculpt ideas and shape paragraphs that you now discover do not add strength to your document. What kind of information should you cut first?

ELIMINATING EMPTY INFORMATION

The theory of information flow can help you decide what to cut. So far, you've learned about developing information flow by starting with the old or familiar and moving to the new or unfamiliar. But there's another important element: empty information. **Empty information** consists of words, phrases, sentences, and maybe even paragraphs that add no value for your reader.

At first glance, empty information may seem like an irrelevant category. However, writers often include empty information on the way to discovering their message. While composing, a writer may see value in information that adds no value for the reader. While editing, a writer needs to identify key points and evaluate the message from the reader's point of view. Information that is insignificant to the reader should be cut.

Joseph M. Williams, author of *Style: Toward Clarity and Grace,* identifies various types of unnecessary information.[2] Williams uses the term **meta-discourse** in reference to the language a writer uses to describe his or her own thinking process. A great deal of meta-discourse is empty information. Here are some types of meta-discourse to avoid:

- Background thinking
- Your opinions and beliefs
- Reader's perception

Background Thinking

Background thinking is *how* you arrived at your conclusions. Explaining background thinking is different from explaining an issue or giving evidence to support a point. Here is an example:

POORLY WORDED

After our meeting, I went back to my office and continued to think about our discussion about employee morale. This is such a timely topic because every department has experienced some of the issues we discussed, such as absenteeism and high rates of attrition. I now realize that I could have been more supportive in developing ideas and a consistent program of rewards. I don't know why I was resisting this idea. In fact, after the meeting, I started doing some research about what other companies are doing and found that a reward program could have a positive impact on our employees and even our bottom line. Let's do more research and then get together to draft a pilot program.

REVISED

After our discussion about employee morale, I started doing some research on what other companies are doing. A reward program could have a positive impact on our employees and maybe our bottom line. Let's do more research and then get together to draft a pilot program. Let me know what you think.

Your Opinions and Beliefs

You do not need to tell how you feel about the points you make. When you can, delete phrases such as *I think, I feel,* or *I believe.* Sometimes these phrases make writers sound indecisive. Get right to the point.

Weak	Revised
I think that you have good ideas.	You have good ideas.
I believe we ought to go ahead with the project.	We ought to go ahead with the project.
I feel that now is the time to address the issue.	The time to address the issue is now.

However, leaving out *I believe, I think,* and *I feel* will change the tone of your document. Some writers may choose to soften the tone by leaving them in. (In those situations, it is still a good idea to avoid overusing *I* statements.)

Also, at times you may use these phrases in conjunction with someone else's position. Rather than boldly telling someone what to do, you can soften the tone and sound less assuming by leaving in the *I* statements.

For softer tone: I believe this issue is important to you.

I think you should go to the meeting.

I feel you should consider the proposal.

Otherwise, your comments might sound as if you are boldly telling someone what to do rather than offering your advice.

May sound too bold: Go to the meeting.

Consider the proposal.

▸Language Diversity

Spoonerisms: Sometimes a slip of the tongue can yield humorous results. In the case of spoonerisms, two slips of the tongue are required. Named for the Reverend W. A. Spooner (1844–1930), a former dean of New College at Oxford, England, a **spoonerism** is a phrase, sentence, or pair of words with swapped sounds. As an example, consider the following spoonerism, attributed to Reverend Spooner: he said, "You've tasted two worms," when he meant to say, "You've wasted two terms."

Can you determine the intended meanings of the following spoonerisms, all attributed to Reverend Spooner himself?

EXAMPLE Spoonerism: A well-boiled icicle

A well-oiled bicycle

1. Is the bean dizzy?

2. It's roaring with pain.

3. I caught a flutter by near that nosey little cook.

4. It is now kisstomary to cuss the bride.

5. Wave the sails.

Reader's Perceptions

Do not tell your reader *how* to interpret your message; such added comments may give the reader the impression that you are unsure of your message or that you lack confidence. Therefore, remove phrases or sentences that tell your readers *how you think* they will react. Here is an example:

POORLY WORDED I'm thinking this may not be the right time to bring up this issue because you are busy with a lot of other projects. However, it has been on my mind for a while, so even if you don't think we should address this issue now, I'm hoping that you will at least consider putting it on the agenda for discussion at our next meeting. Employee morale seems to be a problem, and a rewards program might go a long way in improving our current situation.

REVISED Employee morale seems to be a problem. Could we put this topic on the agenda for our next meeting? I'd be interested to hear what other department heads feel about this and also to hear about their possible solutions.

REVISING SENTENCES

Even successful writers sometimes take their own words too seriously, thinking there is one "right way" to state information. Most ideas can be stated in many different ways, each having a slightly different effect on the reader. It's a matter of syntax and choice.

By presenting the same information in different ways, you can examine how readers might be affected by the differences. Once you put an idea in writing, regardless of how rough, you have completed the most difficult part of the process. Try not to become attached to a specific sentence. To loosen up your revising skills, let's examine how to portray the same information in many different ways.

Here is the same information written in several different ways:

> Our team of financial advisors welcomes you as a new investor to our family of clients.
>
> Our firm is pleased with the decision you made to become our investment client.
>
> Thank you for becoming a client with our financial investment firm.
>
> We appreciate your business and look forward to helping you invest your hard-earned resources.
>
> You will not be sorry about your decision to invest your funds with our reputable firm.
>
> You will be pleased about your decision to invest your funds on the basis of the recommendations of our qualified financial analysts.
>
> Our financial advisers will make sure that your new account with us will be a source of financial reward.

With which of the above sentences would you have started your letter? Why did you choose that sentence? Could you have stated the same information in a more effective way? For the example below, see how many different versions you can develop.

> We cannot accept your application for admission because it was not received before the deadline.

1.

2.

3.

4.

▸Language Diversity

Palindromes: Palindromes are words or phrases like *racecar* or *madam, I'm Adam* that read the same in both directions (changes to punctuation and spaces between words are generally ignored when identifying palindromes). Numbers or other sequences of units (such as DNA strands) that have the property of reading the same in either direction are also considered palindromes.

Ancient cultures have left evidence of early interest in palindromes, including Greek inscriptions, Hebraic writings, and Chinese poetry. Below is an example of a Roman palindrome

SATOR

AREPO

TENET

OPERA

ROTAS

in which the word square can be read in four different ways, horizontally or vertically from bottom right to top left and horizontally or vertically from top left to bottom right. (The palindrome phrase *Sator arepo tenet opera rotas* translates to "The sower Arepo holds the wheels at work.") Here are a few more examples of palindromes:

Words

eye level radar stats

Phrases

"A man, a plan, a canal. Panama"	(referring to Theodore Roosevelt's vision for the Panama Canal)
"Able was I ere I saw Elba"	(referring to Napoleon's first exile)
12/02/2021	(the date December 2, 2021)
tattarrattat	(knock on the door, from James Joyce's *Ulysses*)

never odd or even

Don't nod.

Some men interpret nine memos.

Some palindromes use words as units rather than letters:

Fall leaves after leaves fall.

First ladies rule the State and state the rule: ladies first.

PRACTICE

Instructions: Revise each of the sentences below in three or four ways. Use principles you have learned to make changes; for example, change voice (active or passive), turn nominals into verbs or verbs into nominals, change the point of view, and add or eliminate redundancy. You may even add words or gestures to improve the tone (such as words of appreciation or apology) or turn one sentence into two sentences.

As you proceed, analyze the changes you are making and indicate whether the syntax is getting better or worse. Be creative; your goal is *variety,* not clarity.

1. An error occurred in your account, and you have our apologies for any inconvenience this may have caused you.

2. We have an opening in our sales department.

3. Sylvana did not complete the report.

4. A package has arrived for you, and it should be picked up from the mail room before 4 p.m.

SECTION B CONCEPT CHECK

1. Describe some of the qualities of the revising process.

2. What are some categories of empty information?

3. Is there one "right way" to state information?

Review the original letter in Box 9.1 and determine the kinds of changes you would make to improve it before examining the revised version.

BOX 9.1 The Editing Process

BEFORE

November 2, 2007

Mr. Robert Skoda
Commissioner
Biltmore Fire Department
1315 Jefferson Street
Biltmore, MA 02110

Dear Bob:

Janet Sparacio informed me that you are heading the Biltmore Fire Department's diversity initiative. I would like to take this opportunity to congratulate you on your new and exciting appointment as commissioner. Let me start by telling you that my team and I had the honor of meeting with the executive management team last year. In that meeting an open discussion was held on the diversity issues and objectives of the Biltmore Fire Department and enclosed you will find a copy of that discussion document for your review.

We, at Managing Diversity, would appreciate the opportunity to meet with you personally to have a discussion of your objectives. Based on what we understand, it sounds as if there is a commitment to move forward with the diversity initiative in 2008. We look forward to being part of the RFP process and the possibility of working with you on this critically important organizational goal.

Enclosed are some background materials on Managing Diversity.

Sincerely,

Marcia Cristi
President

Enclosures

AFTER

November 2, 2007

Mr. Robert Skoda
Commissioner
Biltmore Fire Department
1315 Jefferson Street
Biltmore, MA 02110

Dear Commissioner Skoda:

Congratulations on your new position as commissioner. A mutual associate of ours, Janet Sparacio, suggested that I contact you because you may be moving forward with the Biltmore Fire Department's diversity initiative.

My team and I had the honor of meeting with the executive management team last year. In that meeting, we had an open discussion on the diversity issues and objectives of the Biltmore Fire Department. Enclosed is a copy of our notes from that discussion.

We at Managing Diversity would appreciate the opportunity to meet you personally to talk about the diversity initiative. We look forward to being part of the RFP process and possibly working with you on your critically important organizational goals to:

- *Achieve success* at all levels through team building.
- *Train your staff* to understand the legal repercussions of discrimination.
- *Instill team spirit* across all lines of diversity, including age and gender.

Managing Diversity is your first line of defense, and our experienced trainers and coaches are at your service. Enclosed is additional information on the Managing Diversity approach.

I will call you in a week or two so that we can discuss a convenient time to meet. In the meantime, you can reach me at 617-555-1212.

Sincerely,

Marcia Cristi
President

Enclosures

SECTION C: STRUCTURE—BEGINNING, MIDDLE, AND END

All documents, even short ones, have a beginning, a middle, and an end. It might sound trite to discuss this topic; however, many writers think basic structure applies only to longer documents or formal ones.

- The *beginning* of any document should connect your purpose with your reader. With short, informal documents, the beginning sets the tone of the message. Thus, beginnings are important even with the shortest, simplest documents, such as e-mail. Of course, with formal documents, the introduction is critical and must be developed thoroughly to meet the expectations of the particular audience and genre.

- The *middle* contains the body of evidence and examples that support your purpose, validating its relevance. Every time you give the reader excess or irrelevant information, you diminish your purpose. If a bit of information does not support your purpose, cut it.
- The *ending* brings closure for the reader and indicates next steps, defining action for the reader and/or writer. For formal documents, the ending should tie back to the problem initially posed in the introduction. The conclusion may reveal new questions for readers to explore, opening the door for further discussion and research. For informal documents such as e-mail, you may bring closure in much simpler ways by ending with a short closing.

For an academic essay, some writing models recommend a specific number of paragraphs. For example, a five-paragraph essay would include one paragraph for an introduction, three for the body, and one for the conclusion. This model may be a good point of reference for academic writing; however, no writing model provides such an absolute formula for business writing.

In business, all writing must be tailored to its purpose, and purpose varies from piece to piece. As a result, the number of paragraphs will vary from document to document. Whether you are writing a business letter, an e-mail, a memo, a proposal, or a research paper, the purpose will determine the length and format of your document.

Let's review the purpose of each part:

Introduction

- States the purpose and provides an overview.
- Explains why the purpose is relevant.
- Connects the reader to the purpose.
- At times, poses questions.

Body

- Breaks the topic into component parts.
- Covers all main points.
- Supports main points with evidence, examples, and details.
- Answers questions that may be posed in the introduction.

Conclusion

- Summarizes and draws conclusions for readers.
- Clarifies and restates main points.
- Reinforces the introduction, solidly establishing the purpose.
- At times, reveals new questions and suggests additional research.

The introduction is usually the most difficult part of any document. A good beginning captures the essence of the entire document, but you may be unclear about your purpose when you begin to write. Once you have composed your document, your purpose should be clear and meaningful to you. Let's take a moment to examine how this relates to the process of writing.

PROCESS AND STRUCTURE

When you are composing, the easiest way to start writing is to draw on your current understanding. This means that starting with the body, rather than the introduction, can be a good idea. In the body, you are immersed in research, discovering the main points of your topic. As you develop the body of evidence and evaluate data, your thinking evolves.

VOCABULARY: SOUNDALIKES

Precedence/Precedents: Both of these words are derived from the word *precede,* which means "go before." A *precedence* is a priority; a *precedent* is an example that serves as a model for subsequent actions.

We will make your visit a *precedence.*

By allowing these changes, you are establishing *precedents* that may not improve our situation.

These insights will lead to the conclusion. After writing the conclusion, your purpose will be clear to you and you will be able to articulate your key points clearly to your audience.

When you finally have a deep understanding of why your topic is relevant, you may even feel intense about what you have learned. Translate this excitement to your introduction; this critical piece sets the stage for how the reader will perceive everything that follows. If you wrote your introduction first, go back and read it freshly after you have completed the body and conclusion. Does your introduction reflect your vision?

We will now examine how to structure information through a model. Though writing shouldn't follow a recipe, a model can help you organize your ideas as you are composing and revising.

THE PEER MODEL

You are familiar with peer editing, but now *peer* will be used to assist you in structuring information. Rather than relying on introduction, body, and conclusion, the **PEER model** breaks down each part on the basis of purpose. Use this model during the composing or revising stage of writing for documents of any length.

If you loosely apply the PEER model as you compose, your content will be somewhat structured before you revise:

P What is your *purpose?* What points are you making, and why are they relevant?

E What *evidence* demonstrates your main points? What are the facts and details?

E What *explanation* or *evaluation* do you need to make? What *examples* do you need to provide so that the reader understands the evidence and its significance?

R What main points do you need to *recap* for the reader? What conclusions do you need to draw or *recommendations* do you need to make?

By breaking down each part according to purpose, the PEER model can serve as a memory tool. Use it as a self-check to ensure that you have developed all relevant aspects of your documents. Here is how the paragraph on coaching (see Practice, page 276) breaks down:

Purpose	Our company piloted a coaching program for managers. This intense program allowed managers to take an active role in their own development.
Evidence and Explanation	Managers and coaches met weekly for feedback sessions about employee relations. During

▸Language Diversity

Southern American English: Southern American English is a group of dialects spoken across the southern region of the United States, from the Atlantic coast to central Texas and from northern Virginia and central Kentucky to the Gulf Coast.

These dialects include the Virginia Piedmont, Coastal Southern, Baltimorese, Highland Southern, Ozark, Cracker, Gulf Southern, and Mississippi Delta dialects. There are variations in these local languages—Texans speak a slightly different dialect than South Carolinians—but there are more similarities than differences, thus leading to the dialects being grouped together as Southern American English.

The southern dialects also share commonalities with many of the dialects previously discussed, including Appalachian, Gullah, Cajun, and African-American Vernacular English, all of which share historical ties with the American South.

Southern dialects originated with immigrants from the British Isles who moved to the South in the seventeenth and eighteenth centuries from the West Midlands of Britain. As settlers in the United States spread west, so did the influence of southern dialects. As a result, there are places in Kansas, New Mexico, Colorado, Arizona, California, and Alaska (particularly in areas with ties to the oil industry) where language is heavily influenced by Southern American English.

Below is a list of terms as they are pronounced in Southern American dialect. How many can you identify?

1. ever what
2. over yonder
3. hit
4. young'un
5. reckon
6. jawjuh
7. y'all
8. all y'all
9. fixin'
10. knowed

Southern American Dialect:	Reckon he's fixin' to leave.
Business English:	I think he's getting ready to leave.
Southern American Dialect:	I got y'all's assignments here.
Business English:	I've got the assignments for all of you.

meetings, coaches gave managers assessments and inventories so that managers could define their management style. These innovative professionals also advised managers on how to deal with resistance and difficult situations.

Recap This intense pilot program improved employee morale as well as the bottom line.

When you are composing, use these parts as *side headings* as you rough out your ideas. When you are revising, make sure you have developed each aspect of your topic, giving specific evidence and adequate examples.

EXPLORE

Instructions: Read an article in a recent publication and summarize it. Use the PEER model as a template to organize and prioritize your ideas as you read and compose.

SECTION C CONCEPT CHECK

1. What are the basic parts of a business message? What kind of information does each part contain?

2. Identify the elements of the PEER model.

3. Which part of a document is generally the most important? Why?

SECTION D: TRANSITIONS AND CONNECTORS

Transitions help readers make connections and find meaning. Good writing makes those connections for the reader through transitional words, phrases, sentences, and even paragraphs. Transitions connect the reader's thinking with the writer's intention. When good transitions are missing, the reader may need to stop, question the meaning, and reread a section. At times, readers may argue with a narrative because the writer has not drawn a sufficient connection between ideas.

Think of transitions as connectors: they are the elements that bridge ideas between sentences and paragraphs. After a short review of transitional words, we will examine larger transitions, such as transitional phrases, sentences, and paragraphs.

CONJUNCTIONS AS CONNECTORS

As you have already seen, the three types of conjunctions—adverbial, coordinating, and subordinating—function as bridges between ideas. Since you learned about these conjunctions in previous chapters, only a few points are included here. However, you will see how another category of conjunction also bridges ideas: correlating conjunctions compare and contrast information in a unique and effective way.

Adverbial conjunctions provide transitions between sentences and paragraphs. Each signals the meaning of the ideas that follow. Here are some of the roles adverbial conjunctions play, along with examples of the conjunctions:

Contrasting:	however, nevertheless, conversely, on the other hand
Drawing attention:	indeed, accordingly, as usual, in any event
Adding information:	furthermore, in addition, also, what is more, moreover

Drawing a conclusion:	consequently, as a result, therefore, thus, of course, in general
Concluding:	in summary, in conclusion, finally
Illustrating:	for example, for instance
Showing reaction:	fortunately, unfortunately, regrettably
Summarizing:	in short, in summary

Subordinating conjunctions define the relationship between ideas. The subordinating conjunction shows an inequality between ideas, highlighting one idea over another. Here are a few common subordinating conjunctions and their roles:

Contrasting:	even though, although, if, whereas, though
Indicating time:	after, before, while, as soon as, during, as, when, until
Drawing a conclusion:	whereas, since, because, unless, so that, in order that

Coordinating conjunctions also provide transitions between ideas. These conjunctions can help smooth the flow of choppy writing. For example:

And: implies equality of structure; equal weight is assigned to connected ideas.

But: similar to *however;* the word *but* implies a contrast.

Yet: similar to *even though;* the word *yet* implies an exception.

Correlative conjunctions are pairs of conjunctions that add power to the connection because they place more emphasis on the comparing or contrasting aspect of it. Here are the common pairs:

either . . . or

neither . . . nor

both . . . and

not . . . but

not only . . . but also

When conjunctions come in pairs, the structure following the second part of the correlative must be parallel with the structure following the first part. Therefore, you must create parallel structure, or your writing will be *not only* grammatically incorrect *but also* choppy. For example:

Incorrect: Our product *will* not only *bring* great results but also *will be saving* you money.

Incorrect: Our product not only *will bring* great results but also *save* you money.

Correct: Our product *will* not only *bring* you great results but also *save* you money.

Incorrect: The messenger neither *brought* the new product line nor *the samples.*

Correct: The messenger neither *brought* the new product line nor *brought* the samples.

Correct: The messenger brought neither *the new product line* nor *the samples.*

VOCABULARY: KEY TERMS

Virtual Team Terms: Corporations carry out their mission around the world through *virtual teams;* employees across the globe work together without ever meeting face-to-face. Through *webcasting, videoconferencing,* and *text messaging,* team members hold virtual meetings following some of the same guidelines they would follow if they were meeting in person.

For example, in a *videoconference,* everyone receives a copy of the agenda before the meeting. The participants are able to see one another through monitors as they speak on phone lines.

A *webcast* is the most inclusive type of virtual meeting. A webcast consists of a phone conference, online dialogue, and online presentation—*all at the same time.* During a webcast, participants can view a PowerPoint presentation as the group facilitator talks participants through the presentation. Participant names are listed on one side of the screen; team members can communicate with each other privately through instant text messaging by clicking on another participant's name. Webcasting offers many dimensions of communicating, which can even include body language if videoconferencing is also a component.

Increasingly, companies are turning to webcasts to train their employees. Webcasts and videoconferences enhance operations significantly and thus save companies millions of dollars a year.

PRACTICE

A. Instructions: Correct the following sentences for parallel structure.

1. The report was neither too short nor was it too long.
2. Jessica's promotion was both unexpected and she well deserved it.
3. The merger was not only difficult for the upper management but the lower-level employees also found it difficult.
4. Both Ms. Marcell and Tom Jimenez received promotions after the merger.
5. Your supervisor not only wants punctuality but efficiency.
6. Justin will either take the job in Australia or he might keep his job in Canada.
7. As a supervisor, you must be neither petty nor be intimidating.

B. Instructions: Write three sentences demonstrating correct use of correlative conjunctions. Share them with a partner, and see if you can find any errors. Together rewrite a few sentences by moving elements around while still keeping the sentences parallel.

1. ______________________________

2. ______________________________

3. ______________________________

VOCABULARY: NEW WORDS

New to the *Merriam-Webster's Collegiate Dictionary* in 2006:[3]

identity theft, noun: The illegal use of someone else's personal information (such as a Social Security number) in order to obtain money or credit.

keypal, noun: E-mail pen pal.

NIMBY, noun: "*n*ot *i*n *m*y *b*ackyard"; opposition to having something considered undesirable (an incinerator, a prison) located in one's neighborhood.

TRANSITIONS TO ADD FLOW

You may already use transitional elements effectively but not be aware of it. The objective now is for you to use transitions consciously and purposefully. Without transitions, writing is choppy because no connections are drawn for the reader. Here is an example of writing that is choppy because it does not have transitions:

WEAK The invitation to the meeting arrived on Friday. I forgot to tell my team until this afternoon. They responded before they left for the day. Most will be able to attend. Two people cannot attend because of previous commitments.

Can you easily follow the flow of writing from the piece above? Even without being aware of transitions, a novice writer puts them in. Once you become aware of the function of connectors, you can consciously control how you use them. With transitions, you can combine sentences to achieve rich ideas and maintain an effective flow. Here is the paragraph above with transitions added:

REVISED The invitation to the meeting arrived on Friday, but I forgot to tell my team until this afternoon. They responded before they left for the day, and

> fortunately most will be able to attend. However, two people cannot attend because of previous commitments.

Here's another possible revision:

> Although the invitation to the meeting arrived on Friday, I forgot to tell my team until this afternoon. Fortunately, they responded before they left for the day. Most will be able to attend, but two people cannot attend because of previous commitments.

PRACTICE

A. Instructions: In the following sentences, use connectors to bridge ideas. Develop two or three different versions for each set. **For example:**

Weak: Nancy will recruit new interns. You will train the new interns after that.

Revised: You will train the new interns after Nancy recruits them.

Or: After Nancy recruits the new interns, you will train them.

1. Our team made a great effort to win the competition. We didn't win.

2. Selena will retire next week. Her husband won't retire until next month.

3. John wrote a report. We will need the report for our meeting on Tuesday.

4. The meeting ended. Everyone knew not to mention that the meeting had ended early.

5. Sheila was hired yesterday. You need extra help during the busy summer months.

B. Instructions: Revise (or rewrite) the following paragraph by adding transitions and adjusting the information flow; you may change words as well as add or delete information.

> A new client requested information about our fall line of clothing. We have not finished the brochure that illustrates the styles and colors. It is still early in the development process. We will lose this client if we have nothing to show within the next few weeks. We can solve this problem by putting a few samples on our Web site or in a short flyer. We can indicate when the full line will be ready for display. This project adds a layer of work we did not expect. It is worth the effort.

• WRITER'S TOOLKIT

Consolidating Colors, Consolidating Ideas

One way to rearrange a room so that it looks less cluttered is to group similar-color items together. By consolidating similar colors, a room may appear more cohesive.

The same is true with writing. Readers are confused if writing pulls them in too many directions without bringing them to a point or conclusion. By consolidating similar ideas into paragraphs, the reader gains a deeper understanding more easily. The ideas pull together to demonstrate a point.

Thus, a cohesive paragraph develops the main point its topic sentence presents, leaving diverse ideas as the topics for new paragraphs. *Can you find a paragraph that you've written recently that jumps from idea to idea, lacking a cohesive structure?*

PHRASES AS TRANSITIONS AND CONNECTORS

In Chapter 2, you learned that a phrase is a group of words without a subject and verb (whereas a clause has both a subject and a verb). Phrases can function as transitions for clauses. When a prepositional or verbal phrase (gerund, infinitive, participial) introduces a main clause, the phrase places the clause that follows it in context.

Prepositional Phrases

A preposition is a connective that shows a relationship between ideas. Here are some common prepositions: *to, from, by, with, between, before, after,* and *during*. The following are examples of **prepositional phrases** used as introductory connectors:

> *Between the two representatives,* Mitchell had more work.
>
> *Before that incident,* we were their best clients.
>
> *During the transition,* our department will remain at the LaSalle branch office.

Of course, when a prepositional phrase is used as an introductory phrase, a complete sentence must follow.

Gerund Phrases

Gerund phrases often function as introductory connectors. (A gerund is the *ing* form of a verb that is used as a noun.) Here are examples of gerund phrases that are used as introductory phrases:

> *Removing the folder,* Dr. Malkovich looked serious.
>
> *Speaking only to tellers,* the HR representative explained the change in benefits.
>
> *Communicating effortlessly,* Sarah won the board's approval within a half hour.

When a gerund phrase begins a sentence, be careful to construct the sentence correctly. As you will recall, the subject of the phrase must immediately follow it, making it also the subject of the sentence.

PRACTICE

Instructions: The sentences below have introductory gerund phrases. To correct the errors, you will need to rewrite part of each sentence. Your goal is either to turn the phrase into a clause (with a subject and verb) or to make the subject of the phrase the subject of the independent clause.

> **Incorrect:** Walking into the conference late, the presentation was interrupted by Jason.
>
> **Corrected:** Walking into the conference late, *Jason* interrupted the presentation.

1. Emptying out the supply cabinet, the staples were found by Alice in the back.

2. Listening intently to the speaker, the presentation was enjoyed by everyone in the boardroom.

3. Gathering up her papers, the courtroom was left in a hurry by the attorney.

4. Discussing the possible transaction, the phone call between my client and myself lasted over an hour.

5. Wishing he had spent more time preparing, the presentation given by Jack disappointed the clients.

Infinitive Phrases

Infinitive phrases can also be used to introduce clauses. (An infinitive is the base form of the verb plus the word *to*.) For example:

> *To fit the Web meeting into his schedule,* Jerome needed to cancel our appointment.
>
> *To impress an interviewer,* an applicant must arrive prepared.
>
> *To revise its mission,* a corporation would be wise to involve participation at all levels.

As with gerund phrases, when an infinitive phrase begins a sentence, place the subject of the phrase immediately after the phrase.

PRACTICE

Instructions: Find the errors in the sentences below and correct them. You may need to select a subject that is not in the sentence, such as *you* or *we*. To determine the subject, identify who is the subject of the infinitive phrase; you may need to reword the entire sentence. **For example:**

Incorrect:	To be among the first exhibitors, a vendor's booth must be registered early.
Corrected:	To be among the first exhibitors, *you* must register your booth early.

1. To succeed in this position, a good attitude is needed.
2. To best serve our clients, a new help line should be implemented.
3. To function as an effective supervisor, it is necessary to be understanding yet firm.
4. To finish these orders on time, more temporary employees must be hired.
5. To find the perfect computer system, much comparison shopping will have to be done.

TRANSITIONAL SENTENCES AND PARAGRAPHS

Transitional sentences and paragraphs relate to information flow; they connect old information to new information on a broad level. **Transitional sentences** provide logical connections between paragraphs. The transitional sentence glances forward and links the topic of one paragraph with the main idea of the next. Transitional sentences prepare the reader to understand the content of the next paragraph by "seeding" the purpose of the new paragraph. By the time the reader reaches the new paragraph, key ideas are already familiar.

WRITER'S TOOLKIT

Ernest Hemingway's Quest

Ernest Hemingway had an unusual quest: he was obsessed with writing what he considered "one good sentence." Although the world of literature is graced by many of his eloquent pieces, he was never completely satisfied by the work he produced. In his quest to write one good sentence, he refined his writing and brought it to standards rarely reached.

Hemingway reminds us that writing is a skill that a person never completely masters.

Here are examples of transitional sentences:

> In the next section, a detailed analysis will demonstrate the strengths and weaknesses of the model employed in our study.
>
> Next we will show how communication relates to corporate success.
>
> Although production waste relates to the economy, it also relates to the environment.

In addition to transitional sentences, transitional paragraphs play an important role for readers. **Transitional paragraphs** need to achieve two purposes:

1. Summarize the key ideas of the current section.
2. Indicate how the major theme of the document will be developed in the next section.

Here is a transitional paragraph:

> The next chapter discusses several of Deming's famous 14 points, known as the Deming Management Method, as they relate to workforce diversity and managing change. The following sections discuss barriers that can limit an institution's performance: poorly implemented management systems, disrespectful and fearful work environments, interdepartmental antagonism, and weak leadership.

Internet Exercise 9.2

Document Library: For your convenience, you can view the three business document formats presented in the unit openers of this text—and many others that do not appear in the text—by using the link below. Log on to the Web site at **www.mhhe.com/youngBE.** Once you have accessed the home page, select "Student Activities" and then the "Chapter 9" link to get started.

EXPLORE

Find transitional sentences and paragraphs in papers that you have written (for this class or other classes), textbooks, and newspapers. Then answer these questions:

1. Do some transitions seem awkward to you? Identify why that might be so.
2. Are there cases where an abrupt transition is acceptable, even necessary?
3. How do the transitions in your papers compare with the textbook transitions?

SECTION D CONCEPT CHECK

1. What are some transitional roles that adverbial conjunctions play? List four or five different kinds of transitions that adverbial conjunctions can provide.

2. How do subordinating conjunctions help define relationships between ideas?

3. Correlative conjunctions are pairs of conjunctions that add power to your writing because they place emphasis on the comparing or contrasting aspect of a relationship. What are some common pairs of correlative conjunctions? In terms of structure, what is important to look out for when you use correlative conjunctions?

CHAPTER 9 SUMMARY

In this chapter, you learned about editing and revising paragraphs. Two words that describe effective paragraphs are *cohesive* and *coherent.*

- Cohesive paragraphs present one main idea or topic. All sentences in the paragraph connect to the main idea, having a common purpose: each sentence contains a thread of the common idea. The common idea is introduced in the topic sentence and developed through a topic string.
- Coherent paragraphs develop the main idea in a logical way through a logical flow of ideas. The writer develops the topic in a consistent way by controlling information flow from the familiar to the unfamiliar. Readers can make sense of the content because one idea leads to another.

To adjust a paragraph for information flow, move your most effective sentence to the topic-sentence position at the beginning of the paragraph. Eliminate all empty or redundant information. Then make sure that each sentence starts with the familiar and extends the reader's knowledge to the unfamiliar.

As a composing or editing tool, you can use the PEER model to help you structure your information:

P What is your *purpose?* What points are you making, and why are they relevant?

E What *evidence* demonstrates your main points? What are the facts and details?

E What *explanation* or *evaluation* do you need to make, or what *examples* do you need to provide so that the reader understands the evidence and its significance?

R What main points do you need to *recap* for the reader? What conclusions do you need to draw or what recommendations do you need to make?

In the next, and last, chapter of this book, you will work on a longer project that allows you to apply the principles you learned in this and previous chapters.

CHAPTER 9 CHECKLIST

Have you screened your paragraphs for the following?

___ Cohesive (staying on one topic).

___ Coherent (controlling for information flow).

___ Topic sentence.

___ Topic string.

___ Information flow: old to new.

___ Empty information.

___ Structure: beginning, middle, and end.

___ Transitions and connectors.

CHAPTER 9 END-OF-CHAPTER ACTIVITIES

ACTIVITY 1: PROCESS MEMO

INSTRUCTIONS: Select a paragraph you have written for this or another class. Edit and revise your paragraph, and then write a process memo describing what you did to produce a more effective product: what principles of editing or revising did you apply?

If you have Internet access, you can complete this exercise online at **www.mhhe.com/youngBE** and then send an e-mail to your instructor.

ACTIVITY 2: EDITING SENTENCES

BACKGROUND: When you revise paragraphs, you must do more than adjust for information flow to ensure cohesive, coherent paragraphs. To make your writing clear and powerful, you must also edit paragraphs at the sentence level so that the writing is simple, clear, and concise.

INSTRUCTIONS: Revise the following sentences by removing nominals and putting them in the active voice.

1. Management of the account is the responsibility of the account holder.

2. Our department's implementation of the new dress policy occurred last August.

3. A suggestion was made by our auditing department that December meetings be rescheduled.

4. The expectation of our president is that there will be an acquisition of the Houston corporation by early fall.

5. Will there be a discussion of the new account process at our next team meeting?

ACTIVITY 3: EDITING AND REVISING

INSTRUCTIONS: Revise the following paragraphs so that they are cohesive and coherent. Edit the sentences for active and passive voice, parallel structure, and information flow (old to new). Also cut empty information, such as hedges and emphatics, as well as outdated expressions.

1. Meeting Summary

Our department had a really good meeting this morning about a really interesting topic, which just happens to be management training. Management training was one of the significant factors identified in a survey. A survey was conducted by an organizational development specialist to gain an accurate view of management practices. As per your recommendation, a follow-up call will be made by myself to the human resources director for more information about the survey. The development of management skills in new hires was identified as a key element of management practices that work.

2. Meeting Summary

Investment portfolios were discussed by Gerry at the meeting. A person with experience in accounting and who also has done telemarketing is someone who Percy is seeking to hire. The implementation of new hours will occur at our branch offices next week. An expectation of our president is that training in finance is received by all managers by June. The meeting was held on Tuesday, April 15th by the Project management team. Notes were taken by myself and additional details are available upon request.

ACTIVITY 4: SPEAKING BUSINESS

INSTRUCTIONS: In the following list of words, make note of your normal pronunciation before reviewing the recommended pronunciation. How does your pronunciation differ from the recommended?

espresso	Say *ess-PRESS-oh,* not *ex-PRESS-oh.*
et cetera	Say *ett-SET-ter-uh,* not *ex-SET-er-uh.*
Celtic	Say *KELL-tick* for people and their language.
	Say *SELL-tick* for a Boston basketball player.
herb	Say *ERB* (the *h* is silent).
international	Say *in-ter-NASH-nul* not *in-ner-NASH-nul* or *in-ter-na-SHUN-al.*
library	Say *LIE-brer-ree* not *LIE-ber-ree.*
specific	Say *spa-CI-fic* not *pa-CI-fic.*

Are there any other words that have a challenging pronunciation? Make a list and practice your words with a partner. (If you want to see more examples, refer to Appendix B of *The Gregg Reference Manual.*)

ACTIVITY 5: TOPIC SENTENCES AND TOPIC STRINGS

INSTRUCTIONS: The paragraph below provides information about the Chicago Board of Trade.[4] From this information, write a topic sentence and develop a topic string. (You do not need to include all the information below in your paragraph.) Apply all the editing principles you have learned so far to write a cohesive, coherent paragraph.

> The Chicago Board of Trade (CBOT) is a leading futures exchange in the United States. Corn, oats, soybeans, and soybean oil are some of the commodities traded at the CBOT. Along with gold and other precious metals. A futures exchange is where investors can protect against price changes in commodities and investments and even profit from those changes. The exchange practised only traders meeting face-to-face in trading pits to buy and sell futures contracts. Then its first electronic trading system was launched in 1994 by the CBOT, formally bringing the exchange into the "modern world." The CBOT was established in 1848 primarily so that farmers and other investors could protect themselves from price fluctuations. One of the techniques farmers can use to this day through the CBOT is hedging. Hedging allows a farmer to lock in a profit for a commodity such as corn that the farmer actually grows on their farm.. When the farmer's corn is ready for market, even if the price of corn has gone down by then, the farmer can make the same profit that was locked in at the time that the futures investment called hedging was made. By hedging their cash crop, a farmer can protect their livelihood and property when dramatic fluctuations in the market occur.

____

____

____

____

____

____

____

____

____

ACTIVITY 6: ELIMINATING EMPTY INFORMATION

INSTRUCTIONS: In the paragraph below, cut empty and irrelevant background information and make any other changes or corrections that are needed. These changes will assist the reader in getting right to the point. (Assume you are writing a short thank-you note to someone you interviewed about financial institutions.)

Hey, Mr. Roberts—

As per your recommendation, I went to the web to research the Chicago Board of Trade (which u mentioned was called the CBOT). Subsequent to our discussion, I have learned a lot more about such financial exchanges even existed. I am very excited to learn that there is another place in Chicago where people trade commodities, but they different ones. That's the CME which is really called the Chicago Mercantile exchange and someday I can visit both the Merc and the Cbot. If u want to know more about these financial places uc go to their individual web sites which you can find on the web at www.cme.com for the mercantile exchange but then you have to go to another web site to learn about the board of trade and that web site is www.cbot.com. Pretty cool, huh? Anyway, thnx for telling me about ur part-time job in the trading pits as a runner when u were in college. Lol, BJ

ACTIVITY 7: OLD TO NEW INFORMATION FLOW

INSTRUCTIONS: Revise the following paragraph by changing the information flow and adding transitions that relate to "old" information.

All employees must have a new ID by Monday, September 4, or they will not be allowed access to the building. You will have to visit the security office in Room 327 to obtain your new id. Considering the fact that most companies have tightened security measures since the events of 9/11, we feel it is important for all employees to have photo IDs. Our current system of employee identification consists of visual recognition by our receptionist.

ACTIVITY 8: EDITING REVIEW—PRINCIPLES FOR DECISIONS

BACKGROUND: Wordiness often relates to the following:

Redundancy:	Repeating information unnecessarily.
Empty information:	Irrelevant information; background thinking.
Hedges:	Words that cushion your message, such as *usually.*
Modifiers:	Modifiers that emphasize to the extreme, such as *totally.*

When making decisions about *words,* simplify your document by doing the following:

- Changing complicated words to simpler words.
- Cutting empty and redundant words.

When making decisions about *sentences,* make your document more powerful by doing the following:

- Changing passive voice to active voice.
- Correcting for parallel structure.
- Aligning modifiers correctly.
- Placing the subject and verb close to each other and the beginning of the sentence.
- Limiting sentence length to no more than 22 words.
- Connecting information through transitions: connective words, phrases, and sentences.
- Controlling information flow by building from old or familiar information that leads to new information.

INSTRUCTIONS: With the above in mind, edit the following paragraphs.

1. Qualities of an Effective Paragraph

A paragraph consists of a group of sentences that really only discuss one main topic. The presentation of the main topic is made in the topic sentence. The development of the topic occurs through a topic string. A paragraph is cohesive when it totally stays on the same topic. Old to new information flow is the deciding factor in making a paragraph more coherent. A specific number of sentences for a paragraph is not a requirement. There is no exact recipe in how a person should write a paragraph. Paragraphs are dependent on the content the writer is attempting to convey. A writer shouldn't jump from idea to idea when writing a paragraph. All of the sentences should absolutely support the topic sentence.

2. Qualities of a Good Sentence (You may include a list in your paragraph, if you choose.)

A sentence is a group of words that have a subject and a verb. It expresses a complete thought. The length of a sentence should be between 10 to 22 words. Only one main topic should be presented in a well written sentence. The active voice is often more effective than the passive voice. Avoid nominals by turning them into active verbs. You should try to keep the subject and verb close to each other. Maybe you should even try to keep the subject and verb close to the beginning of the sentence. The reader can become really confused if the subject and verb are way too far apart. Also remember to make an adjustment of the sentence for information flow. New information should occur subsequent to old information. That is some of the information about how to write an effective sentences, even though they will vary. And the bottom line is that sentences should be clear in meaning and correct.

ACTIVITY 9: COMPOSING, EDITING, AND REVISING PARAGRAPHS

INSTRUCTIONS: Follow the steps outlined below:

1. Compose a paragraph about your perfect job.
2. Exchange your paragraph with a partner.
3. Edit your partner's paragraph, and explain why you made your selected changes.
4. What kinds of changes did your partner make with your paragraph?

ACTIVITY 10: "WRITER'S REFERENCE MANUAL" DRILL

BACKGROUND: In the "Writer's Reference Manual," read about forms of address. The word *address* takes on two meanings in this drill. First, the word *address* refers to how you will represent the mailing address. Second, the word *address* refers to the way you personally address someone, as in *Dr., Ms., Professor,* or *Honorable.*

In most cases, the mailing address is the same on the envelope as it is on the inside address of the letter you are enclosing. However, the title you use to address the person in the salutation could differ from the way the name is presented in the mailing address.

INSTRUCTIONS: Fill in the correct forms of address and salutation for each addressee below.

Addressee	Written Address	Salutation
Phyllis Margolis Attorney		
Roberto Gonzales Commissioner		
Liann Chinn Dean		
Ann Walker Governor, Texas		
Klaus Shubert Judge, Pennsylvania		
Rich and Cathy Dugan Married couple		
Stephen Goldberg Mayor, Los Angeles		
Feranda Williamson Ph.D.		
Hamoudi Kalal Physician		
Dorcas Roberts Professor		
Gladys Jossell Representative, U.S.		
Monica J. Williams Senator, Rhode Island		
Reginald Grey Veterinarian		

ACTIVITY 11: VOCABULARY LIST

A. COMMONLY MISSPELLED WORDS

INSTRUCTIONS: Practice the words below until you can spell them automatically and use them correctly.

1. arbitrate (v) to submit or refer for decision
2. assessment (n) the amount of a tax or fine; appraisal, evaluation
3. chronological (adj) sequential, in order
4. conscientious (adj) careful, thorough, meticulous, diligent
5. enhance (v) to increase, add to quality
6. exonerate (v) to relieve of responsibility, to clear from blame

7. functional (adj) efficient, serviceable, practical
8. incongruous (adj) not harmonious, not conforming
9. professional (n) expert, specialist; (adj) proficient, skilled
10. reciprocate (v) to give back, counter, reply, respond
11. reference (n) the act of referring, an allusion or mention
12. reprisal (n) something given or paid in restitution
13. reprimand (n) a severe or formal reproof
14. sporadically (adv) occurring singly here and there
15. transferable (adj) transportable

B. SIMILAR WORDS

INSTRUCTIONS: Use the words below in sentences until their meaning becomes clear.

may be/maybe: *May be* is a verb phrase suggesting possibility; *maybe* is an adverb meaning "perhaps":

He *may be* the next mayor. *Maybe* it will rain tomorrow.

precedence/precedents: *Precedence* means "priority"; *precedents* means "established rules."

They set new *precedents* by completing the project early.

We will put all work aside and make this a *precedence.*

sometime/some time: *Sometime* (one word) refers to *an unspecified time. Some time* (two words) refers to *a period of time.*

He said he would call me *sometime* next week.

We plan to spend *some time* on this account before we contact our client.

THE INBOX

COMPOSING

THE PERSONAL MISSION STATEMENT: Most companies have mission statements that talk about core values and purpose. Likewise, the personal mission statement has become quite a popular and useful trend today. Many ways to write your mission statement exist, but all methods have the same underlying concept: the personal mission statement is based on self-reflection.

Use the guide below to draft a personal mission statement. Share it with someone close to you for feedback. A personal mission statement will change over time; it is a fluid document. The guide below is not the final structure of your personal mission statement; rather, it is a writing prompt to help you prewrite for ideas.

Personal Mission Statement Guide

The achievement in my life that I am most proud of is ___________. Each day I will try to be ___________. I will uphold my personal core values, which are ___________. The most important of these values is ___________. I will strive to live this most important value ___________ by ___________. Each day I will add my contributions to others: my family by ___________; my friends by ___________; my community by ___________; my career or future career by ___________. In the future, I hope my successes will include ___________. To achieve these goals, I plan ___________. The most important thing in the world to me is ___________.

REFLECTING

Consider this statement by the famous fourth-century Chinese philosopher Lao Tse: "Your actions are your only possessions."

List five positive traits you have, five positive actions you can take to enhance those traits, and five positive plans to put those actions into being. Below is an example of one trait. Create your own chart as a positive reinforcement of your mission statement.

Positive Trait	Positive Action	Positive Plan
I am an outgoing person.	I can help students who feel uncomfortable to relax and make friends.	I will talk to three students I don't already know and introduce them to my friends.

DISCUSSING

1. Does your college or university have a mission statement? You will probably find it on the school Web site or in the catalog. Read it together in a small group, and discuss its meaning. Does the mission statement apply to you personally? Who do you think wrote the mission statement? Is the mission statement universal, or is it particular to a specific group of people?
2. In your group, revise the college or university mission statement to reflect your discussion. Is your revision more inclusive than the original? What do you notice when you compare the two?

CAREER-BUILDING PORTFOLIO

PORTFOLIO DOCUMENT 5

After several drafts and revisions of your personal mission statement, use a word processing program to create a graphically pleasing document. You could, for example, center the mission statement on the page and place a border around the page. When you are satisfied with the document, place a clean copy in your portfolio.

PORTFOLIO DOCUMENT 6

1. Visit **http://www.hoovers.com** to research specific companies in your field of interest. Find two or three companies that you would consider working for, and read as much as you can about them. Create a "wish list" of companies that seem promising to you. Record the contact information, and take notes about specific information that interested you. Create a list of questions that you would like to ask a company representative if you were given the chance.
2. Apply the PEER method to a brief oral report on one of the companies you researched. Explain why the company appeals to you. First write the report in paragraph form, and then use note cards for your oral report. You'll need to turn in the written report, with sources cited, to your instructor.

Consider the following in your report:

*P*urpose	What purpose does the company serve? What is its mission? Who benefits from this company? Why are you interested in the company? How do you see yourself contributing to this company?
*E*vidence	Provide some facts about the company, and possibly compare it with some competitors.
*E*valuation	Why did you choose this company over the others? How does this company's vision, goals, or other attributes fit in with your personal mission statement?
*R*ecap	Recap the main points for your audience, and state your conclusion explicitly.

KEY TO LEARNING INVENTORY

1. F
2. F
3. F
4. T
5. b and d
6. T
7. b
8. T
9. F
10. T

CHAPTER 9 ENDNOTES

1. Presentation at ABC conference, Cleveland, Fall 2002.
2. Joseph M. Williams, *Style: Toward Clarity and Grace,* University of Chicago Press, Chicago, 1990.
3. **http://www.merriam-webstercollegiate.com/info/new_words.htm**, accessed on October 3, 2006.
4. **http://www.cbot.com/cbot/pub/cont_detail/0,3206,1027+15564,00.html**, accessed on August 17, 2006.

Chapter Ten

Professional Communication

Anyone who has never made a mistake has never tried anything new. —Albert Einstein

This chapter takes a different approach than did previous ones. So far you've developed writing skill by applying principles of grammar and style to sentences and paragraphs. Now you will review office-style communications in depth.

Though you have already learned about e-mail, memos, and letters, this chapter pulls together loose ends so that you can apply what you have learned in real-world settings. For example, the first part of this chapter presents professional guidelines for using e-mail. Then, later in the chapter, you will examine how to convey various types of communications, such as direct and indirect messages, apologies, complaints, and even thank-you notes.

This chapter reviews formatting but adds an exciting twist: visual persuasion. You can use visual persuasion to make your documents more readable and more attractive. By making key ideas instantly visible for your readers, you are enhancing your message and possibly your business relationships.

The last section of this chapter delves into soft skills so that you know what to expect when you are on the job. You review cell phone use, voice-mail use, and dress in professional settings. You may learn that some things that you take for granted in informal situations can be offensive in an office. As a newcomer to the business world, you may welcome this information, as it can help you avoid culture shock when you get your first job. Now get ready to put the finishing touches on your Business English skills—and good luck on the rest of your journey.

To learn more about The Writing Process, please visit our Web site at **www.mhhe.com/youngBE**

Outline

Chapter 10: Professional Communication

Section A: E-Mail Guidelines

Section B: Basic Letters and Messages

Section C: Formatting—Special Features and White Space

Section D: Diversity and Office Etiquette

Objectives

When you have completed your study of Chapter 10, you will be able to:

1. Apply good office protocol to e-mail correspondence.
2. Use formatting to make key ideas instantly visible.
3. Structure various types of office communications, such as direct and indirect messages.
4. Use voice mail and cell phones effectively in an office environment.
5. Determine appropriate dress for an office setting.

Learning Inventory

1. An attachment to an e-mail is self-explanatory, needing no explanation in the e-mail. T/F
2. When communication is urgent, e-mail is your best choice. T/F
3. When you leave a voice mail, you should state your return number at least two times. T/F
4. Readers appreciate it when writers use formatting to make key ideas stand out. T/F
5. One of the most important features to control in formatting is white space. T/F
6. With e-mail, you state your most important information at the beginning of the message. T/F
7. If company policy allows, you can feel free to send friends and family e-mail from work. T/F
8. You should not change the subject line of an e-mail unless you originated the message. T/F
9. In an e-mail, you use all uppercase for information that you want to emphasize. T/F
10. Visual persuasion consists of tools and techniques for presenting your message effectively. T/F

Goal-Setting Exercises

Think for a moment about your personal and career goals and the new skills that you have learned over the past several months. You have worked hard with your writing and speaking skills. In this chapter, set broader goals. How would you like to use your new skills? What career opportunities do you hope to find when you finish school? What would you like to be doing a few years from now? Write three goals for your future.

1. ______________________________

2. ______________________________

3. ______________________________

SECTION A: E-MAIL GUIDELINES

The most common and demanding writing task today relates to electronic messaging, or e-mail. When used effectively, e-mail enhances a busy professional's ability to communicate and solve problems. Information can be exchanged at a moment's notice. However, just as e-mail can enhance getting a job done, e-mail also adds new challenges. When composing e-mail, writers must make effective decisions quickly. Decisions must also be objective: a business relationship can end with the push of a button.

THE WHEN AND WHY OF E-MAIL

When you are on the job, you will rarely stop to ask yourself if sending an e-mail is the best method to use. In most situations, the answer will be apparent. You will develop a *flow* with communication, and e-mail will be a natural part of that flow.

Here are some reasons to use e-mail:

1. To send details in writing, making information easy for the recipient to access.
2. To send a message to multiple people at the same time.
3. To communicate at odd times of the day when a phone message or meeting is not feasible.
4. To save time; with e-mail there is much less small talk.
5. To convey information when you do not need an immediate response.
6. To give short bits of information.

Do not rely on e-mail if your information has a critical time element. The recipient may not even read your message before the deadline. Also, don't assume that once you send information, the other person is now responsible to take action. When you need a fast response, call to say that you are sending an urgent message that needs an immediate response.

If you find yourself avoiding face-to-face communication with someone, your avoidance may indicate that a problem exists. At those times, an e-mail may not be your best option. The purpose of communication is to build relationships; don't hide behind e-mail. Phone the person, or stop by for a brief visit, if possible.

When sending an e-mail, here are some questions to consider:

- What time frame is involved? How soon do I need a response?
- Would a phone call be more or less effective?
- Do I need to meet with a colleague personally to discuss issues informally?
- Should I schedule a meeting to examine the issues and brainstorm options?
- Would a more formal communication, such as a letter, address the situation more effectively?

THE DOWNSIDE OF E-MAIL

E-mail consumes a major portion of the average professional's time on the job, with about two or more hours each day being wasted. First, many business professionals are not confident in their writing skills and struggle to write effective messages. Second, when unclear and disorganized messages arrive, recipients take time and energy to detangle information before being able to respond.

Businesses started using e-mail in the early '90s, and many business professionals found the transition difficult. Even today, most office workers have not had formal training

FIGURE 10.1 E-Mail

Addressing e-mail: *In an e-mail address, the information before the @ symbol identifies the name of the user of that address; the information after the @ symbol and before the period (referred to as a dot) is the site name; and the information after the dot identifies the domain. (.com, for example, identifies a Web site as commercial).* How many different domains can you name, and what types of sites are found in them?

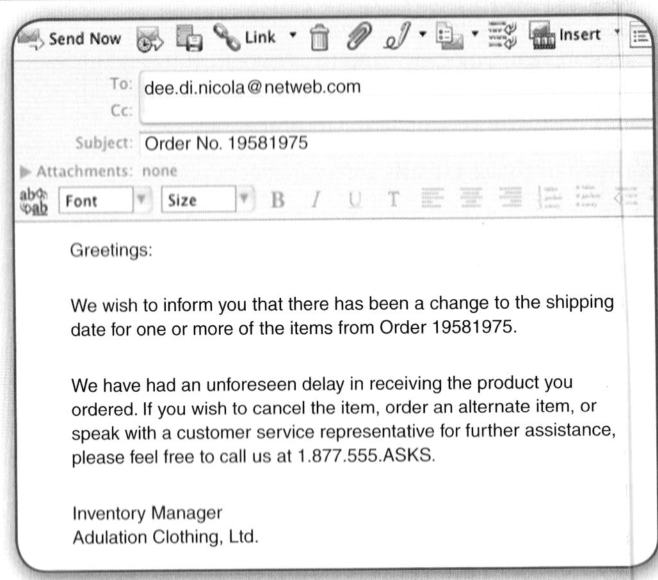

in using e-mail; they learned the hard way, making mistakes as they honed their skills. Used ineffectively, e-mail can create frustrations:

- Long, unedited messages are difficult to understand.
- Controversial messages provoke emotions.
- Messages unrelated to work waste time.
- In some cases, e-mail is used when another type of communication would be more effective.
- Attachments sent unnecessarily or without explanation waste time and cause confusion.
- Untitled or inaccurately titled messages can be confusing and misleading at times.
- Inappropriate use of special features (such as "Read Now" and "Urgent") causes distraction.

Part of the skill in using e-mail is being able to make decisions that keep communication flowing without wasting time and energy. When a phone call would be more efficient, do not spend your time drafting an e-mail. Also, if a communication problem exists, take the time to walk over to a colleague's desk or office for an informal, impromptu chat. Do not let yourself fall into an avoidance trap. When personal contact is the only way to dissolve misunderstanding, don't rely on e-mail.

Some aspects of e-mail are not within your control. Namely, you cannot control the content or tone of someone else's message. Messages that do not meet your expectations may provoke your emotions and waste your energy: some messages sound too direct, while others ramble on without getting to the point. And there may even be the occasional message that sounds accusatory. Stay in control by focusing on the messages that you send and remaining objective about what others write.

Companies monitor employees' use of e-mail without their knowledge. Businesses have the legal right to monitor their workers in this way; they own the equipment and are paying for their employees' time. As a result, every year companies terminate employees for using e-mail and the Internet inappropriately on the job.

E-MAIL GUIDELINES

In general, keep your e-mail messages to the length of one screen. If your message is much longer than one screen, consider using another method of communicating (such as a phone call). Though e-mail standards are still evolving, here are some basic guidelines:

1. Respond to e-mail within a day or two. (Use an out-of-office response when you are unavailable for more than one day.)
2. Use a salutation and a closing, even if the salutation consists of only the recipient's name and the closing consists of only your name.
3. Start the message with the most important information; clearly state the information you need from the reader at the *beginning* of the message.
4. Number items so that they stand out.
5. Use conventional rules for punctuation and capitalization: do *not* write in all uppercase or all lowercase. (All uppercase connotes "shouting" or "screaming"; all lowercase implies that you do not know how to make capitalization decisions.)
6. Avoid jargon, slang, and abbreviations.
7. Use an accurate and updated subject line so that your recipient can refer to your message and file it easily.
8. Avoid using "Read Now" and "Urgent" unless absolutely necessary.
9. Do not send the following types of information via e-mail: extremely sensitive information, confidential information, or bad news.
10. Keep an open mind about messages you receive; if you infer there is a problem, you may actually create one.
11. Stay current about your company policy for e-mail use; even if personal messages are allowed, send them sparingly.
12. Do not send a message about which you have doubts (save it as a draft until you are sure). *When in doubt, leave it out.*

When *forwarding* or *replying to* messages, do the following:

1. Update the e-mail for the recipient by changing the subject line to reflect the new content.
2. If the recipient does not need to know the history, delete the previous message.
3. With forwarded messages, add a note at the beginning to explain how the e-mail relates to the reader and what action he or she should take.
4. Do not press "Reply All" unless everyone needs the information. Most often with messages that are sent to multiple people, only the sender needs the response. Unnecessary replies to *all* create confusion and clutter.
5. Do not respond to controversial or emotional messages until you are clearheaded and objective.
6. Do not forward messages that you consider inappropriate. (Every year, many people lose their jobs as a result of forwarding inappropriate messages.)

Communication Challenges

An Objective Response: Everyone confronts controversial issues. When conflict arises, so do strong feelings. However, in a professional environment, expressing strong feelings in writing is rarely appropriate.

If you are responding to a message that has an emotional charge, your words will convey your feelings as well as your ideas. Even though you successfully address an issue on the intellectual side, you can create problems if you do not present your ideas objectively. In other words, you can win the argument but lose the relationship with your client or the person reading your message.

When someone writes you with emotion, look beyond the obvious. If you respond with anger, expect that the anger will be expressed back to you or that your message will be passed on to someone with higher responsibility. When you cannot present your ideas objectively, wait until you have a clear head before you respond: when in doubt, leave it out!

Consider the following:

- *Avoid being defensive.* Everyone makes mistakes, usually on a daily basis. The best way to correct a mistake is to correct the situation. Some situations will call for an apology. You do not become less of a person for admitting a mistake; some would argue your character becomes stronger.
- *Do not go on the offensive.* There will be times when you receive a message that strikes you the wrong way. When this happens, the best approach is to clarify the message. Though your first inclination may be to "fight back," stay calm and remain objective. *Do not put anything in writing until you are clearheaded and objective.*

CAT Strategy: Connect, Act, Tell

The **CAT strategy** will help you shape your message effectively, taking the above points into consideration. Here's how it works:

- *Connect:* Personalize the beginning so that the message reflects that you are a human being writing to another human being.
- *Act:* For longer messages, list the requested action at the beginning of the message. Readers sometimes glance at a message and then save it to read when they have more time. For time-sensitive messages, list the due date in the subject line of the message. (Or, better yet, make a phone call.)
- *Tell:* Use the remainder of the message to provide information.

Requested action should go toward the beginning of the message because sometimes readers don't read entire messages, especially long ones. Your average message should be about one screen or less in length; if it's too much longer, the information may be too complicated and a phone call might be the best mode of communication. Ask only one or two questions in an e-mail; if you need to address multiple topics, number them or consider presenting each main topic in a separate message. Messages that get to the point make it easier for readers to respond.

Finally, sign off. You can use an informal closing or simply end with your name. If you are writing to an outside client, use an automatic sign-off that gives your mailing address and phone number.

Figure 10.2 is an example of an e-mail that connects with the reader, gets right to the point, and puts the requested action at the beginning. The message also includes a brief explanation and provides contact information in the automatic sign-off.

WRITER'S TOOLKIT

Making Copies

Besides addressing your e-mail message to multiple recipients, you will often need to send copies to recipients who need to be informed but do not need to follow up or take action related to the message. Use the *Cc (courtesy copy)* function for these recipients.

If a recipient needs to take action, you may consider *forwarding* the message instead of sending a Cc; include a note at the top of the message describing the action the recipient needs to take. Otherwise, the Cc recipient may not read the message thoroughly to discover what is expected.

A *Bcc (blind courtesy copy)* is very different from a Cc. With a Cc, everyone receiving the message is aware of all recipients. However, with Bcc messages, the person to whom the message is addressed is not aware that a blind copy is being sent. Be cautious in sending blind copies; a better solution may be to forward the message. (You achieve the same purpose without appearing to be doing something "behind someone's back.")

FIGURE 10.2 Effective E-Mail Message

This e-mail message connects with the reader and takes a direct tone by putting the requested action at the beginning.

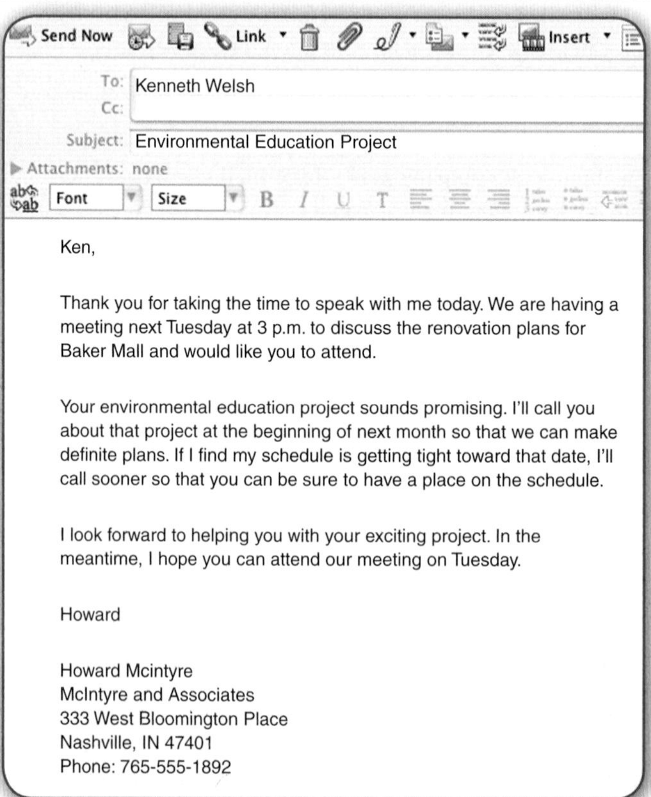

EXPLORE

Instructions: Analyze the following e-mail messages. What would you change about these messages?

MESSAGE 1

Vivian,

I'm having a meeting at 3 p.m. today and need your input. Plse come to my office at about 1 o'clock so we can discuss policy recommendations that you need implemented.

Mike

MESSAGE 2

Mike,

It is now 3:20 in the afternoon and I just got your message. Thanks for the advance notice. I image my input will not be part of the procedures that you discuss. Next time . . .

Vivian

MESSAGE 3

Viv,

I'm sorry about the late notice. The meeting was cncl'd or I would have clled you whn I didn't here from you. But you have put ;me on late notice a few times, so don't get so riled up.

Mike

PRACTICE

A. Situation: The help-wanted ad asks that you apply by e-mail only: *no calls accepted.* However, there's a bug in the system somewhere: the employer e-mails you back and explains that for some reason she isn't able to open either your e-mail or the résumé you attached. She is able to read only the first snippet of your message, about 6 lines of type. You can't figure out the problem with the computer or fix it, but you'd like a shot at the job.

Instructions: Compose a brief e-mail that explains how you will get your résumé to the prospective employer.

B. Read/Respond/Revise: Select one of the scenarios below, and then follow these guidelines:

1. Take 3 minutes to read the message and map your response.
2. Take 6 minutes to compose a brief response.
3. Spend 3 minutes editing and revising your message.

- You have recently gone on a job interview at the local Barnes & Noble bookstore. Write Reed Montel, vice president of human resources, a follow-up note.
- You need to take the next two weeks off because of a personal situation in your family. Write your manager, Ross Ospedale, a request to take a short leave.
- You recently had your car worked on at Speed Auto Service, and the same problem with your car reoccurred within days after the repair. Write the owner/manager, Race Firestone, outlining what happened and how you expect Speed Auto to respond.

• Internet Exercise 10.1

Embarrassing E-Mail: To find out about instances of inappropriate or embarrassing e-mail being made public (and being used as courtroom evidence), visit the Web site at **www.mhhe.com/youngBE**.

At the home page, select "Internet Exercise," and then click on the "Chapter 10" link to begin.

SECTION A CONCEPT CHECK

1. Describe the various parts of the CAT strategy for writing e-mail.

2. When writing e-mail in business, is it ever all right to use all upper- or lowercase letters?

3. List three or more e-mail guidelines that you will start using.

SECTION B: BASIC LETTERS AND MESSAGES

Every piece of business correspondence that you write must be tailor-made for your unique purpose at that moment. For the most part, recipes won't help you: try to be present in the moment when you write or speak. With those points in mind, let's take a look at various traditional approaches to structuring information.

LETTERS

CTA Structure: Connect, Tell, Act

The business letter is an excellent vehicle for building business relationships. Your letters represent you and your company and may be the only image your client has of your company.

Although the content and purpose of letters vary, you can organize most letters successfully by applying the following **CTA structure:**

- *Connect:* In the introduction, connect with the reader as one human being communicating to another. Don't be stiff and abstract. Be friendly, and connect your purpose to the reader's needs and interests.
- *Tell:* In the body, tell your reader details, explanations, and facts. Summarize and highlight information supporting your purpose.
- *Act:* In the closing, state the action or next steps that you will take or that you request the reader to take. Express goodwill; invite the reader to contact you for more information.

Notice how this structure differs from the CAT strategy for writing e-mail messages that you learned about in Section A. In addition to using the basic CTA structure, you also need to determine whether you will communicate information with a *direct approach* or an *indirect approach.* The direct approach is the most common way to convey information; use the indirect approach when your letter conveys news the recipient does not expect or welcome.

The Direct Message

Most letters take a **direct approach** to conveying information, putting the purpose and main point in the first paragraph. (See Figure 10.3.) Once readers understand the purpose, they are able to use supporting information in the body to confirm and expand their understanding of your message.

The bulk of the letter is in the body, which can consist of one paragraph (or as many as it takes to convey your message). Give as many details as necessary, but do not stray from the principle *less is more.* By including too many details, you are making it harder for yourself and more complicated for your reader. Screening out unnecessary details is part of the editing process.

FIGURE 10.3 Direct-Message Letter Example

Dear Ms. Matczak:

Your bank has provided valuable services to me over the years, but an error has been made on my account.

On October 12, I made a direct deposit to my checking account, No. 793 332, for $500. The deposit was made at your Main Street branch. However, the deposit was not posted on my October 30 statement. Enclosed is a copy of my receipt.

Thank you for assisting me with this. Please let me know if I need to take additional steps to reconcile this mistake; you can reach me at 555-9797.

Sincerely,

Bernard Olsen

Enclosure

FIGURE 10.4 Structuring for Message Letters

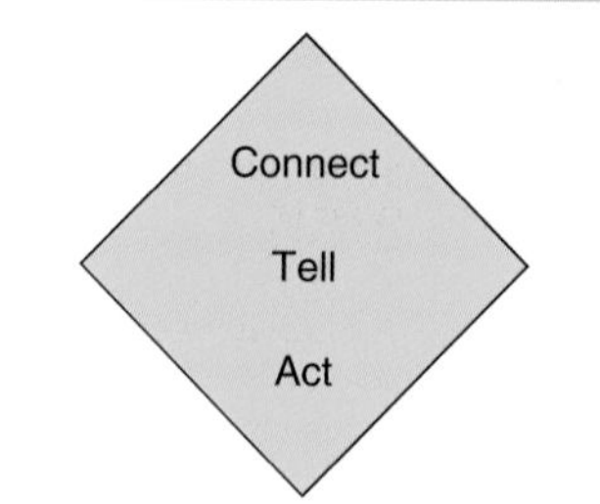

The closing in a direct message is usually short; it states action or next steps that you intend to take or that you request your reader to take. The closing also expresses goodwill and opens the door for additional communication.

Some experts say that it is redundant to close with a statement such as, "If you need additional information, please call me at 555-5567." However, reminding your readers—your clients—that they are welcome to interact with you helps build the business relationship. Especially if you are writing to someone for the first time, state your phone number in the closing.

To simplify the structure, think of the direct message as a diamond, with the top representing a short introduction, the bulk of the information in the body, and the bottom representing a short closing. (See Figure 10.4.)

The Indirect Message

Some letters take an **indirect approach** on purpose. When conveying unexpected or bad news, first explain the rationale before stating your main point or decision. If a reader may not like the message, he or she becomes more equipped to accept the bad news by understanding the logic behind it. The indirect approach is tactful and shows respect for the reader.

With indirect messages, state the purpose in a general way; do not disclose the main point immediately. (See Figure 10.5.) Your main point or bad news will appear in the body or possibly in the conclusion. You need to give enough detail and explanation so that the rationale leading to the news makes sense to the reader (or as much sense as possible).

As in a direct message, the closing paragraph of an indirect message lets the reader know that he or she may contact you or someone else for additional information.

Using a direct approach, the letter in Figure 10.5 might read as shown in Figure 10.6. *What response did you have to each letter? Was the tone of the second letter different from the tone presented in the first one?* See Figure 10.7 for a comparison of direct and indirect messages.

With an indirect message, the explanation softens the message for the reader. Giving the reasoning first not only shows respect for the reader but also shows that you take the situation seriously.

FIGURE 10.5 Indirect-Message Letter Example

Dear Mr. Beery:

We appreciate your business and would like to keep you as a valued customer.

We have considered your request to change the lease agreement on your printer and copier by three months. For several years, our poicy has been that the minimum time frame for leasing office equipment is one year. Part of the reason for the one-year time frame relates to lowering your costs and giving customers the option to buy equipment at a fraction of the retail price. Since you are a valued customer, we would be able to reduce your lease only if a charge is added to your final billing to reflect our increased costs. The fee would equal 25 percent of cost for the unused time left on your contract.

Because of the fee, you may decide that it is more cost-effective to keep the equipment until your contract expires. Let me know if you need more information; I am here to assist you in any way that I can.

Sincerely,

Donald P. Macki

FIGURE 10.6 The Direct Approach

Here is the letter in Figure 10.5, written using the direct approach.

Dear Mr. Beery:

We appreciate your business and would like to keep you as a valued customer.

In response to your request that we change your lease agreement, we must charge you a fee equal to 25 percent of cost for the unused time left on your contract. This fee reflects our increased costs and would be added to your final billing. For several years, our policy has been that the minimum time frame for leasing office equipment is one year. Part of the reason for the one-year time frame relates to lowering your costs and giving customers the option to buy equipment at a fraction of the retail price.

Because of the added fee, you may decide that it is more cost-effective to keep the equipment until your contract expires. Let me know if you need more information; I am here to assist you in any way that I can.

Sincerely,

Donald P. Macki

FIGURE 10.7 Indirect- and Direct-Message Formats

Direct Message	Indirect, or Bad News, Message
Connect with the reader.	Connect with the reader.
State purpose; get to the point.	State general purpose.
Give supporting details.	Give supporting details.
Close with desired actions or next steps.	State main point or conclusion.
	Close with cordial words (and next steps if they apply).

EXPLORE

1. Does it make sense to give a rationale before presenting bad news? Why?
2. Think of situations in which you have had to say no to a friend's or relative's request. How would you draft a letter giving your answer?
3. Determine whether to use the indirect or direct approach for the following letters:
   a. You are writing to let an applicant know that the job has been filled by someone else.
   b. You are formally requesting a leave of absence because of a family illness.
   c. You are providing information about your availability to work part-time.

PRACTICE

Instructions: Use either the direct or the indirect approach to do the following:

1. Draft the body of a letter describing the differences between the direct and the indirect approaches to writing letters.
2. Draft a letter to a relative or friend that explains why you have made a decision different from the one he or she expected. (For example, have you decided on a different career path than the one your parents expected? Have you ever told a friend no?)

Note: Keep your drafts handy; you will use one of them later in this chapter.

TYPES OF MESSAGES

Routine Requests

A common kind of message is one that makes a routine request of a coworker. Routine requests are part of taking care of business. When you are not expecting anything out of the ordinary, you don't need to apologize for asking for a colleague's help.

When making routine requests via e-mail, get right to the point and keep your message short (see Figure 10.8):

1. Present requested action and due dates close to the beginning of the message. If a due date is critical, also mention it in the subject line.
2. Supply only necessary supporting information. Include a comment explaining why the request is important or what the request will help you accomplish.
3. Express appreciation at the end of your message. Also include next steps, if relevant.

In addition to writing routine requests to coworkers, you will often write routine requests to customers. For example, you may have to ask a client to fill out papers so that a signature is on file, or you might have to ask clients to consider additional services your company provides. When writing letters for routine requests, state your purpose for writing and then specify the requested action near the end (see Figure 10.9). Follow this pattern:

1. Connect to the reader, and state the purpose of your letter.
2. Explain the reason for the request.
3. Tell the reader what to do, and supply a due date.
4. Show appreciation to the reader for taking action, and let the reader know that you are available to answer questions.

▸Language Diversity

American Sign Language (ASL): American Sign Language is the dominant language of the deaf community in the United States, in the English-speaking parts of Canada, and in parts of Mexico. ASL is also used in the Philippines, Singapore, Hong Kong, Dominican Republic, Haiti, Puerto Rico, Cote D'Ivoire, Burkina Faso, Ghana, Togo, Benin, Nigeria, Chad, Gabon, Democratic Republic of the Congo, Central African Republic, Mauritania, Kenya, Madagascar, and Zimbabwe.

Standardized sign languages have been used in Europe since the seventeenth century and in America at least since the days of the Plains Indians.

In the eighteenth century, the population of Martha's Vineyard, an island off the coast of Massachusetts, had a higher rate of deafness than the general population of the continental United States. Martha's Vineyard Sign Language was well known by islanders, many of whom had deaf members in their families.

In the early 1800s, Congregationalist minister and deaf educator Thomas Hopkins Gallaudet began the popularization of the hand-signing technique when he founded, with French deaf teacher Larent Clerc, what is now known as the American School for the Deaf. Many of the school's early students were from Martha's Vineyard, and they mixed their "native" sign language with Clerc's French Sign Language; to this brew was added the highly localized sign language systems of other students. And thus was ASL born.

Many of the graduates of this school went on to found other schools for the deaf in North America, spreading the methods of Gallaudet and Clerc and helping to standardize the language. Perhaps because of Clerc's early influence, approximately 60 percent of the vocabularies of ASL and French Sign Language are shared. In contrast, British Sign Language, used in the United Kingdom and many of its former territories, is very dissimilar from ASL.

Signs can be broken down into three rough groupings:

Transparent: Nonsigners can usually correctly guess the meaning.

Translucent: Meaning makes sense to nonsigners once it is explained.

Opaque: Meaning cannot be guessed by nonsigners.

The majority of signs are opaque.

In the United States, sign language interpreters are provided in courts, for college students at important public events, in job training, at social service programs, in mental health service programs, in instruction provided for parents of deaf children, and in sign language classes for hearing people who are learning ASL as a second language.

To learn more about American Sign Language, visit the Web site at www.mhhe.com/youngBE.

FIGURE 10.8 Routine Request via E-Mail

E-Mail Request: Does this e-mail use a *thinker* or a *feeler* approach? *(In the extreme, thinkers tend to base their decisions on hard facts without considering emotional factors; they get right to the point without making an effort to connect with the reader. Feelers, on the other hand, consider emotional factors a priority; they seem to place as much emphasis on connecting to the reader as they do on conveying the information in the message.)* Is the tone appropriate?

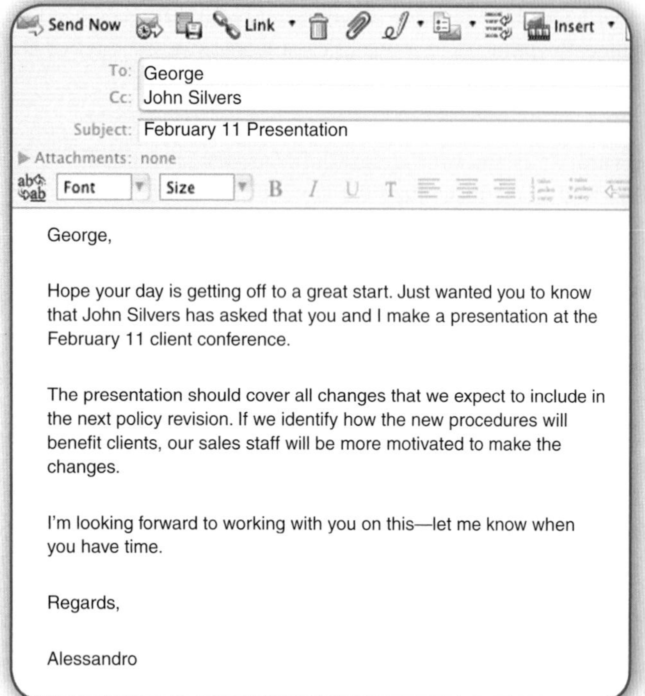

Send Now
Link
Insert
To: George
Cc: John Silvers
Subject: February 11 Presentation
Attachments: none
Font
Size
George,
Hope your day is getting off to a great start. Just wanted you to know that John Silvers has asked that you and I make a presentation at the February 11 client conference.
The presentation should cover all changes that we expect to include in the next policy revision. If we identify how the new procedures will benefit clients, our sales staff will be more motivated to make the changes.
I'm looking forward to working with you on this—let me know when you have time.
Regards,
Alessandro

FIGURE 10.9 Routine Request via Letter

Letter of Request: *What kinds of formatting techniques does this letter apply? Did the formatting get your attention? What response would this letter evoke from you? Are there any changes you would make?*

October 2, 2006

Mrs. Elaine Roberts
1456 West Maple Avenue
Newport, RI 02840

Dear Mrs. Roberts:

I am pleased to inform you that we have honored your request to add your daughter Alicia Roberts Grey to your checking and savings accounts. She now has full privileges as a joint owner with full rights of survivorship.

To validate this request, we ask that you and your daughter please:

1. **Sign your names below** where indicated.

______________________	____________
Elaine Roberts	Date
______________________	____________
Alicia Roberts Grey	Date

2. **Return the signed letter** to us in the enclosed, self-addressed envelope or drop it off at the bank. As soon as we receive your signed form, we will finalize these changes to your account.

If you have questions, please call us at 800-555-5955 or stop by the bank.

We value our relationship with you, Mrs. Roberts, and thank you for this chance to be of service.

Sincerely,

Vincent George
Account Specialist

VOCABULARY SOUNDALIKES

Sight/Site/Cite: When you are referring to your vision or your perception, use *sight.* When you are referring to a location, use *site.* And when you are quoting something or naming a source, use *cite.* For example:

I need new glasses every year because my *sight* changes.

The *site* you mentioned is perfect for our retreat.

Did you *cite* all your references?

If a customer prefers, you can send correspondence as an attachment to an e-mail; your e-mail should explain the correspondence you are attaching (see Figure 10.10).

When you are writing to someone within your corporation who is not a team member, take extra care with routine requests. Though you both support a common mission, someone from another department may not immediately understand the relevance of your request.

Complaints

Making a complaint can be an emotional experience. Agreements or expectations have been violated, and you may have experienced some harm, financial or otherwise. When you have a legitimate complaint, you can handle it in various ways. Depending on the situation and the action you expect, you can make a phone call or write an e-mail or a letter.

Realize that when you take the time to complain, you are actually doing a favor for the ones to whom you are complaining: you are giving them an opportunity to right a

FIGURE 10.10 Routine Request via E-Mail with Attachment

Sending Attachments: *Is there anything in this e-mail message that you would highlight or change?*

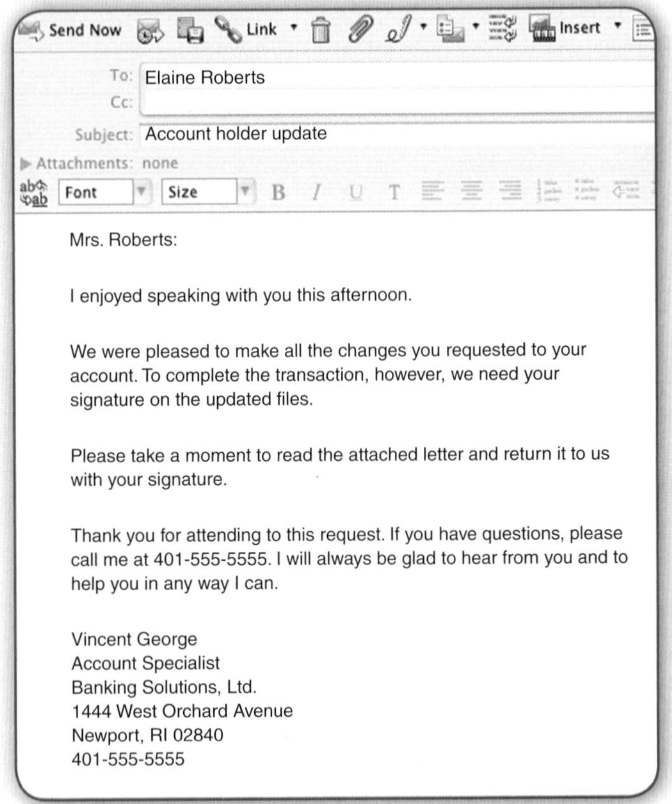

wrong. You are also giving insight into a problem that can then be corrected before others experience the same problem.

A letter is the most formal means of making a complaint and may receive the most attention. However, recipients take all written communication seriously, so don't underestimate the value of sending an e-mail. Both forms can be used as legal documentation, as they contain the details and demonstrate that all parties have been informed. In addition, writing will put the issue into perspective and clarify how to resolve it.

Written complaints traditionally follow an indirect pattern. However, the business world has changed dramatically in recent years: professionals are deluged with correspondence and heavy workloads. Companies are also more service-oriented. Now, in many situations, you can effectively use the direct approach with complaints (see Figure 10.11). However, *direct* does not equate to unprofessional or rude; *direct* means stating the purpose clearly and up front instead of in a roundabout way. Follow these guidelines to present a complaint:

Using the indirect method:	Identify your expectations and the established agreements.
	Give examples of how expectations and agreements were violated.
	Summarize key points.
	State the actions you expect.
Using the direct method:	State the problem.
	Summarize violated expectations and agreements.
	State the actions you expect.

FIGURE 10.11 Letter of Complaint

Internet Provider, Inc., like other ISPs, has worked diligently to prevent spam from reaching the electronic mailboxes of its clients by employing the latest in antispam technology. But the senders of such junk e-mail have worked just as diligently to overcome the antispam efforts. The company's optimistic goal is to reduce spamming by 85 percent before year's end, but, like any other ISP, it cannot promise spam-free service. What are the company's choices in responding to this letter from Jennifer Reed?

February 28, 2006

Internet Provider, Inc.
2003 Bell Drive
Twin Oaks, MI 49117

ATTENTION CUSTOMER SERVICE

For the past several months, I have been receiving tons of unwelcome spam in my e-mail account.

Your customer service department recommended that I open a special spam account, which would intervene so that I do not receive these bothersome messages. Unfortunately, their remedy has not helped the problem but, instead, has made it worse. I still get as much spam as ever; the only messages the spam account intercepts are from friends and associates.

For the past five years, I have been a loyal customer of your corporation, paying my bills regularly and recommending my friends to your service. Unless you resolve this problem within the next two weeks, I will change Internet providers.

Please let me know as soon as possible the changes you can make to my account.

Sincerely,

Jennifer Reed

Assume that the person who receives your complaint will respond. Remain objective; objectivity helps ensure that the problem will be resolved to your satisfaction. Remember, you are dealing with human beings who have feelings; most people do not make mistakes intentionally. Your objective is getting the problem solved, not making those involved feel bad; do not use emotional language that you will feel embarrassed by later.

Emotional: I am angry and upset about the way your bank is handling my account.

Objective: An inaccurate transaction was posted to my account on June 30, 2007.

Consider using the passive voice for "pointed" sentences:

Emotional: You made a serious mistake in my account.

Objective: A serious mistake has been made in my account.

Be honest and do not exaggerate. After you have drafted your letter or e-mail, wait a day or two before sending it. The old saying "You will get more bees with honey than vinegar" applies to complaints. Also, let the reader know you are an asset and a valuable ally when business flows smoothly. You will build less resistance to your cause and be more likely to encourage corrective action. Even when you are correct and another is wrong, you are not justified to act without dignity.

Apologies: Responding to Complaints

As Duke Ellington once said, "A problem is a chance for you to do your best."

Whether you receive a complaint by letter, phone, or e-mail, your response will determine the future of your business relationship with the person making the complaint. It is normal to feel defensive when someone is telling you that you did something wrong. The truth is, mistakes happen. Someone is responsible, and at times that may be you. An honest mistake is one in which you inadvertently broke an agreement or misread the situation.

When someone complains directly to you about a broken agreement or unfulfilled expectation, freewrite your response to reach clarity. Then determine whether you need to make a phone call or draft a letter. Depending on the situation, a formal apology may be in order. (See Figure 10.12.) To make a formal apology to a customer, either call or write a letter (or both). With a coworker, you can be less formal by sending an e-mail, making a call, or stopping by to chat.

FIGURE 10.12 Letter of Apology

Making Reparations: *Suppose you wrote the letter in Figure 10.11 to Internet Provider, Inc.* Would you be satisfied with this reply? Why or why not?

March 5, 2007

Ms. Jennifer Reed
5101 Ford Road
Dearborn, MI 48126

Dear Ms. Reed:

Thank you for taking the time to let us know about the problems you are having with your Internet account.

Our customer services department has received similar complaints recently, and we have taken immediate action. Our software was not picking up new types of spam that have been developed only recently to go "under our radar." Unfortunately, it is in the nature of the individuals and companies who create spam to continually look for methods to overcome the safeguards we have developed against it. When they do find new ways to break through, information we receive from valuable customers like you helps us to gain control of the situation quickly.

Management also approved more stringent procedures to combat the unwelcome bombardment of such ads. Thus, we are proud to inform you that we can now offer the best protection available, including firewalls, subject line detectors, and methods to ban specific addresses and domains.

Because you are a valued customer, we are crediting two months of service to your account. If you need assistance in adding these features to your computer setup, call me or my associate Mabel Johnston at 313-555-1234, extention 43.

Sincerely,

C. S. Cooper
Customer Service Manager

Making an apology implies only that you are a human being. Being able to apologize for your mistake without being defensive is a mature character trait. Here are some guidelines to follow:

- Take all complaints seriously; take extra care if the person drafted a letter.
- Read and then *reread* the complaint so that you are sure of what is being said.
- Respond only when you have regained your balance, and you need to regain it quickly.
- Understand the other person's perspective *before* you make contact.
- Assure the person that you understand what has happened and why it is important.
- Do not go into great detail about why you made the mistake; that could sound defensive.
- Properly acknowledge the person for letting you know about the problem:

  Weak: I received your letter about the problem in your account.

  Revised: Thank you for taking the time to inform me about the problem in your account.

- Avoid using adjectives and adverbs, such as truly and really, or you may sound insincere:

  Weak: I am truly sorry that your account was overdrawn and really appreciate your patience.

  Revised: I am sorry that your account was overdrawn and appreciate your understanding and patience.

- Keep a positive tone and don't make excuses:

  Weak: The mistake should not have happened.

  Weak: I was very busy and not able to meet the deadline.

  Revised: I apologize for the mistake and any inconvenience it has caused you.

- Remain humble and try to reestablish the relationship and regain trust and respect:

  Weak: I will not let this happen again if you give me another chance.

  Revised: I hope that you will give me a chance to regain your confidence.

When you are working with someone who is reasonable, most apologies will dissolve bitter feelings. When you are working with someone who is not reasonable, any apology—whether written or spoken—will not suffice. In such situations, you have to acknowledge that you did your best and then dust yourself off and move on.

Use the direct approach for letters of apology:

1. Start by stating your apology.
2. Let the reader know that you value the relationship.
3. Solve the problem and compensate the reader, if appropriate and possible.
4. Invite the reader to call you to discuss the issue further.
5. Encourage the reader to let you know if the problem resurfaces.
6. Follow up with a phone call to make sure that the problem is solved.

Thank-You Notes

Do not overlook sending coworkers, clients, and prospective clients a thank-you message. Whether it is an e-mail or a handwritten note, your thank-you will be appreciated and will enhance your relationship.

A thank-you note that is handwritten may have the most impact. Your note will make your recipient feel good about assisting you. This type of follow-up is especially important when you are on a job search. Make your letter or message simple, friendly, and genuine. (See Figure 10.13.)

FIGURE 10.13 Thank-You Note

Dear Ruble:

Looking for a job in today's market is extremely stressful, but meeting helpful individuals like you makes the journey easier.

I have contacted Joe, as you suggested, and will keep you informed on my progress. If I can assist you in any way, do not hesitate to contact me. I would be pleased to put my strong computer skills to use on your behalf!

Again, thank you for your valuable time and advice.

Sincerely,

Trisha

Don't use a boilerplate, *one-size-fits-all* message. Customize each letter, e-mail message, or handwritten note by specifically referring to why you are thanking the recipient.

Surprisingly, no matter how often the advice is given or how good the results are when followed, few letters or notes expressing thanks are actually written. Make a decision right now to upgrade that statistic.

PRACTICE

Instructions: To sharpen your skill in writing thank-you notes, do the following:

1. Identify two or three people who have assisted you in a difficult task or situation.
2. Write a thank-you letter to each of them letting the recipient know how his or her assistance helped you.

SECTION B CONCEPT CHECK

1. What is the purpose of the first part of most business correspondence? In other words, what do you wish to achieve before you even present your message?
2. In a business letter, where do you indicate desired action that the reader should take?
3. Under what circumstances would you use the indirect approach when writing a business letter? Why?

Language Diversity

Constructed Languages: A *constructed language* is an artificial language that has been designed by an individual or a small group, rather than having naturally evolved as part of a culture, the way natural languages do. Pig Latin does not qualify.

Esperanto, which is made up of words from various European languages, is an example of a constructed language. Esperanto was devised in the late 1800s by L. L. Zamenhof as a way of opening up communication between European cultures.

Esperanto is also an example of an *auxiliary language,* a language devised for the purposes of simplifying international communication. Similarly, Dutton World Speedwords is a constructed language intended to be used as an international shorthand system.

Constructed languages also appear in fiction and movies. J. R. R. Tolkien spent years devising language systems for various cultures existing in his vision of Middle Earth, including Elvish, Quenya, Sindarin, and Orcish. Klingon, invented for the *Star Trek* movie series, is also a constructed language.

The motivations behind the creation of constructed languages are varied, but they can be loosely divided into four categories:

- *Auxiliary languages,* intended to ease communication between cultures; for example, Esperanto.
- *Artistic languages,* devised for entertainment and aesthetic purposes; for example, Elvish.
- *Engineered languages,* created for the purpose of testing or proving a theory about how languages work; such as, Loglan (which, among its other rules, makes no distinctions between nouns and verbs).
- *Code,* devised for purposes of secrecy.

SECTION C: FORMATTING—SPECIAL FEATURES AND WHITE SPACE

Everything on the page—not just your words—communicates something to your readers, including the space you don't use. Formatting tools and techniques can enhance the meaning of your documents and possibly the relationship with your reader. Here's the idea: By presenting your message more clearly and professionally, you will have more credibility and communication will run more smoothly.

By displaying your key ideas prominently, you can develop an instant rapport with your reader. This kind of visual display is called **visual persuasion.** To use visual-persuasion techniques, package your ideas, break your message into manageable chunks, and give your documents a balanced look on the page. Some of these visual cues allow your reader to scan the document and understand its meaning before actually reading it.

Here are tools and techniques to use to format your documents professionally and to achieve visual persuasion:

- White space
- Bullets and numbering
- Boldface, italics, and underscoring
- Headings and subheadings
- Subject lines

Using formatting to create visual persuasion takes your writing beyond the standard of simple, clear, and concise. When you apply visual persuasion to your well-crafted message, your reader can look at the page and know your main points, and this makes your message easy to respond to.

CONTROL WHITE SPACE

The term **white space** refers to the unused areas of your document, such as top and side margins and the space between lines. Create white space for your reader by breaking information into readable chunks. One way to ensure adequate white space is to limit the number of lines in your paragraphs. Just as a sentence is more readable when it is under 22 words, so is a paragraph easier to read when it takes up fewer lines. In general, for papers consider 8 lines the maximum length for a paragraph. For letters, consider limiting paragraph length to 6 lines; for e-mail, keep your paragraphs to 4 lines or fewer.

White space gives your readers' eyes a place to rest and delineates the various parts of your document. It also gives readers a place to make notes and comments. The most important point to remember about white space is that it controls the way your document looks at a glance. Before you send your document to your client, ask yourself the following questions:

- Does this document look balanced, appealing, and professional?
- Does it look like too much information is crowded into too little space?
- Does the document look lopsided, or does it look as if it has a picture frame of white space?

Documents should look balanced: top and bottom margins should be somewhat equal, as should side margins. A common mistake is leaving too little space at the top of a document, resulting in too much empty space at the bottom. A professional rule of thumb is to aim for a picture-frame look. Use the print-preview feature on your computer to examine how your document will look before you print it. (In Microsoft Word, "print preview" can be found in the File menu on the toolbar.)

Standard guidelines dictate a range of minimum to maximum spacing to leave between parts. After you learn these guidelines for spacing, you will develop a trained eye for document placement. Listed below are some basic guidelines for letters and reports. (Note: For vertical spacing [up and down], 6 lines take up 1 inch of space.)

Letters

- Start most letters 2 inches from the top margin of the paper. (After the 6 blank lines that your computer automatically leaves, count down 6 line spaces from the top of your computer page template.)
- Use the default margins for most letters.
- For short letters, add more space before the date line, between the date and the address, before the signature line, and before the reference initials.
- For long letters, leave less space between letter parts and at the top and bottom.
- Do not justify right margins (readers find justified lines more difficult to follow).

Reports

- Start your first page 2 inches from the top margin (down 6 lines from the default top margin).
- Type the title in 14-point font either all-caps or bold with initial caps and lowercase; type the body in a 12-point font.
- Use 1-inch margins or the default margins.
- Type the second-page continuation heading 1 inch from the top of the page; after the heading, space down 3 lines before continuing the body of your paper.

Memos

- Use company templates or templates provided in personal software packages.
- To start the body of the memo, space down 3 times (leaving 2 blank lines) after the heading.

Research and academic papers must be written according to strict formatting rules; however, these rules vary slightly from source to source. For specifics, consult the reference source your instructor recommends.

Many companies post reference guides on their intranet systems. When you start working at a new company, ask whether the company has a corporate reference guide. Amazingly, many employees remain unaware that their companies provide this critical tool for written correspondence. Check with your human resources department or an informed coworker so that you can be on the cutting edge of your company's policies.

DISPLAY KEY IDEAS WITH BULLETS AND NUMBERS

Even short documents can be improved by displaying key ideas. Bullets and numbers organize and prioritize key points, so your reader does not have to work as hard to find them. In addition, when the important points are highlighted, the reader does not need to reread an entire document to review the key ideas.

- Use bullets to create visual cues for items of equal significance.
- Use numbers to prioritize ideas or to list a sequence of steps that should be followed.

As you compose a document, you may not recognize what needs to stand out. As you edit and revise, select information to display.

Bulleted and numbered points must be displayed in parallel structure, which you have worked with periodically throughout this book. However, now you will work with parallel structure in lists. For example, if you start with an active verb, every item in the list should start with an active verb in the same tense. If you are listing nouns, present all items as nouns. If your items are displayed in complete sentences, make sure they are grammatically correct. Below are a couple of examples of a list displayed in parallel structure. The first example presents the items as nouns:

Here are items to discuss at our team meeting:

- Employee dress policy
- Holiday schedule
- Summer hours

You can represent the same list more specifically by starting each item with a verb:

The topics we need to discuss at our next team meeting are as follows:

- Revise employee dress policy.
- Review holiday schedule.
- Implement summer hours.

Adding *ing* to the verbs turns them into gerunds (a noun form), as shown below:

At our next team meeting, we need to discuss the following:

1. Revising employee dress policy.
2. Reviewing holiday schedule.
3. Implementing summer hours.

For bulleted or numbered items, you have a variety of different styles (size, shape, and indentation) from which to choose. Limit the number of styles you use within the same document and stay consistent, or you will distract your reader. Shift from one style to another only if you have a special purpose for changing styles; for example, use a larger bullet for a major point and a smaller bullet for a minor or subordinate point.

If you present your information in complete sentences or short phrases, you can end your bulleted or numbered points with a period. For more technical questions, consult *The Gregg Reference Manual.*

Let's see how we can apply visual persuasion to make a letter more effective. Look at the short letter in Figure 10.14. Now compare that letter to the revision, with visual persuasion, in Figure 10.15.

FIGURE 10.14 Short Letter with Minimal Formatting

Dear Peter:

James and I enjoyed meeting with you and Emile and appreciate the time you spent with us so that we could learn about your company. You and your staff have done a great job expanding your business.

I'm sure your background and experience lead you to know how important a good banking relationship is for any company. We would be glad to help you explore banking and financing opportunities that could benefit your company. Please feel free to call me at any time. The resources of the First Bank network are here for you to use.

We wish you continued success in your company ventures.

Sincerely,

Gracielle

FIGURE 10.15 Short Letter Formatted Effectively

Dear Peter:

James and I enjoyed meeting you and Emile today and learning about your company. You have all done a superb job expanding your business.

I know you understand the value of a good banking relationship, and we'd like to help you look at banking and financing options to benefit your company. We specialize in serving the commercial banking needs of companies like yours and I'm confident our products and services can help you:

- *Reduce* your costs.
- *Increase* your liquidity
- *Provide* the capital you need to meet your growth objectives.

I will call you in the next few days to discuss the possibility of our working together. In the meantime, please call me at 630-555-6630 if you have questions.

We wish you continued success; thank you again for your time.

Sincerely,

Gracielle

PRACTICE

Instructions: Now you have compared and analyzed the differences in the two letters in Figures 10.14 and 10.15. What differences stand out? What form of visual persuasion was used?

PRACTICE

Instructions: Proofread and reformat the following memo to give it more visual appeal. Start by crossing out unnecessary information.

To: Margola Adams

From: Alex Guireria

Subject: Orrin Keyes' Transfer Application.

Hi Margola:

I heard through the office grapevine that Orrin wants to transfer into our department. I'd like to put in my five cents on his behalf because I think he'd be a great addition to our team. We worked together on the Corona project to link our restaurants, the busy stores and warehouses on a common data systems, and I have only good things to say about his contributions, which include: creating the daily PMIX data verification report for all U.S. stores, producing a resturuant inventory report that is now being used to track inventory for all U.S. stores and restaurants, was an integral part of repopulating the date warehouse in December after the crash, and produced the file we used for the Action Dog promotion to determine supply and demand. Weve used that file for every toy promotion since!

I was so impressed with his work and his attitude, and really, well, you know how it is here. Hard workers don't always get the credit they deserveThere was no proper recognition of the work we did on Corona so you might not know what went into it or who was involved in the aspects of the project. Orrin never hesitated to perform data transformation products during the evenings nor coming in over the weekends as required to keep Corona up and running during daytime hours.

Something to consider.

A. G.

CREATE HEADINGS AND SUBHEADINGS

For shorter pieces of writing, such as letters and memos, writers are hesitant to use headings. However, headings highlight key points so that the reader begins to understand the message at first glance. The worst kind of message is one that leaves the reader struggling to understand the information it presents.

When writers state their purpose clearly and up front, the reader digests information more easily. When the main point is clear, necessary details add effective support. In contrast, details can be tedious when they build to a main point.

To develop a heading, pull out the main point from the topic sentence of a paragraph. If you turned it into a heading, would it add value for your reader? Does it enable you to cut other details in your paragraph, making your message more concise?

INCLUDE SUBJECT LINES

A subject line can enhance reader understanding, regardless of whether you are writing an e-mail, a memo, or a letter. A subject line also enables your reader to file your message for future reference.

Every e-mail message should have a subject line. Don't get stuck trying to think of a subject line before you write your message. Pull out the main point after you have written your message. Short, descriptive subject lines are the best.

Memos require a subject line, but consider using a subject line for letters as well, especially letters that you send to clients you don't know well. A subject line enhances understanding for your reader, and readers are more likely to agree with you when they understand what you are saying.

INCORPORATE SPECIAL FORMATTING FEATURES AND MARKS

Special features include **bold,** *italics,* and underscore; special marks include parentheses and quotation marks (but not all caps). For these elements, follow specific guidelines, and display the elements consistently within your document. Before we look at these features and marks in detail, here are brief explanations:

- *Bold:* Make headings stand out by putting them in boldface type (use bold sparingly to make key ideas stand out).
- *Italics:* Stress words and display book titles or foreign terms in italics.
- *Underscore:* Use underscores in place of italics *only* if you are not writing on a computer.
- *Quotation marks:* Enclose direct quotes and jargon in quotation marks.
- *Parentheses:* Put parentheses around information that gives a brief explanation.
- *Caps:* Follow traditional capitalization guidelines; all-capital letters (all-caps) should *not* be used to make words stand out.

Sometimes, especially in e-messages, writers think they are making an idea stand out by writing in all-caps. Instead, readers may infer that the writer is "shouting" or "screaming" at them. Once again, do not use all-caps in e-mail. The bold feature can also have the effect of "shouting" when it is overused.

Many writers also think that putting a word between quotation marks makes the idea stand out (such as, *It's a really "good" idea*). In fact, placing a word between quotation marks does not stress its meaning. When quotation marks are used for no valid reason, most readers infer that the writer is implying the *opposite* of what the word actually means. So be careful; do not throw quotation marks into a document unless you are clear about what you are doing. For more detailed explanations than provided here, refer to *The Gregg Reference Manual.*

Use Quotation Marks to

1. Insert a direct quote of three or fewer lines within the body of a document.
2. Identify technical terms, business jargon, or coined expressions that may be unfamiliar.
3. Use words humorously or ironically (if you think your reader will miss the humor).
4. Show a slang expression, poor grammar, or an intentionally misspelled word.

Use Italics to

1. Provide a definition of a word or refer to a word as a word; for example, "The word *listen* has many shades of meaning."
2. Emphasize a word, a phrase, or an entire sentence.
3. Display foreign terms (such as *Merci, Grazie, Dobra, Domo Arigato*) and uncommon Latin abbreviations (such as *carpe diem*).
4. Display book titles. (In the past, book titles were underscored. However, now that we have access to the variable spacing and special features of computers, using italics is the preferred method.)

Insert Parentheses to

1. Give a brief explanation within a sentence.
2. Insert a sentence that does not directly relate to the topic of your paragraph.
3. Supply abbreviations.

Using parentheses deemphasizes information. Parentheses also help to break up information flow in a positive way; the writer does not need to give a lengthy discussion of why information is being supplied. Parentheses tell the reader that the information is related to the broader topic without giving an explanation of how or why. By enclosing a few words in parentheses, you can sometimes avoid writing a lengthy explanation.

PRACTICE

Instructions: Edit and reformat the following message, incorporating special marks and bullets or numbers.

Dear George,

Last month, Salaway Home Care sent out a notice regarding a problem we were experiencing with the Coordinator's Notes and the Participation Notes sections of the Canton Manual profile pages. In order to correct this problem we had to edit many of the "note sections" The editing was done by eliminating unnecessary information in those two sections. For example: where Participation Notes state "White Harbor/Canton Medical of Vermont is the Canton of Vermont's active market HMO, please refer to Medicare Risk/Cost members to Senior DelawareCare (DE2M), we have revised to read Canon plus is the active Market HMO for Canton of America. Please refer Medicare members to DE2M-Canton 65." Information such as "coordinator use only" and "direct members access" has also been deleted. Immediate action is requested on your part. Take the next steps: Please visit our web site and print out the new profile pages that have already been edited. You can then review your HMO profile pages and make necessary edits. Also, please advise us of any additional information that can be edited down or deleted.

VOCABULARY NEW WORDS

New Words: Throughout this text, you have encountered margin features describing words that are considered to have been "officially" added to the lexicon as a result of their appearances in an unabridged dictionary, such as the *Oxford English Dictionary (OED).*

New words (also known as *neologisms*) are being coined every day. You might be using them regularly in both professional and personal conversations. Words such as *etailer* and *blog* appear frequently in the media—novels, newspapers, magazines, television and movie scripts, song lyrics, and electronic dictionaries—but they have yet to appear in an unabridged dictionary.

How does a word make it into an unabridged dictionary? A single appearance (or even several appearances) of a word in print does not guarantee relevance: the word may be popular for a short time period before disappearing forever. English dictionaries record how a large number of people use the English language over time. If a word proves to be useful, usage and understanding of the term will spread.

Sources such as Internet databases, subject-specific glossaries, and paper files are searched for occurrences; and their frequency and time span, as well as the range of sources in which they appear, are taken into account. A rule of thumb for *OED* is that any word can be included that appears five times, in five different printed sources, over a period of five years.

This five-year aspect can result in a time lag between the first use of a word and its first appearance in an unabridged dictionary, but it also ensures care in recording the true nature of a word.

CHOOSE FONT SIZE AND COLOR

For most business documents, select conservative fonts and keep them to traditional sizes. Some common fonts are Times New Roman, Arial, and Helvetica. The traditional color for print and e-mail messages is black. However, for e-mail, some business professionals use blue for the body of their message or their automatic sign-offs.

Additional colors may be considered unprofessional; in fact, some business executives are annoyed when untraditional colors or special features appear in an e-mail. These individuals may or may not be justified for feeling this way; however, entrants into the workforce should be aware of possible critics before sending out blazing red or purple messages (or animation), thinking they are being creative. When you use color in e-mail, use it conservatively.

For documents that will be professionally printed, be aware that printing costs increase significantly when more than two colors are used. For documents that are copied, color copiers are now cost-effective and somewhat common. However, continue to be conservative with color, using it sparingly to highlight a document. Otherwise, you may detract from your message. Consult a professional graphic designer if you have questions.

Almost all business documents are formatted in a 12-point font, which means there are 12 characters per inch. This traditional size is a carryover from the typewriter, which had only two sizes (10 and 12 point). Now, with electronic processing, you have a wide range of font sizes.

- Increase font size if you know your reader has visual difficulty. Most e-mail templates are set for a 10-point font; increase the font size to 12 or 14. You may even use the bold feature to make the message especially clear.
- Limit font types to two per document so that your work does not appear cluttered.
- Use a larger-size font (14 point) for the title of your document and major text headings (title, chapter, and section headings).

EXPLORE

1. Look through magazines, textbooks, and other common reading materials. Examine the appearance of a typical page, excluding any advertisements. How many different fonts appear? How many different type sizes? Does the page look clean or cluttered?
2. Surveys have repeatedly shown that the inside column is the least-read section in the paper. That's why a common design for the front page of newspapers places current and breaking news stories in the right-hand column and human interest stories in the left-hand column. When you read letters, where does your eye go first? Do you begin reading immediately, or do you examine the whole document?

SECTION C CONCEPT CHECK

1. What is visual persuasion?
2. Bullets and headings serve what overall purpose in a business document?
3. Why is white space important to the look of a document?

Please review the original memo in Box 10.1 inviting employees to a teambuilding retreat; as you read it, consider the kinds of changes you would make as part of the editing process. Then examine the revised version to see how your changes compare with the new version.

• WRITER'S TOOLKIT

Formatting and Table Settings

When you go to a restaurant, your table setting provides the format for your meal. For table settings that are attractive, practical, and tasteful, the elements are arranged in a way that meets expectations. Properly done, a table setting showcases the food, meets the needs of the diner in a logical way, and provides a natural progression through the dining experience.

Diners base part of their dining experience on the table arrangement. That's why a holiday meal eaten off paper plates may not seem special, while fast food eaten off fine china could seem elegant.

Format every document as if it has been prepared for a special occasion. Your reader will have an easier time understanding your message and responding to it. Also, the reader may interpret the extra care you put into your document as respect.

BOX 10.1 The Editing Process

BEFORE

To: Support Services Staff
From: Ronnie Stevens
Subject: Teambuilding Retreat for Support Services Staff
Date: Sept. 7, 2006

In our on-going effort to create a more effective team within Support Services, we will be conducting a teambuilding retreat on October 11th and 12th, 2006, in Tampa, FL.

We will be working with Terrell Davis from Managing Diversity. In order to ensure the retreat training meets our needs, Terrell will be meeting with each of you on Monday, Sept. 20th to solicity your input prior to developing the workshop training. The individual interviews will be approximately 45 min. and all information is confidential.

As part of the retreat, Managing Diversity will be administering the Managing Diversity Type Indicator. The MDTI is an extremely useful and practical tool to help us in our understanding of each other as team members. The *MDTI* identifies differing styles of perceptions, judgment, energy direction, there are no "right" or "wrong" answers; the indicator simply indentifies different kinds of people who like different things, who are good at different things and who may find it difficult to understand one another. The results of the questionnaire will be given to each team member at the retreat. This informational and fun tool will not only be useful to you in working with your team members but can be extremely valuable in creating a better understanding between family and friends. Please use the scoring sheet for your answers and do not write in the MDTI booklet.

Managing Diversity will also be using the attached Team Feedback Instrument. Please complete both the *MDTI* and the Team Feedback Instrument and return to Terrell at your interview on Monday, September 20th.

Thank you and I look forward to fun and rewarding retreat in Orlando next month.

AFTER

To: Support Services Staff
From: Ronnie Stevens
Subject: Teambuilding Retreat
Date: Sept. 7, 2006

In our ongoing effort to create a more effective team, we will conduct a team-building retreat on October 11 and 12 in Tampa, Florida.

Our team will be working with *Terrell Davis* from *Managing Diversity.* To ensure the retreat training meets our needs, Terrell will meet with each of you so that you can give him your input about the training.

- Terrell will be here from 9 until noon on Monday, September 20. Please let me know the best time for you to meet with him.
- Your individual interviews with Terrell will last about 45 minutes, and all information will be kept confidential.

As part of the retreat, you will be taking the *Managing Diversity Type Indicator (MDTI),* which is a practical tool to help us in understanding each other as team members.

- The MDTI identifies differing styles of perceptions, judgment, energy direction, and communication.
- There are no right or wrong answers: the indicator simply identifies differences so that we can have more success understanding each other.
- Please use the scoring sheet for your answers, and do not write in the MDTI booklet.

You will receive the results of your questionnaire at the retreat. This informational tool will be valuable in creating better communication between you and your team members as well as family and friends.

Managing Diversity will also use the attached *Team Feedback Instrument.* It should be self-explanatory; however, please let me know if you have questions.

- Please complete both the MDTI and the Team Feedback Instrument and return them to Terrell at your interview on Monday, September 20.

Thank you—I look forward to working with you to create an even more successful team than we already have at this fun and rewarding retreat next month in Tampa.

RS

SECTION D: DIVERSITY AND OFFICE ETIQUETTE

In Chapter 1, you learned about the difference between formal and informal language patterns. You learned that speaking and writing Business English were appropriate for the global business environment to aid understanding and communication. Let's take a closer look at diversity so that you can see the role individuality plays in the workplace.

WHAT IS DIVERSITY?

Diversity relates to differences. Whether you realize it or not, you are a unique human being. No one living today is exactly like you: consider your race, religion, gender, education, family, culture, and other factors, such as personality.

Diversity is a big issue in corporate America today. That's because when diversity is not understood or not handled appropriately, the result can be discrimination, conflict among coworkers, or even poor relationships between employees and clients. When problems occur, the company's profit margin may be affected; even worse, lawsuits can be filed that hurt the company financially and project a bad image.

Many companies work to help their employees understand and accept differences by offering training programs on diversity. Diversity programs expand perceptions about personal qualities that are a natural and permanent part of an individual's profile; however, diversity programs do not focus on personal qualities related to choice, such as dress or behavior. For qualities of choice, companies work to establish a culture that supports their individual mission.

WHAT IS A CORPORATE CULTURE?

According to Randall S. Hansen of Quintessential Careers, a corporate culture is "the personality of the organization," or "how things are done around here."[1] Companies express their cultures through a variety of obvious ways. For example, corporate culture is expressed by the way people dress, the hours they work, their work sites, and how they socialize with each other. Corporate culture guides employees on how to think and act.

Companies publish mission statements so that all employees understand the established core values and beliefs that management intends to project to the world. Before you accept a position, try to understand as much as you can about a company's corporate culture. Ask questions about what it's like to work at the company and what the company values in its workers. For example, one important element of every corporate culture is the manner in which employees are expected to dress. You will be much happier if there is a natural fit between your values and the company's values.

> **SPEAKING BUSINESS**
>
> **Self-Check:** Throughout this book, you have reviewed aspects of grammar that relate to speech as much as they relate to writing. Take a few moments to identify characteristics in your speech that you are still working on.
>
> Focus on identifying informal patterns of grammar, pronunciation, and word usage.
>
> Now write five sentences using your informal patterns of speech, and then translate them into formal Business English.

DRESS FOR CAREER SUCCESS

Along with e-mail and phone etiquette, how you dress has an impact on those around you. The first thing anyone notices about you is your appearance. If you want to succeed in the professional arena, you must pay attention to the way you dress. With a little effort, you can look the part and feel comfortable in any professional situation.

According to William Thourlby, author of *You Are What You Wear,* people decide the following ten things about you within the first ten seconds of meeting you:[2]

1. Economic level
2. Educational level
3. Trustworthiness
4. Social position
5. Level of sophistication
6. Social heritage
7. Educational heritage
8. Economic heritage
9. Successfulness
10. Moral character

Always dress appropriately for your position. Interviewers complain that job applicants show up in t-shirts, tattered jeans, and unironed clothing; in addition, the interview is not the time to flaunt a tattoo or body piercing. Know the proper etiquette; employers interpret anything less as disrespectful of the organization and the position. Especially for an interview, wear conservative clothing and jewelry; in other words, wear nothing that would detract from your professionalism. Here is a sample of what some companies include in their dress code:[3]

- Do not wear clothing that reveals too much cleavage or that reveals skin on your back, chest, feet, or stomach.
- Do not wear clothing that is wrinkled, torn, dirty, or frayed.

- Do not wear jeans, sweatpants, exercise pants, shorts, Bermuda shorts, bib overalls, leggings, and any spandex or other form-fitting pants such as bike clothing.
- Do not wear skirts shorter than 4 inches above the knee or sun dresses, beach dresses, and spaghetti-strap dresses.
- Do not wear sweatshirts, midriff tops, or shirts with potentially offensive words, terms, logos, pictures, cartoons, or slogans.
- Do not wear halter tops, tops with bare shoulders, or t-shirts (unless they are under another shirt or jacket).
- Do not wear flashy athletic shoes, thongs, flip-flops, or slippers.
- Do not have any visible body piercing other than pierced ears.

Many companies have dress-down days, on which jeans and other casual clothing may be allowed. Clothing with the company logo is encouraged and can usually be purchased on-site in company stores or through company catalogs.

When an employee wears inappropriate items to work, the employee might be sent home to change clothes and will receive a verbal warning. If the employee continues to violate the dress code, progressive disciplinary action will be taken.

Communication Challenges

Growing Edges: When you are applying for a job, the interviewer is likely to ask you about your weaknesses along with your strengths. Another term for *weakness* is *growing edge.*

Keep in mind that identifying your *strengths* and confidently verbalizing them will get you the job. However, to keep the job and be consistently promoted, your growing edges may become more important than your strengths. That's because *people are usually fired for their weaknesses, not their strengths.* As a result, by honestly working on your growing edges, you will be taking control of your career success.

In addition, most people find a direct connection between their biggest weakness and their biggest strength. Even a good quality expressed in its extreme has both a positive and a negative side. For example, if you are always on time, you may display a lack of patience or become annoyed with others who are occasionally late. Another example is developing creative or innovative solutions to problems: though some of your ideas may dramatically improve the bottom line, others may be a waste of time and money.

Identify your growing edges, and develop a plan to minimize your weaknesses and express them in a balanced way.

Ask yourself: *What are my greatest strengths, and how do they sometimes express themselves as weaknesses?*

EXPLORE

What are some changes in dress that you will need to make to fit into a conservative company culture? As you continue to expand your wardrobe, what are some items you may need to add in preparation for your first job in the business world?

USE VOICE MAIL EFFECTIVELY

Voice-Mail Greetings

Companies encourage their employees to record standard, professional voice-mail greetings. Some professionals change their greetings on a daily or weekly basis, depending on how their schedules change. Here are some guidelines for creating a professional voice-mail greeting:

1. State your name at the beginning of the message, followed by any information you want the caller to leave (such as name and phone number). For example:

    Hi, this is Jack Webb. Please leave your name and number and then a brief message. I will return your call as soon as I can.

2. If you will be out of the office for a day or more, you may wish to update your voice-mail greeting to let callers know you will be out of the office. For example:

    Hello, this is Jack Webb. I will be out of the office from Monday, July 17, until Friday, July 21. Please leave a detailed message, and I will call you when I return to the office.

3. If your schedule varies, you may change your voice-mail greeting on a daily basis. For example:

    Good morning, this is Jack Webb, and today is Tuesday, August 15. I will be in a workshop until noon today. Leave me a brief message, including your phone number and a convenient time for me to return your call this afternoon.

If you leave a specific voice-mail greeting, remember to change it as needed. In the above example, Jack would need to change his message when he returned to his office at noon that day.

Voice-Mail Messages

Too often, very little thought is put into planning phone calls or leaving well-constructed voice-mail messages. If you reach a person at the other end, you want to be prepared to express your message confidently and clearly. However, if you reach voice mail, preparation is even more important. The last thing you want to do is leave a long, rambling message before you get to your point.

Disorganized messages are very frustrating to receive. The caller may or may not include the return phone number; many times, the number is included at the end of the message and is barely audible. When that happens, sometimes the entire message must be listened to again (and again) to retrieve the number.

When you leave a message, do not assume the recipient has your number. Many people access their phone messages without phone numbers at hand; by leaving your number with a brief message, you are making it more convenient for the recipient to contact you. Here are some guidelines for leaving voice-mail messages:

1. Mind-map the message before you call.
2. Start your message by stating your name, company, and phone number (slowly).
3. Prioritize the information, and give the most important details first.
4. Include a time frame: when do you need the information you are requesting?
5. Make sure you include the best times you can be reached.
6. Repeat your phone number *slowly* at the end of the message.

By preparing to leave a voice mail before you make a call, you are also preparing for the call itself. If a real person answers, you can confidently handle the call.

> **VOCABULARY: SOUNDALIKES**
>
> **Complement/ Compliment:** The verb *complement* means "to complete," whereas the verb *compliment* means "to give praise" or "to flatter". For example:
>
> Your tie *complements* your shirt.
>
> Marcel *complimented* me on my tie.

EXPLORE

1. Have you ever left a phone message in which you rambled on? Have you ever received such a message? What are some differences between personal and professional telephone etiquette?
2. Identify a company at which you may someday apply for a position. Use a search engine to find its Web site. At the Web site, find the company's phone number and review basic information about the company. After you have done your research, call the company and ask if you could speak to someone in Human Resources about employment opportunities. Before you make your call, be sure to do a mind map of questions you will ask.

PRACTICE

Situation: You have just found out that there is an opening for a part-time position, and you have all the qualifications. Ms. Kendra Williams is screening applicants for the position, and you are calling to set up an appointment. When you call, you receive her voice mail.

Instructions: Leave a message indicating your interest, and briefly state your qualifications, availability, and a number where you can be reached. (Role-play this activity with a partner.)

FOLLOW CELL PHONE ETIQUETTE

Many companies supply their employees with cell phones, and they expect their employees to practice cell phone etiquette, especially in meetings or other public places.

Though a cell phone or other pocket communication tools may be part of your every waking hour, stop to consider the best way to manage these devices. At an Association for Business Communications conference, Ewuuk Lomo-David presented a list of guidelines for cell phone use.[4] Here they are:

1. Turn ringer to vibrate when in public places.
2. Avoid loud, sensational ring tones that call attention to yourself.

3. Lower your voice when speaking.
4. Wait until you are in a comfortable place to speak.
5. Do not frown when speaking; it indicates a troubled state of mind.
6. Do not answer and speak on the phone while in a line for services.
7. Step about 20 feet away from the public when you must answer your phone.
8. Keep confidential information private (it may be overheard by someone who is familiar with the person or situation you are talking about).
9. Avoid multitasking when you are talking on a cell phone; it could be dangerous.
10. Don't make or receive cell phone calls while attending meetings or classes or driving.

Do not let electronic devices interfere with your relationships or create frustrations for those around you. Right now you may be thinking that these are a lot of rules to follow, and many people don't follow them. Try to remember that it's your success that you need to focus on, not the success or failure of others.

IT'S NOT PERSONAL—IT'S JUST BUSINESS

When it comes to adaptation, you have seen that companies expect their employees to adapt to their culture and not the other way around. Corporations are not democracies: the chief executive officer, the president, and senior management determine how people at their organization will conduct business.

Companies are image-conscious. That's why they develop dress codes and publish guidelines about cell phone and e-mail use. The quality of your work reflects directly on the company you work for. When you start working at a new company, ask Human Resources for company guidelines. You will have much more success if you follow company guidelines, as they are the ingredients that form the company culture. An important part of being successful relates to managing your expectations; and you should now have a realistic idea of what business expects from you. You've worked hard to achieve excellent skills, and you will reap good rewards as long as you continue to grow.

> **• Internet Exercise 10.2**
>
> **Online Career Resources:** To find a list of links to career resources, visit the Web site at www.mhhe.com/youngBE. Once you have accessed the home page, select "Student Activities" and then the "Chapter 10" link to get started.

SECTION D CONCEPT CHECK

1. Imagine you are recording your own voice-mail greeting at work. How would you word it?

2. Describe an outfit that you would wear to an interview or your first day on the job. Be specific about colors, lengths, necklines, jewelry, and even fabric and prints.

CHAPTER 10 SUMMARY

From e-mail guidelines to visual persuasion, you have learned some important concepts to put the finishing touches on your professional correspondence. Remember to make good use of the following:

- White space
- Bullets and numbers
- Boldface, italics, and underscores
- Headings and subheadings
- Subject lines

Now let's shift gears for a moment to think about what you have learned over the last few months. Have you changed the way you speak and write to the extent that you now feel more confident? Do you have a better idea now of what to expect when you arrive on the job?

Growth is a process that will last your entire life. Remain flexible and open-minded; try to keep your passion for learning. Even those who consider Charles Darwin a controversial figure can appreciate the good advice he gave when he said, "It is not the strongest of the species that survive, nor the most intelligent, but the one most responsive to change." Now go out and give the world your best!

CHAPTER 10 CHECKLIST

When writing an e-mail, have you:

___ Used a salutation and closing for your e-mail?

___ Kept your e-mail to one screen in length?

___ Included an accurate subject line?

___ Numbered individual questions to ensure a complete response?

___ Deleted history that isn't relevant?

___ Kept the tone objective and positive?

___ Structured the message using the CAT strategy?

___ Proofread and edited your message so that it is simple, clear, and concise?

___ Used visual persuasion to enhance your message?

Before leaving a voice-mail message, have you:

___ Taken time to mind-map your message?

___ Reminded yourself to speak slowly and clearly?

___ Noted to leave your number at the beginning and end of your message?

___ Prioritized your information?

___ Left a time frame for when you can be reached?

For cell phone use, do you:

___ Turn the ringer to vibrate when in public places?

___ Avoid loud, sensational ring tones?

___ Wait until you are in a comfortable place to speak?

___ Keep confidential information private?

___ Avoid multitasking when you are engaged in a call?

___ Resist making and receiving phone calls while attending a meeting or classes or driving?

CHAPTER 10 END-OF-CHAPTER ACTIVITIES

ACTIVITY 1: PROCESS MEMO

INSTRUCTIONS: Write your instructor a message detailing some of the skills and qualities you have developed during this class. Will what you have learned about writing help you in your future career? Also, write about your career goals. What do you want to achieve within the next six months, the next year, and the next five years?

If you have Internet access, you can complete this exercise online at **www.mhhe.com/youngBE** and then send an e-mail to your instructor.

ACTIVITY 2: EDITING AND REVISING, PART 1

INSTRUCTIONS: Edit and revise the following e-mail message.

> Bill,
>
> I received your invitation to attend the Workshop being held on May 23rd. I am pleased to inform you that i will be able to attend, so that i may coordinate my activities please send me travel information and an Agenda for the meeting. I have enclosed the Form you requested which finalizes the details of my attendance. I am looking forward to spending sometime with you at the meeting, and i look forward to receiving you're information so i can begin planning my visit to NY. Thank you in advance for all of your fine help.

ACTIVITY 3: USING SPECIAL FEATURES

INSTRUCTIONS: Reformat and edit the text below to make it more visually appealing. As you are working, ask yourself: *In regard to special features and visual effects, how much is too much?*

> Eric Diaz
>
> 14 Southern Square Rd.
>
> White Falls, ID 74512, (505) 555-5555
>
> Objective: Seeking permanent middle-school teaching position
>
> Employment History/Work Experience:
>
> 1995 to Present: Substitute Teacher

Working on an emergency credential for the first two years, and credentialed for the remainder of this period, my reputation for working successfully with middle-school students has had me on regular rotation at several middle schools in the area for more than 8 years: Private: White Falls Private School, contact Lynne Scrupp; Jackson Academy, contact Jed Padwa, Helen Loren; Horn Corner School, contact Bill Orman. Public: White Fall Middle School, contact Olsen Dare; Sunnybrae Middle School, contact Evelyn Hartin; Hale Junior High, contact Steve Schabow; and Timber Middle School, Arleen Fukumoto.

1990 to 1995 Playground Supervisor /Athletic Coach

Oakhurn Elementary, 6542 Elkins Ave, Boise, ID (505) 432-4534

Playground Supervisor: Initially working at Oakburn as part of a grant program to encourage development of afterschool programs in local schools, the number of students who could claim they participated in some part of the program increased to include most of the student body. Athletic Coach: A permanent staff position created as a result of the afterschool success allowed me to implement a program that fused the curriculum ongoing in the classroom with playing games, artwork, singing, learn new physical (sports) activities, and music.

ACTIVITY 4: SPEAKING BUSINESS

INSTRUCTIONS: Throughout this book, you have reviewed aspects of grammar that relate to speech. You have practiced changing some grammar patterns, getting rid of slang and colloquial expressions, and even changing the way you pronounce some words.

Take a few moments to identify the changes you have made in your speech patterns throughout this class. Also include your new goals for speech and language use. You have worked hard and deserve to stop a moment to "pat yourself on the back."

ACTIVITY 5: EDITING AND REVISING, PART 2

INSTRUCTIONS: Turn the following rough draft into a correctly written message.

To Dist. Mgt. team:

We will all be having a meeting on Friday, Mch. 12 @ 2: 00 p.m. in the afternoon in the Guangzhu room. The purpose of the meeting will be to define the scope of our process team, for example there are key concerns that need to be address immediately: market process needs to be defined, controlling the flow of generics during promotions and product need display using the most effective marketing tools. This will be a very inter-active meeting so bring thoughts petaining to the following

The customer hold prcess needs to be improved

Time frame for completion needs to be identified

Communication process: ideas for improving

Get back to me quick if you ca'nt attend this vital meeting.

Rob

ACTIVITY 6: FORMATTING AND PARALLEL STRUCTURE

INSTRUCTIONS: Use formatting tools such as numbering and parallel structure to make the following procedures understandable and easy to follow.

PROCEDURES FOR BREAKING DOWN REPORTS

1. Flip through the report until you find the distribution list for vault cartridges. The cartridges that are on the distribution list are pulled and sent for pick-up. The cartridges should be at the out-put window by 9 a.m. You should also send a listing of the cartridges you are sending.
2. Continue going through the report until you find two copies of the packing list. One copy is sent with the cartridges and the second is faxed to New York. The fax number to be used for faxing the second copy over to New York is (212) 555-5555. The fax cover sheet supplied by the data center should always be used when faxing.
3. Bypass all lists until you find the inventory lists. There are three copies of each list. Sometimes you will find all the lists, often only the inventory list.
4. All of the inventory lists are to be sent to data-base. The rest of the sheets should be left in the file.

ACTIVITY 7: "WRITER'S REFERENCE MANUAL" DRILL

INSTRUCTIONS: Proofread and correct errors in the following exercise. You may want to refer to the section on soundalikes in the "Writer's Reference Manual." Look for errors in word usage, punctuation, and grammar.

Our company decided to select a new sight to hold our annual gala event. Last year their wear several complaints about meeting further from work then most employees would have prefer. Even though the distance effect how people thought about the event, we still had alot of complements about the food and décor.

Its not that people like to complain its just that when several employees get together to discuss an event between themselves, they can focus on the negative more then the positive. However they should of considered that management does it's best too provide a nice celebration, loosing site of this can some times give the wrong impression. So let me ensure you; the affect of next years gala event will not only be alright but will be all together well received. And may be next year, a larger amount of personel can attend if its closer to our company.

ACTIVITY 8: VOCABULARY LIST

A. COMMONLY MISSPELLED WORDS

INSTRUCTIONS: Practice the words below until you can spell them automatically and use them correctly.

1. adieu	(n) farewell, good-bye
2. aggregate	(n) total, entire sum (v) to combine, sum up (adj) collective, combined
3. authoritative	(adj) commanding; imposing
4. benign	(adj) kind, mild, not severe
5. collaborative	(adj) cooperative management or leadership style
6. defense	(n) protection, argument, justification
7. excel	(v) to do extremely well, outshine, stand out
8. expedite	(v) to speed up the progress
9. entrepreneur	(n) innovative, risk-taking person who starts a business
10. interim	(n) an intervening period of time
11. miscellaneous	(adj) made up of many different parts or elements (misc.)
12. mundane	(adj) dull, uninteresting
13. regulator	(n) supervisory body, watchdog, controller
14. optimism	(n) hopefulness, confidence
15. transformation	(n) entire change in form, disposition

B. SIMILAR WORDS

INSTRUCTIONS: Use the words below in sentences until their meaning becomes clear.

appraised/apprised: To *appraise* means "to set value on." To *apprise* means "to inform."

The manager was *apprised* before we left the office.

Our neighbors had their home *appraised.*

complement/compliment: *Complement* comes from *complete* and means "to add to"; to *compliment* means "to flatter."

She *complimented* him on his suit and tie.

Your scarf *complements* your outfit.

sight/site/cite: *Sight* refers to vision or mental perception; *site* refers to location; *cite* refers to naming or quoting a source, as in *recite.*

The young girl's *sight* was impaired because of the accident.

That is an excellent *site* for the seminar.

May we *cite* you when we develop our advertisement?

THE INBOX

COMPOSING

You have just had a successful interview for a job that you truly want. During the interview, you talked with Ms. Jameson about your favorite football team. It was nice to talk about football because you both root for the same team, and that put you at ease. Additionally, you both share a similar view on training: you both believe in a hands-on approach. Using this information and the address information below, compose a personalized interview thank-you note to Ms. Jameson. Remember that the interview thank-you note serves two purposes: it sets you apart from others who don't know business etiquette, and it reminds the interviewer about who you are and the positive qualities that came across during the interview. Use a conservative note card or stationery, and handwrite the thank-you note after you are satisfied with the draft. Turn in both a typed copy and the handwritten copy.

Ms. Jameson's business card:

Ms. Paula Jameson
Director, Human Resources
Springville Bureau of Travel and Tourism
2232 Springville Road
Springville, Illinois 60300

213.455.6578
pjameson@springville.org

REFLECTING

Some businesspeople prefer corresponding by e-mail. If you are interviewing for a job, and your contact makes it clear that he or she prefers e-mail, you should send all correspondence by e-mail, followed by a hard copy in the mail if requested. How would you handle a personalized thank-you note as an e-mail?

Use the thank-you note that you wrote in the Composing exercise to create an e-mail. Send the e-mail thank-you to your instructor. Do you think there is a difference between the handwritten note and the e-mail note? Is one better than the other?

DISCUSSING

1. Individually, write the job requirements for any job you've ever held. If you've never had a job, imagine the requirements for a job that you'd like to have.
2. Create a job advertisement, including salary, requirements, and any other information you deem pertinent.
3. In groups of two, practice interviewing each other for various positions. How do you break the ice? What does your body language say? If you feel you are not qualified for the job, can you still produce a positive interview?
4. After spending some time interviewing, discuss in small groups your successes and failures. What was uncomfortable about the process? What did you do well?

CAREER BUILDING PORTFOLIO

PORTFOLIO DOCUMENT 7

Place a clean, typed copy of your thank-you note in your portfolio.

PORTFOLIO DOCUMENT 8

In Chapter 9 you researched some companies that you are interested in. Choose one of those companies and locate the contact information. Write a letter of request addressed to the contact person. Ask for information on job opportunities and internships and any other information you would like about the company. You will actually send this letter, so you should draft and revise it several times. After your instructor approves your letter, print two copies on white or off-white paper. Use your word processing program to print the address on a mailing label or directly on the envelope to make the envelope professional. Keep one copy of the letter for your portfolio, and mail the other one.

PORTFOLIO DOCUMENT 9

1. Depending on your instructor's directions, create a résumé. Your instructor may ask you to create a paper résumé that can be OCR'd or scanned into a computer as is. (A *scannable* résumé is designed to be scanned at the *receiving* end—it has a unique format based on keywords and is "read" by a company's computer.)
2. Place a clean copy of the résumé in your portfolio.

Creating an online résumé is not the same as creating a paper résumé. If you already have a paper résumé, you can alter it for the Internet. If you don't have a résumé yet, create a basic one for this exercise. Here's how:

1. You can use a template available in a word processing program. Once you open the template, fill in the blank areas with your information. You can also find templates on the Internet. A simple search for "résumé template" will turn up thousands of hits; however, **http://www.collegegrad.com** is a good place to start. Be sure to save the document; for the file name, use your first and last name plus the extension *.txt;* for example, *EmilyBerringer.txt.*
   a. Copy and paste the document into a plain text editor (such as MS Wordpad). Most of the formatting should disappear. Clean up the rest of the formatting, making the document as plain as possible.
   b. Make sure to use a font that is easy to read, like Arial or **Veranda**.
2. You can build a résumé using an online service such as **http://www.monster.com**. Click on the "Build a Résumé" tab, and fill out a form. The site will create a résumé for you after you have answered all the questions. It will be in a plain text format.
3. One other option is to create the document in a word processing program, and then choose "Save as Web Page." Doing this will produce an HTML document, like a Web page. When you attach it to an e-mail message, it will open in the receiver's Web browser.
4. When you e-mail the résumé, make sure to note in the message the form or forms you are sending it in. A good practice is to send it in more than one format so that the receiver has a choice of how to view the document.
5. Scanning a résumé with a facsimile machine or a scanner is much the same as e-mailing the résumé. You will want it to be as plain as possible. Of course, you should avoid HTML when scanning or faxing.

PORTFOLIO DOCUMENT 10

The final piece you create for your portfolio will actually be the first piece in the set of documents. You need to create a summary of your portfolio, explaining each document as in an annotated table of contents.

- You may decide how to label the documents: by name, by number, and so on.
- In the summary, include a brief explanation of each document's purpose along with a statement of what you learned from the project.
- Another option is to create a cover page for each document. The cover page can contain the summary for that document.
- Place the summary in the front of the portfolio, or place the cover pages in front of each appropriate document.
- Your instructor might assign a grade to the summary or to the portfolio as a whole.

KEY TO LEARNING INVENTORY

1. F
2. F
3. T
4. T
5. T
6. T
7. F
8. F
9. F
10. T

CHAPTER 10 ENDNOTES

1. Randall S. Hansen, "Quintessential Careers," **http://www.quintcareers.com/employer_corporate_culture.html**, accessed in April 2006.
2. William Thourlby, *You Are What You Wear,* Forbes/Wittenburg and Brown, New York, 2001.
3. Susan M. Heathfield, "Human Resources, Dress for Work Success: A Business Casual Dress Code," **http://humanresources.about.com/od/workrelationships/a/dress_code.htm**, accessed in June 2006.
4. Ewuuk Lomo-David, "Cellular Phone Use and Erosion of Decorum on Campus: A Need for Etiquette and Civility," Association for Business Communication, Greensboro, North Carolina, April 22, 2005.

Writer's Reference Manual

For further detail on any topic reviewed in this reference manual, please refer to *The Gregg Reference Manual*.

CONTENTS

ABBREVIATIONS

Abbreviations are shortened forms of words or phrases, such as *Mr.* (for the word *Mister*) or *R.S.V.P.* (for *Repondez s'il vous plait*). Writers use conventionally accepted abbreviations to shorten repeated references to the lengthy names or terms the abbreviations represent. For example, in a newspaper article about the North American Free Trade Agreement, using the abbreviation *NAFTA* after the first reference saves time for both the reader and the writer.

Abbreviations are also handy for saving space in reference lists, tables, parentheses, illustrations, and footnotes. Sometimes, a reader might be more familiar with an abbreviation, such as *AT&T,* than with the words the abbreviation stands for: *American Telephone and Telegraph.*

Abbreviations that are pronounced as words, such as *NASA* and *AIDS,* are called **acronyms**. **Initialisms** are abbreviations that are pronounced letter by letter, such as *SAT, FBI,* and *IBM.*

Guidelines for Abbreviations

Most abbreviations relate to a specific audience. If you refer to *COLA* in your document, does your audience know whether you're referring to a cost-of-living adjustment or to the Center for Ocean-Land-Atmosphere Studies? Abbreviations familiar to participants in a particular field may be unclear to everyone outside that field.

Here are a few more tips for using abbreviations:

- Spell out the full name on the first use followed by the abbreviation in parentheses; for example:

  The North American Free Trade Agreement (NAFTA) took effect in 1994.

- Rules vary for using periods in abbreviations. Although one custom is to avoid using periods with abbreviations longer than two letters, both *U.S.A.* and *USA* are correct. (*U.S.* is preferred to *US,* to avoid confusion with the pronoun *us.*) In general, the best practice is to be consistent throughout a document.

- Use abbreviations for academic degrees and for common titles when used with a person's name: *Mr., Mrs., Ms., Dr., Jr., Sr., B.A., B.S., M.A., Ph.D., M.B.A.* Other titles, such as *governor, colonel, professor,* and *reverend,* are spelled out.

- Plurals of abbreviations are formed by adding *s* alone. Do not use an apostrophe when forming the plural of an abbreviation.

  My *CDs* are ruined!

  The *ATMs* are being serviced.

- Do not use the ampersand *(&)* as a replacement for *and.* Use the ampersand only when it is part of an official name of a company, a product, or some other proper noun.

- In ordinary usage, do not italicize abbreviations or acronyms.

- If an abbreviation is pronounced as a word (for example, the acronym *MADD*) rather than as a series of letters (for example, the initialism *PTA*), the acronym does not need an article when used as a noun.

  The letter-writing strategy proved effective *for MADD.*

  The bake sale proved to be a moneymaker *for the PTA.*

- Whether to use the article *a* or *an* before an abbreviation is determined by the way the abbreviation is pronounced and follows the general rules for article usage. (See "Articles.")

- Use abbreviations for terms commonly used with numbers, especially times, dates, amounts, and other units of measure.

  12 lb 6 p.m. Vol. 2, No. 8

- Use abbreviations for common Latin terms in footnotes, bibliographies, or parenthetical comments. Both *e.g.* and *i.e.* should be followed by a comma (*i.e.,* as in this note). The exceptions to this rule are *a.m.* and *p.m.*, which are used in all contexts.

a.m.	ante meridian
c.f.	compare
e.g.	for example
etc.	et cetera
i.e.	that is

  Restrict your use of Latin abbreviations to academic work; avoid using even the common abbreviation *etc.* in business correspondence.

- Use the U.S. Postal Service format (two letters, no periods) when you must abbreviate state names. In most documents, and especially if your audience might include international readers, spell out the state name.

The best practice is to use abbreviations sparingly. In other words, if your copy reads like alphabet soup, consider rewriting: when in doubt, *spell it out!*

ADDRESSES (MAILING)

You will need to apply rules for addresses in these three instances: (1) when writing an address in a sentence, (2) when writing an inside address for correspondence, and (3) when addressing the outside of an envelope.

Addresses in Text

When writing out mailing addresses in sentences, use the following style, where a comma follows the street address, the city, and the ZIP Code—but not the state:

> Please fill out the enclosed packet and return to Farmer's Focus Testing, 818 Woodsbury Lane, Chicago, IL 60513, before June 13, 2006.

When using an address block, make sure you put a comma between the city and state:

> Farmer's Focus Testing
>
> 818 Woodsbury Lane
>
> Chicago, IL 60513

Inside Addresses

Whether a letter is going to an individual home or to an organization, start the inside address at the left margin on the fourth line below the date or below a notation that falls between the date and the inside address.

Use single spacing and begin each line at the left margin. Capitalize the first letter of every word in an address except prepositions, conjunctions, and articles under four letters in length.

Letters to Individuals The inside address in a letter to a client's home should include:

First line: the name of the individual you are writing to.

Second line: the street address, post office box number (P.O. Box), or rural route number (RR). If the person lives in an apartment, provide the apartment number after the address or on the line above the address.

Third line: the city, state and ZIP Code.

Mrs. Wanda Helligson
42 Arcane Street, Unit 12
Latham, ID 87654

Ms. Cameron Wells
Apartment 42
21300 Capistrano Avenue
Temecula, CA 99615

- In a letter to two people at the same address, list each name on a separate line:

Mr. Ryan Morse
Mr. Jackson Keane
LTD Rentals
65 Universal Way
Seattle, WA 4423

Letters to Businesses The inside address in a letter to an organization or business should include:

First line *(whenever possible):* the name of a specific person within the business or organization.

Second line: the contact person's job title. If you do not know the individual's name for the first line, begin with the job title or department for the person you wish to contact.

Third line: the name of the company or organization.

Fourth line: the street address, post office box number (P.O. Box), or rural route number (RR).

Fifth line: the city, state, and ZIP Code.

Mr. Ilia Balter
Marketing Representative
Farmer's Focus Testing
818 Woodsbury Lane
Chicago, IL 60513

- If you do not have a name or an office suite, put the name of the business on the first line. Then put the street address or post office box number on the second line and the city, state, and ZIP Code on the third. If the address includes a suite number, a floor number, or a room number, include that information at the end of the street address. If it does not fit on that line, put that information on the line above the street address.

OfficeStock Data Systems
Suite 321
600 Avenue de Los Colimas
Sedona, NM 87213

Fleetly Freight Services
543 Charles Arden Memorial Drive
Arden, SD 71212

- In a letter to two people at the same address, list each name on a separate line; show a business title with each name only if the titles can fit on the same lines as the names.

Addresses on Envelopes

The two styles commonly used for addressing envelopes are the *traditional style* and the *all-cap style*. The traditional style is still favored by individuals and businesses, even though the USPS has endorsed the all-caps style as the only one that should be used.

Traditional Style The traditional style for addressing envelopes uses capital and lowercase letters as well as punctuation. This style follows the formatting used for an inside address. If an attention line is used within the letter itself, it should appear as the first line of the address on the envelope.

The return address should be single-spaced and aligned at the top left of the envelope (about ½ inch from the top and side edges). The return address should include:

First line: the name of the sender.

Second line: the name of the organization (if the sender is writing as a representative of a company or organization).

Third line: a street address or post office box number. (If the return address includes an apartment number that is too long to fit on the same line as the street address, put the apartment number on the line above the street address.)

Fourth line: the city, state, and ZIP Code.

If a note such as *Personal*, *Please Forward,* or *Hold for* is used, type it three lines below the return address. Align the notation at the left with the return address. Begin each main word with a capital letter and use boldface or underlining.

All-Cap Style The United States Postal Service (USPS) uses machines to process mail. When an address cannot be "read" mechanically, the letter has to be manually processed, which can slow delivery times. Although the sorting machines do process mail that is addressed in the traditional style (upper- and lowercase letters), the USPS encourages customers to print envelope addresses in all-capital letters to increase the efficiency of the system.

Here are some examples of all-cap style:

Return Address

WALTER CHARON

25678 MARTINDALE AVE

SYCAMORE, PA 32123

Destination Address

HELEN SHABAZZ

432 SAN ANSELMO DRIVE

NEVADA CITY, CA 90425

USPS Guidelines The USPS offers the additional advice listed below. Senders of bulk mail are required to follow these guidelines. For individual senders of mail, the guidelines are suggestions. The USPS promises to do its best to deliver any piece of mail that a client drops into its system.

- Type or machine-print all address information. Make sure print is clear and sharp.
- Ensure address characters do not touch or overlap.
- Never place an attention line, telephone number, or other entries after the ZIP Code line. Place the attention line at the top of the address.
- Make sure the recipient's street address appears on the line immediately above the city, state, and ZIP Code line.

- Include floor, suite, and apartment numbers whenever possible. Place them on the same line as the street address.
- Place the city, state, and ZIP Code in that order on the last line. *This must be the last line.*
- Do not abbreviate international addresses. Use the complete spelling of a foreign city, province, or country. Place the name of the country on the last line and use all-capital letters.
- When using window envelopes, the address must be visible through the window. Make sure the address insert fits the envelope to prevent shifting. Make sure the complete address is always visible, even if the insert moves. Try to keep ¼ inch clearance between the address and the window edge.
- When addressing envelopes larger than regular letter-size envelopes, always place the address lengthwise in the center of the envelope.
- Never tape a letter envelope on the outside of a flat or package.
- *Common errors to avoid:* Address lines out of order, script typeface or handwriting, address not visible through window, address slanted, left margin not flush, other information below address line, characters touching, and not enough contrast.

AFFIXES (PREFIXES AND SUFFIXES)

An English word can be made up of three parts: the *root,* a *prefix,* and a *suffix.* The **root** is the part of the word that contains the basic meaning (definition) of the word. A **prefix** is a word element that is placed in front of a root. A prefix can change the word's meaning or make a new word. Hundreds of prefixes can be applied to thousands of words. The opposite of a prefix is a **suffix.** A suffix is a word element that is placed after the root. The suffix changes the word's meaning as well as its function. Prefixes and suffixes are called **affixes** because they attach or *affix* to a root.

Prefixes

Here are some common prefixes:

Prefix	Meaning	Example
bi-	two	To an extent, we are all *bi*dialectal.
de-	not	The train *de*railed in Montgomery.
dis-	not	The plans are in *dis*array.
im-	not	That road is *im*passable.
mis-	not	I *mis*placed the proposal copy.
pre-	before	The *pre*face of a book can set the stage.
re-	again	The team will *re*engineer the concept.
un-	not	The project's goals are *un*realistic

Adding Prefixes to Words The trend in business writing is away from using hyphens with prefixes. However, here are a few guidelines to follow:

- For prefixes, do not use a hyphen when combining a prefix with a word starting with a consonant (*melodrama*, for example).
- Use a hyphen to join a prefix to a capitalized word *(anti-Reagan)* or to join doubled prefixes *(sub-subrental).*

Suffixes

Here are a few common suffixes:

Suffix	Meaning	Example
-able	able to	The materials were very dur*able*.
-er	doer of	Mr. Jonas is an excellent teach*er*.
	more	The report is long*er* than we expected.
-ful	full of	The office is peace*ful* in the mornings.
-ly or *-y*	like	The sales assistant was very friend*ly*.
-ment	state of	I trust the contractor's judg*ment*.
-ness	state of being	Contrari*ness* runs in the family.
-ous	full of	The whole explanation is ridicul*ous*.

Adding Suffixes to Words As with prefixes, hyphens are generally not used with suffixes.

Spelling rules for adding suffixes are complicated for the simple reason that none of the rules are absolute—there are many exceptions. See "Spelling Rules" for more information. If you are truly in doubt about the spelling of a word, consult a dictionary: when in doubt, *check it out!*

ARTICLES

The words *a, an,* and *the* are articles (a type of adjective). English has two types of articles: definite *(the)* and indefinite *(a, an). A* and *an* are indefinite articles because they refer to something in a less specific manner. *The* is a definite article because it usually precedes a specific noun. Articles are also part of a group of words called *determiners* (see "Determiners") because they are usually followed by a noun and help to determine the qualities of that noun.

Indefinite (*a* or *an*)	Definite *(the)*
Singular	
a desk (any desk)	*the* desk (that specific desk)
an envelope (any envelope)	*the* envelope (that specific envelope)

You will find many situations where more than one option is correct. If English is your second language, you may find using articles challenging at times. In those instances, ask a friend to help you decide what sounds right.

Incorrect:	Waxed hallway can be slippery.
Correct:	Waxed hallways can be slippery.
	A waxed hallway can be slippery.
	The waxed hallways can be slippery.

Indefinite Articles: *A* and *An*

A and *an* signal that the noun modified is indefinite, referring to *any* member of a group. Use these indefinite articles with singular nouns when the noun is general; the word *some* is the corresponding indefinite-quantity word for plural general nouns.

Singular	Plural
a desk	*some* desks
an envelope	*some* envelopes

Use *a* or *an* depending on the initial sound of the word that follows it (which is most often a noun, but can also be an adjective). Here are some guidelines:

- If the initial sound of the word is a consonant sound (or long *u* sound), use the article *a:*

  a Xerox machine

  a red convertible

  a utility company (*utility* begins with a consonant *y* sound)

  a once-in-a-lifetime offer (*once* begins with a consonant *w* sound)

- If the initial sound of the word following the indefinite article begins with a vowel sound, use *an:*

  an escalator ride

  an exciting presentation

  an hour-long line (*hour* begins with a vowel *o* sound; the *h* is silent)

Definite Article: *The*

The definite article is used before singular and plural nouns when the noun is particular or specific. *The* signals that the noun is definite: it refers to a *particular* member of a group.

The plant in *the* front lobby is leaking water.

Here are a few rules for using *the*:

- Use *the* with specific nouns, especially when the noun represents something that is one of a kind:

  the Pentagon

  The Earth circles *the* Sun.

- Use *the* when the noun represents something in the abstract:

  The European Union has encouraged *the* use of public transit as opposed to *the* use of private transportation.

  the law of the land

  the upcoming elections

- Use *the* with certain kinds of proper nouns:

  Pluralized names (geographic areas, families, teams): the Hawaiian Islands, the Smiths, the New York Jets.

  Public institutions, facilities, or groups: the Lincoln Memorial, the Hyatt Hotel.

  Newspapers: the *Los Angeles Herald,* the *Times.*

  Nouns followed by a prepositional phrase beginning with *of:* the chairman of the board, the supervisor of our team.

  Names of rivers, oceans, and seas: the Amazon, the Atlantic.

  Points on the globe: the South Pole, the Equator.

  Geographic areas: the South Pacific, the East.

  Deserts, forests, gulfs, and peninsulas: the Gobi Desert, the Gulf of Mexico, the Inyo Forest, the Florida Peninsula.

- Do *not* use *the* before:

  Names of countries (*except* the United States, the Netherlands).

  Names of cities, towns, or states: Tokyo, Manitoba, Marseille.

  Names of streets: Roosevelt Boulevard, First Street.

  Names of lakes and bays: Lake Wobegon (*except* a group of lakes such as the Great Lakes).

  Names of mountains: Mount McKinley, Mount Baldy (*except* ranges of mountains such as the Andes or the Rockies or unusual names such as the Matterhorn).

  Names of continents: Africa, Australia.

  Names of islands: Molokai, Balboa, Key West (*except* island chains such as the Aleutians, the Hebrides, or the Canary Islands).

Choosing the Correct Article

- *First and subsequent references:* When we first refer to something in written text, we often use *a* or *an* to modify it. Use *a* or *an* to introduce a noun when it is mentioned for the first time in a piece of writing. Use *the* each time you mention that same noun again. For example:

  > *A* commencement ceremony at the university would not normally have attracted so much attention. However, when it was rumored the Secretary of State would be giving the commencement address, interest in *the* ceremony intensified.

- *Generic reference:* Use any of the three articles to refer to something in a general way, or accomplish the same thing by omitting the article altogether.

  A cat makes a great companion.

  An Abyssinian is sometimes a rather skittish feline.

  The Burmese cat can be a wonderful companion for a small dog.

  Oriental cats tend to have shorter hair than other breeds.

- *Reference without article:* **Zero article** means that either no article would be appropriate with the kind of noun referred to or no article is necessary with that kind of noun. The names of languages, for example, do not use an article. Neither do the names of sports (soccer, football) or the names of academic subjects (mathematics, science).

CHARTS

Charts add visual interest to a report or PowerPoint presentation and underscore important points. You can use any of several different kinds of charts to illustrate or emphasize key points in your business writing. Below is a brief summary of the most commonly used charts: bar charts, pie charts, flowcharts, and organization charts. (For graphs, see "Line Graphs.")

Bar Charts

A **bar chart** enables you to compare and contrast two, three, or more different items. If you are showing the relationships over a period of time, you can cluster several different groups of items.

FIGURE RM.1 Bar Charts

Bar Chart Tips: *Bar charts may be horizontal or vertical.* ***(a)*** *Horizontal bar charts provide more room for labels.* ***(b)*** *Vertical bar charts are preferred for portraying information over time.* ***(c)*** *In a* grouped, *or* clustered, *bar chart, two or more bars are grouped side by side. The bars may be joined together or separated by a narrow space; avoid overlapping bars because they can distort the comparison.* ***(d)*** *Practice caution with segmented charts: visual comparisons are more difficult between the second, third, and ensuing segments because they do not align at common baselines.* For example, judging by the data presented in chart (d), have sales of the Mini Mojo Motorbike increased or decreased since 2001?

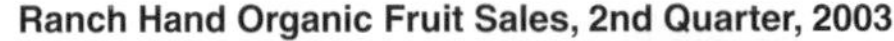

Ranch Hand Organic Fruit Sales, 2nd Quarter, 2003

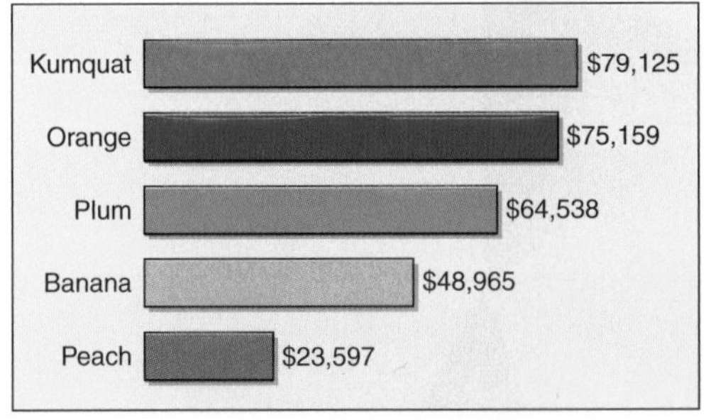

(a) Horizontal

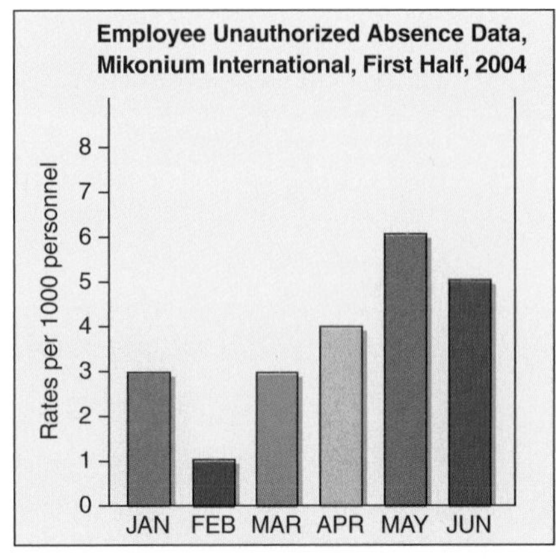

(b) Vertical

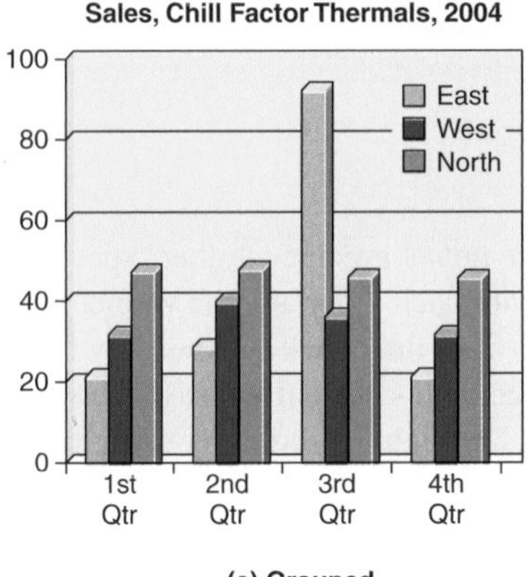

(c) Grouped

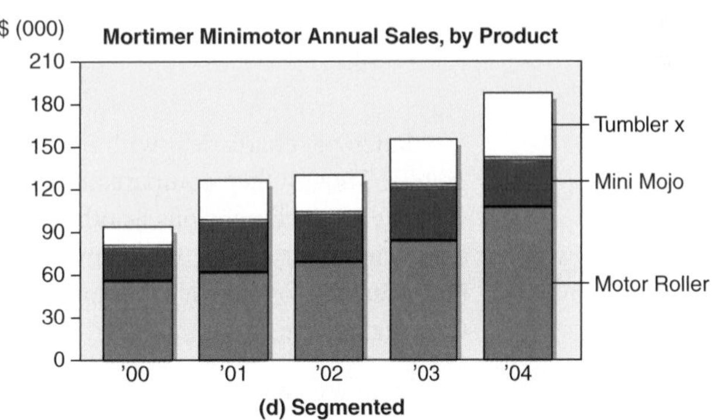

(d) Segmented

With a bar chart, you can display relationships horizontally or vertically. (See Figure RM.1.) Use a different color for each category, and use it consistently throughout your document. If you do not have a color printer, shades of gray or different patterns can achieve a similar purpose. Here are some other tips:

- Limit the number of bars to six.
- Make sure bar widths and the space between them are equal.
- Arrange bars in a logical order (by length, by age, by date) to make comparisons easier.
- Place categories such as "other" or "miscellaneous" at the end of the series of bars.

Pie Charts

Use **pie charts** when the various components discussed add up to 100 percent. A pie chart shows the relationship of one item to another and simultaneously shows how all parts relate to the whole. (See Figure RM.2.)

FIGURE RM.2 Pie Chart

Slicing It Up: *Although pie charts are useful for conveying simple, broad messages, bar charts display complex data more effectively. For viewers to make clear and specific visual distinctions, the pie segments need to differ by more than 5 percent. For example,* in this pie chart, if the percentages in the labels were removed, would you be able to tell whether Shogun or Lily Rose was the second-best-selling rice on the market?

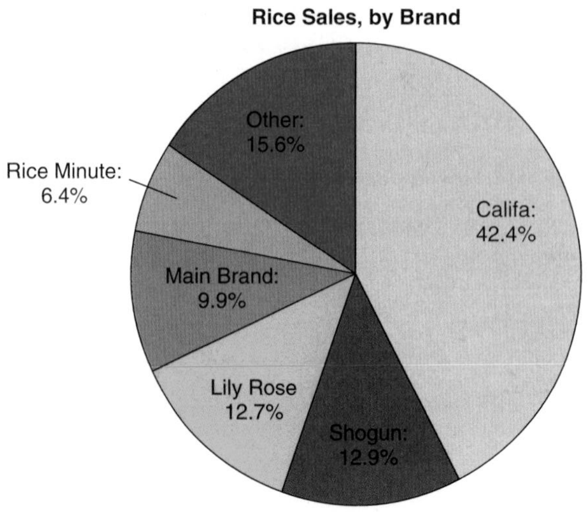

Since pie charts deal with percentages, they are not as precise as other types of charts or graphs. Though they compare and contrast items with each other and the whole, they do not show as many dimensions as other types of graphs. This drawback is especially true of three-dimensional pie charts, which most authorities agree tend to visually distort the information they present. To make a pie chart more interesting, highlight a section by dragging it out. Once again, use color.

Here are some guidelines for creating pie charts:

- Limit the number of categories to six; if you have more than six, try to combine them.
- Label categories directly and add percentages. Avoid using a key, if possible.
- If you are emphasizing a point, place the most important section at the 12 o'clock position.

Flowcharts and Organization Charts

Flowcharts and organization charts are graphic devices with more limited applications than bar charts, pie charts, and tables. A flowchart (see Figure RM.3) depicts a process, usually using shapes or boxes to represent separate steps in the process; an organization chart, on the other hand, displays the structure of an organization or company in terms of hierarchy, supervision, and employee rank (see Figure RM.4).

Both types of charts generally feature boxes connected by lines or arrows, and both, in a sense, provide step-by-step information; the flowchart depicts the flow of a process, while the organization chart depicts the flow of authority.

When creating a flowchart, keep the display simple by focusing on the general process instead of every detail. This will help you limit the number of steps in the flowchart; too many boxes, shapes, or steps in the process can undermine the effectiveness of the display. Your chart should flow from top to bottom, or from left to right. Clearly label all shapes, and for further clarification, create a legend to ease understanding.

FIGURE RM.3 Flowchart

Graphic representations such as this flowchart can make a very complex process seem simple. Flowcharts depict relationships between processes and people rather than numbers. The organization chart in Figure RM.4 is another type of flowchart.

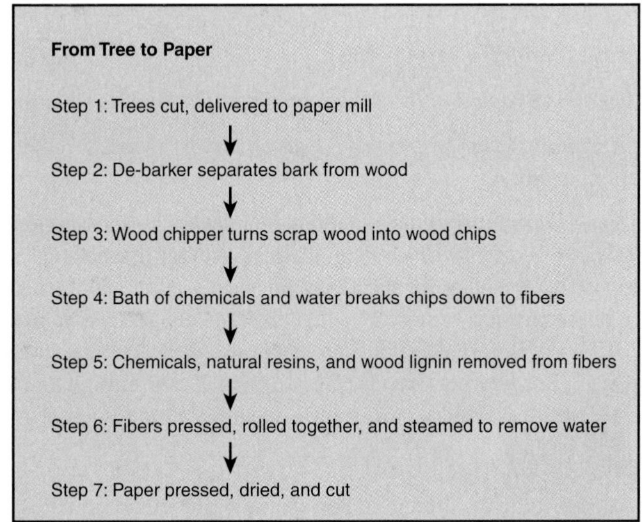

FIGURE RM.4 Organization Chart

An organization chart is a flowchart that maps the structure of a company, organization, or event. The normal layout places the highest-ranked person or position at the top level and subordinate positions in the levels underneath. Why do you think it is good practice to use the same-size boxes at each level of an organization chart?

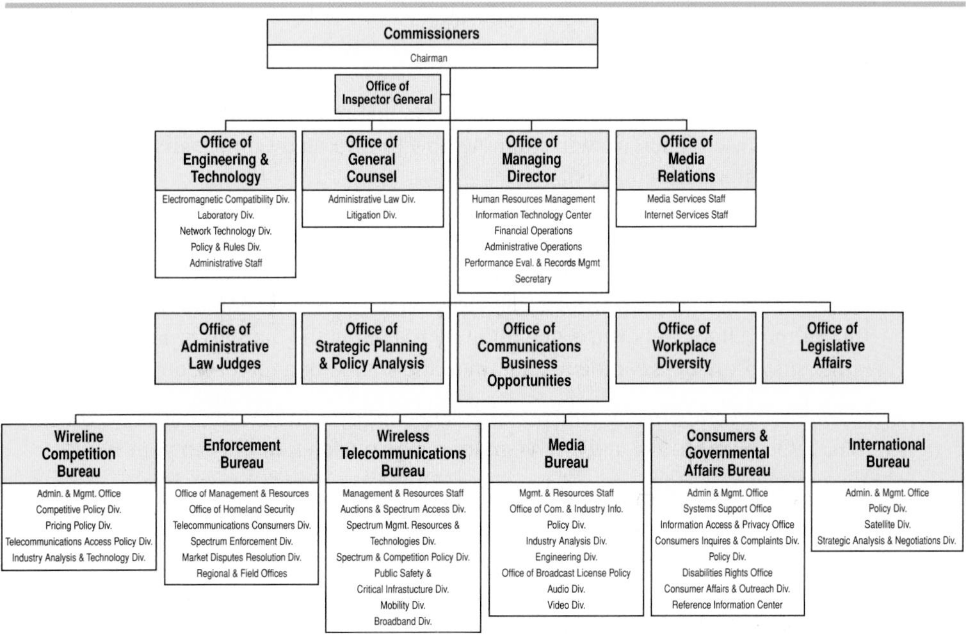

An organization chart can be an effective tool for clarifying job responsibilities and determining reporting relationships within a company or organization. When creating an organization chart, use rectangles to represent top-level positions and circular designs to depict mid- and low-level positions. Take special care when assigning varied shapes to maintain consistency and avoid misclassifying a job position.

CITING RESEARCH

There are four common systems for citation in business, social sciences, and humanities. They are outlined in the following:

- *The Gregg Reference Manual* (GRM)
- *The Chicago Manual of Style* (CMS)
- The *Publication Manual of the American Psychological Association* (APA)
- The *MLA Handbook for Writers of Research Papers* (Modern Language Association, or MLA)

The Gregg Reference Manual presents citation guidelines for business writing applications. *The Chicago Manual of Style* offers two sets of guidelines: one for fine arts and humanities (academic) applications, and the other for social and physical science applications. If you go on to study in medicine or the physical sciences, you are likely to cite references in the Council of Biology Editors (CBE) style. Before you start your citations, check to make sure you are using the correct referencing style. (See Internet Exercise 2.1, on page 35, for information about the Web sites of the books listed above as well as other online documentation resources.)

What to Credit

Not all information needs to be documented. For example, information that is considered common knowledge (something generally known to everyone) or facts available from a wide variety of sources need not be credited. According to the *New St. Martin's Handbook,* the following information needs to be documented:

1. Direct quotations and paraphrases.
2. Facts that are not widely known or assertions that are arguable.
3. Judgments, opinions, and claims of others.
4. Statistics, charts, tables, and graphs from any source.
5. Help provided by friends, instructors, or others.

Let's first take a look at the two most common elements that require formal citations: direct quotations and paraphrases. Then we will examine how to give credit informally and how to assign legal claim to information in business.

Formal Credit

- *Direct quotation*: A **direct quote**—the use of someone else's exact words—needs to be set off from your own words. For short quotes, use quotation marks; for quotes of four or more lines, set off the quotation by indenting the margins at least ½ inch on either side. Provide a complete citation to the source of a direct quote.
- *Paraphrase*: Paraphrasing is expressing someone else's ideas in your own words. When you **paraphrase** and cite your source, you add credibility to your work.

What paraphrasing is not: making a few changes in word order, leaving out a word or two, or substituting similar words. True paraphrasing occurs when you read material, digest it, and then write about the concepts in your own words. However, the idea still belongs to the original author and needs to be credited. Paraphrasing incorrectly can be considered a form of "cut and paste" plagiarism.

Informal Credit In business, when you are conveying another person's ideas, give credit in an informal way by mentioning that person's name. Generally, it's the idea and action you take that counts, not the "who said what, where, and when." However, make it your practice to attach names to ideas: if you credit others for their ideas, you will gain trust and esteem among your colleagues.

Trademarks, Patents, Copyrights, and Incorporation Individuals and businesses can register names, ideas, designs, logos, slogans, and complete works with the federal government to obtain trademarks, patents, or copyrights. They can file with state governments for incorporation.

As you can see, when a business does keep track of ownership, it does so in a legal way. This type of branding protects ownership of information deemed integral to doing business. Not all information can be trademarked or patented. At times, a business ensures legal control of a name by incorporating under that name.

A Working Bibliography

Though each system of documentation has slight variations from the others, they all contain similar information. To save yourself time and frustration, compile a **working bibliography** (use note cards, a small notebook, or a special file on your computer) as you collect your research. Here is the kind of information you will collect regardless of the style you use:

For Books

Author

Title

Publisher and location

Year of publication

Page number

For Periodicals

Author

Title of article

Title of journal

Date of publication (or volume and issue numbers)

Page number

For Web Sites

Author (if known).

Title of document.

Date the information was posted on the Web site. (If available, this is sometimes found at the bottom of the home page.)

The uniform resource locator (URL) network address, including any path and file names. (Enclose the URL in angle brackets to avoid confusion for the general reader. However, brackets are unnecessary and may be omitted when your readers are familiar with URLs.)

Date on which you accessed the information.

If the information was previously published in print, the date of that publication.

Electronic sources are relatively new in the world of communication; as a result, the standards for documenting them are not yet fixed and are sometimes confusing. This situation is complicated because electronic sources are ever changing; if you do not collect exact identifying information as you access each source, you may never find it again. To save yourself time and energy, print out a hard copy or download the accessed information.

Some Common Elements

All citation systems require that sources be cited in the text where the material appears and be fully referenced elsewhere as footnotes, endnotes, or a bibliographic list. Both references together provide the reader with complete information through cross-referencing. Here is a summary of the terminology used by major reference systems:

The Gregg Reference Manual (GRM)	Footnotes, endnotes, textnotes, bibliography
The Chicago Manual of Style (CMS)	Footnotes, endnotes, bibliography

Modern Language Association (MLA)	In-text citations (author and page number enclosed in parentheses), works-cited list, works-consulted list
American Psychological Association (APA)	In-text citations, references

Whether you display source information as footnotes (at the bottom of the page) or as endnotes (at the end of each chapter or the end of the work), place a raised number (superscript) at the end of the sentence in which the cited material occurs.

For all citation methods, you may cite one book several times in your manuscript (showing that you are paraphrasing, quoting, or drawing ideas from its content in several places). However, you need to include the complete source note (author, title, publisher, and so on) only one time in your bibliography, works-cited, or reference list. (See "Textnotes" for more information.)

In a bibliography or reference list, you can list sources that you do not actually cite in your work. However, if you are using the MLA system and you consult important sources that you do not actually cite, add a *works-consulted* page to your references. Only include significant references to your list if you did not cite them. Figure RM.5 displays an example of a work-cited page; Table RM.1 (on page 359) provides examples of styles for citing various sources in in-text citations using different citation systems; and Table RM.2 (on page 360) provides examples for citing sources in end-of-document reference lists using each of the major citation systems.

FIGURE RM.5 Works-Cited List

Source Citations: *A works-cited list is the MLA format for documenting the sources you refer to in your project or research paper. It can include books, magazine articles, journal articles, media sources, and electronic sources. Entries should be arranged alphabetically by the author's last name; numbering is not necessary.*

WORKS CITED

Colvin, Geoffrey. "Stop Blaming Bangalore for Our Jobs Problem." *Fortune* 19 Apr. 2004: 68.

Cooper, James C. "The Price of Efficiency." *BusinessWeek* 22 Mar. 2004: 38–42.

Dobbs, Lou. "The Jobless Recovery." *Money* Apr. 2004: 45–46.

Dolan, Kerry A., and Robyn Meredith. "The Outsourcing Debate: A Tale of Two Cities." *Forbes* 12 Apr. 2004: 94–102.

Gottheil, Fred M. *Principles of Economics.* Australia: South-Western, 2002.

Hagel III, John. "Offshoring Goes on the Offensive." *McKinsey Quarterly* 2 (2004): 82–92. *Business Source Elite.* EBSCOhost. 11 May 2004 <http://web1.epnet.com>.

Kleiman, Carol. "Outsourcing: A Matter of Many Sides." *Chicago Tribune* 11 Mar. 2004. 13 Apr. 2004 <http://infoweb.newsbank.com>.

Mintz, Steven. "The Ethical Dilemmas of Outsourcing." *CPA Journal* 74.3 (2004): 6–9. 13 Apr. 2004 <http://www.nysscpa.org/cpajournal/2004/304/ perspectives/nv1.htm>.

Nussbaum, Bruce. "Where Are the Jobs?" *BusinessWeek* 22 Mar. 2004: 36–37.

Rosencrance, Linda. "Offshore Moves Can Bring Benefits, but Not Without Pain." *Computerworld* 19 Apr. 2004. 11 May 2004 <http://www.computerworld.com/printthis/2004/0,4814,92291,00.html>.

Sowell, Thomas. "Outsourcing." 16 Mar. 2004. *Townhall.com* 6 Apr. 2004 <http://www.townhall.com/columnists/thomassowell/ts20040316.shtml>.

Source: Courtesy of Lynita Perry, DeVry University.

TABLE RM.1 | Styles for In-Text Citations

	GRM (Business Style)	CMS (Scientific Style)	APA	MLA
Single author—not named in text	A closer examination of the increase in worker's productivity at the company reveals the reason for the change.[1]	A closer examination of the increase in worker's productivity at the company reveals the reason for the change (Hennessey 2004, 14).	A closer examination of the increase in worker's productivity at the company reveals the reason for the change (Hennesey, 2004).	A closer examination of the increase in worker's productivity at the company reveals the reason for the change (Hennesey 14).
Single author—identified in text	Carrera argues against strict enforcement of company Internet use policy.[2]	Carrera (2003, 45–96) argues against strict enforcement of company Internet use policy.	Carrera (2003) argues against strict enforcement of company Internet use policy.[2]	Carrera argues against strict enforcement of company Internet use policy (45-96).
More than one author—not named in text	To apply these concepts to business communications, emphasis has fallen on the role of context in business introductions, disagreements, and information processing.[3]	To apply these concepts to business communications, emphasis has fallen on the role of context in business introductions, disagreements, and information processing (Lambert, Elashmawi, and Zabron 2000, 87).	To apply these concepts in business communications, emphasis has fallen on the role of context in business introductions, disagreements, and information processing (Lambert, Elashmawi, & Zabron, 2000).	To apply these concepts to business communications, emphasis has fallen on the role of context in business introductions, disagreements, and information processing. (Lambert, Elashmawi, and Zabron 87).
Multiple sources	Multiple studies conducted by industry analysts have consistently supported the need for tougher standards.[4]	Studies (Gordon et al. 1998, 53) conducted by industry analysts have consistently supported the need for tougher standards.	Studies (Gordon & Knight, 1998; Ishan, 2000; Lornin, 2002) conducted by industry analysts have consistently supported the need for tougher standards.	Studies (Gordon & Knight 53, Ishan 20, Lornin) conducted by industry analysts have consistently supported the need for tougher standards.
More than one author—named in text	According to Giles and Fleming,[5] this is the perfect moment to establish a connection with the audience.	According to Giles and Fleming (2001, 72), this is the perfect moment to establish a connection with the audience.	According to Giles and Fleming (2001, p. 72), this is the perfect moment to establish a connection with the audience.	According to Giles and Fleming, this is the perfect moment to establish a connection with the audience (72).
Unidentified author	Employers view the Flex Time program as a viable method for boosting worker morale.[6]	Employers view the Flex Time program as a viable method for boosting worker morale. ("Flexing Your Horizons," 2004, 28)	Employers view the Flex Time program as a viable method for boosting worker morale ("Flexing Your Horizons," 2004).	Employers view the Flex Time program as a viable method for boosting worker morale ("Flexing" 28).
Direct quotation	Dr. Ralph Tyler found that to be true in the field of education; he stated, "It takes about 20 years . . . to apply in an average classroom what is discovered through research."[7]	Dr. Ralph Tyler found that to be true in the field of education; he stated, "It takes about 20 years . . . to apply in an average classroom what is discovered through research" (1964, 116).	Dr. Ralph Tyler found that to be true in the field of education; he stated (1964), "It takes about 20 years . . . to apply in an average classroom what is discovered through research" (p. 116).	Dr. Ralph Tyler found that to be true in the field of education; he stated, "It takes about 20 years . . . to apply in an average classroom what is discovered through research" (116).

Source: GRM—William A. Sabin, *The Gregg Reference Manual,* 9th ed., Glencoe/McGraw-Hill, Westerville, OH, 2001; CMS—*The Chicago Manual of Style,* 14th rev. ed., University of Chicago Press, Chicago, 1993; APA—*Publication Manual of the American Psychological Association,* 5th ed., American Psychological Association, Washington, DC, 2001; MLA—Joseph Gibaldi, *MLA Handbook for Writers of Research Papers,* 6th ed., Modern Language Association of America, New York, 2003.

TABLE RM.2 | Styles for End-of-Document References

	Bibliography (GRM)	Bibliography (CMS)	References List (APA)	Works-Cited List (MLA)
Annual report	"Annual Report 2002," AT&T Wireless Services, Redmond, 2004.	AT&T Wireless, *Annual Report 2002,* Redmond: AT&T Wireless Services, Inc., 2004.	AT&T Wireless. (2004). *Annual report 2002.* Redmond: AT&T Wireless Services, Inc.	AT&T Wireless, *Annual Report 2002,* Redmond: AT&T Wireless Services, Inc., 2004.
Book—single author	Csikszentmihalyi, Mihaly, *The Evolving Self: A Psychology for the Third Millennium,* HarperCollins Publishers, New York, 1993.	Csikszentmihalyi, Mihaly. *The Evolving Self, A Psychology for the Third Millennium.* New York: HarperCollins Publishers, Inc., 1993.	Csikszentmihalyi, M. (1993). *The evolving self, a psychology for the third millennium.* New York: HarperCollins Publishers, Inc.	Csikszentmihalyi, Mihaly. *The Evolving Self, A Psychology for the Third Millennium.* New York: HarperCollins Publishers, Inc., 1993.
Book—two authors	Howard, V. A., and J. H. Barton, *Thinking on Paper,* William Morrow and Company, Inc., New York, 1986.	Howard, V. A. and J. H. Barton. *Thinking on Paper.* New York: William Morrow and Company, Inc., 1986.	Howard, V. A. and Barton, J. H. (1986) Barton. *Thinking on paper.* New York: William Morrow and Company, Inc.	Howard, V. A. and J. H. Barton. *Thinking on Paper.* New York: William Morrow and Company, Inc., 1986.
Book—three or more authors	Gefvert, Constance, et al., *Keys to American English,* Harcourt Brace Jovanovich, Inc., New York, 1975.	Gefvert, C., R. Raspa, and A. Richards. *Keys to American English,* New York: Harcourt Brace Jovanovich, Inc., 1975.	Gefvert, C., Raspa, R., & Richards A. (1975). *Keys to american english.* New York: Harcourt Brace Jovanovich, Inc.	Gefvert, Constance, Richard Raspa, and Amy Richards. *Keys to American English.* New York: Harcourt Brace Jovanovich, Inc., 1975.
Book—organization as author and publisher	*Evaluation as Feedback and Guide,* Association for Supervision and Curriculum Development, NEA, Washington, D.C., 1967.	Association for Supervision and Curriculum Development, NEA. 1967. *Evaluation as Feedback and Guide.* Washington, D.C.:,1967.	*Evaluation as feedback and guide.* (1967). Washington, D.C.: Association for Supervision and Curriculum Development, NEA.	Association for Supervision and Curriculum Development, NEA., *Evaluation as Feedback and Guide,* Washington, D.C.: Association for Supervision and Curriculum Development, NEA, 1967.
Journal article	Belder, Craig, "Global Discourse: Finding the Rosetta Stone," *World Monthly,* Vol. 8, April 2004, pp. 45–73.	Belder, Craig. 2004. Global discourse: Finding the Rosetta Stone, *World Monthly,* 8: 45–73.	Belder, C. (2004). Global discourse: finding the Rosetta Stone. *World Monthly, 8,* 45–73.	Belder, Craig. "Global Discourse: Finding the Rosetta Stone." *World Monthly* 13 Apr. 2004: 45–73.
Magazine article	M'Salan, Bernadette, "Underneath the Bottom Line," *Fiscal Sense,* February 8, 2001, pp. 78–86.	M'Salan, Bernadette. 2001. Underneath the bottom line, *Fiscal Sense* 8: 78–86.	M'Salan, B. (2001, February 8). Underneath the bottom line. *Fiscal Sense, 24,* 78–86.	M'Salan, Bernadette. "Underneath the Bottom Line." *Fiscal Sense,* 24, Feb. 2001: 78–86.
Newspaper article—unsigned	"Business Finding Ways to Reach New Customers," *Sun Daily,* November 3, 2004, p. C12, col. 4.	Do not include in Bibliography. Citation is made in-text: "An article titled 'Business Finding Ways to Reach New Customers' in the *Sun Daily,* 3 November 2004 describes the current . . . "	Business finding ways to reach new customers. (2004, November 14). *Sun Daily,* p. C12.	"Business Finding Ways to Reach New Customers." *Sun Daily.* 3 Nov. 2004: C12.
Reference work article	"Global Competition," *Workplace Language Companion,* 5th ed., 2004.	Do not include in Bibliography. Citation is made in-text: "The fifth edition of the *Workplace Language Companion* describes global competition as . . .	Global competition. (2004). In *The workplace language companion* (pp. 234–236). New York, NY: Hernan.	"Global competition," *Workplace Language Companion,* 5th ed. New York: Hernan Press, 2004.

TABLE RM.2 | Styles for End-of-Document References (Continued)

	Bibliography (GRM)	Bibliography (CMS)	References List (APA)	Works-Cited List (MLA)
Government document	National Institute for Occupational Safety and Health, *Preventing Lead Poisoning in Construction Workers,* DHHS Publication 91-116A, U.S. Government Printing Office, Washington, D.C., 1992.	National Institute for Occupational Safety and Health. 1992. *Preventing lead poisoning in construction workers.* Washington, DC: U.S. Government Printing Office, Washington. DHHS Publication No. 91-116A.	National Institute for Occupational Safety and Health. (1992). *Preventing lead poisoning in construction workers* (DHHS Publication No. 91-116A). Washington, DC: U.S. Government Printing Office.	National Institute for Occupational Safety and Health. *Preventing Lead Poisoning in Construction Workers.* DHHS Publication No. 91-116A. Washington, DC: GPO, 1992.
Interview	Olinger, Jared, personal interview, January 12, 2004.	Olinger, Jared. 2004. Interview. [12 Jan. 2004].	Olinger, J. (2004, Jan). Personal interview.	Olinger, Jared. Personal interview. 12 Jan 2004.
Paper presented at a meeting	Young, Dona, "Kill the Outline," paper presented at National Business Writer's Association meeting, Seattle, August 28, 2003.	Young, Dona. 2003. *Kill the outline.* Seattle, WA: National Business Writer's Association. Paper presented 28 August 2003.	Young, D. (2004, August). Kill the outline. Paper presented at the meeting of the National Business Writer's Association, Seattle, WA.	Young, Dona. *Kill the Outline.* Paper presented at the meeting of the National Business Writer's Associa-tion, Seattle, WA, 28 Aug. 2003.
Television/radio broadcast	Crane, Yvonne (Producer), *The KTBR News Break,* Orange Broadcasting Group, Chicago, March 22, 2004.	Crane, Yvonne (Producer). 22 March 2004. *The KTBR News Break,* Chicago: Orange Broadcasting Group.	Crane, Y. (Producer). (2004, March). *The KTBR News Break.* Chicago: Orange Broadcasting Group.	Crane, Yvonne (Producer), *The KTBR News Break.* Chicago: Orange Broadcasting Group, 22 Mar. 2004.
CD-ROM article	Bair, Jolan, "Good Writing," *Quality Business Writer's Guide* (CD-ROM), Quality, Inc., Livonia, Mich., 2002.	Bair, Jolan. 2002. "Good writing," Livonia, MI: Quality, Inc. *Quality Business Writer's Guide,* CD-ROM.	Bair, J. (2002). *Good writing.* Livonia, MI: Quality, Inc. Retrieved from Quality database (*Quality Business Writer's Guide,* CD-ROM).	Bair, Jolan. "Good Writing," *Quality Business Writer's Guide.* CD-ROM. Livonia, MI: Quality, Inc., 2002.
World Wide Web page	Montrae, Diedre K., "Exler Lobbies for New Contract," June 3, 2003, <http://www.exlertemp.com/UPDATE/2003.html>, accessed on July 12, 2003.	Montrae, Diedre K. 2003. *Exler lobbies for new contract* [online]. Houston: Exler Inc., 2003 [cited 12 July 2003]. Available from the World Wide Web: http://www.exlertemp.com/UPDATE/2003.html	Montrae, D. K. (2003, June 3). Exler lobbies for new contract. Houston: Exler. Retrieved July 12, 2003 from the World Wide Web: http://www.exlertemp.com/UPDATE/2003.html	Montrae, Diedre K. "Exler Lobbies for New Contract," *Exler Inc. Home Page,* 3 June 2003. 12 July 2003. <http://www.exlertemp.com/UPDATE/2003.html>.
Online database article	"Ranking the Healthcare Providers," <http://www.healthupdate.org/statistics.gov/ind.lib/tab-8315.html>, accessed on January 14, 2002.	*Ranking the Healthcare Providers.* 2002. In Health Update [database online]. Concord: Health Update [cited January 14, 2002]. Available from the World Wide Web: (http://www.healthupdate.org/statistics.gov/ind.lib/tab-8315.html)	Ranking the Healthcare Providers. (n.d.). Retrieved January 14, 2002, from Health Update database on the World Wide Web: http://www.healthupdate.org/statistics.gov/ind.lib/tab-8315.html.	"Ranking the Healthcare Providers," *Health Update.* n.d. 14 January 2002. <http://www.healthupdate.org/statistics.gov/ind.lib/tab-8315.html>.
E-mail	Veljovich, John R. (jrveljo@elegy.net), "Response to Administrative Advisory," e-mail message, November 23, 2004.	Veljovich, John R. 2004. "Response to Administrative Advisory." Personal e-mail [cited November 24, 2004).	Do not include in Reference list. Citation is made in-text: "J. R. Veljovich (personal communication, November 23, 2004) suggests that . . . "	Veljovich, John R. <jrveljo@elegy.net> "Response to Administrative Advisory" Personal e-mail. 23 Nov. 2004. 24 November 2004.
Electronic discussion message (including Listservs and newsgroups)	Kabee, Ellen <lkabee@orcus.com>, "Stepping Up to the Plate," October 24, 2002, <http://chats.orcus.com/group/personnel/message/23>, accessed on December 9, 2004.	Kabee, E. 2002. "Stepping Up to the Plate," Online posting [December 9, 2002]. Available from the World Wide Web: http://chats.orcus.com/group/personnel/message/23.	Kabee, E. (2004, October 24). Stepping Up to the Plate. Message posted to http://chats.orcus.com/group/personnel/message/23	Kabee, Ellen. <lkabee@orcus.com> "Stepping Up to the Plate." Online posting. 24 Oct. 2002. 9 Dec. 2004. <http://chats.orcus.com/group/personnel/message/23>.

Source: GRM—William A. Sabin, *The Gregg Reference Manual,* 9th ed., Glencoe/McGraw-Hill, Westerville, OH, 2001; CMS—*The Chicago Manual of Style,* 14th rev. ed., University of Chicago Press, Chicago, 1993; APA—*Publication Manual of the American Psychological Association,* 5th ed., American Psychological Association, Washington, DC, 2001; MLA—Joseph Gibaldi, *MLA Handbook for Writers of Research Papers,* 6th ed., Modern Language Association of America, New York, 2003.

CONJUNCTIONS

A conjunction is a word that links words, phrases, or clauses. There are three major categories of conjunctions: *coordinating conjunctions, subordinating conjunctions,* and *adverbial conjunctions.* There is also a fourth category, *correlative conjunctions,* which consists of pairs of conjunctions.

Conjunctions are transitional words that help the reader make connections between ideas. Conjunctions can indicate the relationship between the elements in a sentence. Without them, we would not see the relationship. Some conjunctions help compare and contrast information *(yet, on the contrary, rather, instead);* other conjunctions show sequences *(afterward, finally);* and so on.

Adverbial Conjunctions

Adverbial conjunctions provide *transitions.* If you place an adverbial conjunction at the beginning of a complete sentence, the sentence will still be complete. There are many adverbial conjunctions; here is a detailed list:

therefore	in summary	that is	consequently
however	as usual	in conclusion	as usual
for example	in addition	of course	on the contrary
fortunately	hence	otherwise	unfortunately
furthermore	in general	thus	

Here is an example of how adverbial conjunctions show relationships between ideas and provide a transition:

They canceled our meeting. They approved the project.
(choppy, no bridge between the clauses)

They canceled our meeting; however, they approved the project.
(*However* provides a transition between the two actions and shows the relationship between them.)

When ideas are connected effectively, readers are able to follow the line of thought. Adverbial conjunctions also help the reader understand a writer's intent, giving readers a clue to the meaning of a sentence or paragraph *before* they read it.

Each adverbial conjunction signals the meaning of the ideas that follow; here are some of the roles adverbial conjunctions play:

Adding:	in addition, also, besides, furthermore, too
Affirming:	by all means, of course, indeed, yes
Showing consequence:	according, as a result, consequently, hence, thus, therefore
Contrasting:	however, on the other hand, even though, although
Drawing attention:	indeed, accordingly, as usual, in any event
Adding information:	furthermore, in addition, also, what is more, moreover
Drawing a conclusion:	consequently, as a result, therefore, thus, of course, in general
Concluding:	in summary, in conclusion, finally
Illustrating:	for example, for instance
Regretting:	unfortunately, regrettably
Sequencing:	first, second, next, in the first place
Showing reaction:	fortunately, unfortunately, regrettably
Summarizing:	in short, in summary

Coordinating Conjunctions

Coordinating conjunctions join items of equal grammatical structure: they connect independent clauses or items in a series. There are only seven coordinating conjunctions, and some people remember them because together they spell the acronym "FANBOYS": *F*or *A*nd *N*or *B*ut *O*r *Y*et *S*o.

Here's an example of how a coordinating conjunction connects thoughts of equal value:

Suzi will be running the panel, *and* Elise is coordinating the event.

Coordinating conjunctions also provide transitions between ideas. These conjunctions can help smooth the flow of choppy writing.

and: implies equality of structure; equal weight is assigned to connected ideas.

but: implies a contrast; similar to *however.*

yet: implies an exception; similar to *even though.*

Coordinating conjunctions may join single words, or they may join groups of words, but they must always join similar elements; for example, subject + subject, verb phrase + verb phrase, sentence + sentence. When a coordinating conjunction is used to join elements, the elements become a *compound element.*

Connecting nouns:	We have passes for the movie *and* the concert.
Connecting verbs:	Have you seen *or* heard the musical based on the movie?
Connecting adjectives:	The junior *and* varsity soccer teams practice on Tuesday.
Connecting dependent clauses:	If the employees show patience *and* the product works, morale will be raised.
Connecting independent clauses:	Two hundred applicants applied for the jobs, *but* only four were hired.

Subordinating Conjunctions

Subordinating conjunctions are words and phrases that introduce dependent clauses. Subordinating conjunctions show relationships between the ideas they connect. Here are a few common subordinating conjunctions:

after	because	unless	as soon as
although	before	until	while
as	even though	since	so that

Subordinating conjunctions are used to emphasize an inequality between ideas, highlighting one idea over another. Also known as *subordinators,* subordinating conjunctions can be classified according to their use in regard to time, cause and effect, opposition, or condition.

Time	**Cause and Effect**	**Opposition**	**Condition**
after	as	although	even if
before	because	even though	if
since	in order that	in case (that)	only if
until	now that	though	unless
when	since	whereas	whether or not
while	so	while	

Here are two examples of how a subordinating conjunction shows a relationship:

Weak:	Arisa became our new administrative assistant. She organized our files.
Revised:	*When* Arisa became our new administrative assistant, she organized our files.
Weak:	I was waiting in line for the Picasso exhibit. I ate my lunch.
Revised:	*While* I was waiting in line for the Picasso exhibit, I ate my lunch.

Correlative Conjunctions

Correlative conjunctions are pairs of conjunctions that add power to the connection between words because they place more emphasis on the comparing or contrasting aspects of it.

Correlative conjunctions connect sentence elements of the same kind; however, unlike coordinating conjunctions, correlative conjunctions are always used in pairs. Here are the common pairs:

either . . . or

neither . . . nor

both . . . and

not . . . but

not only . . . but also

When conjunctions come in pairs, the structure following the second part of the correlative must be parallel with the first part. Therefore, you must create parallel structure or your writing will be *not only* grammatically incorrect *but also* choppy.

When joining singular and plural subjects, the subject closest to the verb determines whether the verb is singular or plural.

Connecting nouns:	*Both* my aunt *and* my cousin play the violin.
Connecting verbs:	The coverage will *not only* bring you peace of mind *but also* save you money.
Connecting adjectives:	The local government shall provide *both* financial *and* medical assistance.
Connecting prepositional phrases:	Lemonade is made *either* by squeezing lemons *or* by mixing a can of frozen concentrate.
Connecting independent clauses:	*Not only* did the fox jump over the dog, *but* he *also* chased the cat.

DETERMINERS

Determiners are words placed in front of a noun to make it clear what the noun refers to. For example, the word *cubicle* by itself is a general reference to an office space. If someone says *this cubicle,* we know which office space he or she is talking about.

There are several classes of determiners:

Defining words:	which, whose
Definite and indefinite articles:	the, a, an
Demonstratives:	this, that, these, those, all, both, half, either, neither, each, every
Difference words:	other, another

Numerals (cardinals):	one, two, three, ten, thirty, *and so on*
Possessives:	my, your, his, her, its, our, their
Quantifiers:	a few, a little, much, many, a lot of, most, some, any, enough
Question words:	which, what, whose
Sequencing words (ordinals):	first, second, third, last, latter, next, previous, subsequent
*Predeterminers:**	such, what, half, rather, quite

Here are some examples:

all entrances	*few* reasons	*some* soft drinks
any airplane	*many* boxes	*that* tree
both animals	*next* week	*those* avocados
each book	*no* exit	*this* newspaper
enough time	*previous* appointment	*whichever* room
every afternoon	*several* windows	

Numbers as Determiners

The most common way to express quantity is to use a number. Numerals are determiners when they appear before a noun. In this position, cardinal numerals express quantity:

one book *two* books *20* books

When they do not come before a noun, numerals are a subclass of noun. And like nouns, they can take determiners:

the three of us *the last* of them

FORMS OF ADDRESS

Table RM.3 shows the title of addressees, the inside address, and the salutation to use in writing formal letters.

INFINITIVES

The **infinitive** of a verb is the basic form of the verb preceded by the word *to (to sing, to run).* Infinitives have two main tense forms: present and perfect. The perfect infinitive expresses action that has been completed before the time of the main verb.

I am sorry *to have caused* you so much trouble last week.

(The act of causing trouble was completed before the act of expressing regret; therefore, the perfect infinitive is used.)

The present infinitive is used in all other cases.

Incorrect: I planned to have left early.

Correct: I planned *to leave* early.

(*The act of leaving could not have been completed before the act of planning.*)

* Predeterminers appear before determiners.

TABLE RM.3 | Forms of Address: Inside Address and Salutation

Addressee	Inside Address	Written Salutation
Ambassador, U.S.	The Honorable *Full name,* Ambassador of the United States	Sir/Madam *or* Dear Mr./Madam Ambassador
Ambassador to the U.S.	His/Her Excellency *Full name,* The Ambassador of *Place name*	Excellency *or* Dear Mr./Madam Ambassador
Assemblyman/woman	The Honorable *Full name*	Dear Mr./Ms. *Last name*
Associate Justice, U.S. Supreme Court	The Honorable Justice *Full name*	Dear Justice *Last name*
Attorney	Mr./Ms. *Full name,* Attorney at law or *Full name,* Esq.	Dear Mr./Ms. *Last name*
Cabinet member	The Honorable *Full name,* Secretary of *Department name*	Dear Mr./Madam Secretary
Certified public accountant (CPA)	*Full name*, CPA	Dear *Full name*, CPA
Chief Justice, U.S. Supreme Court	The Honorable *Full name,* Chief Justice of the United States	Dear Chief Justice
Commissioner	The Honorable *Full name*	Dear Mr./Mrs. *Last name*
Dean	Dean *Full name*	Dear Dean *Last name*
Dentist	*Full name,* D.D.S.	Dear Dr. *Last name*
Governor	The Honorable *Full name,* Governor of *State name*	Dear Governor *Last name*
Judge, federal	The Honorable *Full name,* Judge, United States District Court	Dear Judge *Last name*
Judge, state or local	The Honorable *Full name,* Judge of the Court of *Place name*	Dear Judge *Last name*
Man	Mr. *Full name*	Dear Mr. *Full name*
Married couple	Mr. and Mrs. *Husband's Full name* Mr. *Husband's First name* and Mrs. Wife's *Full name* Mr. *Husband's Full name* and Mrs. *Wife's Full name*	Dear Mr. and Mrs. *Husband's Full name* Dear Mr. and Mrs. *Husband's Full name* or Dear *Husband's First name* and *Wife's First name* Dear Mr. and Mrs. *Husband and Wife's last name*
Mayor	The Honorable *Full name,* Mayor of *Place name*	Dear Mayor *Last name*
Military and naval officers (all ranks)	*Rank Full name,* USA/USN/USCG/USAF/USMC/USPHS/NOAA	Dear *Rank Last name*
Ph.D.	Dr. *Full name*	Dear Dr. *Last name*
Physician	*Full name,* M.D.	Dear Dr. *Last name*
Pope	His Holiness the Pope	Your Holiness *or* Most Holy Father
President, university	President *Full name*	Dear President *Last name*
President, U.S.	The President	Dear Mr./Madam President
President, U.S., former	The Honorable *Full name*	Dear Mr./Madam *Last name*
Professor	Professor *Full name*	Dear Professor *Last name*
Priest, Roman Catholic	The Reverend *Full name* *or* The Reverend *Full name,* S.J.	Dear Reverend Father *or* Dear Father
Rabbi, man or woman	Rabbi *Full name or* Rabbi *Full name,* D.D.	Dear Rabbi *Last name or* Dear Dr. *Last name*
Representative, state	The Honorable *Full name,* *State name* House of Representatives	Dear Mr./Ms. *Last name*
Representative, U.S.	The Honorable *Full name,* United States House of Representatives	Dear Representative *Last name*
Secretary-General, United Nations	His/Her Excellency *Full name,* Secretary-General of the United Nations	Dear Mr./Madam/Madame Secretary-General
Senator, state	The Honorable *Full name,* The State Senate, *State Capital*	Dear Senator *Last name*
Senator, U.S.	The Honorable *Full name,* United States Senate	Dear Senator *Last name*
Speaker, U.S. House of Representatives	The Honorable *Full name,* Speaker of the House of Representatives	Dear Mr./Madam Speaker
United Nations. representative, U.S	The Honorable *Full name,* United States Representative to the United Nations	Sir/Madam or Dear Mr./Ms. *Last name*
United Nations representative, foreign	His/Her Excellency *Full name,* Representative of *Place name* to the United Nations	Excellency or My dear Mr./Madam *Last name*
Vice President, U.S.	The Vice President of the United States	Dear Mr./Madam Vice President
Veterinarian	*Full name,* D.V.M.	Dear Dr. *Last name*
Woman Maiden name	Ms. *Full name* Miss *Full name*	Dear Ms. *Full name* Dear Miss *Full name*
Married	Mrs. *Full name*	Dear Mrs. *Full name*

Tips for Using Infinitives

- The passive form of the present infinitive consists of *to be* plus the past participle. Do not omit *to be* in such constructions.

  The crates were scheduled *to be moved.*

- When two or more infinitives appear in a sentence, the word *to* may be omitted after the first infinitive unless special emphasis is desired.

  Carlos needs *to* copy the relevant documents, distribute them to the managers, and keep a record of the managers' comments.

- The word *to* is usually dropped when the infinitve follows such verbs as *see, feel, hear, help, let,* and *need.*

  Incorrect: Please help me to move this cabinet.

  Correct: Please *help me move* this cabinet.

- Avoid splitting an infinitive—inserting an adverb between *to* and the verb—when it results in an awkward sentence. In such cases, the adverb will work better in another position in the sentence.

  Weak : It was challenging to even locate the biggest of the balloons.

  Revised: It was challenging *to locate even* the biggest of the balloons.

- The verbs *can, may, shall, will,* and *must* do not have infinitives. The combinations *to be able to, to have to,* and *to be going to* are generally used in these cases.

  Incorrect: I want him to can do it.

  Correct: I want him *to be able to* do it.

INSTANT MESSAGING

An *instant messaging (IM)* program is one that can instantly send messages from one computer to another. IM is a form of *instant e-mail* that is growing in popularity. An instant-messaging program can let you know when anyone who is on your private sender list is online; you can then send the person short messages, similar to sending a text message on your cell phone. Popular instant-messaging programs include:

.NET Messenger Service	ICQ	Skype
AOL Messenger	Jabber	Trillian
Excite/Pal	MSN Messenger	Yahoo!Messenger
GoogleTalk	Qnext	Windows Live Messenger
iChat	QQ	

Instant-messaging programs allow people to communicate in real time over the Internet, much like a telephone conversation but using text-based rather than voice-based communication. Some programs allow many people to chat at the same time, much like a private chat room.

Instant messaging allows easy collaboration. Unlike the case with e-mails or phones, the parties know whether a peer is available. Most systems allow the user to set an *online status* or *away message* so that peers are notified when the user is available, busy, or away from the computer. Thus, people are not forced to reply immediately to incoming messages. This way, communication via instant messaging can be less intrusive than communication via phone, which is one reason why instant messaging is becoming more and more important in corporate environments.

Guidelines for Instant Messaging

- Organize your contact lists to separate business contacts from family and friends. Eliminate even the remote possibility that a social contact could be included in a business chat with a partner or customer—or vice versa.
- Avoid using instant messaging to share sensitive or confidential information. IM is better suited to quick information about project status, meeting times, or a person's whereabouts.
- Avoid making statements about other people, your company, or other companies that could damage your reputation or credibility or your company's credibility. Again, be careful what you say.
- Do not conduct excessive personal messaging at work. Conduct personal chats during breaks or your lunch hour—unless the chats generate new clients or revenue for the business.
- Be aware that instant messages can be saved. One of the parties to your conversation can copy and paste the entire chat onto a notepad or Word document. Some IM services allow you to archive entire messages.
- Be aware of virus infections and related security risks. If you collaborate on documents for your business, file transfer is important. To decide whether or not to restrict transferring files through IM, learn more about the quality of your own firewall protection.
- Keep your instant messages simple and to the point, and know when to say good-bye. Get to the point and avoid unnecessary blather.
- Avoid confusing your contacts with a misleading user name or status. IM user names, like e-mail user names, should be consistent throughout your company.

Text-Messaging Abbreviations

With the increasing popularity and use of instant messaging, Internet chat rooms, and text messaging, a new language has emerged, tailored to the immediacy and compactness of these new communication media. If you have ever been in a chat room or received an instant message or text message that seemed to be in its own foreign language, the list in Table RM.4 will help you decipher the lingo.

Smileys

A **smiley** (also called **emoticon**) is often used in text communications to convey an *emotion* with a message. Smileys are used in text messages in the same way facial expressions and voice changes are used in face-to-face or telephone conversations.

To create a smiley, use your standard keyboard characters and punctuation marks. In messages, text smileys appear sideways. Here are some basics to get you started in understanding what smileys are:

colon	= sideways eyes **:**
close parenthesis	= sideways smile)
colon + close parenthesis	= a smiley **:)**
colon + hyphen + close parenthesis	= smiley with a nose **:-)**
semicolon + close parenthesis	= winking smiley **;)**
semicolon + hyphen + close parenthesis	= winking smiley with a nose **;-)**
number *8* + hyphen + close parenthesis	= smiley with sunglasses **8-)**

Table RM.5 lists some commonly used smileys and their meanings.

TABLE RM.4 | Common Text-Messaging Abbreviations

Abbreviation	Meaning	Abbreviation	Meaning
AAP	always a pleasure	n00b	newbie
ADD	address	NBD	no big deal
AFAIK	as far as I know	NE1	anyone
AISB	as it should be	NIMBY	not in my back yard
AML	all my love	NM	nothing much / never mind
ASAP	as soon as possible	NMH	not much here
AYEC	at your earliest convenience	NOYB	none of your business
B4	before	NRN	no response/reply necessary
BAK	back at keyboard	NW	no way
BBS	be back soon	OIC	oh, I see
BFN	bye for now	OO	over and out
BM&Y	between me and you	OOH	out of here
BRB	be right back	OP	on phone
BTA	but then again	OTL	out to lunch
BTW	by the way	OTT	over the top
COB	close of business	OTW	off to work
CRB	come right back	OVA	over
CUA	see you around	PDQ	pretty darn quick
CWYL	chat with you later	PLS	please
CYO	see you online	PM	private message
DL	download	PMFJI	pardon me for jumping in
DQMOT	don't quote me on this	PROLLY	probably
DV8	deviate	PTMM	please tell me more
EMA	e-mail address	Q	queue
EOD	end of day	QT	cutie
EOM	end of message	RSN	real soon now
F2F	face to face	SC	stay cool
F2T	free to talk	SIG2R	sorry, I got to run
FC	fingers crossed	SLAP	sounds like a plan
FISH	first in, still here	SNAFU	situation normal all fouled up
FITB	fill in the blank	SOL	sooner or later
FRT	for real though	SPST	same place, same time
FYEO	for your eyes only	SS	so sorry
G2CU	good to see you	SSDD	same stuff, different day
G2R	got to run	STW	search the Web
GAL	get a life	SUP	what's up?
GFI	go for it	TA	thanks a lot
GIAR	give it a rest	TAM	tomorrow a.m.
GIGO	garbage in, garbage out	TBH	to be honest
GL/HF	good luck, have fun	TC	take care
GOI	get over it	THX	thanks
GR8	great	THNQ	thank you
GTG	got to go	TIAD	tomorrow is another day
H2CUS	hope to see you soon	TMB	text me back
HAND	have a nice day	TMOT	trust me on this
HOAS	hold on a second	TNSTAAFL	there's no such thing as a free lunch
IB	I'm back	TPTB	the powers that be
ICBW	it could be worse	TTTT	these things take time
IDTS	I don't think so	TTYS	talk to you soon
ILBL8	I'll be late	TY	thank you
ILU	I love you	TYVM	thank you very much
IM	instant message	UKTR	you know that's right
IMO	in my opinion	UR	your / you're
INAL	I'm not a lawyer	WAM	wait a minute
IRL	in real life	WAYF	where are you from?
IUSS	if you say so	WB	welcome back
IYSS	if you say so	WK	week
JMO	just my opinion	WOMBAT	waste of money, brains, and time
KISS	keep it simple, stupid	WRUD	what are you doing?
KOTC	kiss on the cheek	WUCIWUG	what you see is what you get
KWIM	know what I mean?	WWYC	write when you can
LERK	leaving easy reach of keyboard	WYSIWYG	what you see is what you get
LOL	laughing out loud	YA	your
LTNS	long time no see	YKWYCD	you know what you can do
MSG	message	YW	you're welcome
MTFBWU	may the force be with you		

TABLE RM.5 | Common Smileys

Smiley	Meaning	Smiley	Meaning	Smiley	Meaning
:)	Standard smiley	>-)	Evil grin	:-<	Super sad
:-)	With nose	{:-)	Toupee smiley	:-@	Scream
:-E	Buck-tooth	:-!	Foot in mouth	:-0	Yell
:-#	With braces	:-D	Laughter	I-O	Yawn
:'-)	Happy Crying	:@	Exclamation "What???"	%-(	Confused
;)	Winking smiley	:(	Sad or frown smiley	@>—;—	Rose
;-)	Winking smiley with nose	:-(	Sad with nose	:-($)	Put your money where your mouth is

LATIN TERMS

a.m.
(ante meridiem)
"before noon"
Use lowercase letters and do not space between the letters.

et al.
(et alia)
"and others"
Use *et al.* when you are writing a bibliography or citing a legal case to indicate other names were omitted. Avoid using it in sentences; instead, write out *and others.*

e.g.
(exempli gratia)
"for example"
Use lowercase letters and do not space between the letters.

etc.
(et cetera)
"and other things of a like kind" or "and the rest"
Avoid using *etc.* by substituting a description of the items you are leaving out or by using *and so on* or *among others.*

ibid.
(ibidem)
"in the same place"
When citing the same source consecutively, use *ibid.* directly under the citation that gives the author's name (or other identifying information).

i.e.
(id est)
"that is"
Use lowercase letters and do not space between the letters.

op. cit.
(opere citato)
"in the work cited"
When the same work is cited after intervening works are cited, put the author's name (or the other identifying information) followed by *op. cit.*

per
"to, for, *or* by each," "by means of," "through," or "by"
Use *per* correctly in common expressions such as *miles per hour* or *cost per day.* Also use it correctly in Latin phrases such as *per diem* ("by the day"). Avoid using *per* in general writing; for example, for "per our discussion" substitute *as discussed.*

p.m.
(post meridiem)
"after noon"
Use lowercase letters and do not space between the letters.

[sic]
"so," "thus," "in this manner"
The term *sic,* within brackets, indicates that an error in a quote was made by the original author, not the current writer. (Brackets [ ] are used around any words added to another's quotation.)

LINE GRAPHS

A **line graph** is unique in pointing out trends. (See Figure RM.6.) Following the stock market, tracking incoming funds over a period of time, or charting the course of an illness are all conducive to being represented in a line graph.

FIGURE RM.6 Line Graphs

Making a Case: *Line graphs are the most effective format for presenting data, particularly time-related data, but they can also be deceiving. In* ***(a),*** *a simple line graph, the company Solar Shingles, Inc., presents its sales data for the years 1997 to 2005 and appears to be an unprofitable enterprise. However, in* ***(b),*** *a multiple line graph that includes company expenditures, it is apparent that while sales are indeed shrinking, the company's costs have dropped dramatically and profit has increased.*

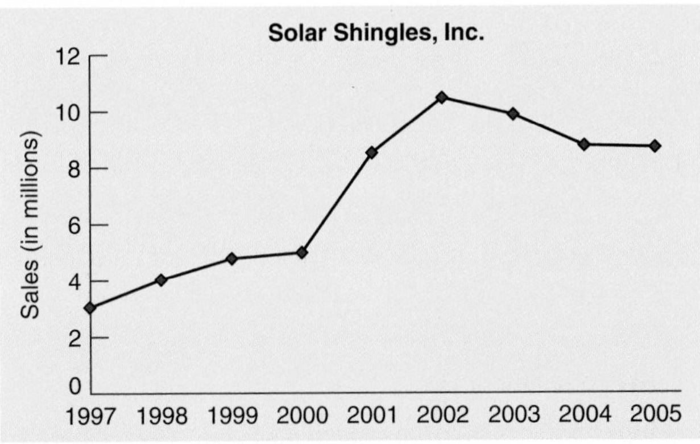

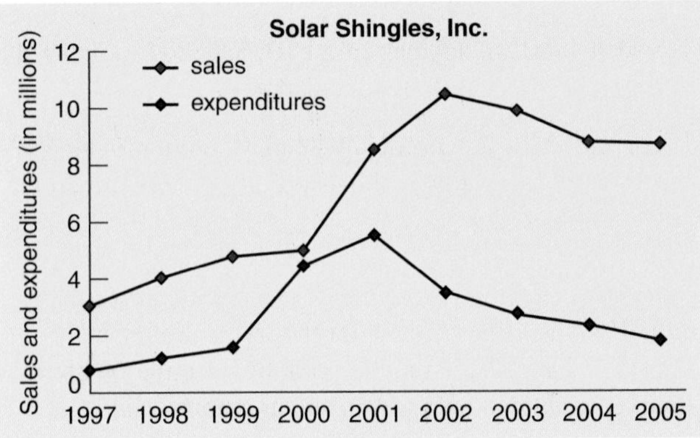

Here are a few guidelines to remember when using line graphs:

- For line graph titles, use left-justified, 10- or 12-point bold type, and clearly state the data that are illustrated.
- Clearly label the axes. (In a time graph, the horizontal axis always indicates time, and the vertical axis displays the units of measurement.)
- Start the vertical axis with zero (unless there is a good reason not to).

ONLINE ADDRESSES

There are two kinds of online addresses: a uniform resource locator, or URL, and an electronic-mail address, or e-mail address.

URL Addresses

A **uniform resource locator (URL)** is a unique address for a file with respect to its location on the Internet. The information contained in a URL address consists of two parts: the *protocol* (http, or HyperText Transfer Protocol, is the most widely used protocol) and the *host name,* which is the name of the host computer where the material is stored.

The host name, also called the domain name or IP address, describes where the resource is located. When you are seeking specific information from a Web site, such as a document or a graphic file, the host name will often be followed by a slash and by information relating to the specific file you are seeking, called a pathname. For example, suppose you accessed a report at **http://www.grabinfo.com/read.document**. The first part of the address, or *http://*, indicates the protocol used to find the pathname that connects to the file called "read.document," which is located on a computer at the address *grabinfo* on the *World Wide Web*.

The *.com* part of the domain name, known as a top-level domain or TLD, refers to the owner or manager of the host computer.

Although the rules are not strictly enforced or adhered to on the Internet, in general these categorizations are true: *.net* (network associations, such as ISPs), *.org* (nonprofit organizations), *.gov* (government agencies), *.edu* (educational institutions), *.int* (international organizations), and *.info* (information services). There are many other TLDs; however, these are the ones most frequently used online.

- A URL may also include, after the host name, one or more elements that provide information regarding the electronic path to be taken in order to locate the desired file.

  www.ebay.com/antiques/desk

- Although URLs are usually typed all in lowercase letters, follow the style of any particular URL exactly as shown in order to locate the file described.
- Spaces between words in any part of a URL have to be signified by means of an underline or some other mark of punctuation.
- The protocol *http://* is often omitted when URLs are provided in documents; the fact that the host name begins with *www* indicates that the protocol is *http://*.

E-Mail Addresses

In an e-mail address, the information before the @ symbol identifies the name of the user of that address; as with URLs, the information after the @ symbol is the host name. The name before the dot is the name of the host computer; and the information after the dot identifies the domain. For example, *.com* identifies a Web site as commercial.

Division of Online Addresses

When writing out a lengthy online address, do not insert a hyphen (or any other mark) to break the address at the end of the line; inserting characters into an address will make the address inaccurate. If you must insert a hyphen to make the address fit, do so after the double slash that follows the protocol.

PERCENTAGES

Express percentages in figures, and spell out the word *percent*. For percentages at the beginning of a sentence, spell out the number that begins the sentence, as well as any related numbers. Reword the sentence if the number requires more than two words when spelled out or if figures are preferable for emphasis or quick reference.

> *Five percent* of our clients lost power for an hour.
>
> My client expected a *25 percent* discount.

- *Fractional percentages*: When writing out fractional percentages greater than 1 percent, use figures:

  > The bank is offering a home equity loan with a *6¼ percent* interest rate.
  >
  > The bank is offering a home equity loan with a *6.25 percent* interest rate.

  For fractional percentages less than 1 percent, spell out the information.

  > The rate is *one quarter of 1 percent* lower than last week's rate.

- *Percentages in a series:* When writing out a series of percentages, use the word *percent* after the last figure in the series only.

  Depending on the size of your order, you might save *5*, *10*, or *15 percent* on your invoice.

- *Amounts:* Separate the figure from the name of the measure with a space, but do not separate % or $ from the figure with a space.

  3.4 hr $22 50%

  Note: Unless the abbreviation of a measure falls at the end of a sentence, do not use a period after the abbreviation.

PLAGIARISM

The word *plagiarism* is derived from the Latin words *plagiarius,* "an abductor," and *plagiare*, "to steal." One type of plagiarism is taking another person's words and using them verbatim without crediting the source. Another is using another's ideas without crediting the source. In whatever form it takes, plagiarism is unethical.

Advances in technology have made plagiarism easier to accomplish, but also easier to detect. Teachers have a knack for knowing the difference between what their students write and what professionals write. A student's vocabulary, spelling, grammar, and syntax all become familiar through only one or two writing samples. In addition, teachers can identify plagiarism through online subscription services.

Plagiarism has serious personal consequences. Rather than learning concepts related to the selected topic, the plagiarist walks away focusing all energies in unproductive directions: plagiarism is emotionally draining, intellectually fruitless, and professionally devastating. Follow an ethical, professional course of action. Learn the details and present them correctly. You may spend a bit more time on your work, but you will get the grade you deserve; your energy will be high and integrity intact, preparing you for success wherever you go.

QUANTIFIERS

Like articles and determiners, **quantifiers** are words that precede and modify nouns. They tell us *how many* or *how much.* Selecting the correct quantifier depends on understanding the distinction between count nouns (for example, *trees*) and noncount nouns (for example, *dancing*).

The following quantifiers will work with *count nouns:*

many, a few, few, several, a couple of, none of the

The following quantifiers will work with *noncount nouns:*

not much, a little, little, a bit of, a good deal of, a great deal of, no

The following quantifiers will work with *both count* and *noncount nouns:*

all of the, some, most of the, enough, a lot of, lots of, plenty of, a lack of

Guidelines for Quantifiers

- In formal academic writing, use *many* and *much* rather than phrases such as *a lot of, lots of,* and *plenty of.*
- Unless it is combined with *of,* the quantifier *much* is reserved for questions and negative statements:

  Much of the rain has already evaporated.

  How *much* rain fell yesterday?

  Not *much.*

- The quantifier *most of the* must include the definite article *the* when it modifies a specific noun, whether it's a count or a noncount noun:

  Most of *the* tellers at this bank can help with your account.

  Most of *the* food is gone.

  With a general plural noun, however (when you are *not* referring to a specific entity), the *of the* is dropped:

  Most buildings have their own evacuation policy.

SOUNDALIKES

accept/except: *Accept* means "to receive" or "to approve of"; *except* means "to exclude" or "to leave out."

Everyone has *accepted* the invitation *except* Sam.

access/excess: *Access* means "to have contact or admission"; *excess* means "surplus."

Do you have *access* to the decision maker?

We have an *excess* of participants, so we do not have enough supplies.

advice/advise: *Advice* is a noun meaning "counsel" or "recommendation"; *advise* is a verb meaning "to give advice" or "to make a recommendation."

I *advise* you to follow your instructor's *advice.*

affect/effect: *Affect* is a verb meaning "to influence"; *effect* is a noun meaning "result." However, *affect* is also a noun, used in the field of psychology, referring to "emotion." *Effect* is also a verb meaning "to cause to happen" or "to bring about." *Affect* is usually used as a verb (substitute the word *influence* to check if you are correct); *effect* is usually a noun (substitute the word *result* to check if you are correct).

Her mood *affected* our attitudes.

The *effect* of the storm was devastating.

That policy will *effect* important change.

The doctor diagnosed her as having an *affective* disorder.

a lot/alot: *A lot* is always two words; *alot* is a spelling error.

We have *a lot* of things to discuss.

alright/all right: The correct spelling is *all right.* To remember, think of something as being either *all right* or *all wrong.*

altogether/all together: *Altogether* means "wholly, completely"; *all together* means "in a group, everyone assembled."

These training materials are *altogether* mine.

Let's keep the training materials *all together* in one box.

complement/compliment: *Complement* is derived from *to complete; compliment* means "to flatter."

She *complimented* him on his suit and tie.

Your scarf *complements* your outfit.

ensure/insure/assure: Use *ensure* when you want *to make certain;* use *insure* when you are referring to insurance and you want *to protect against loss;* use *assure* when you are speaking to someone and you wish *to give confidence* (the object of *assure* should always be a person).

Martin *ensured* (made certain) that the project would be completed on time.

I *assure* you (give you confidence) that everything will go well at the meeting.

You should *insure* your ring (protect against loss) before you wear it.

everyday/every day: *Everyday* means "ordinary" or "daily" and is a modifier; *every day* means "each day"; if you can insert the word *single* between *every* and *day,* use the two-word form.

That is an *everyday* routine.

We do that procedure *every day*.

farther/further: *Farther* refers to distance that can be measured; *further* means "to a greater degree or extent."

She lives *farther* from work than you do.

We are *further* along on this project than we expected.

its/it's: *Its* is the possessive form of the pronoun *it:* Everything in *its* place. *It's* is the contraction for *it is* or *it has*: *It's* raining. *It's* begun.

loose/lose: *Loose* is an adjective meaning "unfastened" or "not tight" or a verb meaning "to release" or "to untighten." *Lose* is a verb meaning "to misplace" or " to be defeated."

You should *loosen* the rope on the boat, but don't *lose* it.

may be/maybe: *May be* is a verb phrase suggesting possibility; *maybe* is an adverb meaning "perhaps."

Winston *may be* the next mayor.

Maybe Winston will be the next mayor.

past/passed: *Past* means "time gone by" and can be used as a noun, an adjective, or a preposition. *Passed* is the past tense of the verb *to pass* and means "to go by" or "to exceed."

Martin walked *past* the correct address. As he *passed* it, he noticed his mistake.

Margarite *passed* the book to another student.

In the *past,* time seemed to go by more slowly.

personal/personnel: *Personal* relates to a particular person. *Personnel* refers to a body of persons employed by a business, as in *Personnel Department* (which is now commonly replaced by *Human Resources Department*).

Don't bring your *personal* problems to work.

The Human Resources Department will address all *personnel* issues.

sometime/some time: *Sometime* is *an unspecified time. Some time* refers to *a period of time.*

Call me *sometime* next week.

We can spend *some time* working on our project.

than/then: *Than* is a conjunction used in comparisons (a subject and verb usually follow it); *then* is an adverb relating to time (when you think of *then,* think of *when*).

You are taller *than* I am.

When you agree, *then* I will have more time.

their/there/they're: These three words create a spelling issue.

Their is the possessive form of they: *their* house, *their* proposal.

There is used as an adverb or an anticipating subject: over *there; There* are calls to make.

They're is the contracted form of *they are*: *They're* happy. *They're* certain.

themselves/theirselves: *Themselves* is a plural reflexive or intensive pronoun: They hurt *themselves. Theirselves* is a local-language form of *themselves.*

to/too: *To* is a preposition. *Too* is an adverb relating to quantity, as in *too much; too* also means *also*.

> I have been given *too* much information.
>
> You should go *to* the meeting *too*.

sight/site/cite: *Sight* refers to vision, mental perception; *site* refers to a location; and *cite* is a verb that means "to quote, to name."

> The young girl's *sight* was impaired due to the accident.
>
> That is an excellent *site* for construction.
>
> May we *cite* you when we develop our advertisement?

threw/thorough/through/thru *Threw* is the past tense form of *throw; thorough* means "comprehensive, carefully, or completely"; *through* means "by means of, finished, from beginning to end, during" (as in *throughout*); and *thru* is an incorrect spelling of *through* (use it as a hyphenated form, as in *drive-thru*).

> Feel free to look *through* this brochure.
>
> John *threw* the ball to the umpire.
>
> We all did a *thorough* job on the report.

SPELLING RULES

In English, there are no rules for spelling words that hold true without exception; however, the following guidelines, albeit with exceptions, more often than not prove helpful to know. When you are in doubt about how to spell a word, the best practice is to look it up in the dictionary.

Doubling Final Consonants

When adding an ending to a word that ends in a consonant, check to see if you need to double the final consonant.

The final consonant of a word is doubled when you add *ed, ing, er,* or *est* in the following cases:

- Double the final *b, d, g, l, m, n, p, r,* and *t* at the end of words.

rob	robbing	prefer	preferred
submit	submitting	flap	flapped

  Note: This rule does not apply to verbs that end with *x, w, v,* and *y,* consonants that cannot be doubled.

	snow	snowing	
BUT:	rev	revved	revving

- Words of more than one syllable have their consonants doubled *only* when the final syllable is stressed and that syllable ends in a single vowel followed by a single consonant.

	begin	beginning
	defer	deferring
BUT:	relent	relenting

Dropping the Final *E*

When adding an ending to a word that ends with a silent *e,* drop the final *e* if the ending begins with a vowel.

> advancing
>
> surprising

- **Exception:** If the ending begins with a consonant, keep the final *e*.

  advancement

  likeness

- **Exception:** If the silent *e* is preceded by another vowel, drop the *e* when adding any ending.

  argument

  argued

  truly

- **Exception:** The final *e* is kept in words such as *mileage* and words where the final *e* is preceded by a soft *g* or *c: changeable, courageous, management, noticeable.* (Try pronouncing any of these words without the *e.*)

Dropping the Final *Y*

When adding an ending to a word that ends with *y,* change the *y* to *i* when it is preceded by a consonant. Most nouns and verbs that end in *y* have plural or third-person singular conjugations that change to *i.*

supply	supplies
worry	worried
merry	merrier
party	parties
happy	happily

- **Exception:** This does not apply to the endings *ing, ism, ish*, however.

cry	crying
study	studying
boy	boyish

- **Exception:** Nor does it apply when the final *y* is preceded by a vowel.

obey	obeyed
say	saying
stay	stays

Putting *I* Before *E* Except After *C*

This rule, even with its exceptions, is relatively simple and worth remembering.

achieve	believe	chief	fiend	patience

- **Exception:** Words pronounced with an "ay" sound:

neighbor	freight	beige	sleigh	weigh

- **Other exceptions**:

either	neither	seizure	foreign	forfeit
height	leisure	weird	seize	

Changing *IE* to *Y*

When a word ends in *ie,* change the *ie* to *y* before adding *ing.*

vie	v*ying*
lie	l*ying*

Adding Prefixes

In general, adding a prefix to a word does not change its spelling.

spelled misspelled

TABLES

Though not as fancy as other types of displays, tables can compare and contrast complicated data very effectively. (See Table RM.6.) Tables have fewer limits than other types of displays: the numbers of columns and rows are limited only by the size of the paper and the print.

A note of caution: Too many details on a table may camouflage your important points. As you analyze data, pull out the important information and turn it into another type of display that highlights your main points or the concepts you wish to stress.

TELEPHONE NUMBERS

A telephone number is, in essence, an address. Each number consists of three blocks: an area code of three digits, a prefix of three digits, and a line number with four digits. The area code designates a geographic region of the United States; the prefix refers to the switching device that a specific phone line connects to; and the line number is the number assigned to your specific phone line.

When writing an area code with a number, you have several options:

234-555-2424	hyphens
(234) 555-2424	parentheses around area code
234.555.2424	periods instead of hyphens
234 555 2424	spaces instead of punctuation
234/555-2424	slash after area code; hyphen between numbers

If you are placing a phone number within parentheses, choose an option that does not require parentheses; for example: (you can call me at 234-555-2424).

Guidelines for Writing Telephone Numbers

- If a business expresses its phone number as a word, follow the company's style, for example, CALL-MCI, GOFEDEX
- When writing an extension number (Ext.), attach it to the end of the phone number: (555) 555-2424, Ext. 13.

TABLE RM.6 | Tables Talk

CHANGE IN REAL HOURLY WAGES FOR ALL WORKERS BY EDUCATION, 1973–2001

	Less Than High School	High School	Some College	College	Advanced Degree
HOURLY WAGE					
1973	$11.66	$13.36	$14.39	$19.49	$23.56
1979	11.62	13.04	13.94	18.27	22.31
1989	9.99	12.17	13.67	19.16	24.71
1995	9.04	11.95	13.37	19.84	26.18
2000	9.40	12.65	14.30	22.10	27.90
2001	9.50	12.81	14.60	22.58	28.14

Source: Mishel, Bernstein, and Boushey, *The State of Working America 2002/2003.*

When dialing long distance within the United States, enter a *1* before the area code; this prefix is the country code for the United States. When a phone number includes the country code, connect the blocks with hyphens.

1-524–629–6000 1-215-PAINTER

Every country has its own country code. To place a call to another country from within the United States, before dialing the phone number, it is usually necessary to first enter "011," the international access code exclusively for calls originating within the United States, then the country code of the number you are calling, and, finally, in some cases, a city access code. Phone calls between the United States and certain countries, such as Canada, do not require an international access code.

Use hyphens to connect the blocks when writing out international numbers. When writing your phone number for a recipient outside the country, you can use a plus sign to represent the recipient's international access code:

+ 1-524-629-6000

TEXTNOTES

In a report or manuscript that contains source references and a complete bibliography at the end, short parenthetical citations may be inserted within the text. Parenthetical textnotes include the author's last name and the appropriate page number in parentheses:

(Ogden 217) (Ogden, p. 217)

The reader who wants more complete information can consult the full entry in the bibliography.

It is important to create an in-text note whenever you use another source's words, facts, or ideas. Also, for each source cited in the text, complete source information must appear in the bibliography or works-cited list. (See Figure RM.5 on page 358 for an example of a works-cited list.)

- If some of the information called for in a source reference (such as the author's name) is already provided in the main text, there is no need to repeat it in the textnote.

  William Sargent, in his recent book, *Under a Microscope*, describes the risks to an organization from an overzealous manager (p. 28).

  Some authorities omit *p.* and *pp.* as well as the comma between the name and the page number; for example:

  You should refer to Sargent's book on micromanagement (28).

  Smith recommends that only one supervisor be present for the procedure (178).

- If you do not include the author's name in the text, include that information in the textnote.

  It is recommended that only one supervisor be present for the procedure (Smith 178).

- If more than one publication by the same author appear in the bibliography, use an abbreviated title in the textnote to identify the relevant publication. The textnote should include the author's last name, the abbreviated source title, and the page number.

  (Sargent, *Microscope* 28), (Sargent, *OfficeSpeak* 134)

- *Multiple authors:* For a publication by two or three authors, include all names and join the last two by using the word *and.*

  (Sargent and Becks 80) (Smith, Cohali, and Vinson 63)

For four or more authors, use the first author's name followed by *et al.*

(Smith et al. 23)

- When two or more authors with the same last name are listed as authors in the bibliography, include the authors' first names in the listing.

  (F. Kale 37), (J. Kale 321)

  According to a recent book on micromanagement (W. Sargent, p. 28), the . . .

- *Group or corporate authors*: Use a group or corporate author's name just as you would use an individual author's name.

  (United Nations 42)

  If the name is long, then either include the full name or shorten words that are commonly abbreviated and place in the parenthetical citation.

  (United Nations International Children's Enrichment Fund 42) (UNICEF 42)

- *No author:* If no author is listed, use the full title (if brief), or use a shortened version of the title unless the title appears in your text. Make sure you begin the shortened version with the word by which it would be alphabetized in the works-cited list.

  Example for a long article title:

  Use: ("Polar" 85)

  Instead of: ("Polar Temperature Measurements Since the 1950s" 85)

  Example for a long book title:

  Use: (Foundations 218)

  Not: (Foundations of Business Communication: An Integrative Approach 218).

- *Source within a source:* If you are citing a source that is found in another source, use the abbreviation *qtd. in.*

  Joleps stated that a physical examination was a requirement at this stage (qtd. in Arnold 42).

- *Citing more than a single work in one note:* Separate the citations with a semicolon.

  (Sargent 28; Foynes and Wotar 5578)

- *Citing two or more sources within a single sentence:* Place the parenthetical citation right after the specific statement it supports.

  > What draining the lake revealed were issues far more troubling than the anticipated reduction of vegetation in adjacent fields (Greene 71); decades of dumping by businesses and individuals had left a toxic scar burned into the lake bed (Mortens 43).

TIME

Clock Time

Many of the rules for writing out expressions of time relate specifically to the use of the words *a.m.*, *p.m.*, and *o'clock*, time descriptions that have been a part of the English language for hundreds of years. The contraction *o'clock*—short for *of the clock*—dates at least back to the days of Chaucer and Middle English. The abbreviations *a.m.* (for *ante meridiem*, or *before midday*) and *p.m.* (for *post meridiem*, or *after midday*) have been a part of the English vocabulary since at least the seventeenth century, having been borrowed from the Latin language. During the seventeenth century, these conventions were used together for the most formal of affairs: *Arrive at 6:30 p.m. o'clock.*

Modern English speakers no longer use *a.m.* or *p.m.* with *o'clock*; instead, *a.m.* and *p.m.* are used exclusively with figures. When using these abbreviations, use lowercase letters (avoid using capital letters).

- When writing out expressions of time with figures, a colon separates the hours from the minutes. If there are no minutes—the time is "on the hour"—you can omit the colon and the zeros.

  12:30 a.m.

  6:00 p.m.

  6 p.m.

  You can also use words to express time. When you do so, use a hyphen between the hours and the minutes, except in cases where the minutes must be hyphenated.

  Meet me at one-twenty?

  I'll be there at one twenty-five.

  Twenty after one o'clock, fine.

- Certain time expressions require only words and should not be used with *a.m.* or *p.m.*, a mistake commonly made when trying to achieve a tone of formality.

in the morning	this morning	
in the afternoon	tomorrow afternoon	noon
in the evening	this evening	
midnight	at night	tonight

  Using *a.m.* or *p.m.* with any of these phrases would be redundant. Some of these phrases can, however, be used with the phrase *o'clock.*

  Breakfast will be served at *six o'clock in the morning.*

  The annual Sale event begins at *11 o'clock tonight.*

- When writing out technical information or number-related statistics, use numerals to express period of time:

  a 20-decibel load　　　　a 15-year adjustable rate loan

  However, you can spell out nontechnical references to periods of time:

  three hours later than I thought

  a forty-five-minute delay

  And it is not unusual to find periods of time expressed in both words and figures in legal text:

  payable in sixty (60) days

- There are several formats for referring to decades. In text, spell out the decade, use the full numeric expression, or use an abbreviated form as long as no confusion will result:

  the sixties

  the 1860s

  the '60s

  the eighteen-sixties

When referring to an inclusive period of years, only the last two digits are necessary in the second number, unless the century changes:

1799–1804

2004–06

- Similarly, there are also several ways to refer to centuries:

The 1800s

The nineteenth century

The 19th century

WORD DIVISION

Avoid dividing words whenever possible. Written documents should be easy to read, and the splitting of words at the end of lines can interrupt the reader's flow. As a general rule, no more than two or three words should be divided on any given page, and no more than one word per paragraph.

When dividing words, make your decisions on the basis of both syllables and pronunciation.

Here is the main rule to follow in word division: The first part of the word that is pronounced must be recognizable before the eye reaches the second part in the following line. For example, *liaison* should be split *liai-son;* if it were split *lia-ison,* the reader would incorrectly pronounce the first part of the word *(lia,* instead of *liay)* and would then have to make a mental adjustment on seeing the rest of the word.

Similarly, never split a word so that the second part of the word is unpronounceable. For example, *unpronounceable* could be split *unpronounce-able*, but not *unpronounceab-le.*

Here are a few more guidelines to follow when dividing words:

- Some words should never be split. These include names, one-syllable words *(book, sell),* and words whose pronunciation would inevitably be altered.
- Divide hyphenated words at the hyphen. Words should never contain more than one hyphen.

  de-emphasize (*not* de-empha-size)

- Divide compound words to form the two separate words.

  stop-gap

  house-hold

  prize-winner

- Divide words before a suffix or after a prefix unless the word has double letters.

  judg-ment

  pre-disposition

  set-ting

  swim-ming

- If possible, the first part of any divided word should contain at least three letters.
- Never split two letters that form one sound *(ea, th, sh).*

  bear-able (*not* be-arable)

- Never split the last word in a paragraph, as this would mean that the last line in the paragraph would consist of the second part of a word only.

Glossary

A

abstract noun A noun that describes an abstract or intangible concept; something that is not knowable through the senses, such as *honor, integrity,* or *pride.*

acronym A word formed from the initial letters of a name, such as *NAFTA,* or by combining initial letters or parts of a series of words, such as *radar,* for *radio detecting and ranging.*

action verb A verb that transfers action from the subject to the object. In English, all verbs are considered action verbs except for 11 verbs that sometimes function as linking verbs between a subject and its complement.

active voice As applied to verbs, a term indicating that the subject performs the action of the verb (for example, *Bob wrote the report*). Compare with **passive voice.**

adjective A word that modifies nouns and pronouns, adding color, taste, feel, and other dimensions to the words they describe.

adverbial conjunction A word or phrase that introduces or interrupts independent clauses, building bridges between ideas and providing transitions (for example, *however, therefore, for example,* and *thus*).

adverb Word that modifies adjectives, verbs, other adverbs, and even entire sentences, adding more depth, color, or intensity. Adverbs answer the questions *how, when, where,* and *why.* Here are a few examples of adverbs: *quickly, quietly, friendly, very, more, most, less,* and *least.*

antecedent The word or words to which a pronoun refers.

appositive A restatement; a brief explanation that identifies the noun or pronoun preceding it. See also **essential appositive.**

arbitrary In the case of language, refers to the idea that words are based on mutual agreement; it also refers to the way in which words string together to create meaning. Because meaning is determined by "the agreement of the speakers of a given language," words for the same things can vary greatly between languages.

auxiliary (verb) A verb, such as any form of *be, have,* or *do,* that is used with another verb to convey a different meaning or tense. Also called *helper* verbs.

B

background thinking A person's thoughts about how he or she arrived at a conclusion or how readers will interpret the conclusions; a type of **meta-discourse** that should be eliminated from writing.

base form The "original" state of the verb. See also **infinitive.**

bidialectal Fluid in speaking both Edited American English and a local/community dialect.

block style A formal letter style in which all lines start at the left margin; the standard format for most business letters. Also called *full-block style.*

Business English A form of Standard English used in formal situations in the workplace; also called the language of the boardroom. In the United States, the term *Business English* is used interchangeably with the term **Edited American English.**

cardinal number A number, such as 7, 21, or 500, used in counting to indicate quantity, but not order.

CAT (connect-act-tell) strategy In e-mail messages, a structure that connects with the reader, states the desired action, and then gives supporting information.

clarity Clearness and simplicity.

clause A clause is a group of words that contains a subject and verb. A clause is an important grammatical unit.

coherent A term referring to a paragraph that presents a logical flow of ideas, developing a topic in a rational, consistent way. One idea leads to another.

cohesive A term referring to a paragraph that presents one main topic along with details to support that topic, demonstrating connectedness among the ideas it contains. All the ideas adhere together for a common purpose.

collective nouns A noun, either singular or plural, that refers to a group, such as family, committee, or team. If the members of the group are acting as a unit, use the singular form of the verb; if they are acting separately, use the plural form of the verb.

colon A traditional mark of punctuation; alerts the reader that information will follow to explain or illuminate the information that preceded it.

comma splice A grammatical error in which two independent clauses are joined with only a comma, causing a run-on sentence.

common noun A noun, such as *horse* or *magazine,* that can be preceded by the definite article *(the)* and that represents one or all of the members of a class of things.

community dialect Any local language pattern that differs from Edited American English (Standard English). Most Americans speak a community dialect with family and friends. Informally known as "home talk" or "talkin' country."

comparative form The form of an adjective that is used when two items are compared (for regular adjectives, formed by adding the suffix *er* or by using *more* or *less* before the adjective).

complete predicate Consists of a verb and other elements of the sentence such as objects or modifiers or complements of the verb.

core (sentence) The core of a sentence consists of its subject and verb. The sentence core is the powerhouse of the sentence.

complete subject Includes the simple subject as well as other words that modify it.

composing Creating, inventing, discovering; in writing, planning or mapping a message and drafting ideas on a page.

compound subject When two or more agents make up the simple subject. The words modifying the subject are part of the complete subject but not part of the simple subject.

compound adjective When two or more adjectives come together as a unit to modify a noun.

compound verb When one subject is followed by two or more verbs that create separate lines of thought about the subject.

concrete noun Something that can be experienced through the senses, such as *flower, dog,* or *rain.*

conjunction Part of speech that serves to connect words, phrases, clauses, or sentences. Conjunctions show relationships and building bridges between ideas.

constructed language An artificial language that has been designed by an individual or small group, rather than having naturally evolved as part of a culture the way natural languages do.

coordinating conjunction A word that joins items of equal grammatical structure, such as independent clauses or items in a series. The seven coordinating conjunctions are *and, but, or, for, nor, so, yet.*

correlative conjunction A pair of conjunctions (for example, *not only . . . but also*) that compare or contrast ideas. The information presented after each conjunction should be represented in the same grammatical form (parallel construction).

corporate culture The "personality" of an organization, or how things are done in a particular corporate setting. Corporate culture is expressed by the way people dress, the hours they work, their work sites, and how they socialize with each other. Corporate culture guides employees in how to think and act while at work.

count noun A noun for an object, such as *desk,* or for an idea, such as *experience,* that is singular and can form a plural or occur in a noun phrase with an indefinite article, with numerals, or with such terms as *many.*

courteous request In written communications, a question that prompts the recipient to act rather than respond with words; ends with a period instead of a question mark.

CTA (connect-tell-act) strategy In business letters, a structure that connects with the reader; summarizes details, explanations, and facts to highlight information supporting the purpose of the letter; and then states the action that either the writer will take or the writer requests the reader to take.

D

dangling modifier A modifier that is separated from its real subject, resulting in confusion about which element of the sentence, the subject or object, is being modified. Also called a *misplaced modifier.*

dash A substitute for the comma, semicolon, period, or colon. Used to emphasize the information that follows it; appropriate in both formal and informal documents.

definite article In English, the word *the. The* is a determiner used to restrict the meaning of a noun to make it refer to something that is known by both the speaker or writer and the listener or reader.

demonstrative pronoun A word that modifies nouns by referring or pointing to them. Similar to possessive pronouns, demonstrative pronouns can be used in place of a noun. In English, the four demonstrative pronouns are *this, that, these,* and *those.*

dependent clause A group of words that has a subject and verb but does not express a complete thought; cannot stand alone as a sentence.

determiner A word belonging to a group which includes articles, demonstratives, possessive adjectives, and words such as *any, both,* or *whose,* and, in English, the first word in a noun phrase or the first word following another determiner. These words help to define and determine qualities of the words they modify.

dialect A variety of a language that is spoken by a group in a particular area, or by a particular social group or class; a local language. Dialects follow their own rules of grammar, word usage, and pronunciation to uniquely express group style and identity.

direct address The use of a person's name or title in addressing the person directly.

direct approach In written communications, a style that gets right to the point; conveys the purpose and the main point in the first paragraph; followed by supporting information and details. Compare with **indirect approach.**

diversity The fact or quality of being diverse, different, and unique. No one living today is exactly like any other when considering personality, race, religion, gender, education, family, culture, and other factors.

double negative If you use more than one negative in a sentence, your statement actually becomes positive. The word *not* is the most commonly used word to negate; less common words that negate a statement are *nothing, never, hardly, barely,* and *scarcely.*

drafting Creating a preliminary piece of writing.

E

Edited American English The type of writing and speaking that, for the most part, follows the standard rules of English usage. Used by formal media programs (such as newscasts) and academia. Another term for EAE is Standard American English or Standard English.

editing Improving the flow of writing by changing the wording and cutting unnecessary words to make the writing more concise and readable.

editing strategy An approach to editing that focuses on turning passive, wordy writing into simple, clear, and concise writing.

ellipsis marks Three spaced periods used to indicate the omission of a word or words from a quotation. Add a fourth period if the ellipsis (plural, ellipses) occurs at the end of a sentence.

emphatic An adjective *(incredible)* or an adverb *(really, very)* that places emphasis on the word it describes; emphatics can also detract from the message rather than place emphasis on it, so they should be used sparingly.

empty information Information that adds nothing of value for the reader.

emoticons A short sequence of keyboard letters and symbols—usually emulating a facial expression—that complements a text message. Also called *smileys.*

essential appositive A word or phrase that identifies a particular person or thing in a sentence where the identity would not be clear without the appositive. Do not set off essential appositives with commas.

essential element Any part of a sentence that cannot be removed without compromising meaning or structure; should not be set off with commas. Also called *restrictive element.*

exclamation point A mark of punctuation used to indicate surprise or excitement; can be used after a word, phrase, or complete sentence.

expletive form A word or phrase at the beginning of a sentence that indicates something later in the sentence but adds nothing to the meaning, for example "it is" or "there are."

F

filler An empty word that adds no value to your message (for example, *just* and *like*).

formal voice The language used in textbooks and newspapers, in classroom study, on the local and national news, and in national and international business transactions. In English, also referred to as Standard English and Edited American English.

focused writing A writing technique that involves writing about a topic for 10 to 20 minutes simply to put ideas on the page, without expecting to produce usable material.

fragment A phrase or dependent clause that is incorrectly punctuated as a complete sentence.

freewriting A writing technique that involves writing one's thoughts freely, in a "stream of consciousness" to release feelings and stress and to gain insight.

fused sentence A grammatical error in which two independent clauses are connected without a comma or conjunction.

G

gender bias In writing, the exclusion of one gender by using only masculine or feminine pronouns in contexts that apply to both genders. Plural pronouns and the phrase *he or she* are gender-neutral.

gerund The *ing* form of a verb (for example, *going, seeing, following, communicating*); functions as a noun.

gerund phrase A gerund followed by a preposition, noun, and any modifier (for example, *going to the meeting, communicating with the manager,* or *being on time*); functions as a noun.

grammar The study of how words and their component parts combine to form sentences.

grammatical subject A subject that generally precedes the verb but may or may not be the agent or actor that performs the action of the verb; in an active-voice sentence, the same as the real subject.

H

hedge A word or phrase that qualifies a statement by making it less than universal (for example, *sort of* or *kind of*); can weaken the message, so should be used sparingly.

helper (verb) See **auxiliary (verb).**

highly formal Passive voice; complicated language; abstract references; no contractions; Latin abbreviations.

homonyms Words that sound alike but are spelled differently and have different meanings (for example, *need, knead, kneed*).

homophone Used to describe one of a pair or one of a group of words that have the same sound.

I

idiolect An individual's unique language pattern; differs from others' patterns on the basis of grammar, word use, and pronunciation.

imperative mood Expresses commands, direct requests, and prohibitions, such as "Stop!" or "Don't go there!"

indefinite article An article, such as *a* or *an,* that does not fix the identity of the noun modified, but instead refers to the noun in a general manner.

indefinite pronouns A word such as *one, anybody, both,* or *several.* Challenges in usage arise in determining whether an indefinite pronoun is singular or plural. The indefinite pronouns *all, none, any, some, more,* and *most* may be singular or plural, depending on the nouns that they refer to. The pronouns *each, every, either, neither, one, another,* and *much* are always singular. When they are used as subjects, they take a singular verb.

independent clause A clause that has a subject and verb and expresses a complete thought; can stand alone as a sentence.

indicative mood A mood, grammatically unmarked, that represents the act or state as objective fact.

indirect approach In written communications, a style that presents details and explanations before getting to the main point; often used in messages that convey bad or unwelcome news. Compare with **direct approach.**

infinitive The base form of the verb preceded by *to* (for example, *to go, to see, to be, to follow*); functions as a noun, adjective, or adverb.

infinitive phrase An infinitive along with an object and any modifiers (for example, *to go to the store, to see the latest book reviews*); functions as a noun, adjective, or adverb.

inflection (1) An alteration of the form of a word by the addition of an affix, as in *cats* from *cat,* or by changing the form of a base, as in *hears* from *hear,* that indicates grammatical features such as number, person, mood, or tense. (2) Alteration in pitch or tone of voice.

information flow In writing, the transition between ideas. Presenting old information that leads to new information creates smooth transitions and ensures that messages are cohesive and coherent.

initialism An abbreviation pronounced letter by letter, such as *IBM* and *NYPD.*

intonation Describes the rise and fall of the voice pitch.

intransitive verb A verb that cannot transfer action to a direct object. Compare with **transitive verb.**

irregular verb A verb that forms its past and past participle in an irregular way (for example, *fly, flew, flown*).

L

linking verb See **state-of-being verb.**

local language A term applicable to any language pattern that differs from its standard version; local language is spoken in casual environments with family and friends. See **dialect.**

M

malapropism Refers to any sentence in which one word has been used incorrectly in place of another.

main verb The last verb in a string of verbs; in English, as many as five verbs can string together to form meaning.

micromessages The unspoken, subtle, and somewhat unconscious messages that tell what a speaker or writer really thinks; the meaning one gets from reading "between the lines"; micromessages can lead to either microadvantages (positive results) or microinequities (negative results).

meta-discourse As coined by Joseph Williams, author of *Style,* a term that refers to the language a writer uses to describe his or her own thinking process; usually consists of unnecessary information.

misplaced modifier Occurs when a modifier is separated from the word it modifies; can result in not only a grammatical error but also an ambiguous meaning.

modifier A word or group of words that describe another part of speech or even a complete sentence.

mood In grammar, a set of verb forms or inflections used to indicate the speaker's attitude toward the factuality or likelihood of the action or condition expressed (for example, the indicative mood used for making factual statements, the subjunctive mood for indicating doubt or unlikelihood, and the imperative mood to express a command).

N

new information Information that the reader does not already know and that the writer wants to convey to the reader.

nominal A noun that originated as a verb; often formed by adding *tion* or *ment* to the base form (for example, *development* from the word *develop*).

nominative case Also called *subjective case.* The form of pronouns that function as subjects of verbs. Must be followed by a verb, either real or implied.

noncount nouns Items that cannot be counted, such as *sand, water,* and *paint.*

noun A word that is used to name a person, place, thing, quality, or action and can function as the subject or object of a verb, as the object of a preposition, or as an appositive.

O

object A word, phrase, or clause that follows a verb and receives the action of the verb.

objective case The form of pronouns that function as objects of verbs and prepositions (for example, *me, him, her, them*).

old information Information that is obvious, or has already been presented, or that the reader already knows.

open punctuation Style of punctuation used in business letters in which no punctuation appears after the salutation and the complimentary closing.

ordinal number A number indicating position in a series or order. Ordinal numbers end in *d, nd, rd, st,* or *th,* as in *first* or *second.* Write ordinal numbers in words if they can be expressed in one or two words.

oronym A word or string of words which is homophonic with another word or string of words; for example, *some others* and *some mothers* or *ice cream* and *I scream.*

P

parallel structure Relates to using identical or equivalent constructions with corresponding sentence elements, such as words, clauses, and phrases in lists; parallel structure creates flow and consistency.

passive voice As applied to verbs, a term indicating that the subject does not perform the action of the verb (for example, *The report was written by Bob*—the subject, *report,* did not perform the action, *was written*).

past participle A verb form that consists of the past form preceded by a helper verb (for example, *have worked, have walked, have met*).

past The simple past form of a verb, used without a helper verb. For regular verbs, formed by adding "ed" to the base of the verb. For *walk,* the past tense and past participle are *walked.*

PEER (purpose, evidence, explanation, recap) model A guide to structuring information while composing or revising; define *purpose,* provide *evidence,* give an *explanation* or *examples, recap* main points.

period A punctuation mark used to indicate the end of a statement; also used with some abbreviations and with Web addresses. Also called *dot.*

phrase A group of words that form a unit but do not usually include a subject and a verb and cannot stand alone as a sentence; functions as a noun, adjective, or adverb. Types include prepositional, gerund, and infinitive phrases.

planning In writing, organizing and prioritizing key ideas; clarifying purpose and audience.

portmanteau word A word that fuses two functions, such as *Spanglish* (fusing *Spanish* and *English*), *brunch* (*breakfast* and *lunch*), and *telecommunications* (*telephone* and *communications*).

possessive case The form of pronouns that shows possession of nouns or other pronouns; for example, pronouns show possession, and a noun usually follows them: *my, mine, his, hers, its, theirs.*

predicate The part of a sentence that expresses something about the subject.

prewriting Prior to writing, researching, reading, and discussing a topic to gain insight; taking notes and mapping; thinking reflectively.

prepositional phrase A preposition along with an object and any modifiers, for example, "*with* Bob" or "*to* the store"; functions as a noun, adjective, or adverb.

preposition Word that shows the relationship of a noun or pronoun to some other word in a sentence; prepositions are "go betweens" and result in prepositional phrases, having a noun or pronoun as their object.

professional (writing) A direct style of writing characterized by use of the active voice, simple words, personal pronouns (for example, *I, you,* and *we*), and at times contractions; used in most business communications.

progressive tenses Verb tenses in which the main verb ends in *ing* and is preceded by a helper verb; used to indicate continuous action in the past, present, or future.

pronoun A word (for example, *I, you,* or *me*) that is used in place of a noun or another pronoun; must agree with its antecedent in number, person, and gender.

pronoun case Determines how a pronoun such as *I* or *me* will be used in a sentence; the main cases, or categories, of pronouns are **subjective, objective, possessive,** and **reflexive.** There are also more categories of pronouns, such as *demonstrative* and *relative.*

proofread Correct grammar, punctuation, spelling, and word usage; part of the editing process but also stands on its own as the final, critical step in producing a document.

proofreader's marks A table of established marks that editors and printers use to indicate changes to be made in a document.

proper adjective An adjective derived from a proper noun, such as "American," "Bostonian," or "Machiavellian." Proper adjectives are always capitalized.

proper noun The official name of a particular person, place, or thing; for example, the days of the week, the months of the year, and the "Declaration of Independence."

Q

question mark A punctuation mark used to indicate a question the writer expects the reader to answer; sometimes can occur after individual words and after sentences structured as statements.

R

real subject The actor or agent that performs the action of the verb but may or may not appear in the sentence; in an active-voice sentence, the same as the grammatical subject. Compare with **grammatical subject.**

reflexive case The form of pronouns that reflect back to subjective case pronouns (for example, *myself, yourself, ourselves*). Also called *intensive case.*

regular verbs A verb that forms its **past tense** and **past participle** by adding **–ed** to the base (for example, *walk, walked, have walked*).

revising Improving the way written ideas are presented by moving sentences or paragraphs and ensuring the major parts of the document achieve what is intended, intertwined with edting as the document progresses but on its own as a final check before proofreading. Restructuring, rethinking, or reorganizing content so that your message is effective.

retronym A new term coined for an old object or concept whose original name has come to refer to something else or is no longer unique (for example, *AM radio, acoustic guitar, black-and-white television, regular coffee,* and *hard disk*).

run-on sentence A run-on sentence consists of two or more independent clauses that run together without punctuation.

S

semicolon A punctuation mark used to separate two independent clauses and sometimes items in a series; stronger than a comma, but weaker than a period. Can be considered a "full stop" that is not "terminal."

-*s* form The third-person singular form of a verb in simple present tense (for example, *listens, speaks, has, does*).

sentence A group of words that has a subject and verb and expresses a complete thought. One or more independent clauses, with or without one or more dependent clauses.

set of commas A pair of commas that set off nonessential information in a sentence.

simple, clear, and concise The characteristics of a writing style that is effective for business writing.

slang Informal, nonconventional language, for example, jargon, colloquialism, that reflects a dialect rather than Standard American English; not acceptable in multicultural communication exchanges.

Standard American English The type of written and spoken language that follows the standard rules of English usage; used in most books, in classrooms, and in public and professional forums. See also **Edited American English.**

standard punctuation In letters, a punctuation style in which a colon follows the salutation and a comma follows the complimentary closing; the most common punctuation style for letters.

state-of-being verb A verb that does not transfer action but instead links a subject to a subject complement, rather than to a direct object. Any form of *to be (is, are, was, were), appear, become, seem,* and at times *smell, taste, feel, sound, look, act,* and *grow.* Also called a **linking verb.**

style In writing, the overall manner or presentation in a document; determined by many individual writing decisions that contribute to the total effect.

subject Together with the verb, the core of the sentence; can be a noun, phrase, or clause. See also **grammatical subject, real subject.**

subjective case The form of pronouns that functions as subjects of verbs (for example, *I, you, he, she, it, we, they, who*); subjective pronouns must be followed by a verb (either real or understood). Also called **nominative case.**

subordinating conjunction A word or phrase (for example, *if, when, as, although, because, as soon as*) used to connect a dependent clause to an independent clause; defines the relationship between the ideas in the clauses.

superlative form The form of the adjective that is used when comparing three or more items, For regular adjectives, form the superlative by adding the suffix *est* or by using *most* or *least* before the adjective.

syntax The orderly arrangement of words. Also called **grammar.**

systematic With language, describes the patterns of grammar, wherein words and the way they can be strung together follow a structure, such as *subject-verb-object* in English.

T

tag-on An unnecessary preposition at the end of a phrase or a clause (for example, *Where do you live at?*); grammatically incorrect and should be eliminated.

theory/practice method A learning technique that involves first learning a principle and then applying it; enables a learner to connect how something *is* used with the principle that defines how it *should be* used and thus develops analytical, critical thinking skills.

topic sentence A broad, general sentence that gives an overview of a paragraph.

topic string A series of sentences that develop the specific idea captured by a topic sentence.

transitional paragraph In a document, a paragraph that summarizes the key ideas of the current section and indicates how the major theme of the document will be developed in the next section.

transitional sentence A sentence that provides a logical connection between paragraphs.

transitive verb A verb that transfers action and must have a direct object to be complete.

U

understood subject Sentence structure that occurs when the subject, either *you* or *I,* does not appear in the sentence but instead is implied, or "understood."

V

verb parts The **basic forms** of a verb (for example, past and past participle).

verb Together with the subject, the core or nucleus of a sentence; conjugated on the basis of subject and tense. Verb usage indicates whether an event *happened* in the past, *is happening* at the present, or *will happen* in the future. See also **action verb, intransitive verb, state-of-being verb, transitive verb.**

vernacular (see **dialect**)

W

white space The term *white space* refers to the unused areas of your document, such as top and side margins, and spacing between lines.

Index

J

K

L

M

Q

R